Kate forshall

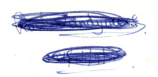

MEDIEVAL EUROPE

MEDIEVAL EUROPE

Martin Scott

SECOND MASTER OF WINCHESTER COLLEGE

LONGMAN

LONGMAN GROUP LIMITED
London

Associated companies, branches and representatives
throughout the world

© Martin Scott 1964

First published 1964
New impression 1971

ISBN 0 582 31397 X

PRINTED AND BOUND IN ENGLAND BY
HAZELL WATSON AND VINEY LTD
AYLESBURY, BUCKS

FOR MARY

PREFACE

This study of the medieval west may seem something of an irrelevance in the 1960s. For too long, some would urge, our eyes have been in European blinkers. Today the histories of Russia, with her roots in Byzantium and eastern Christianity, of China, with her non-European traditions, and of the United States should seem to be of more significance than the repetition of the affairs of the feudal monarchy of France or of the medieval papal curia. Since 1918 Europe has ceased to contain the centres of world power, and since 1945 most—if not all—Europeans have recognized the fact. That more Russian and Chinese history should be both taught and written is not open to question, though few indeed there are qualified to undertake the task. Yet whether it can or should replace the history of our own society is certainly questionable. To make the effort of imagination necessary to bridge a gap of only a few centuries in the history of our own ancestors is difficult enough, but at least the present is full of practical and linguistic reminders of the past. To attempt the same sort of reconstruction for societies which at the time had little or no connection with our own demands a formidable degree of insight in both teacher and taught if the result is to be neither incomprehensible nor merely trivial. The history of the medieval west may not in itself explain many of the problems of the modern world, yet, since the present is no island cut off from the past, the middle ages do in some measure illumine and explain our own age. Nor indeed is such an apology necessary. The period has its own interest, and therefore its own intrinsic value.

Practically, the aim of this book has been to fill what seemed to the author a gap by producing in one volume a history of western Europe from the time of Charlemagne to the middle of the fifteenth century. Such a task has necessarily posed a considerable problem of compression. Purely on grounds of space English history as such has been excluded, but the affairs of England, at least from the time of the foundation of the Anglo-Norman monarchy, were so closely interlinked with those of the rest of Europe that it would have been neither sensible nor possible altogether to have excluded them. In the same way, while the main theme of the book is the story of western Christendom, the lands owing allegiance to the western Church, this society, although a meaningful reality, was never a totally separate entity. Penetration of, and interchange with, other societies beyond its borders was taking place on an increasing scale throughout the period. With its older Christian neighbour, Byzantium, the West preserved an active love-hate relationship which was to end by the destruction of the senior partner in the name of their common religion. The Crusades were only one facet of a continuing, and in some ways fruitful, relationship with Islam. The Slavonic peoples of eastern Europe had every reason to know of the existence of their German neighbours, whose gradual penetration of their lands by military and by peaceful methods formed a central theme of their history for three hundred years. Franciscan missionaries in the fourteenth century were even to spread western influence as far as Pekin. All these have demanded inclusion. Only to the lands across the Atlantic did Christendom remain a closed society.

Any reader at all familiar with the period will see for himself the extent of the author's dependence on the various standard authorities. Most of these have been included in the short list of books attached to the end of the work. Although this has been kept to works in English, or at least reasonably easy to obtain in translation, it remains true that a competence in French and German is much more than a desirable aid to the would-be medievalist, and that without Latin he is cut off from most of his sources. There is no greater threat to the future of medieval studies than the general decline in the study of Latin.

My grateful thanks are due to the Headmaster and Council of Clifton College and to the Worshipful Company of Goldsmiths who together made it possible for me to take a term of absence for the completion of this book, to the staff of the Library of Bristol University who have dealt with a variety of unreasonable demands with unfailing efficiency and good humour, and to Mr. Arthur Hibbert of King's College, Cambridge, who read the whole manuscript and gave me more than generously of his time and skill. The customary acknowledgment that the faults of the work remain my own, but that any virtue it may possess are largely his, is much more than a mere formality. I am grateful, too, to Miss Mary Hall who has typed the whole manuscript for me. For the 1971 printing the bibliography has been extended and updated with the help and advice of Mr. Jonathan Shepard of New College, Oxford, to whom grateful thanks are due. Finally—and I am again conscious of the very real truth which lies behind the customary form—I am more than grateful to my wife who has put up with this book so patiently and so long.

CONTENTS

MAPS

ACKNOWLEDGEMENTS

We are grateful to Chapman & Hall Ltd. for permission to use material from *The Decameron* by Boccaccio translated by J. Payne.

For allowing us to include genealogical tables compiled from tables in their books we are grateful to the following:
Professor Lionel Butler, Mr. R. J. Adam and Macmillan & Co. Ltd. for material from R. Fawtier, *The Capetian Kings of France* used in the table on the Succession to the French Throne in 1328; Eyre & Spottiswoode Ltd. for material from H. A. L. Fisher, *History of Europe* used in the table on the Welfs and Hohenstaufens; Longmans, Green & Co. Ltd. for material from R. H. C. Davis, *A History of Medieval Europe* used in the table on the Carolingians; and Methuen & Co. Ltd. for material from Z. N. Brooke, *History of Europe* and C. W. Previte-Orton, *A History of Europe* used in the tables on the Saxons and Salians and the Capetian Kings of France.

I

The Background

Medieval Christendom was a blend of three great forces. To the Greco-Roman world, politically unified since the first century B.C. in the Roman Empire, had been added two vital modifications. The Christian Church, at first apparently a persecuted mystery religion from the eastern provinces, had taken its persecutor captive, and since the time of Constantine (306–337) had been the established religion of all civilized Europe. At the same time the gradual infiltration of the tribes from beyond the northern and eastern frontiers of the Empire had inevitably altered its whole structure. The tribesmen had come not to destroy Rome but to enjoy her, but if they had tried hard to be Romans they had ended by making something very different out of the old Roman Empire. Some understanding of these three forces is necessary before the history of the Middle Ages can make sense.

The Romans had long known of the Germanic tribes who lay beyond the frontiers of their empire. As early as the first century Tacitus had made a systematic attempt to describe the nature and customs of these neighbours of the Empire whose lands stretched from the shores of the Baltic to the banks of the Danube. Divided by geography into several tribes, such as the Saxons and the Franks in the north and the Goths farther east, these two main branches of the Teutonic race did not differ significantly in their customs. Belligerent in their way of life the Germans might be, but for so long as the internal condition of the Empire remained healthy the Roman legions proved quite capable of containing them. In the middle of the third century an attempt by the Goths to invade the Empire had been defeated at the battle of Naissus (269), and, remaining in occupation of Dacia (much of modern Rumania), the Goths had caused no more trouble to Rome for nearly a century.

But it only required a weakness within the Empire itself, or pressure upon the Goths in their turn from the East, for the danger of Gothic invasion to be renewed. During the second half of the fourth century these two circumstances coincided. From the steppes of central Asia the savage armies of the Huns came forth across

I

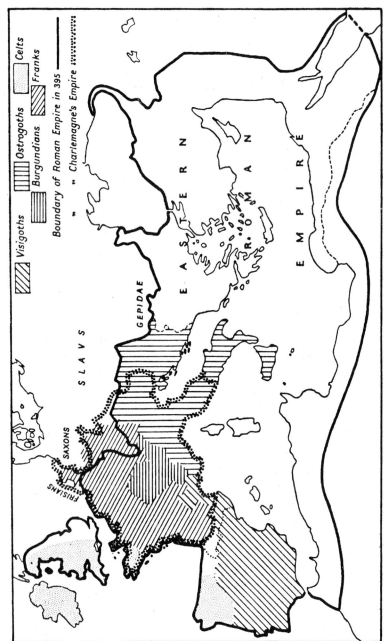

THE ROMAN EMPIRE AND THE BARBARIAN PEOPLES

Legend:
Visigoths
Ostrogoths
Celts
Burgundians
Franks
Boundary of Roman Empire in 395
" " Charlemagne's Empire

SLAVS

GEPIDAE

SAXONS

FRISIANS

EASTERN ROMAN EMPIRE

R.

Russia to throw the eastern neighbours of Rome into confusion. By 376 the Visigoths were crossing the Danube to seek the protection of Rome, and when this was not everywhere freely granted they took up arms against their hosts, and at Adrianople (378) the emperor Valens died at the head of an imperial army. The Goths had come to stay.

The Romans who confronted them were unfitted by the very success of the Roman peace itself for a supreme military effort. Nor were the emperors of those decades, shadowy figures like Arcadius and Honorius, fitted to give leadership in years of crisis. The next hundred years saw a constant succession of barbarian invasions. The Visigoths under Alaric reached Rome to sack it in 410, and the withdrawal of the legions for the unsuccessful defence of the capital had merely opened the floodgates for the northern tribes, Alans and Vandals and the like, to pour into the Empire. By the time of the deposition of the last Roman Emperor of the West in 476, the whole western Empire had become a battlefield of warring German tribes.

The collapse of the western Roman Empire in the fifth century A.D. seems to be one of the obvious turning points of history. Yet to contemporaries the deposition of the miserable puppet Romulus Augustulus in 476 had no such importance. For five hundred years, a longer time than separates us from Bosworth Field, Rome had given comparative peace, law, and stability to much of modern Europe, and not to Europe alone. The Roman world had been centred on the Mediterranean, and her sway had covered the whole of the north African coast from the Pillars of Hercules to Alexandria and all the countries of the eastern Mediterranean. To all these lands the Roman legions on the frontiers had given protection and a period of peace the like of which they were never to know again. The Roman law and the Latin language had given unity, and the Roman roads had given a system of communications not to be bettered until the eighteenth century. In every part of the empire educated men had shared the same staple intellectual fare, based on the Greek thought of the fifth and fourth centuries B.C.. Rome had also brought a measure of religious unity to her world. Over all the diverse religions of the Empire, with the single irritating exception of Judaism, she had imposed the cult of emperor worship as a common bond for those who worshipped so many different gods. When Constantine (312–337) by stages recognized Christianity as the religion of the Empire, it must have seemed to many that this was but a further extension of

3

that unity which it seemed her mission to bring. To Christians certainly it seemed that the Empire was no mere accident of history, but a vital part of God's scheme for the salvation of the world. Without Roman law and order how could the Christian faith have been spread so far and so fast? Writing early in the fifth century, at the very time when Roman political domination was beginning to break up, Prudentius thought of the Empire in terms such as these: 'This is the meaning of all the victories and triumphs of the Roman Empire; the Roman peace has prepared the road for the coming of Christ. For what place was there for God or for the acceptance of truth in a savage world in which men's minds were at strife and there was no common basis of law?'[1] To non-Christians the most damaging accusation that could be brought against Christianity was that it was serving to weaken the semi-divine power of the Empire; it was this accusation which at about the same time led Augustine of Hippo to make his defence of the Church in the *De Civitate Dei*.

It is not surprising that the idea of the Empire was an unconscionable time in dying in men's minds, but two other factors helped its persistence for a thousand years. The first was that, until the time of the Muslim invasions of the seventh century, it was not challenged by any other idea of a world order. The Germanic tribes who came first as unwelcome guests and later as conquerors to the Roman lands in the west were essentially local and tribal in their ideas, and had no conception of how to administer the lands to which they had come except in so far as they could adapt for themselves Roman ideas and methods. For their administration they were largely dependent on cultured Romans, like Cassiodorus, who could be persuaded to accept service under them. These officials were often moved to accept by their belief in the importance of carrying on Roman traditions so that one day the Empire might be fully restored. In language, religion, and ideas of government the barbarians had nothing to offer that was not palpably inferior to the Roman; it is not surprising that in every case they learned much from those they had conquered.

The second factor was that in one very real sense Rome remained unconquered. Constantine had shifted the capital of the Empire to the new city of Constantinople (330), and this city was not taken by the barbarian tribes. Indeed throughout the Middle Ages it was to

---

[1] Quoted from *The Making of Europe, A.D. 400–1000*, Christopher Dawson. Sheed and Ward, London, 1932, p. 23.

remain a large city even by modern standards; at no stage before the twelfth century had it less than half a million inhabitants, and for much of the time it probably numbered around the million mark. The West never had anything to compare with this. Moreover the Byzantine Empire deliberately preserved Roman traditions and methods of government for the whole long course of its history. It was natural therefore that the collapse of the Empire in the West should seem not to be the collapse of the Roman Empire, but merely the temporary loss of its western provinces. The career of the emperor Justinian in the sixth century must have strengthened the belief in the probable reconquest of the lost provinces by Roman legions, and in the West it must have been hoped that reconquest would be followed by the transfer of the capital back again to its proper home in Rome. It was only the almost complete severance of communications between eastern and western Europe brought about by the Muslim invasions of the seventh century which made it obvious that if there was to be an empire in the West at all it would have to be a purely Western Empire; Byzantium was powerless to help or hinder the process.

The idea of the Roman Empire, of one single political authority based on a new or old Rome, holding sway over all local authorities and backed by the authority of God Himself, is one of the great constants of medieval history; it is as clear to Dante in the fourteenth century as it had been to Prudentius in the fifth. Yet the search for anything that is recognizable as the classical empire in the Middle Ages can lead only to Byzantium. Conditions in the West had become so utterly different from anything that had been known in the first four centuries of the Christian era that any attempted restoration of the Empire could only succeed in producing something new. The classical empire had been essentially urban in the sense that the heart of its political and economic life had been found in the towns. It had depended on large-scale and regular trade. To foster this trade it had successfully maintained an elaborate system of communications, well kept roads along which merchants and legionaries alike could travel, and above all the peaceful Mediterranean itself as the great central artery of its economic life. It had depended, too, on the existence of a large professional army controlled from the centre, an army on which the whole *pax Romana* rested, and on the existence of a large class of highly educated laymen from whom a body of professional administrators could be drawn; Pontius Pilate is only the most well known of these essential links in the Empire.

None of these conditions would be true for any attempted restoration of the Empire after the seventh century. The Germanic tribes who had invaded it were not by nature traders, and the general political confusion of the fifth, sixth, and seventh centuries had resulted in a startling fall in the level of economic activity. This, combined with the drop in population which was in itself one of the causes for the collapse in the West, had meant that society itself had become rural. It would not be true of course to say that trade ceased altogether; there was never a period in which new coinage was not being struck somewhere in the West, and the existence of coinage is proof of the existence of trade. Nor did all the towns disappear, for many lingered on with much reduced populations as local ecclesiastical centres, housing a bishop or a monastery. But all over Europe many towns were abandoned altogether, and those that remained were no longer in any sense the centres of an economic life which was now based on subsistence agriculture. With the decline of trade the motive for keeping the roads in repair had gone, and they rapidly deteriorated, thus making any form of remote political control extremely difficult. Now that the West was importing and exporting so very much less the Mediterranean sea routes were much less used, and with the decay of a central authority much less well guarded. The barbarian rulers were, after all, landsmen with little conception of the importance of sea routes to a mercantile empire. Piracy at the expense of such shipping as survived became more and more frequent in the fifth, sixth, and seventh centuries, and caused it more and more to hug the land and avoid long sea passages. Finally the Muslim capture of the whole north African coast, and penetration of Spain in the eighth century, turned the Mediterranean into a frontier controlled by the ships of a hostile faith, while at the same time it made communication by sea with the Eastern Empire extremely uncertain. This in itself was enough to dictate an entirely different way of life to the society which was coming to be based on north-western Europe.

Education gives a similar picture. The urban schools which the Empire had supported gradually broke down; they had been dependent on a level of economic prosperity which no longer existed. The Latin culture died hard, and in the sixth century men like Boethius and Cassiodorus were still to be found writing in the old tradition of Latin letters in defiance of the barbarism of those whom they felt it their duty to serve. But it was doomed. The future of education, almost of civilization itself, lay with the Church; it is significant that Cassiodorus himself ended his long life in a monastic community at Vivarium. The supply of educated laymen slowly ran dry, and with it disappeared the possibility of resurrecting anything like the old imperial civil service. Instead the situation came about which was to last for most of the Middle Ages in which the Church had a monopoly of education and learning. Latin, the language alike of civilization and government, came to be the monopoly of clerics. The laity came to use languages which, although they were in some areas vulgarizations of Latin, were for long spoken and not written.

With the disintegration of imperial power went the disintegration of the imperial army. Not that in the new state of affairs military power was of any less importance than before; it was if anything more important. But it underwent a process of localization. Power now resided with local kings and chieftains rather than with any central body. Men followed the local leader who in their particular area could give them protection from enemies from outside and whose good will was essential for the security of their families and lands. Effective political power came to rest with smaller and smaller units; the power of the empire faded into the power of the barbarian kingships, and they in their turn let the more important of their subjects gain virtual independence of them. In Gaul, for instance, during the seventh century the rule of the Merovingian kings who had replaced the imperial authority became more and more nominal, partly at any rate because the area they had to control was too large for such governmental machinery as they had; real power passed into the hands of the Neustrian and Austrasian mayors of the palace, who were building up a power, firmer because more locally based. This extensive fragmentation of power would make any restoration of a central political authority extremely difficult.

For all these reasons any restoration of the Roman Empire in anything like its original form was very unlikely, yet it continued to retain its hold over the minds of men. In them Rome would remain as the symbol of the order, prosperity, and peace which seemed so largely to have passed from the earth, and any ruler who gained sufficient power would be bound to think in terms of restoring the ancient imperial glories.

In the first three centuries of its existence Christianity had been subject to sporadic and somewhat inefficient persecution at the hands of imperial authorities who had disliked and distrusted this new eastern religion. It apparently forbade its followers to carry out the very reasonable modicum of emperor worship, which was the only limit Rome imposed on freedom of religion within the empire. Christians had been widely suspected of encouraging immorality at their secret meetings, and the dangerous teaching that in Christ there was neither slave nor free, coupled with the fact that a large number of early Christians, including at least one pope, had been of slave status, had convinced many that the religion represented a dangerous threat to social stability. In its turn the early Church had reacted to persecution by adopting an attitude in which other-worldliness was blended with a deep suspicion of the Empire, sometimes indeed identifying it with Antichrist himself.

But well before the conversion of Constantine it had become clear that the imperial policy of persecution was not bringing results, and there had been long periods in which the Church had been free to develop in peace. Understandably this had led to a changed attitude towards the pagan world and the storehouse of ideas and knowledge it contained. Despite the fulminations of those like Tertullian, (†240), who insisted that all the Christian needed to know was Christ crucified, there had been a substantial body of opinion, led by Clement of Alexandria, which looked upon the works of the human reason as being in themselves works of God, inferior indeed to the revelation which came through Christ, but complementary to it. It thus followed that the study of the thought of Greece and Rome was a perfectly proper occupation for Christians, and that its methods could be applied to Christianity itself. There thus appeared a Hellenistic form of the Christian faith which was long to endure. Not only did it make possible the appearance of a Christian theology, for without the use of the abstract terms of Greek thought this would have been impossible, but it provided the main interest of the Christian Byzantine Empire for the whole of its history. Gregory Nazianzen, writing in the fourth century, describes how in Byzantium the man wishing to buy a loaf of bread will be told instead of the price that the Father is greater than the Son, that the changer of money will discuss the Begotten and the Unbegotten rather than giving his change, and that the bath keeper will embark on a discussion of whether the Son proceeds from the Father.[1] Despite such apparent absurdities this attitude of acceptance towards Greek modes of thought was to perform a most valuable service for Christianity. For many centuries it was to remain mainly the preserve of the speculative East rather than the practical West, but in the twelfth and thirteenth

[1] See Dawson, op. cit., pp. 110-111.

centuries Aristotelian ideas from the eastern Mediterranean were to enable the West in its turn to produce a Christian philosophy.

The conversion of Constantine necessarily changed the whole attitude of the Church towards the Empire. Whatever his motives, Constantine associated the Church closely with the government of the Empire, and his example was naturally followed by very many others. Christianity no doubt lost much in quality by the sudden arrival of armies of time-servers to augment the ranks of what had so recently been a persecuted minority, but it was clear that the old attitude of hostility or withdrawal from the secular power was no longer practicable. Now the Church, with its basic concern still the salvation of the souls of its members, was on the same side as the Empire, with its concern for their temporal welfare. Some formula for their relationship had to be formed. Constantine by his conversion had created the problem of the relationship of spiritual and temporal, of pope and emperor, which was to dog much of the Middle Ages. At first sight there does not seem to be any problem; in the teaching of Pope Gelasius (492–496) Christ had foreshadowed a solution in His dialogue with the apostles at the time of His arrest. 'Here are two swords,' they had said, to which He had made reply, 'It is enough,' thus signifying divine approval of the two authorities which should care respectively for men's bodies and souls.[1] But in practice the definition of what was spiritual and what was temporal was to prove very difficult, and the ideal of close co-operation between the two could only really be achieved when one or other of the partners was clearly dominant.

At first there was little difficulty in the relationship; the Church had been exalted by the Empire, and felt nothing but good will for its benefactor. It was content to limit its attention fairly narrowly to the spheres of religion and morals, though to its credit it was prepared to exercise its discipline in these fields even on emperors. S. Ambrose while bishop of Milan was quite prepared to excommunicate the emperor Theodosius for his violations of morality. But as the imperial machinery gradually ran down in the fifth and sixth centuries the Church found itself increasingly drawn into the field of politics. This was a matter of necessity rather than of any conscious choice. If the central authority was no longer in a position to resist the barbarians or to negotiate with them, somebody had to make the necessary decisions. The Church, with its organization modelled largely on that of the Empire, was the only body still existing which

[1] See Luke 22: 38.

could take such decisions. So Sidonius Apollinaris, the bishop of Clermont in the four-seventies, organized the defence of the whole of his area of central Gaul against Euric, leader of the Visigoths, and Leo I, bishop of Rome in 452, succeeded in persuading Attila, the leader of the Huns, to withdraw from Italy to the Danube—or so one story had it. The Church could not have refused to take such initiative when the spiritual and temporal consequences of a failure to do so would have been so catastrophic, but in so doing it got its own members accustomed to the idea that political action was something in which it could properly indulge.

Two other great institutions of the Christian West, the Papacy and monasticism, call for comment here. About the early history of the Papacy there rests much of the dust of battle between Roman Catholic and Protestant historians, but certain things seem clear, to the writer at any rate. Among the bishoprics of the early Church a few carried much greater prestige than the rest, either from the political importance of their sees or from outstanding personalities among their early incumbents. Most notable among these bishoprics were those of Antioch, Alexandria, Carthage and Rome. The inclusion of Rome in this list is not hard to understand. The bishopric of the capital city of the Empire would inevitably have something of a special position, but to this was added the well-established tradition which made Peter, the chief of the apostles, not only with Paul a martyr in Rome, but the first of its bishops. In Rome the words of Christ to Peter: 'Thou art Peter, and upon this rock I will build my Church',[1] were soon seen to have a special significance also for the successors of Peter, though the claim that this gave Rome any authority over other Churches would be disputed in the East, notably at Antioch, which could also claim Peter among its early bishops.

To these obvious claims to respect from the Christian world Rome could add another. While the other Christian centres concerned themselves largely with the speculations which led gradually to the formation of Christian doctrine, the practical problem of Church organization and the spiritual needs of ordinary Church members were the main concern of the bishop of Rome. A good example of this is to be found in the reaction of Rome when Tertullian of Carthage, most puritanical of the early fathers of the Church, tried to get certain specific sins—murder, fornication, and idol worship—made grounds for permanent excommunication from the Church when they were committed by Christians after baptism. Admirable

[1] Matthew 16:18.

10

no doubt as was his hatred of sin, the widespread adoption of this rule by the Church surrounded by a pagan world could only have led to the Church remaining a small body of the spiritual élite, and it is not easy to see how a Church which claimed to serve a merciful God could have refused to accept the genuinely penitent. That at any rate was the view of Pope Callixtus, who in strongly opposing Tertullian can be seen to be upholding the practical commonsense view of the Church concerned with men as they are, as much as with men as they should be. To some extent, no doubt, this contrast between Rome and the other Churches is only the contrast between the practical West and the speculative East, between Rome and Athens. But the Latin tradition had its theologians too; perhaps the greatest of all the early fathers, Augustine, belonged to the Latin tradition. It was also the result of the accident which brought to the most important see in the Western world a succession of men of high practical ability; in particular this was true of the period when the power of the Empire was disintegrating. In the middle of the fifth century and at the end of the sixth the papal throne was occupied by two men, Leo I and Gregory the Great, who would have been quite outstanding in any post of authority at any time. Under such leadership Rome took the lead not only in negotiating with the barbarians but also in the task of converting them. It is not surprising that Rome emerged from the whole process with a much enhanced prestige.

Moreover as far as western Europe was concerned her rivals were eliminated: Carthage was first sacked by pagan Vandals and then with the rest of North Africa swamped by the Muslim invasions. Obviously neither Alexandria nor Carthage could put forward any claim to leadership of the Christian world. Moreover, as in economic life so in religion, the domination of the Mediterranean, first by Vandal fleets and then by the Muslims forced the West and the East to develop along different lines. Doctrinal differences were to develop between the East and the West, but they were the result, not the cause, of the split. In the East the Church continued the tradition of Constantine's Empire and remained heavily dependent on the Byzantine Emperor; in the West it had no emperor to rely on, and so had to develop independence. For this western Church, Rome was the only possible head, and the see of Rome became exalted above all other bishoprics. The degree of effective control it was able to exercise over other parts of the Catholic West would naturally vary: in times of extensive political disorder or when the Papacy itself fell into unworthy hands it might be a very nominal headship, particularly in the more outlying parts of the West, but throughout the western world in the Middle Ages there is no question that the Church is the *Roman* Catholic Church. The only question at issue is the degree to which the Pope wished or was able to extend his authority over the rest of the Church.

Monasticism is the other great institution of medieval religion which should be considered here. Until the fourteenth century at any rate the religious, the man bound by a religious rule, stands as the type of the Christian who is attempting the .Christian life at its hardest but potentially best. The story of Mary and Martha was often taken as an allegory of the proper relationship between the religious and the ordinary lay Christian. Both were in their own ways serving Christ, but Christ bade Martha remember, 'cumbered about with much serving' as she was, that Mary in choosing to talk with Him rather than to help her sister had chosen the better part.[1] So the monk or the nun, in choosing the spiritual life of prayer and contemplation and of such direct contact with God as is possible for human beings, has chosen the better part. Not all will be suited to it, but those who choose the active life of work in the world and ordinary human relationships must remember that those who have chosen differently are pursuing a higher not a lower ideal. Today, when the ideal of the Christian life is normally taken to be that of active charity towards one's fellow men, it is perhaps hard to grasp the idea, but it should be recognized that monasticism is not just a quirk of Christianity at one stage of its development; most of the world's great religions, some older than Christianity, practise it. Indeed if the reality of prayer as a means of access to God is acknowledged, it is hard to deny that a life dedicated to prayer is justified.

The development of Christian monasticism should be associated with the excessive luxury and corruption of the city life of the Roman Empire in the period before the barbarian invasions. The sins of the world and the flesh seemed very real to Christian converts in such an atmosphere, and as early as the third and fourth centuries quite large numbers of Christians had fled from the world to deserts and solitary places where, living in great austerity, they could devote themselves to the life of prayer. Such moves were regarded with great hostility by those who still held to the social conventions of the classical world; those who went to the desert renounced all obligations, military or financial, to the Empire, and followed an ascetic way of life quite foreign to classical counsels of moderation. To many

[1] Luke 10: 38–42.

Christians, however, there seemed something miraculous about this voluntary renunciation for Christ of all that the natural man values most, and the deserts of lower Egypt, the area most favoured by these early monks, became one of the recognized sights to be visited by the reasonably intrepid traveller from the civilized world.

The monasticism of Egypt was to last long: indeed not until the time of the Suez War of 1956 did President Nasser expel the last Christian monks from Egypt. But for the most part it belonged to the type of monasticism known as *eremitic*, and did not form the direct pattern for that of the West, most of which is technically known as *cenobitic*. The monk in the eremitic tradition is essentially solitary, pursuing God alone in his cell, away from the distraction not only of the world but also of his brother monks. In its extreme form he is simply a hermit, and although many of the Egyptian monks grouped themselves into communities like the one over which S. Anthony of Egypt presided as abbot, they still remained essentially solitaries, meeting together for common worship only on comparatively rare occasions. The point of such a monastery was largely that it should stimulate its members to emulate each other in acts of holiness. The eremitic life, valuable as it may be for a very small minority, was open to two very grave objections. However high the original enthusiasm which led men to the desert, men, as Aristotle had taught, are by nature social animals, and only very rarely profit by a life cut off from human society. For many, long periods of physical inactivity became also periods of spiritual sloth. The monk who had gone to the desert to wrestle with angels might end by merely vegetating, a victim of *accedia*, 'weariness of soul the noontide demon' as Cassian was to call it, the state of spiritual torpor which was always the worst enemy of the monastic life in all its forms. Clearly the eremite, with no definite rule to keep and no definite authority to detect the symptoms of decay when they appeared, was in far greater danger.

The other danger was perhaps even worse. The early eremites were encouraged to compete against each other in acts of holiness and austerity, and the competition often seems to have got near becoming an end in itself. The widespread interest in the lengths of austerity to which they would go did not aid them. But it is difficult to feel that the spectacle of Simeon Stylites perched for thirty-three years on his pillar in Syria was particularly edifying, or likely to lead to anything but a sharp attack of spiritual pride in the man who undertook it.

These dangers were realized by some in Egypt itself, and attempts were made, notably by S. Pachomius, to introduce a corporate life there. They were certainly in the forefront of the mind of the father of western monasticism, S. Benedict of Nursia. He had himself tried the eremitic life as a young man about 500, in a cave at Subiaco in the Apennines, and knew that for him it was not the way of holiness. When he came to found his own monastery at Monte Cassino in 529 he took care to make it fully cenobitic. Monte Cassino was itself a highly successful religious house which still stands, despite its periodic destruction at the hands of foreign invaders, as a monument to the foresight of its founder. But the peculiar importance of S. Benedict lies more in the Rule which he wrote to regulate the life there. The Rule of S. Benedict is one of the really important documents of the Christian religion; it gave the pattern for the future of western monasticism, and the later attempts at monastic reform which form an important part of the history of the Middle Ages were in the main concerned with getting back to the purity of the Rule. There is little doubt that it deserves its importance. S. Benedict's aim was to produce 'a school for the service of God' designed not for spiritual supermen but for quite ordinary Christians, who could train for spiritual perfection there. Compared with the austerities of the desert the life of the Benedictine house can sound almost self-indulgent. The Rule for instance decrees quite generous quantities of food and drink, and even allows the provision of an alternative main course at dinner, '*so that he who does not like the one may partake of the other*', an indulgence not always to be found in communal meals today. But the Rule once undertaken was to be kept for life. It was not to be open to a monk to go off in search of a more agreeable environment after a year or two. Considerable discretion is allowed to the abbot within the Rule to adapt it to local conditions, but for the monk there is to be no question of personal austerities or relaxation. Obedience indeed, with poverty (the complete absence of personal possessions) and chastity, is one of the three vows which, after proper time for consideration on both sides, every monk must take. Clearly the Rule places a heavy responsibility on the abbot, and the process of selecting abbots is thus of great importance. The arrangements for the election of abbots, and the method by which the danger that they might allow power to go to their heads is guarded against by making them answerable for their actions after their period of office is over, seem to have been inspired by the custom of the Eastern Church. Both the detailed regulations and the more general passages as to how authority is to be exercised are admirably suited for their purpose.

The *Opus Dei*, the life of regular prayer and praise built round the seven daily services, was at the centre of the Benedictine life, but ordinary men cannot be expected to live a life of uninterrupted prayer. The day was thus divided up into three roughly equal portions. The *Opus Dei* made up about a third of it, meals, sleep and recreation made up another third, and the rest was work. There was remarkably little opportunity for accedia. S. Benedict seems to have envisaged manual work in the fields as being the normal form of this work, and the monastery as a self-contained agricultural community, but in course of time other forms of work, some of them more suited for the aged and the infirm, were also introduced. Thus many houses came to have a *scriptorium*, in which monks were engaged in the copying of manuscripts of the Bible and the works of the early fathers of the Church, and often of secular classical authors as well. The very survival of many works of Latin writers through the Dark Ages can be attributed to these *scriptoria*. Quite incidentally to their main purpose the black monks managed to make a whole series of later renaissances possible; that European civilization survived the disintegration of the classical empire at all was largely their work. As the world outside the cloister gradually relapsed into barbarism, great monasteries, such as Bobbio or Vivarium, could carry on a more cultivated tradition. At Vivarium in the sixth century monks were occupied in putting into Latin versions a number of Greek works, as though they had advance knowledge that Greek would soon be an extinct language in western Europe. Many of these early monasteries were not subject to the Benedictine Rule: Bobbio for instance was an off-shoot of the flourishing Christianity of Ireland. But the genuine merits of the Rule came to be seen, and the foundations of the eighth century, like Reichenau on Lake Constance or Fulda in Hesse, were all followers of the Rule. The degree to which each monastery was self-governing and economically self-contained made it possible for an individual house to preserve far higher standards than the world or the Church outside it. They came to provide little islands of educated men headed by abbots who were accustomed to some of the problems of administration and government. Compared to the educated Roman World they were on a pitifully small scale, but the monasteries could at any rate provide a nucleus. When in more settled times the Church and the monarchies alike were faced with the problem of building up larger scale organizations again, it was inevitable that they should look to the monasteries to provide them with personnel.

The third big factor which went to the making of the middle ages was provided by the barbarian tribes themselves. It can be exaggerated. Anglo-Saxon historians of the nineteenth century sometimes liked to see in the pure blood and manly customs of the Germanic tribes a contrast with the effete and decadent ways of the later Empire. They could be regarded as the origin of most of the laudable institutions of northern Europe, from Magna Carta to Protestantism. The career of Hitler finally exploded this Nordic myth, and in truth there was little in it biologically or historically. The infusion of new blood the tribes brought with them may have improved the European stock, but if so it was only because they rapidly intermarried with the existing inhabitants and lost their identity, not because they retained their purity. The most striking thing about the barbarians was the speed with which most of their traditions evaporated when brought into contact with those of Rome, so infinitely higher even in decline.

Yet the barbarians did have a contribution to make. Their way of life was quite different from that of the Empire, but the two had been in contact long before the *Völkerwanderung*, the great movement of the tribes in the fourth and fifth centuries which had burst into the Empire. From its early days quite large numbers of barbarians had percolated into the Empire from Germany, and Romans were not entirely ignorant of their ways even beyond the frontiers. At the end of the first century A.D. Tacitus, the shrewdest of the Roman historians, had written a description of them in the *Germania*, and although he had his own social motives in writing it, much of what he said was clearly true of the same tribes three centuries later. Two points in particular he noticed about them. Unlike the Romans, they did not form cities but preferred to live in widely scattered village communities. This clearly was to become a characteristic of the Latin world after the time of the invasions. Then too he noticed the importance of the tribe as the social unit. The allocation of land, for instance, was done on a tribal basis. The family holding of land was part of a larger holding, which was that of the tribe itself. The basis of the tribal idea is a blood relationship. Often before their conversion to Christianity the kings or chiefs traced their descent from some god of the tribe, and the king was regarded as the father of his people in something more than a purely metaphorical sense. The relationship between a father and his children is a two way one; he has responsibilities towards them, they have duties towards him. It is also essentially a relationship between unequals. What was true of the barbarian king and his subjects was also true of the relationships between those subjects. Under the Empire three main categories of subject had been recognized: the free citizen of the Empire, the member of one of the subject peoples without citizenship, and the slave. All of them were under the law which gave the same rights to every member of each group, small as these might be in the case of the slave. Among the Germanic tribes there was no idea of an abstract law which should be the same for all. Their law, or customs, for they had not yet codified a law, was a complicated network of duties and responsibilities. Neither freedom nor slavery had any place in German ideas. No man was free, for every man had his obligations to superior members of the tribe right up to the king himself, and he had duties towards the whole tribe. Similarly, no man, except perhaps the captive of another tribe taken in battle, was a slave, for every man had duties owed to him.

This was to remain true of most of Europe for most of·the middle ages: it is one of the chief characteristics of feudalism. Except at the borders of Christian Europe slavery was very rare, but until the revival of town life in the eleventh and twelfth centuries the free man is almost equally rare. When he does occur the free man is pitied, not envied. He is the man who has the great misfortune to have no lord to protect him. In this at least the tribalism of Germany had triumphed over the Roman idea of citizenship.

It would be wrong to exaggerate the influence of ideas of blood and loyalty in this. Obviously the development of what later came to be known as feudalism owed much to the economic facts of life in the period between the fourth and eighth centuries. The fall in the population and the disappearance of the cities had meant that slavery was no longer an economic institution. The Romans had used slavery to produce large quantities of unskilled labour, needed by industries such as mining or in the simple processes involved in the large scale production of staple crops, such as grapes or olives, for an export market. The *latifundia* of southern Italy are good examples; parallels can be found in the use of slaves by the cotton farmers of the American South or the sugar growers of the West Indies in the eighteenth century. Once trade had dwindled and the export markets had disappeared, slaves became a liability and their liberation an act not of charity but of common sense. In the same way during the long years of the Roman peace the freehold farmer of the Empire had no need of protection either from his stronger neighbours or from outside enemies; it was already provided by the Roman law and the Roman army. But when these had ceased to exist the prime need came to be protection, and the way to obtain this was to gain the support of some more powerful local landowner in return for services rendered to him. So he came to be somebody's man. The process is known as *commendation*. This can be seen happening in the later days of the Empire itself. S. Augustine, bishop of Hippo in the early fifth century, was fully Roman in his ideas, but there is no better description of the advantages to be found in feudal commendation than his account of the attitude of the client of a powerful patron in his day: *'So long as my lord here is safe and sound you can do nothing against me.'* Indeed something like it is bound to appear whenever a central authority breaks up. The villeins and serfs of later feudalism were sometimes the descendants of slaves who had been given their freedom, sometimes of free farmers who had been forced to seek protection. The same thing was true of the higher ranks of society. The way to political power lay through strength in battle, and the strongest in battle would be those who commanded most men. For the weaker the best hope of survival lay in pledging themselves to fight under a stronger than themselves, and the knight service of the Middle Ages comes into being.

Few words in the English language are so constantly misused as 'Feudal'; it has become stock journalese for out of date or inefficient. The historian cannot afford to use it so loosely. For him it must mean a system of land tenure of which the main feature is that land is held not in return for a money rent paid, but for services rendered. Those services can be of two main kinds, labour services in the form of agricultural work on the land of the man to whom the services are owed, or military service to an overlord. In this sense it is clear that feudalism came into existence in the period between the fifth and the eighth centuries. In some measure it developed from German tribalism, and at the same time it answered the political and economic needs of its time. In the context of a disordered society in which central government was impossible it was well adapted to provide the basic needs of protection and military power.

The history of the various peoples who went to make up the *Völkerwanderung* cannot be discussed here. In any case most of them were not sufficiently numerous to retain for long a separate identity when in contact with a higher civilization than their own. But one

thing about them was of vital importance for the future. At the time
of the invasions many were already Christians, at any rate in name.
Many of them owed their conversion to Ulfilas, himself a Goth
from the Empire, who had been made bishop of the Goths in 341.
Ulfilas and his followers had succeeded in converting all the Gothic
tribes to Christianity; in the process he had to invent a new alphabet
for them so that the scriptures might be translated. With a nice sense
of the character of his own people he omitted the books of Kings; his
people were already sufficiently warlike. Unfortunately Ulfilas himself belonged to a heretical branch of Christianity, that known as
Arianism. The Arians believed that Christ was not Himself God; He
was perfect Man but not perfect God, in contrast to the Catholic
belief that He is 'very God of very God'. It should not be supposed
that many of the Vandals or Goths were much interested in argument
about the nature of Christ; their conversion to Arianism rather than
orthodoxy was accidental, though it has been argued that a victorious
and militaristic people would have found the idea of a God who
allowed Himself to be butchered on a cross repugnant. But it set up
a barrier between the invaders and the Catholic Church in the West.
The parallel between God's Empire put to shame at the hands of
wicked men and God Himself crucified on a cross may have struck
the Christian citizens of the Empire. The religious split between
Catholic Romans and Arian barbarians prevented any confidence
between the Church and the new political rulers of the West, and
confronted the Papacy with the imminent danger of domination by
peoples who were not only aggressive and uncultured, but heretical.

One barbarian race alone was an exception, the Franks. They had
taken part in the *Völkerwanderung*, but in a comparatively unspectac-
ular manner. Whereas the journeys of the Vandals from the Black
Sea to the Sahara were to be reckoned in thousands of miles, the
Franks had only expanded gradually from their territories in the
Rhineland into Gaul. They had managed to do so without severing
their connection with their homeland. Distant from the Christian
Mediterranean, they had resisted conversion to Christianity longer.
When it came through the conversion of their King Clovis (c.
496–506), it was to orthodox Catholicism and not to heresy. Almost
alone among the barbarian tribes the Franks had the same religion as
the Romans. This is the first fact which accounts for their historical
importance. The second can be found in their sheer distance from
Rome. The Franks had the same military traditions as the other
barbarian tribes, and even orthodox barbarians in Italy would

probably at times be an embarrassment to the Papacy. But even when they had extended into all Gaul the Franks were safely shut away from Italy by the Alps. They could be used as allies by the Church without the fear that they would come to dominate her.

Clovis's conversion to Catholic Christianity was certainly strategically sound. According to Gregory of Tours, after his conversion Clovis said to his men, 'It troubles me that these Arians hold part of Gaul. Let us go forth then, and with God's aid bring the land under our rule.'[1] 'God's aid' could be practically expressed through the alliance of the Church and that large number of Catholics of Gaul who had resented heretical rule. By the middle of the sixth century the Franks controlled most of modern France, which with the Low Countries and their original home in the Rhineland gave them a solid block of territories from the Rhine to the Mediterranean. They had the full support of the Church in trying to govern them. The bishops moved into that place in the royal administration which was later to cause so much difficulty, yet without them the Franks would have been quite unable to govern so large an area. Their methods of government were in any case only adapted to the rule of their own tribe, and Gaul presented a curious contrast of two societies, the Frankish and the Roman, existing alongside each other. A parallel can perhaps be found in occupied territories after modern wars, where the troops of the victorious power, responsible to their own codes of military law, dominate a conquered population. Until a peace settlement is reached the victors are responsible for all policy decisions affecting the defeated territories, yet at the same time the normal processes of government continue for the defeated civilians. The Franks in the more heavily Romanized southern portions of Gaul had something of the position of an army of occupation; the old Roman administration, now functioning largely through bishops themselves often descended from Roman senatorial families, continued to exist, but it had no part in the high politics of the kingdom. These were played out at the Frankish court.

There were two main Frankish dynasties, known as the Merovingians and the Carolingians respectively. The former were the direct descendants of Clovis; the latter, descendants of Arnulf, bishop of Metz, started as servants of the Merovingians but ended as their controllers. The Merovingians were singularly unfitted to rule a large kingdom; indeed the very word has become a synonym for

[1] Quoted from Gregory of Tours. *History of the Franks,* Trans. O. M. Dalton. Oxford U. P., 1927, vol. ii, p. 75.

impotence. Their power was centred on central and southern France, where Frankish occupation was never sufficiently thick to provide a hard core to the kingdom; they regarded the kingdom primarily as a source of income to themselves, and were only too ready to grant *immunities*, by which in return for a grant of money from the inhabitants large areas of the kingdom were exempt altogether from royal control; above all their practice in succession followed the custom of the Franks. They had never known *primogeniture*, the system by which all a man's land passes intact on his death to his eldest son. Their practice was to divide a man's land equally among his surviving sons. When applied to kingship this must be fatal, for it leads continually to the disintegration of power. Indeed if the Merovingians had not indulged in fratricide and judicious assassination to a truly remarkable extent their power could never have lasted even as long as it did. The history of the Merovingians is rather like the modern history of the Kremlin. Apparently strong figures suddenly disappear without trace, and over the whole story rests the same pall of obscurity.

The Merovingians continued to reign until 751, but for more than a hundred years before that they had no real power. While they had been concentrating on their family quarrels power had passed to those of their nobility who could base it on firmer support from limited areas. The kingdom had been divided up into three main sections, Burgundy, Neustria, and Austrasia, each of which had its own palace to act as a centre of administration. Obviously there were dangers for the kings in such a process, but they were powerless to stop it. Each palace was controlled by a 'mayor'; the word originally meant little more than 'major domo' and indicates the idea of personal service to the king which lies behind most Frankish institutions. These mayors, local men who could command the loyalty of the local nobility, soon came to count for more than the kings themselves in their areas, and the struggle for power in the kingdom came to be between the mayors. The Merovingian kings became ineffective spectators dependent for their continued existence on such ideas of loyalty to their persons if not their powers as might continue to exist. In this struggle the mayors of the Austrasian palace had great advantages. Their area was larger than that of either of the other two mayors, and if it was originally less heavily populated, this could be remedied by energetic men who were prepared to clear the forest and found new villages. Moreover since it included the original territory of the Franks they were less troubled by divided loyalties than those

21

who had more Romanized areas to control. Loyalty to the Austrasian mayors of the palace was increased by the presence of an external enemy lacking in the rest of the kingdom: at the end of the sixth century Pepin I, the third of the Carolingian line of mayors of the palace, had taken the lead in repelling attacks by Frisian invaders of Austrasia, and in so doing had strengthened the popularity of his house in that area. By a series of discreet marriages and by rewarding successful warriors with generous grants of land, known as fiefs, in return for their promise of continued military aid, they had increased their power. By 687 they had established their domination over the other mayors, and made themselves the real rulers of the whole kingdom.

They were only stopped from making themselves kings in name as well as fact by two factors. The whole tradition of the Franks was that kingship was a matter of blood; it might be obtained by murder, but only if the murderer himself stood next in the line of succession. The blood relationship could not be manufactured. Also the Merovingians, *Rois Fainéants* though they might be, were supported by the Church, and the co-operation of the Church was one of the pillars on which Frankish power rested. It was not worth risking its hostility.

It required a catastrophe to enable the Carolingians to gain the trappings of power. That catastrophe was provided by Islam. The prophet Mohammed had died in 632. Eight years later his followers controlled all Palestine and Syria and some of Asia Minor. By 670 they were at the walls of Constantinople itself, and by the end of the century the whole of the north African coast, once one of the most fertile and populous parts of the Roman Empire, was in their hands. They did not stop there. By 711 most of Spain was in their hands and they were preparing for the invasion of France. The danger for Christian Europe was a very real one; the Mediterranean itself was no longer safe for Christian ships, and there were raids on the coast of Italy. No help could be looked for from the eastern empire, which was desperately struggling for its own survival. Yet the Arabs could not be met by negotiation; inflamed with the idea of the Jehad, the holy war, their force could only be met with force. Neither the Merovingian puppet kings nor Eudes, the duke of Burgundy who had been seeking to make himself independent in southern Gaul, were in the least likely to be able to do it. For eighteen years, from 714 to 732, the Arabs ravaged southern Gaul, destroying many towns. There was a spirit of defeatism in the Christian ranks; some local rulers preferred to submit to the Arabs rather than risk defeat, and it looked as if France was.going the same way as Spain. Then in 732 another great Muslim, host surged forward from the Pyrenees under 'Abd ar-Rahman, this time with the intention of attacking northern France as well. Near Tours they met a Christian army under the Carolingian mayor of the palace,. Charles Martel, and at the battle of Poitiers (or Tours) were utterly defeated, and their leader slain. Poitiers is one of the really decisive battles of European history. Although it was many years before the Arabs were safely confined again behind the Pyrenees, it marked the ultimate limit of their advance and decided that Europe north of the Pyrenees should be Christian. For once their forward advance was checked, disunity in the Arab world came to the help of Christendom.

Any debt the Franks owed to the Church was amply repaid, and Charles must have felt himself fully justified in the various confiscations of Church property he carried out to make himself stronger to carry on the war against the Arabs. By any test of hereditary right Charles Martel had little claim to be even mayor of the Frankish palace, for he was only the illegitimate son of his father, Pepin II. His position rested on his acceptance by the Frankish nobility, now confirmed by the services he had rendered to them and to Christendom. But what he had achieved must have raised in his mind and in those of others the question of whether there was much point in continuing the puppet Merovingian monarchy. When the· Merovingian king died in 737 Charles Martel did not replace him, and ruled for the last four years of his life as mayor of the palace to a non-existent king. At his death he left two sons, Carloman and Pepin III. This may explain why he did not take the monarchy for himself, for if he had followed Frankish custom they would both have had to be kings on his death. As it was they ruled jointly as mayors of the palace, even restoring a Merovingian king, Childeric III, as a figurehead. In 747 Carloman simplified matters by retiring to a monastery, and the way was clear for Pepin to join the Crown to the reality of power.

All that now remained was to get the approval of the Church for the transfer; Childeric's views were of no account. The Carolingians stood well with the Church as the saviours of Christendom from Islam. If Charles Martel had ridden rather roughshod over clerical privileges and immunities in France, his son Pepin was well regarded by the Church. He was constantly seeking the advice of the Englishman S. Boniface of Crediton, the greatest churchman of his day, and was supporting him in the great missionary effort he was starting to convert the pagan Saxons and Frisians. Pepin's motives in this were no doubt strategic as well as religious. He gave back, too, some of the Church property his father had confiscated. All this contrasted most favourably with the conduct of the Germanic tribe with whom the Papacy had to deal in Italy, the Lombards. They had arrived in northern Italy in 568, and in some ways were the most savage of all the barbarian invaders. Such Christianity as they had picked up was originally of the Arian variety and though they had subsequently been converted to Catholicism, they never showed much respect towards the bishop of Rome. Latin civilization in Italy had depended largely on such aid as could be furnished to it by the eastern emperor, but the Moslem invasions had now diminished that support. The Papacy was in great danger of losing its lands in central Italy and even Rome itself, and becoming a puppet of the Lombards. In this distress it turned to the Franks. In 739 Pope Gregory III had appealed to Charles Martel when the capture of Rome by the Lombard king Liutprand had looked imminent; on that occasion his appeal had gone unanswered, and the danger had in fact passed. But by 750, when the Lombards were again under the control of an aggressive king in Aistulf, it had been renewed. From the papal point of view it was most important that Pepin should prove more ready to come to the aid of Rome than Charles Martel had been. Anything that was likely to ingratiate the Franks would be good papal policy.

This was the situation when in 750 Pepin sent the Frankish bishop Burchard to Rome to consult Pope Zacharias as to whether the Merovingian kings should be overthrown and the royal title given to those who exercised power. Zacharias agreed that this was so. There were after all plenty of Old Testament precedents for priests making kings. With this authority behind him Pepin could summon a council of the Frankish nobility at Soissons in 751 which confirmed the change, and Pepin could be anointed as King of the Franks by S. Boniface. Childeric was dispatched to end his days in a monastery. The Carolingian monarchy had arrived.

The events of 750 and 751 were to be of much importance in the future, and it is important to be clear about what happened then. The Papacy obviously only conferred the monarchy on Pepin because it hoped that in return the Franks would assist it in its struggles with the Lombards. It was an open invitation to them to intervene in Italy, an invitation which was to be pressingly renewed only three years later. Much of later medieval history centres on the interventions first of the Carolingians and then of the German kings and emperors in Italian affairs; the origin of these interventions came not in a Frankish attempt to dominate Italy, but in a papal attempt to get them to come there. The two processes involved in making Pepin king are also of importance. In the future it would be possible to interpret this either as the act of the Frankish people acting through their representatives the nobility, who had 'elected' Pepin, or as the act of the Church, which had 'chosen' and consecrated Pepin king as Samuel had chosen and consecrated Saul. At present there was no divergence between the two views, but in the future they would lead to much strife.

2

The Carolingian Empire

The coronation of Pepin by S. Boniface was only the first of a series
of acts which marked the close alliance between the Papacy and the
Franks. The successor of Zacharias, Pope Stephen III, remained in
great danger from the Lombard King Aistulf, and in 753 he left
Rome to cross the Alps and interview Pepin in person. Once more it
was a matter of the Papacy making an approach to the Franks, and
not vice versa. Stephen remained in France for more than six months,
and the results of the visit were highly satisfactory to both parties.
Taken by itself the mere fact of the Vicar of Christ coming as a
suppliant to the Carolingian court would have done much to
legitimize the usurping dynasty, but Stephen did more. Pepin was
anointed and crowned again by the pope, and his two sons, Charles
and Carloman, were also crowned as a token that the Church's
favour was extended to Pepin's heirs. His privileged position was
confirmed by the revival of the old title *Patricius Romanorum* for his
use; the new king of the Franks was given a special position which in
the eyes of the Church exalted him above all other Christian kings,
and any doubts which may have lingered about the propriety of
deposing the previous line were dispelled.

Stephen's motive was not empty admiration for Pepin. The
Patricius Romanorum was charged with the responsibility of protecting
the see of Peter and the lands which belonged to it. Later in the same
year (754) the army of the Franks led by their king moved into
Italy, defeated the Lombards, and forced them to return their
conquests, including Ravenna, long the capital first of the Ostrogoths
and then of the Lombards, to the Papacy. Aistulf was forced to
recognize Pepin as his overlord, and his attempt in the next year to
break free from these humiliating terms was similarly defeated. The
position of the Papacy in Italy no longer depended on a shaky moral
prestige; it had now demonstrated that it could call to its aid the
strongest army of the West. The relationship which had thus been
set up between Rome and the king of the Franks was bound to
affect that older relationship which since the time of Constantine had

linked the Papacy with the Emperor. For many years now this had been purely nominal, and strained by differences of doctrine, and the extreme difficulty of communication now that the Muslims controlled the Mediterranean meant that the Emperor in Byzantium could not be of much assistance to the Pope in Rome even if he wanted to be. That the eastern emperor Constantine V realized the danger of the new papal favourites succeeding to his traditional position in the West is shown by his dispatch of three embassies to Pepin, with the aim either of getting him to acknowledge imperial overlordship or of creating differences between him and the Papacy; they were, however, of little effect.

In other ways Pepin continued what had already become the historic role of his house, the protection of Europe from further attacks from the East or the South. The recapture of Narbonne in 759 marked the end of the process of clearing the Moors from France which had been begun by Charles Martel. Two big expeditions against the Saxons in 753 and 768 turned them into tributaries of the Frankish crown, while the work of Christianizing the tribes beyond the frontier went on with his support and made them less dangerous for the future.

Pepin died unexpectedly in 768, but before his death he was able to make the division of his lands between his two sons, required by Frankish custom. That he felt obliged to follow the custom, when the political advantage of an unified monarchy must have been obvious, is a clear indication of how far the Franks were still a tribal people. The division he made gave to Charles, the elder son, all the frontier territories of the kingdom, including the entire coast of France and the Low Countries and all the German border lands. Carloman the younger got a solid block of lands from Paris in the north to the Mediterranean coast in the south, and extending to the east so as to cover Switzerland and much of southern Germany. Clearly the principle was to give to the elder son the more exacting share of the kingdom, that in which constant fighting was to be expected. The division might well have led to war between the two brothers; it was perhaps fortunate that Carloman died in 771. As it was, though they maintained separate courts, Charles was always the dominating brother and it would be fair to regard him as the king of the Franks from 768 to his death in 814.

The reign of Charlemagne appeared to his contemporaries and even more to those who lived after him, a period of magnificent achievement; among the many 'Greats' of history no other has had the title permanently incorporated in his name. This reputation rests on the extent to which he embodied the qualities which went to make up the ideal ruler by the standards of the ninth and tenth centuries. The most important of these was that he was a great warrior, and a warrior in the cause most worth fighting for, the Christian faith. Although the gentle scholar Alcuin might have his doubts about the forcible baptism of whole tribes of pagan Saxons or the execution by beheading of 4,500 pagan rebels at one ceremony, the attitude of Charles's friend and biographer Einhard is far more typical of his age. To him it was nothing short of splendid that hardly a summer passed without his hero taking the sword and smiting the enemies of the Cross wherever they might be. He was then the great Christian soldier. But he was more than that; he was the friend and patron of scholars as well, to whose court wise men came from all over the world. Finally he was the man to whom belonged the honour of restoring the great Roman Empire so long decayed, but now by God's providence and the might of the Franks risen again. How far were these three reputations justified?

There is little doubt that Charlemagne's military fame was justi-fied. His kingdom was surrounded by hostile peoples who made repeated raids on it; often he must have been sorely taxed as to which of two or more conflicting calls on his army should be answered in any one summer. But it is only necessary to look at the map to see the success of his efforts. At the beginning of his reign the Pyrenees was a hostile frontier from which further Arab attacks into France could be expected; after it a Spanish March had been established including Barcelona and most of north-east Spain, from which the reconquest of the rest of Spain could be started. At the beginning of his reign Saxon raids were liable at any moment to break into the Rhineland; by the end of it the frontier of the empire ran along the Elbe and the Saxons themselves have been put firmly under the Christian yoke. In Italy, where before the Franks had appeared only rarely as an invading army, the Lombard Kingdom had been smashed and the remaining Byzantine settlements, Venice alone excepted, had been withdrawn from the north; the frontier of the Frankish empire now lay well to the south of Rome. On the Danube, where at the beginning of the reign Bavaria was much harassed by the raids of the Avars, a central Asian people, by the end of it their power had been broken, the frontier had been advanced deep into modern Yugoslavia and a Pannonian March established which extended Frankish influence even further to the East.

The constant campaigns which brought these results were all planned by Charlemagne, who often accompanied the armies himself. From May, when the grass first grew long enough to enable his cavalry to live off the country, until the autumn he was usually campaigning somewhere on the boundaries of the empire. Clearly their extension owed much to him. This is the more true since at no time did he have the resources for a professional army. The host he had had to be provided by the local landowners he summoned to serve in person or to provide men to serve in their stead. It was not large, and must often have been outnumbered, for the king normally only called out the host in those areas which were likely to be affected by the particular menace with which he was going to deal. There were probably two reasons for this. The lack of any central supply system meant that his armies had to live off the country when the supplies of food they had taken with them were exhausted, and even during the three months its original food was meant to last the obligation to provide 'fodrum' for the horses must have put a strain on the local resources. A really large army might have been as disastrous for the inhabitants of threatened areas as the barbarians themselves. Again it may well have been that the inhabitants of southern France, if called on to meet a Saxon threat on the eastern frontier, would not have responded. Charlemagne had no machinery with which to compel them to answer his summons; in the last resort he depended on their loyalty to him and their own sense of the necessity of a campaign. But this constant change in the personnel of his army must have meant that experienced units could not be built up. He was in a very different position from any Roman general, and his achievements were the more remarkable.

As in most medieval warfare until the fourteenth century Charlemagne's army was essentially a cavalry army. It was made up of knights armed with lances and heavy swords for attack, and defended with cuirasses and small round shields; some of them were also equipped with bows and arrows which could be fired from the saddle, a skill which had been introduced to Europe by tribes like the Huns, who had more or less lived on horseback. Such infantry as there were played a very subsidiary role. The knight was essentially an offensive weapon, the medieval equivalent of the tank in recent wars, and his use dictated an offensive strategy. The aim was to seek out the enemy and disorganize them by a cavalry charge. The battle then turned into a multitude of single combats, in which the heavier arms of the Franks gave them an advantage. Charlemagne's armies were by no means always victorious; indeed the most famous of all his battles was to be a defeat, the destruction of the whole rearguard of his army at Roncesvalles in the Pyrenees in 778, later to be made the subject of the best known of all medieval epics, the *Chanson de Roland*. But he accomplished enough under very difficult conditions to justify his claim to be one of the great commanders of history.

Next we should turn to the revival of religious, literary and artistic life which took place under Charlemagne and his successor Lewis the Pious and which is sometimes known as the Carolingian Renaissance. Renaissance is a word inclined to be over used by historians today; when it is used a comparison is immediately suggested with the Italian Renaissance of the fifteenth century, and it is important to realize the differences between them. The Carolingian movement was on a far smaller scale. Instead of influencing the whole governing class of society it was confined almost entirely to a small section of the clergy. Again it differed from the Italian movement in being the work of churchmen and essentially Christian in its inspiration. Yet there certainly was a revival, and its connection with Charles himself is clear. Charles's interest in it seems to have been twofold: he was interested in learning for its own sake, and he was interested in the possibility of building up a class of educated administrators for his kingdom. His own inclination and the needs of the kingdom pointed in the same direction. The task he faced was formidable. The lay culture of the empire was practically dead, and the number of laymen who could even read must have been minute. If a revival was to be started at all it must be through the Church. Yet even here the outlook was dark enough. Very few of the parochial clergy had any education; a minority of the monasteries alone seemed to offer any hope. Charles' policy was twofold. He sought to attract to his court men of learning from wherever he could find them throughout Europe. When he had secured them he hoped to use them in the work of civilizing his still largely barbarous kingdom. Peter of Pisa and Paulinus of Aquileia came from Lombardy; Theodulf from Spain; Angilbert from France; Alcuin, the greatest of them all, from York. They were attracted no doubt by the generous patronage the king was known to extend to scholars, but they were attracted also by the personality of a king who really was interested in the things of the mind. These men were the inner circle of the king's friends. With them during the winter months he was able to relax in a world of literary allusions, in which the king became David, Alcuin Flaccus, and Angilbert Homer. In the correspondence between them and in the poems they so frequently exchanged there breathes something of the close literary friendships of the world of Erasmus seven hundred years later, yet the atmosphere is more intimate and less torn by internal dissensions than that later world. They were the civilized world, or at any rate that small part of it which still remained among the living, and that consciousness bound them together.

Yet they were not there merely to enjoy each other's company; the king had a great task of education for them. The career of Alcuin can be taken as an example of the nature of this work. He was an Englishman, the product of that vigorous culture in northeast England in the eighth century which had the monastery at Jarrow on Tyneside as its centre and the Venerable Bede as its most famous product. He had himself been a pupil of the cathedral school at York, a school which possessed what was at the time probably the finest library in northern Europe. As a young man Alcuin first met Charles when he was travelling on the Continent with Aelbert the librarian of York. In 767 he became master of the school at York and in 780 he was sent by a new archbishop of York to collect his *pallium*, the cloak which acted as the sign of an archbishop's authority, from Rome. On his way back he had met the king again at Parma; the friendship between the two was immediate and lasting. Alcuin indeed seems to have been one of those rare men whom to know is to like. In 782 he accepted the post of master of the Palace School attached to the Frankish Court. Apart from two short visits to his homeland, the rest of his life was to be spent in Frankish territory. When he retired from his post in 796 he was made abbot of Tours, where he died eight years later. The Palace School was a vital part of the king's educational reforms. Before Alcuin's day it had been little more than a military training establishment for the sons of some of the chief Frankish knights, but under him it became something very different. While it continued to take children it broadened its scope to include adults as well, and concerned itself with the mind as well as the body. If the manuals Alcuin left behind him are to be trusted the education given was largely in the form of discussion between master and pupil, the method of Socrates himself. 'School' indeed now probably suggests something too formal for what must often have been the conversation of friends rather than the instruction of pupils. Yet the list of those who shared Alcuin's teaching and friendship is a distinguished one; it includes Einhard, Charles's biographer, and the ninth-century poets, Rabanus Maurus and Grimald of S.

Gall. Many of them wrote of their master later, and always in terms of affection and respect. But the Palace School performed a political function as well by creating at the centre of the kingdom a group of men who valued the mind and who had influence well beyond the court.

The Palace School was only one of Alcuin's responsibilities. He seems to have acted as the Crown's educational adviser, and his influence can be seen in many of the edicts issued by the Crown known as *capitularies*. These covered a wide range of subjects, but a surprisingly large number of them were concerned with education. The schools with which they were concerned were of three types, the monastic school, the cathedral school, and the village school. The monastic schools were mainly concerned with the training of oblates and young monks for the life of religion, and while every effort was made to see that the larger monasteries had *scholae claustri* for this purpose, they could not affect the world outside the cloister very directly; only in a small number of cases is there evidence also of a *schola exterior*, concerned with those who were not destined to be monks. Yet the monk might always be chosen later in life for some post outside the cloister, and in this way even the *schola claustri* might have its effect on the general life of society. The cathedral schools had as their object the supply of a suitable number of educated clerks for the needs of the Church as a whole, and men so trained could be used in the service of the kingdom as well. Finally there were the schools sometimes kept by priests in the villages for the sons of any who wanted their children to be literate. Charlemagne is sometimes credited with the intention of founding a universal system of elementary education; if so what was achieved inevitably fell very far short of the mark. The vast majority of the inhabitants of the kingdom remained illiterate. Yet there were bishops who were stirred by the king or by Alcuin to attempt something of the sort. Theodulf for instance, who became bishop of Orleans, ordered that there should be a school set up in every village of his diocese. Whether this in fact took place is another matter; even in a fortunate diocese only a minority of the priests would have been capable of conducting the simplest of schools. But, however small the total effect of Alcuin's reforms, they represent the first attempt made by a government to restore some of the educational standards of Europe in co-operation with the Church. They gave the possibility of an educated class, without which the more powerful monarchies of the future could not have existed. Their importance should not be minimized.

Charles and Alcuin concerned themselves with other aspects of cultural life. In an age when all learning had to depend on verbal tradition or on fallible copyists, the documents of the past could become mangled beyond recognition. Great efforts were made to secure uniform and accurate texts of the Vulgate, the Latin version of the Bible, and the works of the early Christian Fathers. Without them the scholars of the twelfth century might well have been faced with a hopeless jumble. At the same time a uniform script, known as the Carolingian minuscule, was introduced to prevent future mistakes; this proved to have such virtues of clarity and grace that it came to be the basis of most later writing. A similar task of ensuring uniformity was performed for the Liturgy, the form of church services, and the plainsong music used in these services.

Charlemagne also took a personal interest in the art of illuminating manuscripts on vellum. There too the link with England, where a vigorous school of illumination had flourished in Northumbria in the seventh and eighth centuries, is clear. In the Frankish kingdom the English school of design could come into contact with Byzantine and Italian as well as with German work. A number of different styles of illumination grew up in his reign and the next. They were centred on some of the large monasteries in whose scriptoria the work was done; those at Tours, Wurzburg, and S. Gall are among the best known. All of them had their own individual styles, and together they serve to make the illumination of the Carolingian period perhaps the finest of the Middle Ages. It is full of flowing lines, life and vigour, much of which would be lost in more intricate designs of later centuries. Without the political achievement of the king it would have been impossible.

The same can be said of the literary output of the age. It contains perhaps no obvious masterpiece, but much of it is of lasting value. In prose Einhard's life of his friend and master stands in a class by itself. Its author's warm regard for his subject is clear in every page, but it stops short of uncritical adulation. He has criticisms to make of his hero's conduct on several issues. But above all he brings the king to life, as neither a bare narrative of events nor a conventional 'stained glass window' type of portrait could have done. Einhard took the Roman historian Suetonius as his model; not since classical times had so clear a literary portrait been drawn. The age contained other good historical writing. Paul the Deacon, a Lombard who spent some of his life at Charlemagne's court, wrote a 'History of the Lombards' which was deservedly to remain a great favourite

33

for much of the Middle Ages; it combines a good understanding of the complicated story he is telling with a collection of vivid stories about the personalities of the past. Only in the trifling matter of dates is Paul less valuable. But it is in poetry that the finest works are to be found. One of the most remarkable features of Carolingian poetry is the sheer bulk of verse produced, not perhaps very surprising when one minor poet of the ninth century, Milo of S. Amand, could produce 2,118 hexameters on the not particularly rewarding theme 'On Sobriety'. Naturally enough much of it is uninspired and consists of the rather sterile imitation of classical models. But there were some who succeeded in breathing freshness and originality into the classical forms. Alcuin himself and Theodulf among Charlemagne's contemporaries, and Rabanus Maurus and Walafrid Strabo in the ninth century, were much more than versifiers. Their best work is to be found in their shorter poems, in Alcuin's poem for his lost nightingale or in Rabanus Maurus's farewell to his old friend Grimald, abbot of S. Gall, the poetry of friends for friends.[1] It is perhaps, like illumination, a minor art, but of its kind there is no doubting its quality, and on the Continent at any rate the preceding centuries had seen nothing to equal it. Limited as its scope and achievement may have been, there is no doubting the reality of the Carolingian Renaissance in literature.

But it is time to move back to the world of politics. The central event of the reign was the coronation of Charles by Pope Leo III as Holy Roman Emperor on Christmas Day 800. The first thirty-two years of the reign all led up to this; its consequences shape the rest of the Middle Ages. For the next five hundred years at least European politics revolve around the knowledge that the Roman Empire is not merely a glorious memory of the past nor a distant city on the Sea of Marmora, but something alive still and present in the West. All political thinking was conditioned by this belief, and although the capital of this empire was only rarely in fact at Rome, most men shared the belief of the Romans themselves that it should be there.

Pepin had died in 768 without solving the problem of Italy. His defeat of Aistulf had quietened the Lombards for a time, but they were still capable of revival. If they once more threatened to dominate the Papacy the services of the *Patricius Romanorum* would again be called on. At first Charles hoped to deal with the Lombards by diplomacy, and Pepin's widow Bertrada, a considerable influence on the early years of his rule, arranged a marriage for him with the

[1] See Helen Waddell, *Medieval Latin Lyrics*. Constable, 1929, pp. 88 and 108.

daughter of Desiderius, now the Lombard king. This, the first of his four marriages, was not a success. Desiderius was not deterred by his matrimonial link with the Franks from trying to dominate Rome and regain the lands the Lombards had been forced by Pepin to restore to the Papacy. In 771 Charles repudiated his Lombard wife, and made it clear that he was prepared to follow in his father's footsteps as the protector of the Papacy against Lombard attack. As a Christian no doubt he objected to the idea of a Papacy that was a Lombard puppet, but there were also solid political reasons for his decision. Past history showed clearly that an over-strong Lombard kingdom would be likely to attack his dominions in southern France. His promise was soon taken up. In 773 he received a request from the new pope Hadrian I (772–795) to come to his aid, and led his army over the Alps to Italy for the first time. The operation was an entire success; a large part of the Lombard army surrendered in Pavia. Carloman's two children, who had fallen into Lombard custody, were retrieved, and Hadrian was restored to his lands. At a ceremony in Rome in 774 Hadrian and Charlemagne not only exchanged oaths of mutual loyalty, but the king made an extensive grant of lands, known as the Donation of Charlemagne, to the pope. Since this grant included lands in the south such as the Duchy of Benevento over which neither king nor pope had any control, and Venetia in the north which was still Byzantine territory, it cannot have been much more than an expression of continued good will at the time, but it was to be important in the future. In making it Charles probably felt that he was doing no more than confirming the Donation of Constantine. This was a document which related how the great emperor Constantine, stricken with leprosy, had been cured of his disease by the prayers of Pope Sylvester. In his gratitude he had not only accepted conversion to Christianity, but on transferring the capital of his empire to the East, 'because where the princedom of bishops and the head of the Christian religion has been established by the Heavenly Emperor it is not just that an earthly Emperor should have power', he had given to Sylvester and all succeeding popes 'all the provinces, districts, and cities of Italy and the West, to be subject to the Roman Church for ever'. This was of course the merest legend. The Donation of Constantine was written probably at Rome, at some time in the eighth century. But until it was conclusively proved to be a forgery on stylistic grounds by Lorenzo Valla in the fifteenth century, it was fairly generally accepted as a genuine document, and formed one of the main grounds for papal claims to temporal power. It is worth adding that the Donation of Constantine and other noted forgeries of this period, such as the Forged Decretals of the ninth century, do not necessarily represent infamous conduct by their perpetrators. They seem to have regarded their actions as the reconstruction of historical documents which had no doubt existed, but had unfortunately been lost; they should not be judged by the moral code of modern historians.

The pattern of events in 773 and 774 was to be repeated at frequent intervals in the succeeding years. No less than four separate expeditions had to be made to Italy in the years between 775 and 788, and in each case the protection of the Papacy and its lands was a major cause of war. It began to be clear that the restoration of the Papacy by the *Patricius Romanorum* could not be a single operation. What was needed was a permanent guard over it in Rome. If the Carolingians had been justified in displacing the Merovingians as Kings because those who had the power should have the authority also, would not the king on precisely the same grounds now be justified in taking for himself the imperial power in the West, where Byzantine authority had long been largely mythical? The idea of restoring the Empire in the West must have occurred to Charles in these years. It is said that when Hadrian died in 795 Charles wept 'as one who had lost a father', but in fact during his lifetime the positions had been the other way round. Charles had even been prepared to receive appeals from the inhabitants of the papal lands against their master. Hadrian was succeeded by Pope Leo III, who was not long in running into difficulties. On 25 April 799, he was attacked by the relatives of the late pope, who are said to have tried to blind him and cut out his tongue. Leo escaped and took the by now well-worn road across the Alps to seek for aid from the king of the Franks. He found Charles at Paderborn, and asked him as protector of the Papacy to restore him to Rome and to punish his enemies. Shortly afterwards messengers arrived from the other faction in Rome also with a request for the king, that he should depose Leo for a variety of crimes, including perjury and adultery. Somebody had to judge between the two parties, and that person could be none other than the king to whom they had both appealed. Alcuin writing to his friend the king at this time points out that of the three authorities who are highest in the world, the Papacy is rent by faction, and the Emperor has been deposed by those of his own household (he referred to the recent deposition and blinding of the emperor Constantine VI by his mother Irene); only the Kingly Dignity remained. He ends, 'The welfare of the Church is now in danger and rests on you alone: you are the avenger of evil deeds, the guide of those who go astray, the comforter of those who mourn, the glory of the good.'[1]

Charles had to go again to Rome, not this time to protect the Papacy from its enemies but to save it from itself. He investigated the charges against Leo and found them to be unjustified. Leo was allowed to clear himself by swearing a solemn oath that he was innocent. This took place two days before Christmas 800. On Christmas Day itself the king went to S. Peter's to hear Mass. As he was rising from prayer before the tomb of S. Peter, Leo approached him and crowned him with a diadem, the symbol of imperial authority. The congregation of Romans then broke into acclamation of the new Emperor, wishing 'long life and victory to the great and pacific Emperor of the Romans'.

From the ninth century until today there has been much dispute about the exact significance of what happened on Christmas Day 800. The Royal Annals of the Franks written very shortly after the event treat it as nothing exceptional; the pope was paying a fitting act of homage to the king and in so doing happened to use the title *Imperator*. Writing some twenty-five years after the event, Einhard even says that Charles did not know he was going to be crowned and was much displeased with the manner in which it was done. The implication is clear: the Pope did not make Charles emperor. He was emperor the whole time even if he did not use the title. All that happened at S. Peter's was that the Church publicly recognized the fact through its head on earth. However, the *Liber Pontificalis*, the chief authority from the Church's viewpoint, makes it clear that in the eyes of the Papacy, Charles was 'made' (*constitutus*) emperor by the act of coronation itself. The significance of this for the future is obvious. What the pope could do he could presumably undo.[2]

Whatever actually happened on that Christmas Day there is no doubting what it meant to most men at the time. The Byzantine episode in the history of the western Empire was over and it was back where it belonged, in Rome. Now at last the two swords of which Pope Gelasius had spoken could be seen as they should be seen, the temporal sword of the emperor guarding the Church, the

---

[1] Epistolae Alcuini (Mon. Germ. Hist. Epistolae IV) no. 174, quoted in *The Era of Charlemagne*. Easton and Wieruszowski. Van Nostrand, Princeton, 1961.

[2] For an excellent brief discussion of the coronation, see *A History of Medieval Europe*, R. H. C. Davis. Longmans, 1957, pp. 149 f.

spiritual sword of the pope sanctifying the Empire. Yet this happy state of affairs in reality rested on two conditions. As the events of the last three years had shown, Charles was so immeasurably stronger than Leo in the purely temporal sense that there could be no question of the pope resisting him. He happened too to be a man of genuine piety who regarded the welfare of the Church as one of his main aims. Both these conditions might be temporary. What would happen when the emperor grew weaker and the Papacy found itself other temporal allies, or when an emperor ruled to whom the spiritual welfare of the Church meant little or nothing?

The historian is bound to ask how real this restoration of the Empire in the West was. Only to ask the question is to suggest at once the large number of ways in which the restored empire fell short of its original. The first and most obvious is size. Charlemagne's Empire even at its greatest extent at the time of his death was less than a quarter the size of the old empire. It did not contain anything to the south or east of the Mediterranean. Even in that north-west segment of the old empire to which his power was restricted, he had no control over Muslim Spain or the Byzantine lands of Sicily or southern Italy, nor, apart from a very nominal and temporary recognition in Northumbria, of Britain. But small as it was in comparison with the classical empire, Charlemagne's was yet far too large for the machinery he had. The Roman Empire had been based firmly on a capital at Rome, the centre alike of government and communications. Rome, at the furthest extreme of the Carolingian Empire, would have been a most unsuitable capital for it; but the new empire had no fixed capital. Charles had a number of palaces; that at Aix-la-Chapelle, sometimes called his capital, was merely his favourite palace. But it was no use the emperor hoping to remain in any one place and to get his instructions obeyed in areas hundreds of miles away. Communications were very bad, and there was no trained civil service at the other end to carry instructions into effect, even if they arrived. Moreover after four hundred years of continually increasing localization of government, the tradition of obedience to the edicts of a central authority had come near to disappearing. The only sure way he had of getting instructions obeyed was by going to the place himself. The 'capital' of the Carolingian Empire was a moving court of the king and the officers of the royal household; it was a poor substitute for Rome. Incidentally the system imposed an intolerable strain on the emperor. Even modern statesmen travelling in comfort have been known to break down under the stress of too

38

much travel. It might work with a man of Charlemagne's exceptional physical and mental energy, but given an old, ill or idle emperor it must collapse.

The lack of any class of educated laymen to act as a civil service has already been seen. Charles tried to remedy it by using churchmen in their place. His warm relations with the Church helped him to do this, but the task of supervising the administration of the Empire was very nearly an impossible one. In the classical empire the authority of the emperor was exercised locally by the governor, an official appointed by Rome and replaceable at any time. In the Carolingian Empire it rested with the count. The count indeed owed an allegiance to the emperor, but since his power was rooted in his position in the local community and not in his appointment by the Crown, local rather than imperial considerations were likely to dominate his mind. A count was in any case likely to be less efficient than a Roman governor, for most of the Carolingian counts must have been illiterate. Various methods were tried to secure obedience from them. Very full and detailed instructions were sent to the counts in the form of capitularies from the court—the emperor must have spent a large part of his life dictating to his travelling clerks. Often such capitularies were issued at a great council attended by as many great magnates as he could get together, so that they should have the added authority of as many as possible of the most important men of the realm.

Even so many of the capitularies were ignored, and the system of *missi dominici* was perfected to try to remedy this. The empire was divided up into large areas, and to each area two *missi dominici* were sent. Very frequently these consisted of one lay noble and one great churchman, so that they could deal with church as well as lay matters. Their terms of reference were wide, probably too wide. Besides seeing that capitularies were being obeyed, they were entitled to hear complaints against the counts and generally to supervise the local administration. Indeed they seem to have been expected to set all wrongs right in the course of a few weeks off from their normal occupations. Since so much of the law of this Empire consisted of local custom they had to be men from the same general area they were appointed to supervise, and this would obviously increase the risk of local favouritism. Above all they had no force which they could easily invoke if their instructions were ignored. It is easy to show the failings of the *missi dominici*, but difficult to see what other system would have worked better. Like the rest of the Carolingian

39

administration it worked after a fashion—so long as Charles himself was alive to direct it.

In the last resort all empires depend on force, the direct force given by an army and the indirect force given by the possession of greater supplies of money than can be controlled by any subject. The Roman Empire had had both a professional army and a highly efficient system of taxation. Charles had neither. His revenue was pathetically small in comparison with that of the Roman Empire. Most of what he did get was in kind rather than money. Just as his army was made up of men who were rendering service in return for land they or their lords held, rather than of professional soldiers serving for money, so his income was largely in the form of grain or other agricultural produce, rather than of money. Except to mark a very few special occasions Charles issued no gold coinage, and the only silver coin he struck was the penny (*denier*). The *solidus* (twelve *deniers* = one *solidus*) is often used as an accounting device, but very often it is the 'solidus of grain', the quantity of grain which could be purchased for twelve deniers. The reason for this is clear. The inhabitants of the villas on the royal demesne could not be expected to pay a money rent, for they were not selling any produce. But they could provide the food and other supplies the court would need in its travelling existence. The capitulary *de Villis* is concerned with the supply of grain and beer, pigs, oxen and horses, and with the furniture the court would need when it came to a villa; it is not concerned with money.

There was indeed a royal treasury, guarded over by the chamberlain, who with the chancellor was the most important of the officers of the household travelling with the emperor. In Charles's time much of its contents seems to have been made up of war booty. So long as the army continued to win great victories a quantity of assorted loot would continue to come into the treasury. It is true that direct taxes and customs on trade continued to be levied in certain areas, but the revenue from these was comparatively unimportant. There just was not enough trade going on, and in any case the machinery for raising such revenue as was possible was not efficient. For example the incorporation of much of Italy into the Empire ought to have led to a significant rise in the royal revenue, for town life of a sort was fairly widely continued there; but this does not seem to have happened. There are, indeed, indications that the Carolingian period saw something of a revival in the economic life of the West. The deniers struck were of good quality, and some of the capitularies show a realization of and an interest in local trade which had been lacking in the days of Merovingian decrepitude. But the Emperor remained a very poor man.

In all these ways the Carolingian Empire cannot be considered a restoration. The resources available to it and the methods of government it had to adopt were nothing like those of the classical empire. There can be no surprise that it broke up. But it is not fair to castigate it, as one modern historian has done, as 'the futile and indeed ridiculous attempt to establish a Germanic Roman Empire'[1]. If it failed to survive Charles's son it achieved two very important results. For the whole length of his reign Charles successfully defended the Christian West at a time when new barbarian invasions might well have wrecked it, and in the East by successfully extending his frontier he made the danger of such a disaster in the future much less acute. Again if Charles did not succeed in fulfilling a tradition, he certainly succeeded in founding one. For many centuries men would look back to the age of Charlemagne as the period when the concept of the Christian Empire really worked. This was the ideal, and subsequent conflicts of Pope with Emperor were deviations from it.

The last years of Charles's reign were occupied with two main problems. The question of the relationship of the recreated Empire in the West with the previously existing Empire in the East had to be solved, and the succession had to be settled. It was not to be expected that the Byzantine emperors, rulers over far richer and more civilized dominions with a continuous tradition of government back to classical times, would regard the new 'emperor' in Rome as anything but an impudent upstart. But it was not impossible that they might be brought to give it some recognition. The early years of the ninth century were worrying times for the Greek emperors. Internally their peoples were divided by the Iconoclastic movement, on the issue of whether the use of images in Christian worship was permissible; it was typical of the East that such a dispute should destroy the peace of the Empire. Externally they were menaced by the savage attacks of the Bulgars on their northern frontier, as well as by the continuing struggle with the Moors in Asia Minor. They were most unwilling to wage a further long conflict with the West in defence of their territories in Italy. At first the shock of seeing a usurper ruling over a large portion of what was their empire, even if they had had no control over it for some hundreds of years, was

[1] See *The First Europe*. C. Delisle Burns. Allen and Unwin, 1947, p. 618.

too much for them. The years between 800 and 814 saw repeated fighting between the two emperors, fighting in which the control of Venice, already mistress of a considerable Adriatic trade, was the central issue. In this, as in his attempts to control Moorish raids for slaves on his southern coasts, Charles felt his comparative lack of sea power; the Franks had no naval tradition. The war was damaging to both empires, and at last in 814 a peace was signed between them. The Byzantines were allowed to keep Venetia, and their provinces in the toe of Italy, and Sicily. Over Venice their control was always to be slight, but Greek continued to be the spoken language of the extreme south of Italy until Renaissance times. Charles was able to guard against future Byzantine attacks in Italy by forming a close alliance with the Duchy of Benevento, which acted as a buffer between the two empires. In return the Eastern Emperors undertook to recognize the Emperors in the West. The negotiations were not finally concluded until just after Charles's own death, but the final act of recognition made a not unsuitable epitaph to his career.

The succession question looked sure to be difficult. It was not likely that one who indulged so freely in matrimony would leave only one son; for some years it looked as though he would be survived by three legitimate sons, Charles, Pepin, and Lewis. Until the end of his days Charles's power rested mainly on the Franks, and as has been seen Frankish custom demanded the division of a man's lands between his sons. On the other hand the whole idea of the Empire demanded that it should be indivisible; constant division would soon reduce it to absurdity. It cannot be known whether Charles would have felt strong enough to violate the customs of his own people. In 806 the Ordinance of Thionville had arranged for the division of his territories between his three sons as kings on his death, but it had not mentioned the Empire. Probably he had in mind an arrangement by which the eldest son had the title of emperor, exalting him over the other two. But Fate harshly solved the problem for him. In 810 and 811 both the elder sons died, and the way was clear for the survivor to succeed as emperor to the whole of the undivided empire. Bernard, the only surviving son of the two dead brothers, could be provided for making him king of Italy, but it was unlikely that he would be a menace to his uncle. The coronation of Lewis, the future emperor, was carried out in his father's lifetime so that there should be no doubt about what should happen when he died. It took place at Aix-la-Chapelle in the autumn of 813, and Charles himself placed the crown on his son's head and recited to him the duties of kingship. This time there should be no question of the Papacy 'making' the Emperor. Even the place is significant. The Frankish Emperor is crowned not in Rome, but in the heart of Frankish territory.

Charles had been ill for some time, and the coronation of his son was his *Nunc Dimittis*. Early in 814 he died, and was buried at his favourite palace at Aix. At the time of his death his lands were at peace for almost the first time. The long road which led from the conversion of the barbarian leader Clovis to the establishment of a great Christian empire under those same Franks had reached its end. The Carolingian Empire may not have been Roman, but Charles deserves his title.

3

The Second Dark Age

The days of Charlemagne's successors were evil: within three years of his death civil war was rending the Empire; by the end of the century the very title of Emperor had become extinct in Western Europe. It might survive as a potent symbol in men's minds of an age of Christian peace at home and knightly valour against the infidel on the borders of Christendom—indeed the further Charles passed into legend and away from history the more admired he became. But the Empire itself disintegrated.

Nor is this surprising. As has been seen the real problem about the Carolingian Empire is not why it collapsed, but how it ever held together. Lacking any real internal unity and threatened from north and south and east by savage and land-hungry enemies, it had only been maintained at all by the genius of its founder. Only a succession of such rulers could have saved it. Yet the speed of its disintegration was dictated by some curiously incompetent statesmanship by his successors.

Lewis the Pious (814–840) started his reign under the most favourable auspices. As the only surviving son of his illustrious father there could be no question of disputing his right to the succession. Moreover, he had already been crowned and generally accepted before Charles's death. But he lacked the strength of personality and the military skill which had made his father so formidable. Charles had had good advisers, but throughout his reign the important decisions were taken on his own initiative. He was an autocrat in an age in which there was everything to be said for strong and undivided control. Lewis by contrast seems to have been a man easily swayed by those around him; in the earlier years of his reign he was much under the influence of the Church, while later he was notoriously ruled by his second wife, Judith of Bavaria. Thus ultimate power came to be exercised by those who had different and perhaps opposed interests from those of the Empire itself. Nothing could have been more destructive of imperial power.

Not that there was anything necessarily weakening about a close alliance with the Church. Indeed it was essential that the only two

44

institutions in the West which served a universal rather than a local ideal should co-operate with each other. This had been a main cause of Charlemagne's success, and later medieval history was to show that on the whole those rulers, such as S. Louis of France, who succeeded in enlisting ecclesiastical support for their government were successful, while those like the Emperor Frederick II who courted the opposition of the Church ended in failure. Yet there is a clear difference between the 'greatness' of Charles and the 'piety' of Lewis. The latter concentrated in the earlier years of his reign on the affairs of the Church to a dangerous extent, neglecting those cardinal duties of defence and secular administration which were the main temporal justifications of the Empire. In 816 Lewis consented to have himself recrowned by the Pope. If this served to show that he was a dutiful son of the Church, it also tended to belittle the coronation he had already received at the hands of his father and to suggest that he owed his position more to clerical support than to his position as hereditary king of the Franks. Yet an emperor who had not got the backing of the Frankish tribes would be nothing.

As his chief adviser in these years Lewis took the Spanish monk S. Benedict of Aniane (†822), for whom he secured the abbacy of Kornelimünster, near Aix. To Benedict the supreme problem of the age was the reform of the Church, or more particularly of those spiritual centres of the religious life, the monasteries and cathedrals. Certainly there was a need of such reform: the extreme decentralization of Benedictine monasticism, by which each abbot and each house was a law unto itself, made it easy for innumerable local variations to appear. To eradicate corruption once it had become established in a house was almost impossible since there was no method of mutual inspection and reform. It was easy, too, for houses to fall completely under the domination of local landowners, who treated them as their own property and often installed themselves or their relations as lay abbots. Around the cathedrals were gathered what was too often a disorderly rabble of clerics, much given to disputes about each other's property. The monks had a Rule (that of S. Benedict) which they did not keep; the cathedral canons had no rule, but in the view of Benedict of Aniane needed one. Various attempts had been made during the eighth century to reform both monks and canons, and Benedict himself at his first house of Aniane had shown the way to a stricter and more literal following of the Rule of S. Benedict.[1] But

---

[1] That the Benedictine Rule was recognized even in theory before Benedict of Aniane's reform now seems questionable.

such reform could only be partial and local unless it had stronger backing behind it. In later ages the Papacy was often to be found as the directing force behind Church reform, but in the ninth century it had neither the prestige nor the machinery to undertake such a rule. Benedict, therefore, looked to the one institution which did seem to possess the necessary power for such a task, the Empire, and Lewis responded enthusiastically to the challenge. In 816 a council summoned by the emperor ordained that cathedral clergy should in future be bound by rules (*canons*) enforcing celibacy and the common possession of cathedral goods on them, and in 817 a similar council enforced a stricter interpretation of the Benedictine rule on all monasteries. Two years later both decisions were incorporated in a capitulary, making them binding throughout the Empire.

There was of course a big difference between ordaining this and being sure that it was actually carried out; old established communities like that of S. Denis at Paris could resist the changes, and when confronted by mass disobedience there was nothing much that the emperor could do. The reforms of Benedict and Lewis were much less effective in bringing about a radical change in the life of the Church than the great reform movement of the eleventh century. Yet such as it was it was a genuine attempt at one of those periodic and necessary reforms by which the medieval Church was renewed. In other ways Lewis showed himself aware of his obligations to the Church: he donated large areas of land to it, thus reversing the methods of his father who had not hesitated to use Church lands as a means of securing lay support; and he carried out an attempt at moral purification of the court, which involved amongst other things the removal of Charlemagne's notorious if admired daughters to nunneries.

Yet if this favour shown to the Church must have commended the emperor to many clerics, in other ways it weakened him. Even the attempt to purify monasticism had its dangers. A capitulary of 817 issued by Lewis at Benedict's instigation laid it down that in future monastic schools should be limited strictly to novices and oblates (i.e. future monks) of the monasteries themselves, and not extended to a wider public. If this capitulary was effective it must have been a blow to one of the standard sources of supply for the Carolingian administration. But much more serious was the loss of confidence which gradually developed between the emperor and the Frankish armies on which the real power of the empire rested. In an often quoted letter Agobard, archbishop of Lyons, used the Christian argument that since 'there is now neither Gentile nor Jew, Scythian nor Aquitanian, nor Lombard, nor Burgundian, nor Alaman, nor bond, nor free. All are one in Christ',[1] so also there should be no difference of laws and custom within the Christian Empire. The idea was an exalted one, and seems to have lain behind much of Lewis' policy. But if it seemed good to Agobard, who was himself of Visigoth descent, it was much less acceptable to Franks, particularly in those west German lands where the real roots of Carolingian power were to be found. To them the empire was a Frankish empire, established and still protected from disaster from the east by Frankish armies. It might be nominally Holy and Roman, but it must remain actually Frankish. The omission from his formal title of the words *Rex Francorum* must have seemed a sign of the forgetfulness by the emperor of the source of his power. Nor did Lewis improve matters by drawing his chief councillors from the western and southern portions of his lands, in men like Benedict himself or the Aquitanian chancellor Helisachar, further emphasizing his break with the historic past of the Franks.

Thus it seems fair to infer that Lewis was weakening the power of the Empire from the beginning of the reign, but it was his handling of the succession problem that did the most damage. At the time of his accession Lewis had three sons surviving by his first wife. Unless two of them died there would inevitably be a succession problem. Frankish custom demanded that the lands of a father should be equally divided among his male children, unless any of them by treason against his parent should justify his disinheritance. But if this division were to happen the Empire would clearly cease to exist. Carolingian authority would disintegrate in exactly the same way as that of the Merovingians had done. Moreover, Lewis' clerical advisers, such as Benedict, were counselling him that at all costs the unity of the Empire must be preserved. To them the Empire and the Church were alike indivisible; indeed the one was only the temporal expression of the other. The authority of Caesar was as well established in holy Scripture as that of Christ, and schism against either was deadly sin.

If the Empire was worth saving Lewis was right to stand by this principle of unity, even at the almost certain cost of civil war. The question was first raised at the general assembly of the Frankish nobility in 817, and Lewis gave a clear answer. Lothar, the eldest son, was to inherit the Empire undivided and to rule as its sole emperor.

[1] M. Deanesly, *A History of Medieval Europe, 476–911.* Methuen, 1960, p. 433.

The two younger sons, Pepin and Lewis, were to be kings of Aquitaine and Bavaria respectively, but they were to be clearly subordinate to their brother in the same way that their cousin Bernard had been left as a subordinate king of Italy by Charlemagne.

This apparently sensible arrangement certainly involved a risk of civil war, for both the younger brothers might feel that they had been cheated out of their birthrights, and neither would have any difficulty in collecting support. The suspicions which Lewis had already aroused of not being a true Frank at heart were strengthened tenfold. Perhaps Lewis was right to feel that the issue had better be settled at once even at the risk of war, rather than left vague in the Micawberish hope that something would turn up. If he had made no disposition of the Empire at all war after his death would have been certain, and all three sons would have had equally good claims. As it was there was a reasonable hope that there would be sufficient loyalty to the new tradition of Empire to outweigh the old Frankish custom and avoid war. At worst he should be capable of decisive victory. But it was certainly unfortunate that loyalty to the Emperor and to his division of lands should have been weakest in the areas of the Empire where military traditions were strongest.

It is impossible to tell if Lewis's policy would have succeeded, for he proceeded to wreck what chances he had by an act of gross stupidity. The immediate result of the division of 817 had been a revolt by Bernard in Italy; he seems to have thought, rightly or wrongly, that his rights there were threatened by the failure to guarantee them in 817. This revolt had been satisfactorily defeated, Bernard had been captured, and, no doubt to the gratification of his relations, had died from the effects of having both his eyes put out. But the good effects of his victory were immediately wiped out by Lewis. Recently widowed by the death of his first wife, Irmengard, he proceeded to marry again. His new wife was a Bavarian princess called Judith, and in 823 she gave him another son, the future Charles the Bald. The new child of course had no rights under the division of 817, but, instead of ignoring the issue of his unfortunate lapse for succession purposes, Lewis proceeded to claim for this new child not only a share but a disproportionate share in the inheritance. After the death of Benedict of Aniane in 821 Lewis, weak-willed and sensual for all his piety, fell completely under the influence of his wife, and she naturally enough wanted her son favoured above his half brothers. The pattern is that of many a sordid family quarrel, but here it spelt the ruin of an empire. While Charles was still a young child he was given large territories at the expense of his elder brothers; meanwhile the claims of the emperor elect Lothar were increasingly ignored even though he had already (823) been crowned by the Pope. By 829 Lothar's name was being omitted from all imperial edicts where before it had been included and it began to look as though Lewis intended his youngest son to succeed him as emperor. It was only natural that Lothar and his supporters should turn to arms to protect their rights.

A confused civil war followed in which the elder brothers were fighting not only against their father but amongst themselves, and a number of new 'settlements' were announced, none of which had any effect. One incident alone can be quoted for the contrast it gives with the strong days of the Empire under Charlemagne. In 833 Pope Gregory IV intervened in the war to try and bring peace to the Empire. Only a generation before the Franks had been intervening in Italy to settle the disputes of the Papacy; now the roles were reversed. There could be no clearer sign of the decay of imperial power. The only difference was that while Charlemagne had been successful in his intervention Gregory failed. In 838 one of the sons, Pepin, died, and in 840 Lewis followed him. But neither of these two deaths put an end to the futile, dismal struggle. The bloodiest of the war's battles seems to have been between Lothar on one side and Charles and the young Lewis on the other in 841.

> O the grief and the bewailing! There they lie, the naked dead,
> On their bodies wolves and crows and vultures ravin and are fed
> There they lie, unburied horror, idle corpses that were men.[1]

About this slaughter of Christian Frank by Christian Frank there could be none of the exaltation that accompanied the deeds of Charlemagne against the Infidel; it was an unmitigated disaster for the Empire and for Christ.

Peace came at last, as so often, through the exhaustion of all the contestants rather than because any decisive victory had been won. Indeed the terms arranged by the Treaty of Verdun in 843 were curiously similar to the original partition Lewis the Pious had intended in 817, before his marriage to Judith of Bavaria had brought chaos. Once more there were three sons to be considered, Charles the Bald

---

[1] *O luctum atque lamentum! nudati sunt mortui,*
    horum carnes vultur, corvus, lupus vorant acriter;
    orrent, carent sepulturis, vanum jacet cadaver.

Quoted from Angilbert, 'On the battle which was fought at Fontenoy'.
                    Helen Waddell, *Medieval Latin Lyrics*, Constable, 1929, p. 104.

simply inheriting the share which had been given to the now dead Pepin. To him went all modern France except the Rhone valley and the Riviera, the mountainous areas in the East (the French Alps, the Vosges, and the Ardennes), and an area in the north-east near the modern Belgian frontier. Charles also held territory to the south of the Pyrenees, the remains of that Spanish March Charlemagne had set up to hold the Saracens of Spain in check. To Lewis, called the German, a kingdom of Eastern Franks was devised for the most part from what today are German-speaking lands. Its eastern frontier was the ill-defined line between Christians and the pagan untamed Slavs of the forests in the east; in the north this frontier ran roughly along the river Elbe; further south Lewis' domain included the upper reaches of the Danube. The western frontier of Lewis' kingdom was the Rhine in southern Germany, but further north it cut back to reach the Baltic coast at Bremen. Between these two kingdoms of the west and the east was to lie a third, to which historians have given the name Lotharingia. It included the Low Countries, the lower Rhine basin, and the territories of eastern France, modern Switzerland and the kingdom of Italy. This central kingdom contained both Rome, the traditional capital of the classical empire, and Aix, Charlemagne's most favoured seat of government, and to its king was given the imperial title. Lothar was thus exalted in status over his brothers but given no effective control over them.

It is easy for the historian to be smugly wise after the event. Lotharingia was to have a short and unhappy history as an independent power. Far from dominating its neighbours, by 869 most of it had already been divided between Lewis the German and Charles the Bald. For more than a thousand years that part of it which lies north of the Alps has remained of uncertain allegiance, a political vacuum fatally attracting its stronger neighbours. When the German empire was strong and the French monarchy weak, as in the tenth century, much of it came under German control; when the roles were reversed, as in the age of Louis XIV, the French would dominate. Once in the fifteenth century, when both happened to be weak at the same time, the duchy of Burgundy nearly succeeded in reviving Lotharingia. But it is an area which has never had political stability; it has remained a troubled no-man's-land, site of Bouvines and Rocroi, Sedan and Verdun, and all the other battles which marked the relationships of eastern and western Franks down the ages. There has been no difficulty in finding 'inevitable' reasons why this should have been so. Lotharingia was the wrong shape, being too long for its breadth, so that it had far too long frontiers to defend with not enough hinterland behind them, and dangerously extended communications. The Alps, impassable in winter and difficult at any time of the year, cut its territories in two. Nor were there any racial or linguistic bonds to bind its peoples together. What possible links were there between the Frisians of the Dutch coast, the Romanized Gauls of Provence, and the Lombards of the Po valley? Yet much the same arguments applied to the other two kingdoms united at Verdun. France and Germany too had no sort of linguistic or geographic unity in 843. But the men of Verdun were not trying to create modern nation states, succeeding in two out of three cases but dismally failing in the third. They were seeking rather to build up three approximately equal kingdoms, in which each king would be supported by a sufficient number of tenants-in-chief who were already his men. At the same time they hoped to arrange that each king had an adequate revenue of his own. Thus they thought much more of the problems of vassallage than of modern political geography, and there is no reason to think that in terms of vassallage Lotharingia was not as sensible a creation as either France or Germany.

What of course could not be arranged at Verdun was that all three kings should live to a ripe age and leave behind them one, and only one, son. As things turned out Lothar the emperor died first in 855, twelve years after Verdun, leaving behind him three sons. They showed themselves true Franks by immediately dividing the inheritance. The imperial crown could not be divided, and passed to Lothar's eldest son, Lewis II. The consequences are not surprising. Now that the emperor was much weaker than either Lewis the German or Charles the Bald they could both proceed to enlarge their territories at the expense of Lotharingia. The central kingdom gradually disintegrated, and the imperial title, now of little account, was bandied about among rulers such as the Italian, Guy of Spoleto, and Arnulf of Carinthia. When the latter died in 899 not even the Papacy, in the ninth century always the champion of the imperial idea, thought it worth renewing. The Carolingian Empire had come to an ignominious end.

So far this chapter has dealt with the Carolingian decline as if the Empire was its own self-contained world. This was far from the case. Indeed one reason why men were content to see it disappear was that since the death of Charlemagne it had so markedly failed to solve the problem which was its real *raison d'être*, the problem of defence. In their earlier days the Carolingians had saved Europe from the menace

51

of Islam by their exertions; now with the danger scarcely less great they had come to concentrate solely on the internal struggle for power.

As in the reign of Charlemagne, the empire under his successors remained threatened by barbarian attack. Now indeed the whole western and northern seaboard was open to Viking attack. But whereas in the earlier period the emperor had been able to bring the main Frankish host, if not to the rescue, at any rate to avenge plundered areas, now the host had largely disappeared; what was left of it was being dissipated in civil war. Local leaders were left to cope with the problem of defence as best they could with local resources. It is not surprising that they were not always successful.

There were three main types of invader during the ninth century, the Arabs of the Muslim world, the Magyars and the Norsemen. Of the three the Arabs were probably the least serious. In the eighth century Islam had really threatened to swamp Christendom, if not with barbarism, at least with an alien culture. But now the Arab world had passed from the period of violent military expansion into a more settled condition. The Arabs no longer needed any more territory than they possessed and their original enthusiasm for winning all Europe for Allah by the sword had waned. But they remained formidable fighters by sea as well as by land, and their control of the Mediterranean enabled them to profit by any weakness in either the eastern or the western empire. They appear in the history of the ninth century not only as pirates whose activities halted all but the most coastbound shipping, but as raiders who, descending from their ships, often penetrated far inland in Italy and southern France in search of loot and Christian slaves for the markets of the Near East. So feeble were the measures taken against them that they were able to maintain a settled base for a considerable time on the French Mediterranean coast, and from there to send their ships right up the Rhone and so to sack towns in the middle of France. Indeed nothing so clearly illustrates the defencelessness of the Frankish Empire against its external enemies as the fact that some places, notably Luxeuil in Burgundy, were sacked both by Norsemen from the Seine and by Arabs from the Rhone.

The Arabs were also tempted into Italy by its extreme weakness, which offered the hope of good plunder. Sicily was obviously both a tempting prize and a useful base for any Mediterranean sea power, since it can be defended by sea from any attack by land. By 831 they had captured Palermo, and Arab bands were soon operating in southern Italy as well, often making their first appearance as mercenaries on behalf of local princes who valued their military qualities or the use of their ships. The Normans were later to gain a foothold in exactly the same way; Italian princes seem to have put very little trust in local talent. Arab settlements appeared in many places in the south, and raiding parties penetrated further north, reaching, but not taking, the tempting prize of Rome more than once and sacking Monte Cassino, not for the first or last time in its existence. But the urge to make permanent large scale conquests had gone. The chief result of their invasions was the creation of a number of isolated Muslim communities which were to remain a problem for Christian rulers of the South for many generations.

The Magyars were yet another tribe of invaders from the East, who had their origin in the steppes of central Asia and were moving west towards Europe. As the weakness of the Roman Empire in the fourth century had invited attack, so now the weakness of its Carolingian successor acted as a magnet. The Magyars themselves were famous for their horses. Living much of their life on horseback, they were still in a nomadic stage of existence, preferring a life of fighting and hunting to one of cultivation. This made it necessary for them to be always on the move, for no form of existence requires more space in relation to numbers. The skill of their cavalry made them formidable, if dangerous, allies, and like the Goths before them they first appeared in the West by invitation. Arnulf of Carinthia, who had been elected king of the East Franks in 888, tried to use them as allies against the opponents of his rule in Moravia, and so tempted them to leave the Danube plain which had been their temporary resting place. Having tasted conquest the Magyars wanted more, and proved quite uncontrollable as allies. In 899 they carried out a disastrously destructive raid through Lombardy, and later turning north smashed their way into Hungary. Here they were well placed to ravage Germany, and no part of the country was safe from their attacks. The efforts of Lewis the Child, Arnulf's successor, to check them were quite fruitless, and Magyar bands even ravaged Burgundy, which thus had the gloomy distinction of suffering from all three types of invader. Such defence as was possible fell to local dukes. who could organize the construction of castles in which some at any rate of the local inhabitants could take refuge until danger had passed. The days of defence by organized attack under the leadership of one emperor were gone, and no answer was found to the Magyar menace until the power of the Empire was restored in the East by Otto the Great; only when they had been defeated with the sword could they be won to Christianity and to a more settled life as cultivators of the soil.

The third of the assailants of the Empire were the Nortmanni or Vikings. For the historian of western Europe they are by far the most important, for whereas Arabs were contained in their own isolated groups and Magyars were in the end restricted to Hungary, they were permanently to occupy much of Europe. In the process the original Viking stock was absorbed in the course of a surprisingly short time by the peoples they conquered, so that, for instance, the Normans who conquered England seem to be French rather than Scandinavian. Yet the reverse side of this rapid loss of identity was that the Viking characteristics could be rapidly absorbed by a wide circle of European peoples. From the Scandinavian lands to Sicily, from Ireland to the kingdom of Jerusalem the history of the Middle Ages bears everywhere the traces of the Vikings.

The Vikings show marked differences from the other barbarian invaders of the post-classical period. In Scandinavia they had been off the main routes of the *Völkerwanderung*, and their period of movement does not seem to come as a reaction to external pressure. The normal pattern of movement followed by Goths and Huns and Magyars was from east to west. No such pattern is observable with the Vikings: while some go west to England or south to Normandy, others go far east deep into Russia to open up the so-called Varangian route to the Black Sea and Byzantium. The other peoples were migrants, in search of a new homeland. The Vikings were traders and raiders long before they were settlers, and such settlements as they made often grew out of the need for efficient raiding bases. All the other barbarians, the Frisians and Saxons alone excepted, were essentially continental peoples, moving irresistibly across the land but halting when confronted with that alien element the sea. Even the narrow waters surrounding Britain caused an appreciable gap between the withdrawal of the Roman legions and the arrival of the first foreign invaders. The Vikings were a people of the sea, moving great distances in their long boats and appearing unexpectedly from across the vast and trackless ocean. To most Europeans there must have been something unnatural about this strange mastery of an unknown element.

Nor were the Vikings really barbarians in the same sense as the Huns. Certainly they were savage enough, knowing nothing of the

Christian God, but dedicated to fierce pagan deities and despising the man who 'has never given a warm meal to the wolf'. But ruthless destroyers though they were, they showed, as a great American scholar has put it, 'a strange combination of the primitive and the civilized—elemental passions expressing themselves with a high degree of literary art, barbaric adornment wrought with skilled craftsmanship, Berserker rage supplemented by clever strategy, pitiless savagery combined with a strong sense of public order, constant feuds and murders coexistent with a most elaborate system of law and legal procedure'.[1] Without anything but a primitive runic script, they yet had in their sagas a rich oral tradition which could flower into a literature as soon as they had mastered the use of the alphabet. These sagas are the main source of information about the Vikings, and they disclose a strange world, far different from anything in the existing European tradition with its sophisticated urban Latin roots. It is a world in which the mighty are the mighty in battle, and the only virtues are courage and endurance against the foe. Yet the sagas show the Vikings to have been a people of acute imagination, capable of reflecting on the tragedy of human existence in as intense a way as anyone since the Greek tragedians of the fifth century B.C. The prevailing mood is one of doom; the sea is rough and few there are who overcome it. Even those who by prodigious valour triumph for a time must in the end meet their fate. All that a man can do is to quit himself like a man. The same imagination showed in the bold decoration and flowing lines of Norse gold and silver work. In them can be seen the qualities which, when coupled to new techniques and linked with Christian belief, were to cover northern Europe with churches and to revitalize the whole of European architecture.

One other quality of the Vikings calls for mention, their extreme adaptability. In one sense this is a sign of weakness; many of the traditional features of Norse life were quickly jettisoned when they came into contact with the rest of Europe. The Norse gods for instance did not last for long in the face of Christianity, and despite the large extent of Viking conquest there are very few words of Scandinavian root in most European languages. Even Norman French shows that the native population was capable of absorbing the invaders, so that scarcely any trace of Scandinavian remained. This probably shows that, except perhaps in England, there were never very many Norse invaders; their energy and martial skill must have

[1] C. H. Haskins, *The Normans in European History*. Constable, 1959 ed. p. 36.

made them seem far more than they were. But they were capable of turning their original qualities to very different uses. The descendants of the men of the. long ships showed an equal skill in the quite different conditions of feudal warfare in Europe, as heavily armoured knights on horseback rather than lightly armed sea raiders. Later the sons of these men were to adapt themselves to quite different conditions of warfare again on Crusades. In the same way the descendants of the fierce worshippers of Odin were to bring the same fiery zeal to the service of the Galilean god and make themselves the foremost warriors of Christ. Their ideals and their methods changed; the spirit enthusing them did not.

The Viking invasions to the west of Scandinavia began in the second half of the eighth century. They took the form of two main lines of expansion. The northern was to cross the North Sea and establish settlements on the Shetlands and from there to attack Scotland and northern England, and to move on to form settlements in Ireland and Iceland. Later these Norsemen were to go even further, reaching Greenland and in all probability some part of the north American continent. These tremendous sea voyages, undertaken at a time when most European sailors feared to go out of sight of land, are well-nigh unbelievable achievements, but they are of little significance in the mainstream of European history. The other line took Viking ships across the North Sea in a south-westerly direction, so that they struck the east coast of England, the Frisian Islands, the Dutch and north German coasts and both the English and French Channel coasts. The Viking leaders were quite prepared to trade as well as raid; one buried in the Hebrides had a pair of scales included in his tomb, along with his sword and spear and axe. But the extreme weakness of the defences put up to them must have acted as a spur for their more destructive instincts, and it was as destroyers above all that they appeared to contemporaries: 'from the fury of the Northmen, good Lord deliver us' was an insertion in more than one ninth-century litany. Viking attack took a form to which no ruler in Europe had an immediate answer: it was far less predictable even than the attacks of the Arabs or the Magyars. Neither the Saxon kings in England nor the Frankish kings on the Continent had any understanding of sea power or any naval forces. In the Mediterranean there were at any rate some Byzantine Christian ships to dispute the control of the Moorish galleys; in the North there was nothing to set against the Viking long ships. Charlemagne himself by breaking the independent power of the Frisian islanders had unwittingly broken the only force which might have been able to contest the Viking control of the sea. They were thus free to appear at will anywhere along some thousands of miles of coastline, to burn and destroy coastal villages, and as they grew bolder to sail up navigable rivers such as the Rhine, the Thames or the Seine, and bring destruction deep into the heart of the countryside. Even assuming that the feudal host was not engaged in some domestic quarrel elsewhere, long before the ponderous machinery necessary to bring it into existence had taken effect the raiders would be off, only to reappear elsewhere.

At first it was outlying districts that suffered the main weight of these attacks. The comparative strength of Charlemagne's empire no doubt acted as some deterrent. But the success of the Vikings there emboldened them to more ambitious plans, and the disastrous wars over the inheritance of Lewis the Pious made northern Europe an easy target. In 841 a large Viking force suddenly appeared in the Seine, and from then on none of the rivers of northern Europe were safe. Viking settlements appeared on islands off the coast, such as Rhé in the Bay of Biscay or Walcheren in the Rhine estuary, so that the threat became perpetual rather than occasional. Paris was sacked as early as 845, and in the eight-fifties raids by the Northmen were constantly taking place. Orleans and Tours, Nantes and Chartres, there was scarcely a French town of any size which did not suffer from their disastrous attentions, and the Rhine and the Weser proved as easy to navigate as the Seine and the Loire. Some ships even made the journey through the straits of Gibraltar and began raiding the Mediterranean coasts, damaging Christians and Muslims alike.

Effective defence against these attacks was very difficult. It needed a combination of the building of navies and coastal and river defences with the development of highly mobile land forces in constant readiness to move against any new threat. England in the end produced a military genius in Alfred capable of stopping the Norsemen, but Lothar I (843–855), Lewis the German (843–876) and Charles the Bald (843–877) were not men of genius. Even if they had been able to concentrate on the Vikings it is unlikely that they would have found an answer, but the Vikings were only one of their problems. Charles the Bald, king of the West Franks, is a rather pathetic figure. Faced by Vikings in the north and west and by Arabs in the south, he got only the most tepid loyalty from his own alleged vassals; in Aquitaine and Brittany the troubles of the king were selfishly regarded as excellent opportunities for asserting their own independence. Surrounded by enemies Charles nevertheless retained a touching belief in the righteousness of his cause. Early in his reign he was too inclined to follow the disastrous English precedent of Danegeld, paying the raiders to go away. Inevitably, submitting to this type of blackmail only made future raids more certain. But he came to realize the possibility of more effective measures, such as the fortification of Oissel, an island in the Seine (858), or the attempt to build a bridge across the river at Pitres (862). Once the rivers could be blocked the interior of the country would be reasonably safe. He attempted to enforce regulations to bring out all freemen who had arms and a horse to the support of local counts in times of emergency; all must co-operate in defence works, and strict regulations were drawn up against those who tried to buy security for themselves by bartering their arms to the enemy. Yet ultimately these measures were in vain. Near the end of his reign (875) Charles had solved none of his domestic problems, but yet consented to accept the vacant imperial title from Pope John VIII, and with it the role of defender of the Papacy against Arab attack. He would have done better to have kept to his own problems. To make himself free to visit Italy he was forced to revert to the old evil Danegeld policy, and to put his trust in a number of counts whose loyalty to an absentee so-called emperor was very dubious. When he died in 877 his counts had already risen in revolt against him and the Viking problem was as far from a solution as ever. In the reigns of his successors, men such as the feeble Louis the Stammerer and the incompetent Charles the Fat, things only went from bad to worse. It seemed that the kingdoms of the Franks, like the Empire, were doomed to disappear in constant division and anarchy.

Not until 911 does any light appear in the darkness. In that year Charles the Simple, the nominal king of the West Franks, decided to recognize that there was no longer any hope of expelling the invaders. If they could not be driven out he had better recognize them and so perhaps have a better chance of living on peaceful terms with them. The jarl of the particular Viking band which controlled the Seine mouth at that time was Rollo, and since he was regarded by the Vikings of Scandinavia itself as a rebel he may have been the more ready to become Charles's man. By doing homage to Charles the Simple, Rollo became his 'man', pledged to serve Charles as lord and to receive his protection. It is said that at the ceremony Rollo exclaimed 'No, by God' at the moment when he should have placed his hands between those of his new lord, and that the deputy he appointed to take the oath in his place deliberately pushed over the French king. However, this may be, the relationship between them certainly lacked reality, as feudal homage always did when the 'protected' was a great deal stronger than the 'protector'; later French kings were to stand in a similarly anomalous position towards their vassals the Angevin kings of England. But despite this artificiality the ceremony is an important dividing line in French history. The area given over to Rollo as duke in 911 was not very large, consisting only of the area on both sides of the Seine later known as Upper Normandy; the duchy was to be enlarged in 924 by the addition of Middle Normandy (the Bersin), with its capital of Caen, and completed in 933 by the addition of the area of the Cherbourg peninsula (the Cotentin). But the ceremony of homage followed as it was by the conversion of Rollo to Christianity in the next year, marks the beginning of the very rapid progress by which the Vikings of France became Normans.

The immediate impression of the ninth century is one of disintegration. All that the Frankish leaders had achieved from the coronation of Pepin to the death of Charlemagne was lost; by the beginning of the tenth century Europe seemed to be back again in the period of barbarian invasion, and the attempt to restore a unified Christian empire had been shown to be a failure. But every historical period is one of both growth and decline. The Carolingian empire could never have succeeded, but on its ruins were laid the foundations of a new Europe.

4

The Saxon Empire

The last of the East Frankish kings who was a direct descendant of
Charlemagne, Lewis the Child, died in 911. But the powers he had
exercised had been only a faint shadow of those of his ancestor.
Germany had never been so completely Romanized as France, and
the Carolingian attempt to instal methods of centralized government
there had been short lived. By 843 the system of *missi dominici* had
broken down and capitularies were no longer issued for the whole
kingdom. This had left defence as the remaining function of the
Crown, but even here the kings of the East Franks had not been
effective. The task of repelling barbarian raids had devolved more and
more upon the local counts, who were on the spot to organize
resistance. Inevitably the status of the counts had increased as royal
prestige waned. Under Charlemagne the counts had been royal
officials replaceable at least in theory by the emperor; by the tenth
century the descendants of these counts were ruling in Germany,
often as dukes. Within his own territory each duke had far more
power than the king; his office had become hereditary, a fate which
frequently befell medieval offices, and it had become impossible for
any but a very strong king to replace him. Indeed a German historian
has written that 'the German duchies were considered not as offices
derived from the Crown, but as units of independent origin'.[1] The
independence of the duchies was increased by the existence within
each duchy of a different tribal tradition and set of customs, and the
dukes had come to regard themselves as jealous protectors of these
claims to be different.

There were four such great stem duchies in 911. The eastern
frontier of the kingdom was protected in the north by the great
duchy of Saxony and in the south by Bavaria; on these two fell the
main weight of protection against the Magyars and the Slavs. The
duke of Suabia in the south of Germany had had as his original purpose
the protection of the Alpine passes; Franconia lay in the centre of

[1] Mayer, *The Historical Foundations of the German Constitution.* Trans. Barraclough in
Mediaeval Germany. Blackwell, 1948, vol. ii, p. 12.

Germany. To these four might be added a fifth, the western duchy of Lotharingia or Lorraine, poised uncomfortably throughout its history in its allegiance between France and Germany. It must not be thought that the German dukes were opposed to the monarchy; indeed, in so far as it was the origin of their own rights they supported it, but they were in a position to be independent of it.

In 911, of the duchies only Lorraine remained so loyal to the Carolingians that its duke sought out the king of the western Franks, Charles the Simple, and did homage to him. There was not the least likelihood that Charles would be of any use to Germany; he could not even deal with his own invaders in the West. What hope was there that he could help in defeating the Magyars? But if Charles was not to be king, there remained an open problem of succession. It is a tribute to the strength of what was now a respectably old tradition of the Franks, backed by dim memories of the unity of Rome, that the monarchy did not just quietly disappear. Certainly if the Germans had allowed all unity to be lost in a welter of conflicting duchies the defence of the country would have been even more difficult than it already was. In this juncture they reverted to an even more ancient tradition. The kings of the Franks when they had been still a race of nomadic fighters had not been chosen by hereditary right, but by the acclamation of the chief warriors and wise men. So now the new king of the eastern Franks should be chosen by a meeting of all the most notable princes, lay and ecclesiastical, of the whole country.

Such an assembly met at Fircheim in 911. Its choice fell on Conrad, the duke of Franconia, who thus became Conrad I (911–918), the first and last of the Franconian dynasty. The new king received the support of the other dukes—he was indeed proposed by the duke of Saxony—and the blessing of the Church through the sacred oil of coronation. Yet his reign was a complete failure. Conrad was most anxious to assert his authority as a king over the other dukes, but to make this the primary aim of his policy was a grave mistake. The reason for which the monarchy had been preserved was to lead a successful German effort against the enemies who threatened the whole country from the east; a king who succeeded in this would find that prestige and authority within his borders would be added to him. But Conrad's external military ventures were largely directed not against the common enemy, but towards establishing Franconian rule over the duchy of Lorraine, and even in this he was unsuccessful. Understandably the other dukes resented this use of the royal position. At best Conrad's policy was irrelevant to their peoples, at worst it was merely a foretaste of the fate in store for them.

A central feature of Conrad's government was its dependence on churchmen. In part no doubt this was a conscious imitation of Charlemagne's own methods, in part a necessity of any attempts at large scale government in his age. But the dukes outside Franconia were probably right in seeing more in it than that. The Church had always favoured the imperial aim; it too was a European institution transcending local frontiers, and it might be expected to favour the monarchical as against the ducal idea. Moreover, it was a considerable property owner. The duke of Franconia alone could not hope to exercise much power outside his own duchy, but if he stood in close alliance with the Church he would be able to control some power at least throughout Germany. So it was that Conrad trusted the greatest share of the royal government to ecclesiastics. Archbishop Hatto of Mainz, Bishop Saloman III of Constance and Bishop Pilgrim of Salzburg were all in close association with the cause of royal authority; for the two latter at any rate this necessarily meant opposing the authority of their dukes. At a synod called at Hohenaltheim in 916 it was formally proclaimed that any one who sought to lessen the prerogatives of the Crown incurred the full anathemas of the Church. Since after so many years of fluctuating royal authority the precise extent of those prerogatives was inevitably ill defined, this was to bring spiritual weapons into politics with a vengeance.

It is not difficult to understand the resentment this policy caused outside Franconia. Not only did it represent a real threat to the power of the dukes to control their own territories, but to many important landholders it must have seemed that the Crown itself was engaged in fermenting the blackest treachery. For throughout Germany the idea that laymen owned churches was well accepted. That all churches belonged to an impersonal corporation controlled from Rome was very far from being accepted in tenth century Germany; indeed it simply was not true. A priest might owe his spiritual powers to episcopal ordination, but his church, the very land it stood on and its fabric, as well as his appointment to it, he owed to the lay owner of the church. The nearest analogy in more recent times is perhaps that of a domestic chaplain to an aristocratic family in the eighteenth century, and the German landowner would no more expect 'his' clergy to turn against him than a later patron would expect publicly to be denounced by his own chaplain. The system is known as the *Eigenkirche* or 'proprietary church' system, and it gave many laymen from the dukes down to quite humble sub-tenants a feeling of ownership in their churches, and a consequent resentment of any attempt to enlist their churches against what they regarded as being their proper rights. Incidentally this system was strongly enough entrenched to make it very unlikely that Conrad would succeed in mustering the whole German church in support of the Crown. Conrad then was attempting a policy which was certain to bring him into conflict with his own most powerful subjects, without any reasonable hope of gaining enough support to be able to defeat them. A wiser man would have realized that he could not at once dispense with the help of those to whom he owed the Crown itself. In the last two years of his reign he was faced with revolts against royal authority in both Saxony and Bavaria, and in each case was badly defeated in his efforts to try and put them down. When he died in 918 he was king only in name; in reality he was no more than an unsuccessful duke of Franconia.

On the death of Conrad there looked to be every chance that the German kingship would simply cease to exist. To the assembly which met at Fritzlar in the next year to elect a successor came the nobility of only two, Saxony and Franconia, out of the four duchies; the others seem to have decided that a title which gave so much trouble to so little good purpose was not worth maintaining. No attempt was made to continue the Franconian line. Even Conrad himself on his deathbed had realized the hopelessness of this, and had instructed his brother to take the regalia to duke Henry of Saxony. With the assistance of this voice from the grave Henry was recognized as king, but at the time it cannot have seemed as though this king of but half the kingdom could accomplish much. But by their choice at Fritzlar the electors had made the first indisputably great ruler since Charlemagne (leaving out of account the English Alfred). For Henry I (the Fowler, 919–936) stands first in a great succession of medieval German kings and emperors. Even if he lacked the imperial title of his successors, he was to lay the sure foundations on which they built.

Henry's first problem was to gain recognition from the duchies which by ignoring his election implicitly denied his crown. He had already gained enthusiastic acceptance from the nobility of Saxony and Franconia, partly from the gesture at his coronation by which he had dispensed with ecclesiastical coronation. This combined a compliment to the assembled nobility of the two duchies, in suggesting that he who had their aid needed no other, with a welcome sign that he might reverse or limit the ecclesiastical policy of his predecessor.

Having thus secured an army from Saxony and Franconia he was able to use it to bring the other duchies into line. Burchard, duke of Suabia, could be impressed by the mere display of force; no doubt he thought that it was not worth risking war to avoid a recognition which would probably prove to be no more than nominal. Arnulf of Bavaria was more recalcitrant; he is believed to have had designs on the crown himself, and did not give his recognition until he had been defeated by Henry in the field two years later (921). The attachment of Lorraine was secured by a marriage to the daughter of its duke. Henry thus obtained by diplomacy what had eluded the repeated efforts of Conrad's army.

But formal recognition was only a beginning. The problems confronting Henry were the same as those Conrad had faced, made even more grave by his predecessor's failures. But he tackled them in a quite different spirit. Before the monarchy could hope to receive genuine loyalty it must show that it deserved it not from Saxony alone, but from all Christian Germany. In short, it must show that by defeating the invaders from the East it could perform the most deserving service of all for the whole country. In this he was aided by a quite exceptional military skill. Many tenth century kings were capable of fierce courage on the field of battle; Henry the Fowler and his son Otto the Great added a much rarer quality to this native savagery, the ability to think in strategical terms and to plan for campaigns several years ahead. Early in his reign, in 924, he was able to check the Magyar invasions into his own duchy of Saxony, and to arrange a nine years truce with them.

During this breathing space Henry concentrated on a complete reform of the Saxon army. The Magyar victories in the past had been won by the skill of their cavalry and the inability of the German forces facing them to stand up to cavalry charges. Certainly the host which responded to the summons of a ninth century king or duke must have been an inefficient body. It was made up for the most part of infantry, and although those summoned were exhorted to bring horses with them where possible, they were not trained in the use of them for war. Mounted infantry rather than cavalry, and largely untrained at that, they had been no match for men accustomed to live and fight on horseback. Henry now undertook the intensive training of much smaller bodies of men selected from his own entourage to fight on horseback and so to beat the Magyars with their own weapon. At the same time he was arranging the construction of a number of castles on and behind his eastern frontier.

Effective as the Magyar cavalry might be in battle or in ravaging a defenceless countryside, there was little it could do when confronted with a well stocked and defended castle; a defensive system of these castles prepared in depth made the invasion of Saxony a much more hazardous business. Some at least of these castles were large enough to give protection not only to a garrison, but to many of the inhabitants of the surrounding countryside. How much the later development of towns in Europe owes to the existence of these strong points or *burgs*, and how much to purely economic causes, is a hotly disputed point, but it seems certain that many of the towns of central Germany existed as strong points before they became towns.

In two ways Henry the Fowler helped to shape the pattern of war for the rest of the Middle Ages. By showing the value of the castle in defence and of the trained mounted cavalryman, the knight, in attack, he helped to make the wars of the future the affairs of knights and castles which form the popular image of the Middle Ages. Incidentally in so doing he was helping to make warfare in the future much less destructive and costly in human lives. The knights of the Middle Ages, like the tanks of the Second World War, were costly products necessarily in short supply; that they had become vital factors in war helped to prevent the indiscriminate slaughter implicit in large scale infantry operations.

The Magyars had been the inspiration of these changes, and by 933 Henry was ready to try them out. In that year, at the battle of Unstrut, he was able to inflict a major defeat on them which kept them clear of Saxony for a generation. But the methods which were effective against the Magyars could equally be applied against the other enemies of Germany; both Danes and Slavs felt the consequences of Henry's military reforms. Henry's reign can be seen as a vital turning point in the history of the Christian West. For six hundred years, from the Goths of the fourth century to the Magyars of the tenth, the West had been under constant attack. Now the tide was turning and the steady expansion of Europe into the lands beyond the Elbe was about to begin. In future it would be the Christian armies which did the destruction, showing no more mercy than had been shown to them in the past. There was force in the verdict of the Saxon chronicler Widukind[1] that Henry was 'the greatest king of all Europe'.

Henry's victories were won by Saxons fighting for Saxon aims;

[1] Author of *Res gestae Saxonicae*.

they should be regarded as victories for the duke of Saxony rather than for the king of the Germans. Yet in winning them he was serving Germany as well, for inevitably he was strengthening his position as German king. By the end of his reign he had done much to restore the power and prestige of the monarchy. It was hard to deny the right of such a monarch backed by such an army to control his lands throughout Germany. So Henry was able to begin resuming control over the royal estates, which since the days of Charlemagne had been passing from the Crown to the dukes. This had two good effects for the monarchy. On the one hand it gave the Crown an independent income and source of supplies which when united with those of its own duchy made it stronger than any of its individual vassals; on the other by giving it lands within all the other duchies it gave it a lever which could later be used to assert royal authority over the whole kingdom. Henry's victories against the pagan enemies of Germany were also victories for the Christian Church. He could thus rely on the support of the Church as Conrad had done, without the same suspicion that he was using the Church for purely selfish ends. The process of restoring royal power had begun.

Henry's reign was spectacularly successful, but more than a mere eighteen years of firm government was needed to re-establish the monarchy. It was provided by the long reign of his son Otto I (936–973). The unanimity with which his son was elected was a tribute to his father's work, but it needed more than this unanimity and coronation at Aix to ensure its continuance. Even if the dukes by performing ceremonial duties at the coronation feast were prepared to recognize their role as 'servants' of the Crown, this did not mean that they had foresworn the golden opportunity presented by the rule of a young and untried king to regain some of their lost powers. Outside Germany too the news of Henry's death suggested that the moment had come to renew attacks on his kingdom. The first years of Otto's rule were anxious enough.

Fortunately Otto was well suited to face these dangers. Although at the time of his coronation he was, like Charlemagne, illiterate, he had many of the qualities which went to make a successful king in the tenth century. Most notable among these was a physical and moral 'toughness': he was not to be deterred either by the rigours of a life spent largely in campaigning or by any moral scruples in his treatment of his enemies. With this he joined a shrewd common sense, which enabled him to distinguish what were the really important aims to pursue in the highly complicated problems he faced, and a nerve that did not desert him in the numerous crises that he was called to face.

The first few years of his reign were anxious enough. At once there was trouble from the Slavonic tribes on the north-east frontier of Saxony and from the Magyars further south. At the same time he had to face treason by no less than three out of the four dukes. The Saxon army remained loyal to its creator's son, and Otto was fortunate in having to hand a most capable general in Hermann Billung, the strongest of the Saxon nobles. If Billung was to use his power to build up a dynasty which was later to embarrass the German crown, at the time his campaigns served to save Saxony from fresh invasion.

The problem of the duchies Otto handled personally. So long as the dukes remained quasi-independent rulers with their own policies, which might well run contrary to that of the Crown, it was clear that their loyalty to it would be tenuous. Yet any attempt to assert real royal rights over them was likely to provoke them into revolt. Moreover, even if it were possible, the abolition of the duchies did not seem desirable. Suabia, Bavaria and Lorraine formed a defensive ring round Germany; each had a unity of its own, and to break this by enforcing the alien power of the Saxon kings might well lay the whole country more open to attack. The duchies had to be retained, but somehow they had to be made loyal. The only exception was the central duchy of Franconia; it had less deeply entrenched local customs and traditions than the others, and it was the only duchy to have no very obvious defensive purpose. It was expendable, and when in 939 its duke Eberhard, Conrad I's brother, was stirred into revolt by royal assertions of rights over his lands, he was killed in battle, and the office of duke was left unfilled. Instead the Franconian lands were transferred to swell the power of the Saxon royal demesne.

Otto did not attempt to abolish the other duchies, but as opportunity offered sought to set members of his own family at their head. This served two purposes. It checked the tendency for the duchies to become hereditary possessions rather than offices under the Crown, and it put them for the time under men whom he trusted. The device of filling great posts in the kingdom with the next of kin of the monarch is found fairly frequently in the Middle Ages; the French monarchy in the thirteenth century is another example. It did not provide any ultimate solution of the problem of the overmighty subject. Against a weak king even his brother might rebel, and in any case within two generations at most the blood relationship had become a fairly distant one. But as an immediate answer to Otto's problem it had much to commend it. The disloyalty of the existing dukes to the royal power as exercised by the new king was a grave danger to him, but at the same time it gave him a pretext to re-construct the duchies as he wanted. By 949 all the duchies were held by members of his family: Bavaria by his brother, Suabia by his son and Lorraine by his son-in-law. Since this also meant that they were all fairly new to office and unable to count on traditional loyalties, it clearly brought a new balance between the power of the Crown and the power of the duchies all in favour of the former.

This was the more fortunate as in 955 Germany underwent its last great crisis from a barbarian invasion. The Magyar invasion of that year may not have been any more serious than the attacks earlier in the century. But it had been preceded by a comparatively peaceful interval, and just because it was the last attack it was to remain longest in memory, just as in England the London plague of 1665 has remained The Plague. But this time the Magyars found themselves confronted not merely by a strong duchy, but by the whole kingdom. All the dukes co-operated with the Crown, and at a great battle on the banks of the river Lech, Magyar power was finally annihilated. The prestige of Otto had already been high in Germany, but now he became famous throughout Europe. The word 'imperator' even began again to be used of him, and certainly if it was the part of an emperor to use the temporal sword on behalf of the Christian faith, it was a pardonable exaggeration to use it of Otto. If not a true emperor, he was at least a King over kings, which was one usage of the word imperator in the tenth century.

If the extension of royal power through his relations was one half of Otto's domestic policy, the other lay in his cultivation of the Church, which was made central to his government. Nor would this have seemed at all shocking to his contemporaries. There had always been something religious in the concept of kingship among the Franks. In the coronation ceremony it was said that Christ had appointed the king as a mediator between the clergy and the people; as with the ancient Israelites kingship was a religious as well as a secular function, and it seemed right that the king should appoint the high offices in the Church as well as in the kingdom. The objections of a later age that this was an intolerable interference by Caesar in the things of God were not yet heard. The tradition of the Church from its earliest times had been that bishops should be elected by the clergy and people of the diocese. In any modern sense of course such an 'election' was quite impracticable, but the form by which bishops were 'elected' by the clergy of their future cathedral and subsequently acclaimed by the laity was retained. But the appointment of bishops became in practice the concern of the Crown; in exactly the same way the bishops of the Church of England today, though in form 'elected' by the dean and chapter of their cathedrals, in practice are appointed by the Crown acting on the advice of the Prime Minister. All newly elected bishops did homage to the king and became 'his men', just as any other tenant-in-chief was the king's man. In return the king gave the newly appointed bishop or abbot his ring and crozier, the sign of his spiritual authority, with the words '*Accipe ecclesiam*' (Receive the Church). So it was made clear that all authority in the German church ultimately rested with the Crown, even if the king did not normally interfere with the spiritual functions of the clergy.

Having thus established his power over the Church, Otto could afford to treat it with great apparent generosity: lands were showered on it, and large ecclesiastical 'immunities' created, where all rights of taxation and jurisdiction belonged to the Church. Yet these immunities did not lessen the power of the Crown. The abbeys and churches which had thus been placed under the special protection (*mundeburdium*) of the Crown did not cease to render their feudal services of men and supplies to the king. In future, under the control of celibate clergy there would be less risk that hereditary fiefs would be built up which might turn against the Crown; any who attacked the immunities would be guilty of sacrilege as well as treason. In effect Otto was using the clergy to perform the functions of the Carolingian counts; in some cases, as with the archbishops of Mainz and Cologne, the title of count was actually conferred upon churchmen. As with the lay duchies, Otto sought to strengthen the loyalty of these clerical immunities by conferring them on members of his own family; archbishop Bruno of Cologne was his brother, archbishop Henry of Treves his cousin, and archbishop William of Mainz his bastard son.

It is clear that such a policy was only practicable in an age in which the prestige and powers of the Papacy were low. A strong pope would be sure to resent a policy which left so small a part to Rome. But the Papacy was unable to assert its rights in Rome, let alone in Germany. A free and independent Church such as was to be the dream of the reformers of the eleventh century was an impossibility in the conditions of the preceding century. The choice lay only between the 'protection' of the nobility and the 'protection' of the Crown. There is little doubt that royal leadership as exercised by Otto I was the better alternative; it helped to preserve a certain unity in the Church and to prevent it breaking up into mutually hostile local Churches. Moreover the bishops and abbots appointed by Otto were selected with great care. Administrators and even fighters they certainly were, but they also included men of piety and learning, such as Bruno of Cologne himself.

Nevertheless there were dangers about the Ottonian system of government through a *Reichskirche* for both parties to it. The Church very soon became the largest landholder in Germany, but in so doing it was put in a position of dependence on the Crown which might too easily become mere subservience to it. A king who was less careful than Otto about the selection of bishops could do it irreparable harm in a short time. A Church which is a department of state can only too quickly become merely that. Nor was it fully satisfactory from the royal viewpoint. Even an episcopal 'subject' might become hostile to the Crown, and if he did there was the difficulty that, although Otto could make bishops, he could not depose them; this right was reserved to the Pope. The system really required the co-operation of the Papacy. A more serious danger perhaps could not have been foreseen by Otto. The more power he delegated to the Church the more dependent the German monarchy became on it. This did not matter so long as God and Caesar were generally recognized to be allies in the fight for the faith. But if a view were to grow within the Church at some future date that the things of God should be separate from the Mammon of this world, the consequences for the Crown might be disastrous, for it would be left without an administration. The Investiture Contest lay hidden in the Ottonian system of government.

Otto's work in Germany laid the foundations of royal power there for the next two centuries, but he is better remembered for 're-storing' yet again the Roman Empire in the West. Yet his motives for the action of 962 are by no means clear, and have been given very different interpretations by historians. Of course in one sense the assumption of the title of Emperor by the strongest ruler in the West should cause little surprise; it was the traditional title hallowed by all the associations of the past, in an age in which it was axiomatic that the old was better than the new. But on the one hand it has been argued that having had such success in Germany and having saved Europe at Lechfeld, Otto was reaching out to establish a wider domination over all the West: that he sought to restore the empire of Charlemagne, if not that of Augustus. On the other it is argued that his involvement in Italian affairs, which was to force him to take the imperial title, sprang from his efforts to reinforce his government in Germany, and that his first object throughout was to make himself a strong ruler there, rather than to seize universal authority.

Only too often in her history Italy has attracted foreign invaders. The things which attracted invaders in the tenth century were much the same as in the fifth or the fifteenth. The wealth of the towns of Lombardy and Tuscany, the fertile countryside, the lure of classical and Christian Rome, all combined with a complete absence of any effective large scale political organization to make Italy a standing invitation to any ruler hoping to augment his fortunes. It attracted Norsemen and Arabs and Byzantine Greeks from the Mediterranean. But the seaborne raiders of the South were not alone in being attracted by the prize. The Germanic peoples from the north side of the Alps showed the same interest. Naturally those who were nearest were most tempted to intervene, while Saxony more than three hundred miles away seemed remote from Italy. Otto was a Saxon, and it was no part of the traditions of his house to concern itself with Italy. But as a German monarch he could not afford to see any of the duchies making itself so powerful by acquiring lands and revenue outside Germany that it could equal the power of the Crown itself. Early in his reign he had intervened by force in the kingdom of Burgundy to prevent its combination with the kingdom of Italy to make a too powerful neighbour for Germany (947). In 951 he led an army across the Alps to prevent a rather similar occurrence. The kingdom of Italy, the shrunken relic of the once extensive Lotharingia, was no menace of itself. But now it was in the hands of a widowed queen Adelaide, a situation which gave every expectation to those who wished to fish the troubled water of Lombardy to their own advantage. The dukes of Suabia and Bavaria, Liudolf and Henry the Quarrelsome, were both intervening south of the Alps, and if the latter was ostensibly coming to rescue Adelaide from the hands of Berengar of Ivrea, a rebellious vassal who saw himself as king, Otto was not prepared to trust either of them. Liudolf was his son and Henry his brother, but if either Suabia or Bavaria was allowed to build up extensive power in Lombardy, Germany would become more difficult to control. Otto moved into Italy, defeated Berengar, married Adelaide, and united the Italian to the German crown. He did not then obtain imperial coronation from the Papacy, and this seems to strengthen the view that he was seeking not universal dominion, but a strong Germany.

Ten years later Otto was in Italy again, this time in response to an appeal from Pope John XII. In danger from the turbulent nobility of Rome, John asked for the protection of the German king; memories of Leo III and Charlemagne come to mind. Again Otto led his army south; he could not allow the headship of the Church on which his administration now so largely rested to pass into possibly hostile hands. By the end of 961 John was again safely installed on the throne of Peter. Early in the next year he settled his account by crowning Otto emperor. The title of Emperor, never securely attached to any strong political power since the death of Lewis the Pious, was now united with that of king of Germany.

The occasion was marked by an orgy of good will on both sides. In the *Ottonianum* the new emperor confirmed and enlarged all the earlier grants of Italian territory made by his Carolingian predecessors (the Donations of Pepin and Charlemagne). In return John not only consented to the creation of the new archbishopric of Magdeburg, through which royal power was to be extended in the Slavonic lands of eastern Germany, but recognized the imperial right to confirm—or presumably not to confirm—Papal elections. It is by no means clear that either Otto or John knew what it was that the other was doing or intending to do in 962. To Otto the confirmation of the Patrimony of S. Peter seemed to be the conferring of another immunity. Just as the archbishop of Cologne had the free enjoyment of the lands of his diocese, but did not contract out of the German kingdom and was expected to regard himself as the king's man, so now the bishop of Rome was to be the emperor's man. John, no doubt with little knowledge of German administrative methods, saw it as a guarantee of complete independence.

The honeymoon period was short. Only a year later they had quarrelled over Otto's demand for an oath of allegiance to the imperial crown from the rebellious subjects of the Papal territories, and John was seeking to build up a coalition to break the power of the emperor he had so recently created. But all the force of arms was on the side of the emperor, and John, a notorious evil liver, had no moral authority to set against it. He was accused of a bizarre series of crimes, ranging from the castration of a cardinal to swearing by Jupiter and Venus while playing at dice, and deposed in his absence by a synod largely made up of German bishops. Otto presided over the election which followed, and Leo VIII, a more submissive if more respectable successor, was declared to be the new pope. The Roman populace, always easily stirred, resented this foreign interference in the affairs of 'their' Papacy, and after John's death in 964 proceeded to elect a new pope, Benedict V. Otto, however, besieged the city, and compelled the recognition of Leo VIII. The rule of the German emperor might not be popular in Rome, but it was inescapable. The Papacy itself had been reduced to the status of a bishopric in the *Reichskirche*, and the West had no alternative to recognizing that the German kings could indeed style themselves Roman emperors, even if effective imperial authority never extended to France, England, and the outlying Scandinavian lands.

The renovation of the Empire in the West naturally had repercussions in the East at the New Rome. The Byzantines, holding that to them alone belonged the honour of maintaining the imperial tradition, regarded the new emperor as an impudent upstart. Since they still controlled Italian provinces in Apulia and Calabria, their hostility might be more than formal; it would be easy for them to create constant trouble for imperial policies in Italy. At first Otto tried to reduce the Byzantine provinces by force of arms. But operations at the extremity of Italy nearly a thousand miles from the source of his power in Saxony were very difficult for him, and he was unsuccessful. But where war failed, diplomacy succeeded. In 972, the year before his death, he managed to arrange a marriage between his son, the future Otto II, and Theophano, daughter of an earlier Byzantine emperor, Romanus II (†963). This outward and visible sign of acceptance by the Eastern Empire, even if it was not of acceptance as an equal, was the last thing needed to demonstrate the legitimacy of the new Empire in the West.

Otto was not another Charlemagne, despite the similarity between the circumstances which led each to the imperial crown. His empire was something less and something more than that of his predecessor. In so far as Charlemagne's empire had had a capital, it had been at Aix in the future Lotharingia, geographically and politically the centre of his dominions. Otto was based on Saxony far to the east, and if his rule came to include most of what had once been the central kingdom, he never gained or sought control of what was now the feeble realm of France. But if his power extended much less far to the west, in the east he controlled new territories which had never been part of either the classical or the Carolingian empires. Warfare against the Slavs had been the *raison d'être* of the Saxon duchy, and it kept this purpose through its transformation into a German

73

monarchy and a Roman empire. After Lechfeld the Germans everywhere had gone over to the offensive, and already by 973 deep inroads had been made into the previously unsettled lands between the Elbe and the Oder. Like the Crusades later, this was at the same time a military and a religious operation. The lands were to be won for Christ, not so much by the conversion of their Slav inhabitants as by the simpler process of exterminating them and breeding good Christian Germans to take their place. But here, as further to the west, the power of Church and Crown went together; the new archbishopric of Magdeburg represented a victory for both. These new lands bound Otto more closely to the north and east of his empire. Even if it was Roman in name, it remained German in spirit; no mere replica of the past, it was a new phenomenon, a German Empire.

There were of course plenty of elements within the realm which resented both the authority of the Saxon line within Germany and its new imperial pretension. So long as Otto I lived his military reputation discouraged revolt; as soon as he was dead his son Otto II (973–983) had to face risings. There had been no opportunity of disputing his succession to the Empire, for his father had had him crowned co-Emperor six years earlier. But as soon as his father was dead the young man of eighteen found his authority challenged not only by revolts in Bavaria and Lorraine but by an invasion from outside. Harold Bluetooth, the king of Denmark, decided that the time was ripe to renew Norse invasions. In this opening crisis of his reign Otto showed that he had inherited his father's nerve, though a large part of his success must be attributed to the strength of the Saxon army he had inherited also. The Danes were defeated and made tributaries of the Empire (974), and later the two duchies were subdued.

Yet what in Otto I had been a good courage became in his young son rashness. Otto I had made some attempts to reconquer the Byzantine provinces of southern Italy, but finding it more difficult than he had anticipated had turned instead to negotiation. There is little doubt he was right. The Ottonian Empire was German, and to a German Empire the possession of southern Italy could be no more than a luxury. Only for a Mediterranean empire could it be essential. In 980 Otto II decided to revert to military methods. The opportunity seemed favourable. Byzantium was torn with internal dissensions and was unlikely to be able to send effective help to its provinces. Moreover, Muslim attacks from Sicily were increasing. They might well overwhelm the Byzantine forces, and it could be

74

argued that it was the duty of the Christian emperor of the West to defend even eastern Christians. At any rate this made a satisfactory pretext. In the event Otto's intervention was a disastrous military and diplomatic failure. He found himself opposed by both Greeks and Moslems, and in 982 suffered a complete defeat at the hands of the latter. He was lucky to escape with the remnant of his forces to Rome.

The news of his defeat gave new hope to all who had suffered from German arms. The next year there was alarming news from the regents he had left in Germany of dangerous Slav invasions of the new lands in the east and of another Danish attack from the north. Now, if ever, the duty of a German emperor lay in Germany, but Otto with courageous obstinacy turned his mind to raising new forces to avenge his previous defeat. While engaged in this foolhardy occupation he died (983).

The reign of Otto II is thus an apparent failure, and it is easy to see in it only a demonstration of the fatal temptation to meddle in affairs which were no concern of Germany's that the imperial title so often brought with it. Yet, as in Sherlock Holmes' 'curious incident of the dog in the night-time',[1] what did not happen in Otto II's reign is perhaps more important than what did. Despite the prolonged absence of the emperor on a highly unsuccessful foreign venture, the German empire did not disintegrate. Even when Otto broke the first law of medieval kingship by dying so prematurely that his son and heir was only three, the Saxon line still continued. The attempts of Henry the Wrangler, duke of Bavaria, to gain the regency or perhaps the crown for himself were frustrated by a remarkable display of loyalty to the infant Otto III (983-1002). The bishops of the Church united with all the more prominent nobility of the other duchies to resist him. Under the leadership of Archbishop Willigis of Mainz they convinced Henry that he had no hope of securing power, and at the Diet of Rara (984) compelled him to renounce his claims. In return for surrendering the person of the young king, whom he had kidnapped, he was allowed to retain his duchy. It is too early yet to speak of national loyalty, but this loyalty to the crown is eloquent testimony of the way the Saxon line had come to be associated with order and strong government in Germany.

The death of Otto II gave an unexpected importance to his widow, Theophano. She was a woman of character and determination, and came from a Byzantine world in which her sex was not debarred from political interest and activity. She proved capable of preserving

[1] See 'Silver Blaze', by A. Conan Doyle.

some sort of imperial authority in Italy, and after she had come north to Germany of exercising the powers of regency there. She must have been more than competent, for she made a surprisingly good job of what must have been a very difficult task; only perhaps in Blanche of Castile, S. Louis's mother, were the Middle Ages to see her like. Maintaining the close relations of the Saxon house with the Church she succeeded in preserving internal order and in defending the kingdom against Slav attacks in the East and French plans against Lorraine in the West. Yet in one way her influence on the German monarchy may have been unfortunate. Byzantine as she was, the imperial problem cannot have seemed to her wholly, or even perhaps mainly, a German one. The Mediterranean aspect of the Empire must have loomed large in her mind. It is at least possible that Otto III's later preoccupation with a Mediterranean empire owed something to this maternal influence; one at least of his tutors was a Greek, and he certainly cannot have inherited it from his paternal grandfather!

Theophano died in 991, and after her death her place was filled much less efficiently by Adelaide, the elderly widow of the Emperor Otto I. Three years later the young king assumed power himself. He was only fourteen years old, and, although it may be true that Englishmen of the nineteenth and twentieth centuries perhaps mature more slowly than any people the world has known, fourteen was over-young even for a tenth century European to take on the most responsible of all tasks. 'Your young men shall see visions' says the prophet Isaiah, and there was much of this adolescent quality about Otto III. Born to the imperial purple there was really only one vision this particular young man could see. It was of an emperor who would be something far greater than a German king, who only claimed to rule half Europe. Did he not unite in his own person East and West? Was it not his destiny to revive not merely the empire of Charlemagne, but that of Constantine, so that there should again be one Christian emperor ruling over all Christian peoples? He was encouraged in this by his close friend Gerbert of Aurillac (†1003), the former abbot of Bobbio, whom later Otto was to get made pope. To Gerbert, as to Otto, the emperor had a divine mission not only to protect but to spread the Catholic faith; where Otto had spread the faith by extending German influence gradually into pagan lands, Otto III sought to spread it far more rapidly by converting the Slavs themselves into Christians. One sign of this policy was his visit as a penitent and pilgrim to the tomb at Gnesen in Poland of

S. Adalbert, who had been martyred while working among the Slavs three years earlier. He gave his full support to missionary enterprises not only in the lands between the Elbe and the Oder, but in Poland and even further to the east. This spiritual aim expressed itself in a political policy. A bargain was to be struck with the eastern peoples. No longer were they simply to be subjugated by the force of German arms; if they were prepared to accept Catholicism and acknowledge themselves members of the Empire, in return they would be allowed to retain their full rights as independent peoples. An example of this policy can be seen in his treatment of the Magyars. S. Stephen of Hungary (†1038), who had been converted to Christianity in 995, undertook the conversion of the Magyar peoples. In return he was allowed to organize the Christian kingdom of Hungary, which took its place among the Christian peoples of the Empire.[1]

It is difficult not to admire this more humane approach to the eastern problem. But it had a very serious practical disadvantage. The Empire had been accepted in Germany as an effective bulwark against the enemies in the East. The spectacle of an emperor fraternizing with these very enemies was bound to undermine German confidence in the Empire; yet, although Otto might style himself *Imperator Romanorum* or *Servus Jesu Christi*, unless he remained also king of the Germans he was nothing. Even the German Church, accustomed by now to regard itself as the chief prop of royal power, resented the way its claims to a favoured position were ignored in this new pursuit of a universal Christendom.

Naturally a Roman emperor should rule from Rome, but Otto's attempts to make Italy the centre of his government endeared him no more to Italians than to Germans, His first appearance on the Italian scene came in 996, in the by now traditional manner; he was summoned by Pope John XV (985–996) to set him free from the domination of a Roman family, the Crescentii. Death had freed the pope from his troubles before Otto reached Rome, but when he got there he secured the election as next pope of Bruno of Carinthia, who took the title Gregory V (996–999). His choice could hardly have been more unfortunate. The new pope was well under the canonical age, being only twenty-three, and the unpopularity of this youthful

---

[1] In opposition to this view it has been powerfully argued that the real motive of Otto III's 'romanizing' policy was to resist Byzantine attempts at infiltration. See, for example, the pamphlet: *The Medieval Empire. Idea and Reality*, G. Barraclough. Historical Association, 1950.

German was increased by the fact that he was the Emperor's cousin, His appointment looked to Italians as an example of that nepotism from which it had been hoped the emperor might free them. Within a year Gregory was faced by a large scale repudiation of his authority and the erection of an anti-pope. No less than three times in the next six years Otto was forced to lead armies against a rebellious Rome; this does not suggest that he was being successful in his efforts to Romanize his empire. Indeed Italy as a whole was far too broken and unruly to make a firm basis for his government; almost the only thing Italians agreed about was that this strange young emperor was a foreigner, and it seems unlikely that he would have been able to establish his empire securely even if he had not died so young. It is true that by his use of imperial *ministeriales*, often of German birth, he seemed to be striving towards an administration which was not dependent on the whims of the Italian nobility. Through his very close friendship with Gerbert of Aurillac (Sylvester II), after 999 he was able to ensure that key church appointments went to men sympathetic to their common views. The leading English historian of medieval Germany alive today sees in Otto III's policy an attempt to extend the methods of the German empire to Italy, so that in this analysis it becomes a logical development of that of his grandfather, rather than a contradiction of it.[1] Yet there remains an air of unreality about the spectacle of Otto III dining off silver plate alone on a dais in his palace on the Aventine, his mind filled with large schemes for winning the Russian church to the Roman obedience or with doubts as to whether he might not be called to renounce all and become a monk. The contrast between this and the harsher realism of the earlier Saxons in their cruder German court is too acute. The historian can never say for certain what *would* have happened in history, but it may very well be fortunate for Otto that he died when he did.

What is certain is that by dying in 1002, when he was only twenty-one, Otto brought to nothing all his ambitious schemes. He left no son behind him, and perforce the elective machinery of the Empire had to come into operation again. The Saxon line was at an end.

Yet the Saxons had served Germany well. Taking over the kingship at a time when to all appearances it was hopelessly discredited, they had shown that it could perform vital services for the whole

[1] See G. Barraclough, *The Origins of Modern Germany*. Blackwell, 1947. Ch., 3, section iii.

country. By their use of the German Church and by their steady attention to building up demesne lands throughout the country, they had shown that royal administration could be made to work. Whatever the future of the Empire might be, there was now no question of doing away with German kingship.

5

Cluny and the Investiture Contest

Nothing in medieval history is more dramatic than the sudden conflict in the second half of the eleventh century between the Papacy and the Empire, the two God-given authorities over sinful man in a fallen world. Both had many centuries of history behind them; both seemed to be supported by the full authority of God Himself in the Bible. If Peter's successor could point to Christ's words to his predecessor 'Thou art Peter and upon this rock I will build my church',[1] the emperor more than any other earthly ruler could recall the apostle's teaching 'Let every soul be subject unto the higher powers, for there is no power but of God. The powers that be are ordained of God',[2] or recall that even David was not permitted to raise his hand against Saul, the divinely appointed king of Israel. But at first there was no apparent reason for any such comparison. Pope Gelasius had taught that both had their authority from God, and the past seemed to show that they stood or fell together. Constantine, Charlemagne and Otto the Great had revived the Empire, and in each case the Church had benefited directly and greatly from their action. The two waxed and waned together.

Yet, sudden as it was, the conflict arose from causes that were deep-rooted in the history of both institutions. Paradoxically it was just because the two were so closely linked that they had to fight; neither could afford to let the other triumph without seeming to surrender something which was vital to its very being.

Let us take the case of the Church first. During the whole period from 500–1000 the Church had been subject to exactly the same pressures which in the lay sphere had produced a decentralized and feudal Europe. In the conditions of disorder and bloodshed which marked the barbarian invasions the centralized machinery of the Church could not hope to survive any more than that of the Empire. Pagan Saxons or Vikings were no respectors of the rights and property of the Christian God, and churches or monasteries formed some of their most tempting prizes. In such a situation the distant blessing of

[1] Matthew 16: 18.   [2] Romans 13: 1.

80

a Rome, afflicted herself in precisely the same way, was of no avail; what was needed was military help from close at hand, and this could only be provided by local lords. Moreover these same lords frequently founded new monasteries and chaplaincies which were dependent on them from their beginning. The Church remained Roman and Catholic in name, but in practice it came to be feudal and local. Lay lords gave particular churches protection, and in return expected from them service. As in lay feudalism these services were very varied, ranging from the purely spiritual duty of praying for the souls of the protector and his ancestors, to a wide range of more secular duties. Just as the bishops of tenth-century Germany were expected to play their part in royal administration and to provide men for the common defence of Christian Germany, so lower down the scale lay lords might expect a wide range of dues and services from priests who were as much *their* men as any other tenants. As the barbarians themselves became Christianized, so they too founded churches and endowed them with land. In doing so they did not think of themselves as contributing to a vast spiritual corporation whose distant centre was in Rome; such an idea was altogether too abstract for them. Just as their old gods had been their gods, the gods of their own tribe, so now their new churches were to be *their* churches, with the primary duty of securing the spiritual welfare of their own kin and dependents. Over them they would retain extensive rights, including the primary right of appointing the priests who would serve them or the abbots who would rule over their monasteries. It would be fair to say that in the eighth century the whole idea of the Church as one spiritual body was in danger of disintegrating before these local and particular churches.

The process was probably inevitable, but it brought with it grave spiritual dangers. However good the motives of the founder or original protector of a church might be, there was no guarantee that his son would not exploit his churches to his own temporal advantage. If he wished he was of course in a particularly favourable position to do so, since he alone possessed not only the power to enforce the law but through his own courts to say what the law was. Moreover, the temptation to use clerical appointments as a means of disposing of unwanted younger sons in his own family was strong. It can hardly have seemed a temptation. Why should he not do as he liked with his own? Yet such nepotism is rarely an advantage, whether in twentieth century business or in the eighth century church; too often the relation is not fitted for the job to which he is directed by his family.

81

Most serious of all was the difficulty of bringing about any reform in a church which was so localised. Once a parish or a diocese had become corrupt under an incumbent who was unable to stand up to a greedy or violent lay lord, or who was himself incompetent or immoral, how could it be reformed? Rome offered no hope; it was much too far away, and in any case for much of the period was a glaring example of the faults which most needed correction. In many ages the monasteries were looked to for the provision of spiritual men of ability to reform the Church outside the cloister, but now the monasteries were as closely involved in the process of secularization as any other part of the Church.

Charlemagne had seen something of this danger, and his attempt to restore imperial authority in the West had necessarily brought with it some measure of restoration of Papal authority. But with the disintegration of the Empire which followed the death of Lewis the Pious the process had been resumed. By the tenth century the western Church had reached a very low ebb. To give but one example, in 936 the abbot of the great Benedictine house of Farfa in the Sabine hills had been murdered by two of his monks. The guilty pair then proceeded to rule the abbey themselves in an uneasy dyarchy; for a number of years they continued to use up the abbey revenues for the sustenance of their mistresses and numerous illegitimate offspring. Farfa was no great distance from Rome, and it might be expected that here at any rate the Papacy might be able to undertake a drastic reform. But the Rome of the tenth century could reform nothing; its popes were the feeble creatures of lay princes, succeeding each other in a bewildering succession of intrigues and murders. For a time the scene was dominated by the figure of Marozia, who saw both her son and her grandson made pope. If she was not the notorious harlot of Gibbon's imagination the period well deserves the scorn Gibbon was later to heap on it in one of his most brilliantly ironic passages.[1] Until the reformation carried out by Otto the Great the western Church was most rotten at its core.

Reform, when it came, started far from Rome, and, as so often in the Middle Ages, first took the form of an attempt not to remedy the wickedness of the Church, but to withdraw from it. In the year 910 Count William of Aquitaine, impressed by the piety of a Benedictine house at Baume, gave to its abbot Berno the offer of land on which to found a new monastery. Generously he left the selection of a suitable site to Berno, and when the latter elected to build on

[1] See Gibbon, *Decline and Fall of the Roman Empire*, Chapter 49.

the site of the count's hunting kennels at Cluny, William after some hesitation agreed. Neither man can possibly have foreseen that within a generation the new house would work a greater change in the monasticism of Europe than had been wrought since Benedict founded Cassino. The rapid importance Cluny gained was caused by two almost accidental factors; the virtual independence which William gave to the new house he had founded, and the exceptional quality of its early abbots. In the charter William gave to Berno, Cluny was stated to be given 'to the apostles Peter and Paul'; no lay lord was to be its protector, but it was 'to pay to Rome a tribute of x solidi every five years, and to have papal protection and guardianship'. In effect this was a charter of independence. Far away between the headwaters of the Loire and the Saône, Cluny was safe from interference from Rome. Distant too from either the German emperor or the French king, she was free to develop along her own lines.

The Benedictine Rule to which the Cluniacs sought to return puts a very heavy responsibility on the shoulders of the individual abbot. Cluny was exceptionally favoured in her early abbots, and the good sense which led the monks to elect comparatively young men enabled her to get full service out of them. In the first hundred and forty-eight years of her existence Cluny had only five abbots, and of these three at least were men of outstanding ability: Odo (abbot 926–942), Maiolus (954–994), and Odilo (994–1048). The sixth abbot, Hugh, was to rule for more than sixty years and provide further striking proof of the healthful effect of office!

The intention of the early Cluniac abbots may have been to restore the primitive purity of the Benedictine way, but Cluny is no exception to the general rule that genuine restorations are very rare in history. The original Benedictine communities had copied what Professor Knowles has called 'the simple patriarchal family life of Monte Cassino'[1]. They had been made up largely of lay brothers, many of them no doubt nearly illiterate, and manual work in the fields around the monastery had played a large part in their lives. By contrast Cluny was from the first a community of priests, and soon became of very large size. Even more than at Monte Cassino the Opus Dei, the service rendered to God by the monks in the choir of the abbey church, was the overriding concern of the whole community. It came to occupy some six to seven hours every day, and as time passed and the liturgy grew more complicated, the

---

[1] *The Monastic Order in England.* Dom. David Knowles. Cambridge U. P., 1940, 30.

number of feast days on which it occupied much more than this steadily grew. Clearly this had its dangers; by upsetting the balance between work and prayer which had been a characteristic of the original rule it perhaps made later corruption more likely, and modern critics have seen something backhanded in the compliment S. Peter Damian paid Cluny in the eleventh century, when he wrote that the life of Cluny made any sins save those of thought impossible. Yet it is clear that Cluny must have answered some very basic need in the religious life of the age. This is proved not only by the very large numbers who entered Cluniac houses, but by the very similar reforms carried out by houses elsewhere, notably in Lorraine, without any apparent connection with Cluny at all.

Essentially Cluny called men out of the world itself or from the tainted monasticism of decadent monasteries to the full service of God. The biographer of Odo, the second abbot, describes how Odo himself came to Cluny in disgust from Tours, where the monks had become so concerned with the trivialities of dress that they absented themselves from the night office in wet weather lest they should dirty their shoes 'so coloured and shining that they resembled glass'.[1] Because it was concerned to take men out of the world to seek the way of perfection in the cloister, Cluny in its earlier days had no political policy and little interest even in the priest who chose to stay in the world. Even at the height of its fame in the eleventh century Cluny is found to be remarkably detached from the great struggle between Gregory VII and Henry IV; in so far as he played any role in this, Abbot Hugh (1048–1109) was a peacemaker, urging on both sides the duty of not disrupting Christendom. But the real viewpoint of Cluny was that the things of this world were of little account when compared with eternity.

Yet Cluny, however much it may have been built round the idea of withdrawal from the world, is of the first importance in the history of western Europe. The sheer size of the movement it started could not fail to impress very many who were not directly concerned in it. Cluny itself housed as many as four hundred and sixty monks in 1144, making it by far the largest monastery the western Church had ever known. But Cluny was only the centre of a vast European movement. As early as the time of Berno the abbot of Cluny was sometimes called in to help in other houses whose abbots or patrons felt the need of reform. Under Odo (926–942) what had been an

[1] *Vita Odonis a Joanne.* Quoted, L. M. Smith, *The Early History of the Monastery of Cluny.* Milford, 1921, p. 22.

occasional exercise became a major part of his duties. The most
sensational example came in the reform of Fleury. Fleury had been
a Benedictine house of great importance, to which the bones of
S. Benedict himself had been removed for safe custody from Saracen
raiders in Italy. But things had gone badly with it, and by 930 it
presented a classic picture of monastic decay. When Count Elisardus
called in Odo to undertake the work of reform, the erring sheep had
no desire to be led back to the ways of righteousness by their new
pastor, and closed the doors of their monastery against Odo and his
little band, greeting them with abusive epithets and missiles. After
three days Odo braved the barrage alone, riding upon an ass to recall
the entry of Christ into Jerusalem, and managed to gain admittance.
Once inside, the peculiar combination of strength and gentleness
which seems to have marked his character prevailed, and the monks
co-operated with him in introducing the conditions of Cluny to
Fleury. Odo saw it as a part of his duty to try to spread the ordered
life of Cluny as widely as possible; during his abbacy he visited a very
large number of monasteries. They included no less than four in
Rome itself, the first breath of reform in the degraded city of Peter.
In very few cases did he fail to make considerable changes in the
condition of the houses he visited. In the tenth century few of the
houses thus visited were left with any constitutional link with Cluny.
They remained independent abbeys, although sometimes the abbots
of Cluny were invited by courtesy to see how their work had fared.
What was being established was not a Cluniac Order, but a Cluniac
way of life.

Sometimes, inevitably, the good effects of a reform wrought by
Cluny wore off when the monks were left once more to their own
devices, and in the eleventh century there came a change of policy
Under abbots Odilo (994–1048) and Hugh (1048–1109) houses
which once called in Cluny to reform them were obliged to retain
a link with her. Their abbots were made subject to the abbot of
Cluny. Moreover Cluny itself took to making new foundations on
a large scale, and such houses did not become independent abbeys
but priories of Cluny. Thus there came into being the first of the
centralized monastic orders gathered round one head, the abbot of
Cluny. This was the pattern to be followed by all later monastic
revivals, from the Cistercians in the next century to the Jesuits in the
sixteenth. It had obvious advantages. By providing a mechanism for
inspection and reform it became much easier to check decay when it
first appeared; the pattern of individual and autonomous houses was

really only appropriate to a Europe where communications and conditions were so bad that no large scale organization could hope to survive. In the more orderly state of Europe now coming into being there was a clear need for the religious order. It is true that Cluny did not immediately solve all the problems of such an order. In particular no answer was given to the problem of what might happen when Cluny itself stood in need of reform. In the twelfth century the stormy career of Abbot Pontius (1109–1120) showed that the choice of the monks of Cluny, good as it had been in the past, was not infallible, and that an unbalanced abbot might do grave harm to the whole order.

Nor could any constitution-making protect Cluny from what was always the gravest danger to any monastic reform in the Middle Ages. Put briefly this was as follows. Every successful monastic reform based a part of its success on the discipline and austerity it imposed on its members. In almost every case this was at first easy, for the monastery itself was genuinely poor and could not avoid austerity. Yet the more it succeeded in its task, the more it became known to be the home of holy and humble men, the more difficult it became to maintain the original fervour. It was not only that fame brought with it a rush of vocations to the monastic life of whom many might be less suited to it than the original members. The gifts and bequests of the laity wishing to share in God's work or to purchase for themselves spiritual benefits were showered upon the successful abbey or order. It was hard to refuse such gifts, and, S. Francis and the early Cistercians apart, none did. Yet they were a deadly danger: at best they dangerously entangled the monks in the very worldly concerns from which they had fled; at worst they could lead directly to the luxury and vice which would call for another reform. During the tenth and eleventh centuries donors gave very large quantities of land to Cluniac houses, sometimes mingling the idea of protecting it from encroachment by their neighbours with more pious motives. The order thus became a great landowning corporation with all the responsibilities involved in such a state, such as the possession of serfs and the need to exercise various feudal rights. This led to a large variety of disputes with secular landholders, with other monasteries and with the bishops, who understandably resented the removal of large areas of their dioceses from their own jurisdiction. What had started as a protest against secularization of the Church had itself by the twelfth century become largely secularized; the time was ripe for another reform.

Yet Cluny impressed the whole imagination of its age. It might seek to cut itself off from the distractions of the world, but the spectacle of large new abbeys rising over Europe from Spain and Lombardy to England was itself a reminder to all of the things that were not Caesar's. Even in their architecture Cluniac churches spoke of the world that was centred on God. They were built round the altar, the centre of the worship of the monks. It was often raised above the level of the rest of the Church so that anyone entering the building had his eyes immediately fixed on the altar, and round it were grouped all the richest colours of the church, the most highly coloured frescoes, the brightest curtains and the richest patterns in the tiles inlaid on the floor. The whole church was but a shell for the worship that was offered within it. The finest examples of Romanesque architecture in Europe come from Cluniac houses. Even today, when we have lost the capacity to be impressed by sheer size, a great abbey like Vézelay strikes wonder, and the mere ruins of a dependent priory such as Castle Acre in Norfolk are impressive even in decay. Cluny itself we cannot know; it was almost totally destroyed in the French Revolution. But the effect of its vast grandeur on an age accustomed to be moved by material symbols can be imagined. Unconsciously it preached to the world two lessons, the absolute necessity for purity of life within the Church, and the need for spiritual independence from all the works of secular men. These two were linked in the life of Cluny; they were to be linked in the Church as a whole.

A more direct influence on the general reform movement in the Church came from Lorraine, once a part of the middle kingdom of Lotharingia and now divided into two duchies of the German crown. Here a monastic reform very similar in its aims to that of Cluny started at almost the same time. The most prominent of the houses affected was that of Gorze, near Metz. The Lorraine movement differed in one important respect from the Cluniac; the monasteries there never achieved the stroke of fortune which had given Cluny independence from the Church around her. They remained under the control of the local bishops. Moreover, they could not at first hope for complete independence of royal power. The German emperors were far more powerful rulers than the impotent early Capetian rulers of France and were likely to resist any attempt to remove large areas from their kingdom.

These factors prevented the Lorraine houses from developing along Cluniac lines, but at the same time they meant that reformers

87

there could not view the world and its problems with the same detachment. They could not take a purely monastic view of reform; their well-being depended on the well-being of the Church outside the cloister. By the early eleventh century there was a vigorous reform movement centred on Lorraine within the Church. Originally its aims had nothing to do with Rome, which despite the efforts of Odo to show a better way to its monks remained a disgrace only tempered by distance. Nor were they much interested at first in constitutional questions of how the Church should be governed. They were concerned primarily with two moral questions, simony and clerical concubinage. Much is to be heard of them in the conflict ahead.

Simony derives its name from Simon Magus, who in the Acts of the Apostles is described as trying to buy the powers of the Holy Spirit from the Apostles.[1] It is the crime of trading the holy things of God for profit. Clearly as such it was wrong, but as with many sins the difficulty came in defining it more precisely. Take a modern but perhaps not misleading parallel. All men disapprove of dangerous driving, and would agree that dangerous drivers should be severely punished. But many drivers who habitually exceed the speed limit in built-up areas would be shocked and angered to find themselves imprisoned for their offence. Yet on a strict definition speeding could well be considered dangerous driving. In the same way general medieval opinion was always strongly against simony; Dante placed the simoniacs upside down in flames in Hell for their crime of reversing the true order of things.[2] Gross simony had become common in the Church of the ninth and tenth centuries. Large sums regularly changed hands when rival candidates appeared for ecclesiastical office, and all sorts of abuses were common. Philip I of France (1060–1109) could write to an unsuccessful candidate for a bishopric whose bribe had not been large enough: 'Let me make my profit out of him; then you try to have him degraded for simony, after which we can see about satisfying you.'[3] But if such bribes were clearly simony, there remained a large number of practices which were common form but might be considered simony if it came to be defined strictly. To pay a bribe to obtain a living was obviously simony, but what of the fees so regularly paid by a new incumbent on taking office? It was clearly wrong to buy a bishopric, but was there any reason why a bishop should not pay feudal dues to his secular overlord in the way that any lay tenant did? The strictest

[1] See Acts 8. [2] See Dante, *Divine Comedy*, Canto XIX.
[3] Quoted J. P. Whitney, *Hildebrandine Essays*. Cambridge U.P., 1932, p. 7.

definition of simony might make any lay concern in spiritual offices simony, and such a definition would run so contrary to existing practice in many parts of Europe that it could only lead to a violent clash between the Church and lay authorities.

The problem of clerical concubinage was rather similar. In the Eastern Church a distinction had been drawn, and is still maintained, between the monk living under vows of chastity and the ordinary parish priest. All the high offices of the Church were reserved to the former, who had chosen the more excellent way, but the latter were permitted to marry. This distinction had never been made in the West, where all the clergy were expected to be celibate. There were two main reasons for this. Those who were to handle the holy mysteries of faith were to keep themselves free from the pollution of the flesh and to concentrate on the one great vocation they had chosen. Equally important from the practical viewpoint was the danger that once priests were allowed to found families, offices in the Church might follow the common fate of lay posts and become hereditary. The rule of celibacy is hard for human nature to bear, and it is not perhaps surprising that from England in the eighth century to Bohemia in the fourteenth there should have been repeated protests by groups of clergy, who not only broke it but believed they were justified in so doing. In Germany in the eleventh century very many of the parochial clergy had those whom strict reformers, bred in a monastic tradition, might regard as concubines, but who to them were wives. Their behaviour might not be in accordance with the law of the Church, but it was hallowed by long tradition. Any attempt to enforce strict celibacy would be sure to meet bitter resistance.

The Church in the early eleventh century was an institution still full of abuses, nowhere more glaring than in Rome, but it showed also many signs that reform might be on the way. Revitalized from within by the great Cluniac abbeys and with a vigorous reform movement in Lorraine, there was every expectation that an attempt at a reform of the whole body might soon be made.

It is time now to turn to the Empire, the other protagonist in the coming conflict. When Otto III died in 1002 he left behind him no children, and his premature death had not allowed him to make any arrangements for the future of the Crown. Once again the machinery of election had to come into operation. The choice fell on Henry, Duke of Bavaria, a cousin of the later emperor and son of that Henry the Wrangler who had tried to depose Otto II. It remained to be seen if the first of this new line of emperors, the Salian, could rescue the monarchy from the disrepute into which Otto III's imprudent adventures had brought it.

Henry II (1002–1024), known later as Henry the Saint, proved a fortunate choice. In sharp contrast to his predecessor he had no extravagant schemes of universal dominion. As he saw it his primary duty was to restore royal authority in Germany; the extension of his power into Italy was of only secondary importance, undertaken because the tradition of imperial activity there was now too strong to be abandoned. In Germany Henry was very successful. He was able to prevent the forces opposed to royal authority from uniting; the two major threats to his power, an attempt by Lorraine to break away and a rising against him in his own duchy of Bavaria, were suppressed separately and effectively. To an even greater extent than Otto I, Henry relied on the Church to exercise his authority in Germany. His own personal piety, later to lead to his canonization, no doubt predisposed him towards such a policy, but it was shrewd statesmanship as well. He saw himself not as the faithful son of the Church, but as the only effective head of the one policy which was both German church and German monarchy. In the conditions of his age the Papacy could not exercise more than the most nominal headship of the Church in Germany, nor was there any desire among German churchmen that it should do so. The real choice lay between a Church dominated by the secular rulers of the various duchies and a Church largely controlled by the Crown itself. The interests of religion as well as those of the Crown were better served by the latter. Henry interfered considerably in the affairs of the Church. Royal pressure was brought to bear at the election of bishops and abbots, so that such appointments, although in form in accordance with Church law, were in fact his own. Henry took care that the men he nominated were suited for their religious duties, but at the same time he naturally saw to it that they were men who would aid his government. The policies he imposed on the German Church quite often had political as well as religious aims; indeed the distinction is probably not one he would have understood. For instance, his creation of the new bishopric of Bamberg in 1007 and its generous endowment with lands taken from the rebellious comital family of Schweinfurt had a clearly political purpose. The new bishopric was intended both as a royal bastion against possible Slav attacks from the East and as a powerful warning against possible risings within Germany. Later, when more extreme reforming views prevailed in the Church, much that Henry II had done was to seem the grossest interference in spiritual matters by a layman. But this new conception of simony had not yet taken root; at the time he seemed to be fulfilling two goods, the purification of the Church and the strengthening of the Crown.

One quality, however, Henry II lacked; he was not a great soldier. On the eastern frontier he had the misfortune to come up against the most powerful opponent the Germans had faced since Lechfeld. While Otto III had been fighting his last campaign in Italy Boleslav the Mighty of Poland had seen that the time was ripe to resume attacks on German territory. After Otto's death the instability of the system of alliances he had built up to protect the East was revealed. Boleslav was able to advance his frontiers in the north right up to the Elbe, across which raiding parties were able to harry Saxony; further south his armies advanced to occupy most of Bohemia. For fourteen years (1004–1018) Henry's armies were engaged in trying to eject Boleslav from his new territories, and although by the Peace of Bautzen (1018) he consented to withdraw from Bohemia, the Polish frontier remained on the Elbe. The German advance to the East had received a severe setback. Similarly Henry's attempts to extend German power in the West by attaching the kingdom of Burgundy to her by force failed. Nor were his incursions into Italy any more successful. He led three expeditions to Italy in all, and in the course of one of them was crowned emperor in Rome (1014). But he secured no permanent results. Byzantine power was not extinguished in the South, the Papacy was not set free from the turbulent control of the Roman nobility, and no secure foundations for imperial power in the peninsula were laid. But this catalogue of failures should not obscure his success within the borders of Germany.

Henry II left no son, but the election which followed his death went in favour of his closest male relative, Conrad II of Franconia (1024–1039). At first sight he has little in common with his predecessor. He had nothing of sanctity about him; on the other hand he was much more effective than Henry in the field. Two of the problems which had defeated Henry he solved by force. Burgundy was brought under the German crown (1034) and Poland reduced to her former frontiers. In Italy too he had a much more positive policy. He seems to have realized that a German emperor could not hope to control the country by means of occasional and hazardous expeditions across the Alps. What was needed was an administration on the spot which remained permanently loyal to the Crown. After a revolt led

91

by the city of Pavia had convinced him early in the reign that the Italians could not be trusted to provide this themselves, he embarked on a systematic policy designed to Germanize the administration of northern Italy. The Church served him well in Germany; in Italy too it should be made to serve the Crown, and wherever possible the election of loyal German churchmen to Italian sees should be secured. In the same way marriage could be used to link as many Italian marquisates as possible to Germany; one of them, that of Azzo of Este to Kunigunda, heiress to the Welf estates in Suabia, was to bring the Welf connection to Italy, where it was to play a leading role for many centuries. Where marriage could not attain his ends Conrad was prepared to court popularity among the numerous class of sub-tenants, the *Valvassores*, against their tenants-in-chief, the *Capitanei*, in the hope that he could build up an imperial party with promises of the free possession of their estates. Yet his policy was no more successful than Henry's lack of a policy—Germany had no towns which could compare with those of Lombardy, and Conrad did not realize either the military strength of the Lombard towns or their resentment of alien rule. Moreover the Italian Church had not the tradition of subservience to the Empire which marked the *Reichskirche*. Aribert, Archbishop of Milan could combine the two forces. Behind the walls of the wealthiest and strongest of all Italian cities he continued to resist Conrad, for cavalry, the decisive arm in the battles of the north, was of little use in siege warfare. By the time of his death from malaria in 1039, Conrad's Italian efforts had only succeeded in alerting the Italian Church and the Lombard communes to the danger of German domination.

Yet Conrad too can be accounted a successful German king. He was aided by chance deaths causing vacancies in appointments vital to the Crown. For instance both the duchies of Bavaria (1026) and Bohemia (1038) fell vacant during his reign, and in each case he was able to secure the election of his own son, the future Henry III, to the post. Numerous lesser offices were safely filled by men of his own choice, and he began the process of building up a genuine royal administration. A class of '*ministeriales*', new in general royal administration, appears, clerks of quite humble origin drawn for the most part from the royal estates and trained to the duties of an official class. In them can be seen the germ of the royal bureaucracies of the later Middle Ages, which were to find their most developed form not in Germany but in France. But Conrad also used the dignitaries of the Church in his administration; no emperor concerned above all with the problem of the over-mighty lay subject could afford to neglect them. Less spiritually-minded than his predecessor, he took little account of the religious suitability of his church appointments. What had been only potentially an abuse under Henry II became something of an actual one under Conrad.

There was little difficulty about the succession in 1039. Conrad had only one son, and he had already succeeded to many of the duties of Empire before his father's death; his election as king of Germany had been carried out in his father's lifetime. In character the new emperor Henry III (1039–1056) resembled Henry II more than his father. Strengthened perhaps by his second marriage to the highly religious Agnes of Aquitaine, he had the same spiritual view of his duties, and regarded the protection and purification of the Church as the most important of them. Yet, like Conrad, he was also possessed of military skill. By the end of his reign Poland, Bohemia and Hungary were all vassals of the German crown, and the danger of attack from the East seemed to have disappeared; with it incidentally had disappeared one of the strongest reasons for preserving a powerful German monarchy. In the West his main political achievement was the division of the duchy of Lorraine, after a dispute with the new duke Godfrey. The long term effects of this were unfortunate. Not only did it leave Godfrey with a grievance, but it meant that the Crown would now face the problem of controlling a number of semi-independent vassals directly without the aid of a duke in an area where alternative methods of administration had not yet been created.

But Church reform was the cause nearest Henry's heart. In this he was a man of his age. By the middle of the eleventh century many of the nobility of northern Europe had been touched by the flame kindled at Cluny; great noble families, such as the dukes of Normandy or Aquitaine, had become ardent reformers. From the Elbe to the Atlantic new monasteries and churches were being built on an impressive scale, and from the monasteries monks were selected to become bishops and carry the work of reformation to the whole Church. The high regard in which the monasteries were held was shown by the number of those of the highest birth who became monks in youth—for example S. Poppo (978–1048), the close friend of Henry II who later became Abbot of Stavelot—or who, like Godfrey the Bearded, duke of the Ardennes, felt it safer on the approach of death to take vows, and to die, if not to live, in the habit.

93

With all this work of reform the German emperors had long been associated. Cluny, indeed, had little direct contact with the German Church, but great houses such as Gorze and, rather later, Hirsau, had carried a reforming message there. As early as 952 Otto I and his brother Bruno, Archbishop of Cologne, can be found at the Council of Augsburg trying to persuade the German clergy to abandon their 'wives'. Henry the Saint had used his influence to secure reforming bishops in most German dioceses, and had successfully guided a number of synods to reforming conclusions. After an interval under Conrad, who cared for none of these things, Henry III resumed the good work. But in reforming the Church the German emperors acted under one big restraint. Their power rested in large part on the political support of the Church. They could not afford to allow the spread of ideas which taught the absolute necessity of complete separation between the Church and lay power. Nor indeed can they have seen why such a separation should be thought to be desirable. So far in German history the Church had always profited from its connection with the monarchy. While striving to check the more blatant examples of simony, they saw no reason why it should be held to cover all and every secular incursion into ecclesiastical affairs.

It was in Lorraine that the more extreme doctrines of reform were to be found, and it is difficult to be sure what the main motives of the reformers were. In that area, as elsewhere in Germany, 'proprietary' churches and monasteries were common, that is to say churches and abbeys which had been founded by local landowners on their own land, often with the primary object of offering masses and prayers for the souls of the founder and his family. Except that the land so given could not be used for any but a spiritual purpose, such churches remained as much the property of their lay owners as any other part of their land. The reforming monks and canons of Lorraine may have been genuinely concerned by the simony involved in this lay ownership of the things of God, but their lay owners were often worried that the Crown might use the accusations of simony as an excuse for transferring them to the control of the German bishops, and hence ultimately of the Crown. The Crown was not popular in Lorraine, and many of these landowners in the early years of the eleventh century made over the ownership of the churches to the Papacy, as William of Aquitaine had made over Cluny to Rome. In so doing they could both defend themselves against accusations of simony and make it more likely that they could retain some real control over them. Unless the Papacy became very much stronger than it was in the early eleventh century, it was likely that the control of a distant and unreformed Rome would be merely nominal; a German Crown, both nearer and stronger, was a much more real threat. Elsewhere in Germany other owners of proprietary churches followed the example of those in Lorraine. In so doing they were establishing a situation by which, if once the Papacy were reformed and sought to establish a real control over the Church, it would have a powerful lever to use against the royal control of the German Church.

The movement to spread reform from the body of the Church to its head in Rome was largely the work of Henry III; paradoxically nothing in the long run did more to create troubles for the German monarchy. In 1046 he received the call, by now customary for German kings, to come to Rome and resolve a schism in the Papacy. No less than three men were claiming to be the legitimate pope. They included one, Benedict IX, whose life was a public scandal even to the hardened inhabitants of Rome, while the only worthy claimant on moral grounds, Gregory VI, had obtained his 'election' by blatant simony. But on this occasion Henry did not content himself merely with trying to decide which of the three was the least unworthy claimant. At a synod he summoned at Sutri all three popes were deposed, and on Christmas Day 1046 a German bishop, Suidger of Bamberg, was proclaimed pope. Henry was aiming at a permanent reform of the institution and not merely at solving a temporary problem; he had thus naturally chosen a German churchman whom he knew to be a capable man of reforming ideas to start the process.

The new pope took the title of Clement II, and his first public action was the coronation of Henry and his wife as Emperor and Empress. The Romans themselves at first approved of his action, and shortly afterwards they revived the title of Patricius for Henry. The rights attached to this title were vaguely defined, but they were clearly thought to include some sort of supervisory rights over the Papacy and elections to it, for without such supervision the institution might soon slip back into corruption. Since Clement soon died (1047) Henry was called upon again to exercise his rights; four times in the eight years 1046–1054 did Henry nominate German reformers to be pope. At the time the puplic opinion of Christendon supported him in righting what was an obviously intolerable state of affairs; Odilo of Cluny for instance strongly approved of his action in exalting Clement II. Henry could not have foreseen that within a few years a prominent member of the papal court[1] would consider that he was undoubtedly suffering the pains of Hell for his supremely simoniacal action.

The most important of the popes who owed their position to Henry III was Leo IX (1049–1054). The emperor's cousin, before his election he had been bishop of Toul in Lorraine and had made a name for himself there as a leader of reform. When he moved to Rome many of his old colleagues from Lorraine came with him. Several of them were made cardinals, and ensured that the central administration of the Church became dedicated to reform. Such were Cardinal Frederick of Upper Lorraine, a brother of the duke and himself later to be Pope Stephen IX, and Cardinal Humbert, who had been a monk in a reformed monastery in the Vosges. Both were to play a prominent part in shaping the papal policies of the future. But the most dynamic figure who accompanied Leo to Rome was the young monk Hildebrand. It is a common mistake to refer to the whole reforming movement in Rome as Hildebrandine, for at first Hildebrand can have had small say in the making of policy. But he was to remain in Rome for thirty-five years, and for much of that time he was to be the most influential, if by no means the most extreme, of the papal entourage. At the end of it as Gregory VII (1073–1085) he was himself to be perhaps the greatest and certainly the most dramatic of all medieval popes.

In building up this body of dedicated men to run the central machinery of the Church Leo performed a great service for it. At the same time he associated two causes which until this time had had no necessary connection with each other, Church reform and the authority of the Papacy over the whole Church. In the past reform movements had been liable to spring up anywhere in the Church, and often owed more to the initiative of local lay rulers than to any churchman. Even a large scale reform such as that instituted by Cluny in monasticism had had very little to do with the Papacy. But now that the Papacy had put itself squarely at the head of the reforming movement the best prospects for reform obviously lay in an increase of papal power, and those who opposed this growth, even if they claimed to be protecting their own churches, were in danger of seeming opponents of Christianity itself. Annual councils were held in Rome at which the latest batch of reforming decrees for the Church were promulgated. From Rome Legates would take them to all parts of the Western Church to explain them at a series

[1] Cardinal Humbert.

of provincial councils. It mattered little whether local rulers approved of them or not. Henry III, the only one who might have possessed enough prestige and control over his church to forbid them, was an enthusiastic supporter of the new ways; he was himself present at the provincial Council of Mainz in 1049. If many churchmen no doubt had grave doubts as to where all this was leading, they were chary of expressing them lest they too should be denounced as enemies of the truth. Whatever its implications for the future, Leo's short pontificate was supremely successful in Church reform.

In other spheres he was less fortunate. The new stress on unity within the western Church naturally brought to mind those other Christians in the East who knew not Peter. There were doctrinal differences between East and West, but these were the result rather than the cause of the division between Rome and Byzantium. For many centuries the Mediterranean had been a hostile Islamic sea, and the two Churches had necessarily grown apart. Now the communications between East and West were much safer, and the time seemed ripe to attempt to fulfil again Christ's injunction that they should all be one.[1] But Leo's choice of Cardinal Humbert, the most intransigent of all the reforming cardinals, to lead the Western delegation to the Patriarch of Constantinople was unwise; a series of acrimonious discussions ended with Humbert depositing a bull of excommunication on the high altar of S. Sophia, whence the Patriarch duly retrieved it for public incineration. The cause of unity had not been much aided, for personal insults had now been added to historical divisions. Similarly Leo's only attempt to use the temporal sword ended in disaster. Into the complicated politics of southern Italy the Normans had now come as a further disturbing factor. Leo determined to establish papal control over a kingdom which if it were allowed to develop might well menace Rome itself. His attempt to do so met with disaster when he was defeated and taken prisoner by Robert Guiscard, the Norman king, at Benevento in 1053. The Normans had come to stay in southern Italy as dangerous foes and perhaps even more dangerous allies for the Papacy. Soon after his release in 1054 Leo died.

In the closing years of Henry III's reign there was no hint of the coming clash with the Church. Relations between the emperor and the Papacy remained harmonious, and Henry was concerned mainly with the doings of the disgruntled Godfrey of Lorraine, who was trying to compensate himself for his lost lands in the north by gaining

[1] John 17: 21.

new territories in Italy. His marriage to Beatrice, Countess of Tuscany, threatened revolt there, and Henry dealt with the situation firmly, defeating Godfrey in the field and removing Beatrice and her infant daughter Matilda by her earlier marriage to an enforced exile in Germany. But he had not succeeded in driving Godfrey from Lorraine when he himself died suddenly in 1056. It was only his death which revealed his most serious deficiency as a ruler. Any king who did not leave behind him an adult male heir had failed seriously in his duties, and Henry's only son had not been born until 1050. His father had taken the precaution of getting him recognized by the princes and crowned during his own lifetime, but the outlook for a child of six surrounded by greedy magnates was bleak.

The minority of the new emperor Henry IV (1056–1106) lasted until he assumed personal rule on 1065, nine years later. It is a period of the first importance in the history of both Church and Empire. In Germany the consequences for royal power were wholly disastrous. The Empress Agnes attempted to act as regent, but her pious intentions were no substitute for strong masculine government. Everything that Henry III had worked for was shown to depend on his own forceful personality. Godfrey of Lorraine was immediately able to go over to the offensive, and, reunited with Beatrice, who had been most unwisely released by Henry III in a fit of deathbed penitence, he entered again on his Tuscan inheritance. He ruled in the name of the young king, but what Henry III had feared had come about. A strong vassal had united the estates of two different families and could threaten the Crown on two fronts. On the eastern frontier Poland and Hungary both threw off a yoke which could no longer be enforced. What happened in Germany was even more serious. Dangerous revolts took place in Saxony, and even the Church on which the Salian kings had lavished so much attention proved most unreliable when there was no longer a king to direct it. Archbishops Anno of Cologne and Adalbert of Bremen both thought that they should exercise royal powers during the minority, and they intrigued ceaselessly against each other and against the unfortunate Agnes. In 1062 she gave up the unequal struggle and retired to a nunnery. In the course of the struggle all three showed great generosity in giving away large portions of that royal demesne, on which royal power had rested, to their supporters. Henry IV was lucky to survive at all, but by the time he began to try to assert his own power in 1065 the monarchy his father had left was greatly weakened. The relationship between the Roman Church and this enfeebled German monarchy would inevitably be different from that of the earlier age; this is one basic cause of the Investiture Contest.

The results of the regency were no less marked in Rome itself. There was now no emperor to wield his influence there, and the reformers were compelled to make all their own decisions. The line of German popes came to an end with Stephen IX (1057–1058), but the reformers were now strong enough to resist attempts by the Roman factions to revert to the old conditions of mob rule and were able to carry out an orderly election without the help of a *Patricius*. One result of this was seen in the short reign of the Burgundian Nicholas II (1059–1061). In the Vatican Council of 1059 he issued his Election Decree. For the first time a really clear system was laid down for the election of a new pope. Traditionally this had rested rather vaguely with 'the clergy and people of Rome', with nothing to say what happened in the event of a clash between the two; in practice recent elections had been controlled by the imperial authorities. Now the elections were made wholly the responsibility of the cardinals, then about fifty in number and for the most part connected with the Curia itself. They were specifically permitted to hold their meeting outside Rome if conditions in the city were such that they felt they could not reach a fair result there. The 'assent of the people of Rome' becomes merely an act of acclamation of the new pope, a recognition of a *fait accompli*; as such it still survives. While this exaltation of the cardinals was primarily intended to safeguard the Papacy from the threat of Roman demagogues, it would be equally effective against imperial intervention. Henceforth the role of the emperor was to be much the same as that of the people of Rome; he is to give formal recognition to the new pope, but the power of veto which strong emperors had exercised in the past is gone. At the same council further decrees were issued against simony and clerical 'marriage'. Not only were the sins themselves again denounced, but would-be priests were forbidden to get themselves ordained by simoniac bishops and the laity to receive the sacraments from unchaste priests. The intention of these prohibitions was to root out the abuses, but behind them lay a novel doctrine which was being propounded by Cardinal Humbert and the more extreme of the Roman reformers. In his *Libri Tres adversus Simoniacos* (c. 1057) Humbert had argued that the validity of sacraments depended in part on the worthiness of the man who dispensed them; a sacrament performed by a flagrantly immoral bishop or priest was no sacrament. Peter Damian and the moderates were more far sighted. Damian yielded to none in his hatred for sin. Indeed his *Liber Gomorrhianus* (*c.* 1051) lives up to its name, and is a startling denunciation of the more unpleasant vices of the Church. Yet he realized the consequences of adopting Humbert's view; since no man can really judge the sinfulness of another, the effect would be that a general doubt would be cast on all sacraments. No one would ever be sure whether his sins had really been forgiven in Confession or whether he had really partaken of the Lord's Body in Communion. It was well for the Church that his view eventually prevailed, and that it was held that, although an impenitent priest sinned in celebrating the sacraments, this did not rob them of their efficacy.

Nicholas II took one action in the political sphere which had great consequences for the future. At Melfi in 1059 he reached an agreement with the Norman leaders Robert Guiscard and Richard of Capua by which he invested them with the territories they had won in southern Italy and might win in Sicily, while in return they promised to do the pope service, and in particular to protect the cardinals at the time of papal elections should it be necessary. The Treaty of Melfi was much more than a realistic acceptance of the fact that the Normans had come to stay. By it the Papacy added to its newly found moral authority the military strength of what was by now far the strongest power in the western Mediterranean, and this at a time when the power of the Empire was rapidly declining. Moreover if the Empire should ever revive its strength, here was an immediate and serious cause of dispute between it and the Papacy. If the Empire meant anything at all in Italy, it meant that the Papacy had no possible right to give away large tracts of the peninsula. At Melfi can be seen the signs of that problem which was to continue to dog the Papacy for nearly three hundred years, the problem of how to combine military strength in the brutal world of European politics with the moral authority proper to a spiritual institution. Western democracies face a rather similar problem today.

The pontificate of Alexander II (1061–1073) was the calm before the storm. Alexander himself was a peaceable man, content to make haste slowly in the work of reform. At the beginning of his reign he was troubled by the attempt of the Romans to disregard the Election Decree, and, invoking the distant authority of the *Patricius* in Germany, to elect their own pope. But the Normans brought military aid to Alexander, and the anti-pope Cadalus got only tenuous support. Three years later the Empire withdrew its rather nominal recognition of him. Henry for his part had more than enough to do in Germany after he had assumed government in 1065 to worry much about Italian affairs.

In 1073 the monk Hildebrand, who had been a close adviser of the last two popes, was himself elected and took the title of Gregory VII (1073–1085). Oddly enough the circumstances of his own election seem to have violated the Election Decree, the acclamation of the people of Rome playing the decisive part in it. However, there is little doubt that he would also have been the choice of the cardinals. Peter Damian had died in the previous year, and Hildebrand was now the only survivor of the original group of reformers who had transformed the Papacy. No man had as long or as close an experience of the workings of the Curia, and no man had a more continuing zeal for the work of reform. He had indeed chafed somewhat against the comparative inaction of his predecessor; now that he was pope the Lord's work would be resumed.

Gregory VII was a small man of exceptional ugliness and even more exceptional energy. When he first came to the throne he seems to have had no intention of provoking a deliberate clash with the Empire. Indeed he prayed that 'as the times and the position of the Church make it expedient all dissensions and invidiousness between Papacy and Empire may cease'.[1] Yet his intransigent nature made it very unlikely that his prayer would be answered. Immediately he revived Leo IX's policy of annual Roman councils and provincial synods, which Alexander had allowed to lapse, and new and stern decrees against simony and clerical marriage were sent out to the Church. In England they caused little difficulty. William I was himself very sympathetic to reform, and in any case had no need to lean very heavily on the Church in an administration which was based on a firm control of his lay nobility. Moreover, Lanfranc, his archbishop of Canterbury, was known and trusted in Rome, so that there was not the same call for legatine intervention. In France the papal legates Hugh of Die and Amatus of Oleron met little resistance; there was no powerful French king to lead an opposition. But the prelates of Germany were not yet accustomed to taking their orders from Rome, and believed that the Crown would support them in resistance. At first they tried the simple expedient of inaction. If no provincial synods were called, the unpopular decrees could never be promulgated. Gregory was not the man to put up with this dumb disobedience; he immediately suspended archbishops Siegfried of Mainz and Liemar of Bremen until synods were summoned. When

---

[1] Quoted L. M. Smith, *Cluny, in the Eleventh and Twelfth Centuries.* Allan, 1930, p. 58

Siegfried was reluctantly compelled to summon a synod at Mainz in 1075 to proclaim the new decrees he ran into further trouble. The married clergy felt so horrified by the demand that they should give up their wives that they became violent. 'The clerks who sat around rose up and so raved against the archbishop with their hands and with movements of their bodies that he despaired of leaving the synod with his life'.[1] Even those German bishops who were generally sympathetic to reform resented Gregory's apparent arrogance; Liemar spoke for the rest when he said 'This dangerous man orders us about as though we were bailiffs.' The whole temper of the German Church seemed hostile to Rome.

At the same time (1075) Gregory turned his attention also to the lay authorities. At the Lent synod in Rome that year accusations of simony were brought against Henry's most immediate counsellors, five of whom were threatened with excommunication. There is some evidence that some of them had accepted money to influence Henry in his ecclesiastical appointments, but Gregory's failure to consult the king first suggested that he himself might well be the next on the list. At the same synod the practice of lay investiture was condemned absolutely, on pain of excommunication. Since Investiture became the symbol which was the focus of the whole struggle and gave its name to it, the process needs to be explained. Investiture was a common feature of all feudalism. When a lord received the homage of a vassal it was customary for him to hand over to his newly pledged man some material object, such as a banner or a charter, as a symbol of the office or property conveyed to the vassal and as a reminder of whence it came. The practice had penetrated the Church, and it had become customary for the German emperors to invest newly created bishops or abbots with a ring and a staff. Once it was questioned it could be defended on two grounds, that the considerable lands attached to the spiritual office necessarily carried with them feudal responsibilities to the lay overlord, or on the ground that the emperor, sanctified by the holy oil of coronation, was no mere layman but himself had a high spiritual function. Much of the dispute around Investiture arose from a genuine confusion as to which was the real explanation. But once the Papacy had associated itself with a strict definition of simony the practice was clearly questionable, while the emperor for his part could not possibly afford to lose all control of the German Church and the extensive land which went with it.

[1] Quoted J. M. Whitney, *Hildebrandine Essays*, p. 34.

At about the same time Gregory was drawing up the document known as the *Dictatus Papae*; although it was not at once issued, being intended for his own unofficial guidance, it is useful evidence of the way his mind was moving. The *Dictatus Papae* consisted of twenty-seven different phrases or propositions asserting papal power, which together went much further towards pronouncing the complete supremacy of the Roman Church and its pontiff over the whole world than anything previously claimed. Indeed the papal position has significantly altered. The earlier reformers had claimed independence for the Church from the world; now Gregory was claiming control over it. Precedents were put forward to show that in the past the Church had exercised such control. Had not Pope Zacharias deposed the last of the Merovingians and S. Ambrose excommunicated the Emperor Theodosius? Did it not follow that emperors only held office by the good will of popes? Did not the ancient laws of the Church and the conduct of Constantine himself show that this had been known to be so in the past? Much use was made of the Forged Decretals, then generally thought to be genuine documents of the early Church but now known to be eighth-century forgeries. If such ideas became the policy of Rome, a conflict was almost certain, for they amounted to an entirely new relationship between the two major powers of Europe.

The only hope for preserving the peace would have been a pacific emperor; the young Henry IV was not this. His upbringing with an incompetent mother and a gaggle of unscrupulous archbishops could scarcely have been worse, and the accusations later brought against him that he spent his youth in dissipation and low company may well have been justified. Certainly he had already had one brush with the Church before the conflict started, when in 1069 he had tried to repudiate his wife Bertha of Turin, and on this occasion moral right had not been on his side. Unlike Henry II or Henry III he could not claim to speak with the voice of righteousness. That he had good qualities had been seen early in his rule, when he had shown courage and skill in putting down revolts in Bavaria and Saxony, but he lacked judgement and control over his temper. His early successes only led him disastrously to overestimate his power in Germany, and to believe that he was secure enough to try to build up imperial power in Italy.

The point of ignition came in Milan, the strongest and richest of the Lombard towns and the seat of an archbishopric which had numbered S. Ambrose among its earlier occupants. The city had long been disturbed by internal disputes between a feudal nobility who valued the imperial connection, and a popular movement, whose followers, known as *Patarini*, protested alike against their feudal overlords and against the corruption of the Milanese clergy. In 1072 two rival archbishops, Godfrey and Anno, had been consecrated. Godfrey had obtained imperial investiture and was championed by the nobility, while Anno had the support of the Papacy as well as of the *Patarini*. Henry realized that an effective Italian policy demanded the control of Milan, but in 1072 his position in Germany was too serious for him to risk a war in Lombardy. For the moment he gave way.

In 1075 he felt strong enough to take action, and with the support of the nobility he invested a new imperialist archbishop, Tedald. Such an action was an open challenge to Gregory. He immediately sent Henry a stern letter threatening him with excommunication if he did not withdraw Tedald. Henry did not wait to be excommunicated. In January 1076 he summoned a synod at Worms, attended by two archbishops and twenty-four bishops of the German Church. They dispatched a joint letter to Rome; its tenor is clear from the opening lines, where the long string of Germanic names and German sees roll out addressing themselves not to Pope Gregory, but to 'Brother Hildebrand'. They accused him of seizing control of the Church by unlawful means with his 'well-known arrogance'; at first they had kept silence, hoping that his subsequent conduct would belie 'these iniquitous preliminaries'. Instead he has 'thrown the whole Church into confusion'; an accusation was thrown in for good measure that he was under undue feminine influence, and the letter concludes 'since, as thou didst publicly proclaim, none of us has been a bishop, so thou henceforth wilt be pope to none of us'.[1]

When the messenger reached Rome with this letter and a similar letter from Henry, he was nearly lynched by enraged clerics. Gregory was not slow to answer. Henry was declared deposed from the Empire and from the German throne, and using the power to bind and loose first given to Peter Gregory released his subjects from any obligation to obey him. Finally he was declared excommunicate. The war was on.

It was to be fought as vigorously with the pen as it was with the sword. Henry's literary champions, such as Peter Crassus or Benzo of Alba, based their case on the idea of *pax*; God intended that the

---

[1] Quoted from *Documents of the Christian Church*, ed. Bettenson. Oxford U. P., World's Classics, 1943.

peace of the world should be preserved by a divine order, and to this end He had instituted two authorities, for the Empire quite as much as the Papacy was a divine institution. This order Gregory had violated constantly by his rash innovations, and had shown himself to be opposed to the peace God willed for the world. This was the main count against him; his uncanonical election and the issue of investiture itself were only side issues.

The papalists answer to this was that peace was not the highest good in the world; in any case the peace Christ promised His Church was 'not as the world giveth'.[1] The high mission of the Church was to secure *iustitia*, the rule of righteousness on earth. The Emperor had openly supported simoniacs and connived at unchastity; finally he had committed the grave sin of rebellion against God's Vicar on earth. *Iustitia* demanded his deposition. The two views were incompatible, and behind the clash lay the whole question of the government of Europe.

An important difference between the two sides was that whereas Henry's deposition of Gregory was likely to have only a limited effect in Italy and none in Rome, Gregory's excommunication of Henry had grave and immediate effects in Germany. The revolt in Saxony had never been properly extinguished, and elsewhere there were local magnates, such as Rudolf of Suabia and Otto of Forchheim, who were already regretting the apparent revival of imperial power as a check on their own territorial plans. Now Henry's excommunication made rebellion respectable. They became at once rebels and ardent papalists. Controlling much of the south of Germany they blocked the Alpine passes (1076), at the same time announcing that if the emperor was not reconciled with Gregory by February 1077 they would consider all allegiance to him at an end. In the meantime they invited Gregory to come to Germany in the spring of 1077 to ratify his deposition and to nominate a successor.

This is the background of the most famous incident of the Middle Ages. Henry escaped their net, and crossing the Alps in bitter weather with a handful of followers sought out the pope in the fortress of Canossa. There, as a penitent sinner, he besought Gregory to give him absolution. The pope kept him waiting for three days barefoot and clad in the humble dress of penitence, but Henry had left him no choice. No one who took his priesthood as seriously as Gregory could refuse to absolve a penitent. The sinner was absolved and the ban of excommunication lifted (January 1077).

[1] John 14: 27.

Canossa needs no further description, but three comments should be made on it. It became a symbol of German humiliation before an Italian Papacy, so that eight hundred years later the Prussian chancellor Bismarck could boast 'We will not go to Canossa'. Yet at the time it represented a considerable tactical victory for Henry; his penitence was almost certainly spurious, yet by it he succeeded in dividing his enemies when all seemed lost. Nevertheless in the long term the spectacle of the mightiest ruler of Christendom humiliating himself before the pope was sure to increase the prestige of the Papacy. Finally it should be noted that what was lifted was the excommunication; it is by no means clear that Gregory intended to annul the deposition.

The rebellious German nobility alone got nothing out of Canossa. They decided to carry on as if nothing had happened, and met to elect Rudolph of Suabia as king of Germany at the Diet of Forchheim (March 1077). The kingdom dissolved into indecisive civil war between the two parties, and in 1079 Gregory announced that he was sending two legates to Germany to try the issue between the two claimants. If either did not turn up or tried to interfere with the decision the verdict would automatically go against him. Both agreed to it rather reluctantly, for neither was at all sure what answer the Papacy would give. When Henry happened to win a victory at Flarchheim in Saxony (January 1080), he thought himself strong enough to risk announcing that he would not be a party to the conference.

Gregory at once again excommunicated and deposed the emperor, and from this sentence he was never to be absolved. The throne thus made vacant he declared to have passed to Rudolph of Suabia. Meanwhile Henry proceeded to summon a synod of the Church at Brixen (1080) which elected a new pope in the person of Guibert of Ravenna (the anti-pope Clement III, 1080-1100), who already rested under Gregory's ban of excommunication.

It cannot be said that either new appointment was a great success. Gregory prophesied that God would show whose cause He supported by bringing destruction on Henry, but it was Rudolph who was killed in battle in the same year. His successor as anti-king of Germany, Hermann of Salm, gained little support. On the other hand the Synod of Brixen, although quite copiously attended by Lombard imperialist bishops, only showed how extensively the events of the past five years had eroded Henry's control of the German Church. Of the German bishops only seven now appeared in answer to the imperial summons, and of these one excused himself from signing. The association of Rome with Righteousness was too firmly established for most of them to be prepared to support their king in an election which clearly violated all the laws and traditions of the Church. The close partnership of imperial Church and Crown which had started with Charlemagne was at an end.

However, from the military angle Henry had gained control of the German situation. By 1081 he was ready to undertake the invasion of Italy. Matilda of Tuscany remained loyal to Gregory, but her forces alone were not enough, and in the last resort the papal artillery of excommunication and anathema would be ineffective against advancing troops. In that situation there was only one possible answer, to summon up the help of the Normans. Gregory was reluctant to do this, since they had already taken the opportunity provided by the Investiture Conflict to increase their lands in the south at the expense of papal territory; indeed in April 1080 Robert Guiscard too had been excommunicated. But the drowning man will clutch even at a serpent, and in the autumn of the same year Gregory went south to meet Guiscard; the excommunication was lifted, and Guiscard had been enfiefed with the territories he had stolen. The action may have been damaging to the moral prestige of the Papacy, for more clearly than at Melfi the Papacy was conniving at wickedness, but it opened up the possibility of military aid.

Henry laboriously campaigned his way south, but his assaults on Rome in 1081 and 1082 were frustrated by the walls of the city and by the loyalty of its citizens to their pope. However, in 1083 some of the defenders, faced by the tribulations of yet another siege, opened the gates to the imperial forces. By the end of the year Clement III had been enthroned in S. Peter's and had returned the compliment by crowning Henry as emperor. Meanwhile some few hundred yards away Gregory VII and those cardinals who remained loyal to him continued to defend the well-nigh impregnable Castel Sant Angelo.

For this desperate situation appeared an even more desperate remedy. In 1084 Guiscard led his Normans to the rescue of their overlord. Henry prudently did not risk a battle, and withdrew his forces to the north; the pope was free. But it soon appeared that he had only exchanged one kind of captivity for another. For the Normans did not rest content with liberating the Vicar of Christ; they also indulged in a large-scale sack of Rome, burning down much of the city and massacring many of the inhabitants. Captivity had been infinitely preferable to such a liberation. When the time came for them to withdraw it would not have been safe for the pope who had been responsible for their advent to have remained to face the fury of those who so recently had shown their loyalty to him. Gregory had to accompany the Norman forces into exile, and it was in Norman territory at Salerno that he died in the next year (1085). At the end of his life Gregory believed that he had failed utterly and in his last months he came to believe that he was witnessing that reign of Anti-Christ which must precede the end of the world. Yet even in his agony of spirit he never doubted that in all that he had done he had been striving to fulfil the will of God. His dying words were Dilexi iustitiam et odi iniquitatem; propterea morior in exilio.[1] It was this unshakeable belief in the righteousness of his cause that had made him such a formidable champion of papal rights.

The death of Gregory VII did not put an end to the struggle. There was indeed an interlude in which a wiser man than Henry IV would have sought a compromise. The next pope was not elected for more than a year. He was Desiderius, the abbot of Monte Cassino, and since he was not associated with the extreme reformers he might well have been prepared to negotiate a settlement. But the opportunity was lost. Taking the title of Victor III (1086–1087), he went to Rome under Norman protection for his enthronement, and then prudently withdrew to govern the Church from Cassino. When he died the next year the cardinals elected one of their own number, the French cardinal of Ostia, who became Urban II (1088–1099). Urban in earlier life had been prior of Cluny, until Gregory had removed him from the cloister to the papal court. He had served as one of Gregory's legates in Germany and was in full sympathy with Hildebrandine ideas. His first action as pope was to write to Henry's opponents in Germany pledging them full support.

The Emperor's position soon became very difficult. His Italian allies melted away; the Lombard bishops who had supported him found themselves threatened by popular risings with papal support, and one by one made their peace with Urban. Milan started the procession in 1088. The marriage between Matilda of Tuscany and the Welf heir to the duchy of Bavaria strengthened that link between south Germany and Italy that German rulers had so long tried to prevent. Henry found himself practically isolated in Verona for several years, unable to control either the Po valley to the south or

---

[1] 'I have loved righteousness and hated iniquity; therefore I die in exile.' The first sentence is a quotation from Psalm 45.

the Alpine passes to the north. His plight marked the complete collapse of his Italian policy; even more seriously it meant that he lost all control over events in Germany.

Meanwhile his adversary went from strength to strength. Urban had returned to Rome somewhat gingerly, and the winter of 1088–1089 he spent on an island in the Tiber; neither he nor his Norman allies could expect to be loved by the Roman populace. But the success of papal policy elsewhere soon raised his stock in Rome, and he was able to reoccupy S. Peter's. From there he was able to re-establish his authority over the rest of the Church, a process much aided by his own good sense and moderation in not demanding complete uniformity throughout the Church. In 1095 he was at a great council at Piacenza which marked his acceptance by almost all the Italian bishops, and from there he moved into France for the Council of Clermont (Nov. 1095);[1] his spectacular triumph there could not fail to increase papal authority throughout the Church.

When Henry managed to make his escape back to Germany in 1097 it was to find that the royal position after his twenty years of absence was irreparably damaged. There could now be no question of restoring royal rights and authority throughout the kingdom. He concentrated instead on trying to secure that the succession to the Crown remained within his family. The dukes were allowed more or less complete autonomy in return for their promise of support when the time came to elect the young Henry V. But the young man was unworthy of the trust his father put in him. In 1104 he led a rebellion against his father, perhaps with the idea of hastening the moment of inheritance, perhaps because he resented the way the Emperor had squandered the royal rights he had hoped to inherit. Old and ill, Henry IV had to take the field against his own son. During the next year (1105) the father was taken prisoner, not in battle, but by a despicable pretence of reconciliation made by Henry V. He made his escape (1106), but died the same year. The bishops of Germany were instructed from Rome not to give Christian burial to the excommunicate; it was five years before the corpse was permitted to be buried in the cathedral of Speyer Henry himself had built. It scarcely needed this posthumous insult to mark the complete failure of all his policies.

The death of Henry IV was not the end of the Investiture Contest; the quarrel as to who should invest German bishops continued acrimoniously until the Concordat of Worms in 1122. Nevertheless

[1] See Chapter 7.

it marked the end of that stage of the conflict when the real issue was not investiture, but the question of who should govern Europe. The German Emperor as God's appointed guardian for the Church on Earth was now no longer a political possibility; the question had become one of whether he could hope to control Germany. This represented a great triumph for the papal idea. The possibility that the Papacy might in fact be set over the nations to do justice and punish iniquity had suddenly become real. It was the more impressive in that this victory had been won in part at least by the real association of Rome with righteousness. Yet it was a victory which concealed grave dangers for the future. However it might be won, political power could not be kept except by political means; Gregory VII's dealings with the Normans had already shown this. In Canossa the historian can see not only the promise of the might of Innocent III, but a warning of the downfall of Boniface VIII. Christ's Vicar on Earth was now fatally concerned with the things that are Caesar's.

6

The Empire from 1106 to 1152

Henry V (1106–1125) was duly elected and crowned as king of Germany on the death of his father, but the price he had to pay for recognition was a heavy one. Already he had won support for his cause by lavish promises that when he ruled he would respect all the feudal rights of the German nobility. Now when he was king he could only retain a semblance of power by making little attempt to restore royal authority. No effort was made to restore the royal domanial land his father had squandered in the struggle with the Church; indeed the process of its dissipation was continued. Similarly royal rights of jurisdiction and taxation were not enforced, and the failure to enforce rights inevitably led to their disappearance. The Saxon emperors had commended themselves to Germany by their strength; Henry V and his successors tried to retain their thrones through their very weakness. Inevitably this led to even more excessive demands being made by a nobility conscious of the opportunities presented by a weak Crown. The policy of appeasement led to neither peace nor honour.

At the same time this abandonment of the struggle for real power over his German vassals led Henry to feel that the effort to control the Church and the attempt to assert royal authority in Italy could not be abandoned if the Empire was to continue to mean anything. The Italian situation was not without hope from the imperial point of view. If Milan and the stronger cities of Lombardy were firmly opposed to the German rule of the Empire, there were other weaker communes which might feel more threatened by the scarcely disguised desire of Milan to assert her authority over them than by a distant emperor; they might be used to build up an imperial party. Further south the communes of Tuscany, admittedly weaker and less developed than those of Lombardy, were striving to gain their independence from their immediate overlord, Matilda of Tuscany. Since she was a firm supporter of the Papacy, they would be inclined to support the imperial cause. In neither case, of course, were the communes really interested in anything but their own independence, yet it did mean that Henry could look for considerable Italian support if he should resume the struggle with the Papacy.

At the time of his unfilial revolt against his father Henry V had been reconciled with the Church, whose ban had previously covered the whole family. The problem of investitures thus faced him as it had faced his father. The most recent authoritative statement on the subject had been made by Urban II at Clermont (1095); it prohibited both the investiture of bishops with ring and staff by secular authorities, and also the homage often done by newly created bishops to their new lay lords. Yet so far as it applied to the Empire there was a certain unreality about the ruling. The emperor of the day had been an unrepentant and excommunicate schismatic to whom any form of obedience was sin. Now that a new and orthodox emperor reigned, even if he had not yet received papal coronation, it might well be held that Urban's ban did not apply to him. The Emperor, after all, was rather more than an ordinary secular authority, and even in England Henry I was proving very reluctant to accept the papal ruling. Soon after his accession Henry V resumed both questionable practices.

The pope of the time was Paschal II (1099–1118), a man of piety and learning who seemed to have inherited the inflexible principles of Gregory VII; early in his pontificate he had resisted Henry IV's approaches for a compromise solution on the death of the anti-pope Clement III (1100). But events were to show that Paschal had not Hildebrand's strength of will. In 1107 he was in France, and thus comfortably remote from imperial interference he reminded the new German ruler of his obligations to the Church, a warning he repeated the next year when he was in southern Italy. Henry was invited to come to Rome in 1110, and there seems little doubt that Paschal intended to take a strong line with him, offering him coronation only in return for complete renunciation of the two offending practices. But when Henry V came across the Alps it was at the head of a powerful army, and Paschal suddenly realized that he was about to face it alone. The Normans of the south were unwilling to embroil themselves in war; even that most faithful papal ally, Matilda of Tuscany, had welcomed an emperor who after all was coming at the invitation of the Papacy. Indeed she was personally sympathetic to Henry V, and hoped to see a new era of amity between the Empire and the Papacy.

As Henry drew near Rome Paschal panicked, and met Henry at Sutri (1111) with a totally unrealistic proposal. The Investiture dispute only arose because churchmen held so many lay offices and so much land that secular rulers felt that they must retain some control over them. If then the Church was to abandon all its land and all participation in government, the problem would be solved. Lay rulers would not need to invest clerics, and in a state of primitive apostolic poverty the Church would be able to concentrate on the things of the spirit. All this was true enough, but Paschal was no S. Francis to inspire the Church with a devotion to Holy Poverty.[1] There was not the least likelihood that his proposal would find acceptance with the rest of the Roman Curia, let alone with the Church as a whole. The proposal was no more likely to be popular with secular rulers. The political and social life of the time was so bound up with the idea of the Church as a great landowning corporation, performing a wide variety of administrative and governmental functions, that a sudden transformation of this sort could only cause chaos. Many hundreds of families who had given lands to the Church would feel cheated out of their rights if their lands were now handed to the monarchies of Europe, yet the job of restoring them to their previous holders would be impossibly difficult. Moreover, the idea was too obviously not the product of a deep spiritual purpose but a desperate expedient for the particular problem of Investiture.

Henry must have realized that the proposal was impracticable as soon as it was made, but he accepted it and left Paschal to discover the difficulties for himself. Three days later Pope and Emperor entered Rome, and Paschal attempted to announce the changes in S. Peter's. He was greeted with a violently hostile demonstration. An imperial bodyguard which was standing by 'rescued' him, and removed him to the custody of the German army. There the thoroughly demoralized man made another change of front, and consented to do what Henry wished. Two months later he was back in S. Peter's to crown the German king as Emperor; before he did so he stated specifically that the Papacy recognized the imperial right of investiture and that the ceremony should always precede the consecration of a bishop.

Henry had gained his point, and German affairs were soon to call him back over the Alps. Once he had gone (1112) Paschal had to face the fury of a Curia, who saw in him the betrayer of all that his predecessors had fought for; it is not surprising that he changed his mind again and tried to revoke his recent concession. In so doing he gave Henry an excellent pretext for another Italian expedition.

After three difficult years in Germany, Henry was again able to

[1] See Chapter 10.

113

move on Rome (1116). His expedition had been made the more necessary by the death of Matilda of Tuscany in the previous year. She had bequeathed her lands to Henry himself, with the Papacy as overlord, a singularly unworkable arrangement. Paschal did not wait to see what was in store for him at a second meeting, but decamped to the safety of the Norman kingdom. He was to return to Rome in 1118 only to die in the Castel Sant Angelo, and his successor Gelasius II (1118–1119) remained in exile throughout his pontificate. Henry meanwhile had reverted to the sterile policy of his father in the creation of an anti-pope, Gregory VIII (1118–1121). The circumstances of his election were clearly uncanonical, and he gained no recognition outside the Empire and little within it; even Henry himself seems to have had small confidence in him. Gelasius had died at Cluny, and his successor was elected in France. Archbishop Guy of Brienne, who became Pope Calixtus II (1119–1124), was a strong-willed French prelate of illustrious pedigree; he was related to the kings of France, Germany and England. At the same time he was very sensible of the damage the schism was doing to the Church. In 1120 he moved the Papacy back from France to Rome, and in the next year he improved the chances of a settlement by capturing and deposing Gregory VIII.

In Germany too events were moving towards a reconciliation between Emperor and Pope. Without any firm basis there for royal government, Henry had to rely on the free co-operation of the nobility and such support as he could obtain from the German Church. During his father's lifetime all these parties had had a common interest in the humiliation of Henry IV, and until 1111 the new king continued to receive good support. The size of the army he was able to lead to Italy in that year is evidence of that. But that expedition had a bad effect on his position in Germany. On the one hand it gave him the confidence to try to assert royal rights over the princes, a policy for which the Crown no longer had the necessary resources; on the other it made loyalty of the German Church very dubious, for there was widespread feeling that Henry's treatment of Paschal exceeded due bounds. Lothar of Saxony, the strongest of the princes, and Archbishop Adalbert of Mainz, the leading German prelate, became his enemies, and worked together to secure his downfall. Adalbert indeed had been Henry's own chancellor, and Henry had worked to secure his election to the archbishopric in 1111 in the belief that he would secure the loyalty of the German Church. But once he had become archbishop he saw the possibility of establishing himself as a powerfully independent prince bishop, and turned against his royal patron. The first dangerous rising came in Saxony in 1113, and although Henry was able to put it down, the danger remained. The problem of what to do with Adalbert was no easier to solve than the problem Becket later set Henry II of England; neither king found a satisfactory answer, for Adalbert's imprisonment only increased the opposition of the Church. A second and larger revolt started in Cologne in 1114, and this time it was successful. When Henry went to Italy in 1116 he left behind him a Germany where all royal control over the whole of the north of the country had been lost. Southern Germany remained loyal even during his second absence in Italy; that it did so is a tribute to the good offices of Duke Frederick of Suabia, whom Henry had kept as regent.

There seemed little prospect of anything but a prolonged civil war, but at this juncture the princes of Germany intervened to save the country from a fate which in the end would weaken even their own position. It is a sign of the decline in both royal and Church power since 1075 that now the determination of the princes to have peace was the vital factor. A Diet at Würzburg (1121) arranged an armistice between the warring factions, and the princes offered to act as mediators between Church and Empire.

The Concordat of Worms (1122) was the final outcome of this Diet, and the settlement of the fifty-year-old dispute between Papacy and Empire. The terms of the Concordat represent a compromise between the views of the extremists on both sides. Henry agreed to renounce the investiture with ring and staff which had been the original pretext of the dispute, but he was to continue the practice of touching the newly consecrated bishops with his sceptre as a sign that such royal rights as they exercised they received from him. Bishops and abbots for their part were to do homage to the emperor for their lands and to regard themselves in temporal affairs as his men. On the all important question of the election of bishops, the formula devised for the settlement was that bishops should be 'freely and canonically elected', but that this election should be carried out 'in the presence of' the emperor or his representative. Clearly the latter phrase might cover the use of much pressure; an election carried out in the presence of the emperor could scarcely be genuinely free. At first sight the Concordat seems a surprisingly fortunate conclusion for nearly fifty years of unsuccessful imperial warfare against the Papacy. But there were two important restrictions on the concessions made to Henry. In the first place the terms granted were only to apply to Germany; in the other parts of the Empire, such as Italy and Burgundy, the elections were to be free in fact as well as form, and the ceremonies of homage and the conferring of regalia were to come only after election and consecration had taken place. In this the political facts of the situation were recognized. The bitterness of the struggle within Germany had led to a complete loss of control over the lands on the margins of the Empire. The second restriction was even more important. The royal concessions to the Papacy were specifically stated to have been made for ever; those of the Papacy were made to Henry V by name. It would be open for future popes to deny them to his successors. Certainly Henry might have got far worse terms, and both Papacy and Empire could only benefit from the conclusion of a struggle which since the death of Henry IV had had little meaning. Yet the overall effect of the Investiture Conflict had been gravely to weaken the strong empire built up by the Saxons and the earlier Salian emperors. At the death of Henry III the Papacy had been controlled by the German emperor. Now it had made good its claim to independence. But the claim Hildebrand had made for it, that it should reverse the roles and control the Empire, had not been fulfilled; that part was to be played by the German princes.

The events of the next thirty years only illustrate this loss of imperial prestige. Henry V left no son, but on his deathbed in 1125 he nominated as his successor his nearest male relative, his nephew Frederick of Suabia, the head of the house of Hohenstaufen. The two most recent precedents, the elections of Henry II (1002) and Conrad II (1024), suggested that the electors would choose Frederick as the next of kin to the last ruler. If they had done so the hereditary principle would probably have become established in Germany, as it already was in France and England. Instead they chose Lothar II of Saxony (1125–1137). The dominant figure at the election at Mainz was the archbishop, Adalbert, who carried his hostility to Henry V in life beyond the grave by persuading the electors to ignore his last wish. Lothar had been known for his implacable hostility to Henry. He had no imaginable hereditary claim to the Crown, being himself the son only of a minor Saxon count; he had obtained the succession to the Saxon duchy (1106) through his marriage and the subsequent extinction of the house of Billung. It would be clear to all that his possession of the German crown rested on election alone. Moreover he was already fifty and had no male heir; he seemed unlikely to found a royal dynasty, or to interfere with the privileges of the princes from whose ranks he had so recently emerged.

Throughout his reign Lothar acted in Germany much more as the leader of a noble faction than as the king of the whole country. Faced by the enmity of the Hohenstaufen family, who were understandably disgruntled with the results of the Diet of Mainz, he was concerned far more with building up a party than with governing a kingdom. Royal lands were further dissipated to gain allies, and the favour of the Church won by a subservience very foreign to the traditions of the German Crown. Lothar allowed the rights of supervising episcopal elections and of receiving homage alike to pass from the Crown, so that the papal concessions made at Worms disappeared. He married his only daughter Gertrude to Henry the Proud of Bavaria, the leader of the powerful Welf family, despite the danger of thus making himself dependent on a powerful vassal. All these things were forced on him by the weakness of the Crown and the reality of the Hohenstaufen threat. What is more, he was successful in his aim; after eight years of fighting, the Hohenstaufen, Frederick of Suabia and his brother, the future Conrad II, were compelled to acknowledge Lothar as king (1135). But the measures he had been forced to take to secure this result had again whittled away the permanent resources and prestige of the Crown.

Lothar does not present any stronger a figure in Italy. His first Italian expedition (1132-1133) had a double motive: to the desire of every German king for imperial coronation in Rome was added the existence of a papal schism requiring a solution. In 1130 the death of Pope Honorius II (1124-1130) had produced an unusual division in the Papacy. The Election Decree had laid it down that the right of papal election lay with the cardinals; on this occasion both the claimants had been elected by cardinals, and the Decree did not make it at all clear who was the rightful pope. In favour of Innocent II (1130-43) it could be urged that he had been elected first, although by the narrowest of margins, and that more of the 'cardinal bishops', who possessed a certain pre-eminence in the college of cardinals, had participated in his election. Supporters of Anacletus II (1130-1138) could point to the fact that more cardinals had voted for their candidate. At first Anacletus looked likely to prevail. He gained possession of Rome, and Innocent was compelled to withdraw, first from Rome, and then eventually from Italy itself to France. There he met S. Bernard of Clairvaux (1090-1153), and succeeded in convincing him of the justice of his cause; it is interesting to note that Bernard was convinced not by the legal arguments in favour of Innocent, but by his conviction that he was morally more fitted to be pope than Anacletus. Bernard wielded a quite unequalled influence over the Christian West, and his support was worth far more than that of any lay ruler. He had soon persuaded Louis VI of France and Henry I of England that they wished to support Innocent, and then using the services of his admirer S. Norbert of Xanthen, the archbishop of Magdeburg, as an intermediary, he brought Lothar to the same decision. A meeting took place between the king and the pope at Liége (1131), at which Lothar not only recognized Innocent as the rightful pope, but consented to hold the pope's stirrup when he dismounted as a sign of the inferiority of secular to spiritual power. It seems hard after all this that when Lothar suggested that Innocent might like to restore the original papal concessions of the Concordat of Worms he received a severe rebuke from Bernard for his arrogance! By 1132 Lothar was ready to move on Italy to restore Innocent to his rightful capital and to receive coronation himself.

Anacletus meanwhile had been much less successful in obtaining support. Apart from Rome itself the only substantial secular support he gained was from Roger II of Sicily, the powerful Norman ruler who had welded the county of Sicily and the duchy of Calabria and Apulia into a single kingdom. In return Roger required Anacletus to recognize that his lands were an independent kingdom, no part of which was a papal fief.

Lothar moved somewhat tentatively throughout an Italy in which he felt far from secure. The Lombard towns did not welcome the reappearance of a German army in the Po valley, and Lothar must have been very conscious of the insecurity of his communications. He did not reach Rome until the summer of 1133. Once there he wasted no time in getting himself crowned emperor. Again he went out of his way to pay respect to the pope, and papalists could look with satisfaction at an emperor who seemed to regard himself as the pope's man. But Innocent needed practical aid rather than homage, and this Lothar could not give. As soon as he was crowned Lothar hurried back to Germany to complete the reduction of the Hohenstuafen, leaving Innocent to withdraw his court from Rome to Pisa. Anacletus regained Rome, but he had hopelessly forfeited the sympathy of the Church.

Three years later Lothar was again back in Italy (1136) and this time he had not the anxiety of an undefeated Hohenstaufen behind him. Accompanied by his son-in-law Henry the Proud, he moved through Lombardy without incident and passed to the attack on a Norman kingdom still loyal to Anacletus. The operation was entirely successful; Roger II, defeated on the mainland, withdrew to Sicily, an impregnable fortress to an enemy without seapower, and the Norman lands on the mainland were conferred on Rainulf of Alife, a Norman who had supported the imperial cause. The schismatic pope now had no hope of any general recognition, and although Anacletus continued to be recognized in Sicily, his successor Victor IV wisely submitted to Rome (1140). Yet Lothar's apparent success must raise grave doubts as to the wisdom of his Italian policy. The question of whether the newly-won lands in southern Italy should be held as a fief of Empire or Papacy led even this notably pro-papal emperor to a dispute with the Papacy, settled only by the uneasy compromise of joint investiture. It also raises the question of whether Lothar's concentration on southern Italy was not a hopelessly impractical policy for an emperor whose power was based on lands in the north of Germany. His lines of communication crossed not only the Alps but the Lombard plain, where the communes might at any moment become actively hostile; what hope was there that they could be kept open?

Lothar was not to know the answer to this question. He was already a sick man before he left Italy, and shortly after regaining Germany he died (December, 1137). The pattern of events in 1125, so fatal to the stability of Germany, was repeated in 1138. Once more the electors passed over the obvious candidate, Henry the Proud, the head of the Welf family and Lothar's designated heir. Their reason for doing so was the same as in 1125. Just because he was obviously the strongest candidate he might well have become a strong emperor, who did not need to placate the princes with constant concessions. Instead they elected Conrad III of Hohenstaufen (1138–1152), and thus at a stroke made nonsense of the whole of his predecessor's policy. In so doing they preserved their own rights as electors by ensuring that the monarchy should remain elective, but at the same time they condemned it to continued weakness and sentenced Germany to a disastrous feud between Welf and Hohenstaufen. As in 1125 the leading part in the proceedings was taken by a prelate, on this occasion the Archbishop of Trèves.

The reign of Conrad III saw the process of the disintegration of the German monarchy continue apace. His own family lands were centred on Suabia, in the south, and there was now very little imperial domain left in the north. The Welf Henry the Proud, smarting under his own rejection, controlled the duchies of Saxony and Bavaria, and could hardly fail to be a most dangerous overmighty subject. Conrad started with a brave gesture in declaring him dispossessed of both, but he lacked the force to carry out the sentence. By 1139 Henry had cleared imperial forces from the north of Germany and was about to regain Bavaria. His unexpected death in that year was a stroke of luck for Conrad, perhaps saving him from dethronement. It provided an interlude, for his heir was the ten-year-old boy who was to be Henry the Lion. Yet even this boy was accepted by the nobility of Saxony as their new duke, and after a confused period of civil war Conrad found himself forced to recognize him as Duke of Saxony in 1142. It was certain that when Henry came of age he would make some attempt to regain his father's other duchy.

The great event of Conrad's reign was his participation in the Second Crusade (1147-49)[1] as a victim of S. Bernard's passionate persuasion; the disastrous failure of that expedition did nothing to strengthen his position in Germany. He returned to find Henry the Lion insistently pressing his claim to Bavaria, and rest of the reign was occupied in profitless warfare with his vassal.

Conrad never visited Italy, but during his reign the Papacy came to learn that imperial weakness was not an unmixed blessing. For all the disadvantages of German intervention in Roman affairs, a strong emperor could at any rate protect the Papacy from other internal and external enemies. Between 1138 and 1152 the popes had to face these dangers alone. In Rome itself a powerful opposition to papal power grew up. In part this was only the natural desire of the Roman bourgeoisie to attain a republican independence for their commune; why should not Rome follow in the steps of Milan? But it also took the form of a protest against the wealth and corruption of the clergy, and a demand that the Church should be stripped of its wealth and return to apostolic simplicity; the rash suggestion of Paschal II had returned to plague his successors. That such views gained wide acceptance is a reminder that the force had gone out of the reform movement. By their very success the reformers had created the need for another reform. As against the pomp of papal Rome the rebels could take their stand on the supposedly austere virtues of the Roman Republic, and centring their government on the Capitol could organize a republican government under a Patrician of their own election. Lucius II (1144-1145) treated the world to the spectacle of a pope once again summoning Norman aid against his own city, leading an assault against the Capitol—and failing to capture it. His successor Eugenius III (1145-1153), a less militant Christian, was equally unsuccessful. The Romans had found themselves a leader in

[1] See Chapter 7.

Arnold of Brescia, whose firmness of purpose and purity of life were proof even against the apostolic knocks of S. Bernard.

The Italian scene gave the Papacy equally little satisfaction. With imperial armies safely out of the way, Roger II could re-emerge from Sicily and regain control of the mainland duchies. Innocent II's attempt to prevent this process ended only in the indignity of his capture (1139); the price of his release was papal recognition of Roger's right to the undivided kingdom. The Normans were most unwelcome allies for the Papacy; consorting with Muslim infidels and paying scant regard to clerical claims for independence, their alleged respect for the Papacy was always likely to turn to tyranny. Yet the popes had no choice; the only possible rival to Norman power in the Mediterranean was that of the Byzantine Empire. But the Byzantines might be considered schismatics, and the crusading movement was leading to a steady worsening of relations between Eastern and Western Churches. Eugenius III found himself looking expectantly towards the Alps for the appearance of Conrad III, an event which Roger did his best to prevent by aiding the Welfs. The news that Conrad III had died on the eve of his departure for Italy was greeted with consternation in Rome (1152).

The time has come to attempt some survey of the effects of seventy-five years of continuous warfare on the German scene. All medieval societies experienced occasional periods of civil war and anarchy, but the chain of events springing from Henry IV's first quarrel with the Church had involved Germany in a disaster of a quite exceptional magnitude; an English parallel would be to imagine the 'anarchy' of Stephen's reign continued without a break until the death of John. The total of human suffering involved the historian, perhaps fortunately, cannot compute. The march and counter-march of armies brought the usual destruction in their train. Famine was never far distant in the Middle Ages, and the absence of men on military service when the time came to gather crops would mean starvation the next spring. The general insecurity of German life is all the more evident when elsewhere in Europe the tendency of the eleventh and twelfth centuries was towards a more ordered society.

But certain definite effects can be noted. The power of the Crown suffered a blow from which it was never to recover, even under the genius of Barbarossa. Large areas of what had once been imperial territory had no real connection with the Empire by 1152. Burgundy and Provence, Bohemia and Lombardy had made good their claims to independence. Within Germany itself the kings had failed consistently in their first duty of providing personal protection. The large class of free men who had looked to the Crown to defend them had looked in vain; realistically they had sought security from the local nobility and become their vassals. This is the great age of castle building in Germany, but the castles are not as in England built with royal permission. They were put up by the feudal nobility and often used against the Crown. Germany became a country without any centre. While in England London was a real capital and in France the influence of Paris was gradually spreading more widely, no more is heard of Henry IV's attempt to make Goslar the German capital. Germany became only a geographical term, and the centres of real power came to be the castles (*burgs*) of the nobility. This nobility was largely made up of comparatively new families; it has been seen that Lothar of Saxony himself came from a very new family. Their lands corresponded neither with the old tribal divisions, nor with the administrative units of duchy and county through which earlier and more effective emperors had sought to control the country. Families like the Zähringen in the Black Forest area or the Hohenstaufens themselves had built up their lands without considering the problems of governing Germany; all they asked was to be left alone to run their own lands in their own way. Yet they were the effective powers of twelfth-century Germany. The royal title was coming to be a somewhat empty dignity handed round among them.

Two further causes for the increasing weakness of the German crown must be mentioned. Despite its political weakness, twelfth-century Germany shared in the economic growth which elsewhere was such a characteristic of the age.[1] Two ways in which that economic growth manifested itself were in the foundation and expansion of towns in many areas, and in the steady flow of German colonists to the Slavonic lands of the East. The first process was common to the rest of Europe, the second a primarily German process. Both might have brought to the Crown resources of manpower and money and the political power which go with them; from neither did it profit to any marked extent.

The community of interest between kings and towns was one that occurred in many parts of Europe. It is indeed a prime cause for the general growth in the power of monarchies in the twelfth and thirteenth centuries. Kings needed the revenue which could make them capable of ruling their own nobility; the towns alone could provide it. Towns needed protection from a nobility which might

[1] See Chapter 11.

exploit them by constant impositions, or even at worst destroy them utterly in the course of some, to them, meaningless feudal squabbles; the king was the most obvious source of such protection. So in Sicily or France or England the two interests come together, and charters were issued by the Crown on mutually advantageous terms.

In Germany much less is seen of this process, at least until the time of Henry VI. It was not altogether the fault of the German kings. Henry V did his best to build up support from the communes of both Germany and Italy, and his successors also issued charters when advantage seemed to offer. But the circumstances of Germany did not favour the association. A large proportion of German towns were episcopal in origin, and the loss of control over the German Church meant a loss of control over them; sometimes a revolt against the bishop would temporarily bring the townsmen to the support of the Crown, as at Cologne and Mainz in Henry IV's reign, but such a change was only temporary. Even more important was the inability of the German kings to fulfil their side of the bargain. The Crown was involved in constant but by no means always victorious civil war. Alliance with it increased rather than reduced the normal hazards of urban life. Money supplied by the towns was likely to be spent on aims far removed from any interest of theirs, on the prolongation of civil war in Germany or on costly expeditions to distant Rome. To this must be added the necessarily impermanent nature of privileges granted by an elective monarchy. In countries where hereditary succession prevailed the chances were that a son would confirm the charter issued by his father, or at least issue another on not dissimilar terms. But where the succession was liable to pass at any moment to an entirely different family there was no guarantee that this would be done. It is not surprising that towns preferred to have their rights confirmed by some more permanent body, such as the Church or a well established local feudal family, but the loss to the Crown of the support of one of the most potent forces in twelfth-century society was severe.

The causes for the rapid expansion of German settlement in the previously Slavonic lands of eastern Europe during the twelfth century are not easy to determine. The religious element was certainly present, for many of the Slavonic tribes remained pagan and there was no lack of good Christian swords to wield against them. In 1147 the princes of Saxony even managed to persuade Pope Eugenius III that their operations against the Wends deserved the same dignity and spiritual rewards as those who undertook the far longer and more perilous journey to the Eastern Mediterranean. Yet the Wendish Crusade was not in itself a success, and its failure was caused by the predominance of territorial over spiritual motives among the crusaders. Certainly it was important to baptize or exterminate the enemies of Christ, but it was even more important to prevent Christian colleagues from stealing too large a share of the conquests. The leaders of the crusade were bickering about the division of the spoils long before any spoils had been won; their divisions made it possible for the Wends to defend themselves in the forests of Brandenburg and Pomerania against a militarily far superior enemy.

Land hunger, particularly among the class of fiefless younger sons, played its part, and since the settlers came not only from Germany but from as far west as Flanders, genuine overpopulation in certain districts probably gave the movement additional impetus. Certainly by 1200 some of the Flemish towns can be seen to have suffered from a chronic excess of population over the needs of their industries. The lightly peopled lands to the East offered the chance of a better life to such people, and the rulers of the East badly needed more population for the defence and cultivation of their new lands. The role of the colonial lands of eastern Germany in an expanding medieval society can be compared with that of the Frontier in the history of the United States. Like the American West, the German East attracted the more adventurous and less law-abiding, those who were prepared to risk leaving a more settled society for the hazards of the frontier.

The methods of getting new population to the new areas were also curiously similar. In America this job fell to the railroad companies, which were prepared not only to spend money on advertising the new lands on both sides of the Atlantic, but to make generous grants to help settlers start their new life as farmers; the companies knew that once they had started producing they would have no alternative to using their railroads if their grain was to reach a market. In the German East professional *locatores* were employed from about the middle of the twelfth century to secure settlers for the new lands. In return for a generous grant of land for himself the *locator* surveyed the lands to be opened up, divided them into suitable holdings, and decided on sites for towns to act as future markets and on how the produce of the new farms would be transported. Finally the *locator* was responsible for advertising the venture in the West, and often for advancing the necessary capital, so that men would come forward at the right time. The reward for the landowner came not in the possession of more feudal vassals, for one of the attractions offered was that of free status, but in the certainty that the grain and timber and hides the new farmlands produced must pass to market down rivers he controlled; here lay a great chance of increasing his revenue.

Another cause is to be found in the conditions of the East itself. Any political vacuum always invites attack, and there was no sort of unity among the Slav peoples. While some eastern kingdoms like Poland or the Magyar kingdom of Hungary had adopted European ways and the European religion, the Wends were still largely primitive tribesmen, unable to resist the onslaught of armed knights if forced to fight in the open and even less able to withstand the gradual destruction of their forests. As in many parts of Africa today the native way of life was doomed once intensive cultivation had destroyed its natural habitat.

The greater part of German colonization was not a matter of military conquest. The settlers from the West had so great a technological advantage over the Slavs in farming and in industrial techniques that many Slavonic rulers were only too glad to admit them to their lands and to imitate their methods in purely Slav areas. Well beyond the areas of German occupation pockets of German settlement became established, where colonies of German merchants, craftsmen, and technicians appeared on the eastern shores of the Baltic or in the mines of the Carpathians; Germanic names on the map still recall these Teutonic outposts, and the successors of the original settlers often retained their German consciousness to create grave difficulties in the nationally conscious politics of the twentieth century.[1]

This colonial movement was the greatest German achievement of the Middle Ages. Immense areas of marsh and forest which before had provided a scanty living for a few scattered tribes were now turned into prosperous farming land; without it the development of urban communities in the West would have received an insuperable check for lack of food, and the great Hanse cities of the fourteenth and fifteenth centuries would never have existed. But the share of the Crown in this colonization was negligible. Lothar II, it is true, gave much attention to the lands of the East, but he did so as a Saxon prince and not as king. When the title passed from his family in 1137 the lands he had gained were lost to the Crown. Henry V and

[1] For example the 'Sudeten Germans' of Czechoslovakia were the pretext for Hitler's occupation of that country, 1938–1939.

125

Conrad were too preoccupied with trying to maintain their position further west to have the resources to spare for colonial endeavour. The prizes in that struggle were won by those princes who could concentrate their efforts on it. Families which before had seemed remote from the heart of German affairs, such as those of Albert the Bear, Margrave of Brandenburg (1134–1170), or Adolf of Schauenburg, Count of Holstein (1130–1164), gained greatly in importance with their territorial expansion. The Saxon house, freed from the burden of Empire, could console themselves richly in the East under Henry the Lion (1139–1195). The Church took a leading part in the process. There was waste enough to provide all the solitude and hard work even the newly founded Cistercians could require, and they, with S. Norbert's creation, the Premonstratensian Canons, laboured at a task which brought souls to Christ and revenue to the Church at the same time. The Archbishop of Magdeburg took a large if not always very honourable part in the process, and his see and city gained greatly in importance as a consequence. Only the Crown gained no profit.

The colonial movement resulted in a big shift in the balance of power within Germany, from a West torn by civil war to the rapidly expanding lands of the East. Since Crown lands, or what was left of them, were to be found mainly in the south and west, it could only mean a decline in the power and prestige of the German monarchy. Barbarossa was to make some attempt to associate the Crown with the eastern lands, but he was too late; in any case the chain of events since Henry IV and Gregory VII had first quarrelled had enmeshed the monarchy in Italian affairs too deeply for it to be extricated. If the Empire was now to be anything it would have to be more than a merely German power, for it had lost the power to be that. This is perhaps the most far-reaching consequence of the Investiture Conflict.

7

The Crusades

When Urban II proclaimed the first Crusade at Clermont in 1095 he was starting a movement far greater than ever the enthusiasm of the moment can have led him to expect. For the next two hundred years crusading was to occupy a leading place in the imaginations of western Christians. It was to become a secular counterpart to monasticism as the pre-eminently Christian way of life, yet paradoxically it was to destroy the chief Christian buttress against attack from Asia. It was to build the most perfect of all feudal kingdoms in Outremer; at the same time it was to work drastic changes in the history of some of the existing feudal kingdoms of the West. Starting as an attempt to clean the world of the infidel stain, it was to end by breeding in the minds of some at least of its protagonists a new and more sympathetic attitude to the great Muslim civilization.

Such effects could not proceed from one sermon, however eloquent. The Crusades were the outcome of an intricate tangle of causes in which the weaknesses of Byzantium and the divisions of the Muslim world play as big a part as the purely western factors. But it is to the West that we must look first.

It is easy to find a multitude of non-religious causes for the Crusades, and certainly in their later stages they tended to lose much of their religious character, yet in their origin the Crusades were an expression of the religion of the West. The eleventh century had been a period of religious enthusiasm, marked by the penetration of the reform movement to all parts of Europe and by the construction everywhere of churches and monasteries. Christianity perhaps controlled a larger share of the emotions of men then than at any other time in its history, but in so doing it had created a number of tensions. On the personal level the consciousness of sin, which is a mark of genuine religious conversion, demanded some outlet. It is the age of extravagant penances, when men would seek to wipe out the stain of sin with some great work for Christ. Some would seek the cloister and others undertake long and hazardous pilgrimages; Cluny played a great part in encouraging both processes. But the liberation of Christ's

THE CRUSADES

birthplace and Christ's tomb from the hands of His enemies was a
task supremely fitted to the needs of men who loved both Christ and
the sword. For the military nature of western society is one clue to
the whole movement. From its troubled beginnings in the barbarian

invasions the West had been organized for war; its social structure
and its scale of values alike encouraged fighting. At first this had led
to no difficulties with the Church. For so long as the greater part
of the West lay open to savage attack by pagan barbarians the Church
had perforce to share in the general admiration for great Christian
warriors like Charlemagne, who defended the Faith by their exploits.
Yet the days of this acute danger were past, and Christianity is not a
religion which glorifies fighting as a good in itself. Most of the
early Fathers indeed condemn war as merely legalized murder, and

the western Church, if shrinking from such a definition, was yet becoming more and more positive in its condemnation of war between Christians as a grave sin. Signs of this can be seen in two movements of the eleventh century, known respectively as the Peace of God and the Truce of God. By the first the Church sought to exclude the persons and lands of churchmen and the poor from all interference in war, by the second to lay down periods such as Sundays and Lent which, because of their religious significance, should be considered close seasons for fighting. Neither movement was particularly successful in practice; the attempts to enforce the Peace of God indeed led to some particularly bitter fighting, a not unknown fate for peace movements in other ages. But their importance lies in the way that they reveal the dilemma of a society geared to war, without any satisfactory outlet for its energies. The gradual reconquest of Spain from the Moors and the German expansion into Slav lands both provided local solutions to the problem; but the Crusades in the East were the supreme example of a conflict at once bloodthirsty and 'Holy'.

The Crusades were peculiarly under the patronage of the Papacy, and it is not difficult to see the sound papal motives of policy which led Urban to proclaim the first Crusade. Certainly he shared the general enthusiasm for the Holy Places, but he must have been very conscious of the part such a movement might play in uniting a Europe torn by the Investiture Contest. Gregory VII had received an appeal for help from the East, but had been quite unable to do anything about it. If Urban could proclaim a common cause for all Christians, much might be done to heal the wounds of Christendom and to unite imperialist and papalist in one common cause. Even if this did not take place, any large response to the papal summons could not but be a considerable arguing point for the Papacy in the future. Moreover, the summons for aid came from Byzantium, and Urban no doubt foresaw a possibility of fulfilling the aim of Leo IX and bringing the eastern Church to the one fold and the one shepherd. The urge to gain that unity, so dear to the reformers of the eleventh century, by a great united action was a powerful motive behind the Crusades.

It would be foolish to argue that religious causes were alone responsible for even the first Crusade, or to try to discover exactly how much of the enthusiasm it generated came from religious causes; certainly those who participated in it cannot have known the answer to the question. It must be remembered that it was from the East that almost all the luxuries of western Europe came. It was easy to picture even the arid land of Palestine as being a source of temporal as well as spiritual wealth. In the East too lay Byzantium, that great city whose wealth and population made the largest towns of the West seem overgrown villages. Italian traders had brought back reports of the eastern capital which must have awakened a longing spirit among many crusades. Where so much wealth was, could not some be diverted to them? The systematic exploitation of the Crusades for mercantile ends was to come later, but from the first there must have been a hope that God would reward His servants on Earth as He would surely do in Heaven. Many of the humbler crusaders who made up the People's Crusade in 1096 were as weak in geography as in theology. Drawing no distinction between the New Jerusalem, the Golden City of which the saints sang, and the earthly Jerusalem to which their feet were directed, they had no idea of the difficulties which lay before them, but pressed on in the confident expectation that great wealth lay not far ahead.

Any form of overseas expansion generally reflects some pressure of population within a society; the Crusades are no exception. The widespread adoption of primogeniture as the principle of succession to feudal fiefs had meant that the prospects of younger sons were not good. At home they faced impoverishment from which they could only escape by becoming churchmen or by successful rebellion against their own kin. Now they had a chance of carving out new lands for themselves beyond the seas; if they failed they would at least have the consolation of a heavenly crown. In either case they would no longer menace the stability of the societies from which they came. It is not difficult to understand why many of the leaders of the First Crusade, such as Baldwin of Jerusalem, were younger sons, or at least, like Bohemond of Antioch, had little prospect of succeeding to their family lands. Certainly the Crusade had more to offer them than it did to an elder son, such as Robert of Normandy, who could only lose heavily by it.

In Asia too circumstances favoured the First Crusade. The Muslims had not at first shown themselves oppressive rulers. Seeing in Christians and Jews people who were like themselves 'Peoples of the Book', they did not try to force conversion on them, but granted them something of the status of second-class citizens, inferior indeed to the followers of Allah, but permitted to live and worship in peace provided they paid their tribute regularly. To many of the Christians of the Near East indeed Muslim rule had been far preferable to the

Christian rule of Byzantium or Rome, for many of them belonged to heretical sects, such as the Nestorians or the Monophysites, who could only expect persecution from an orthodox Christian government. Even an orthodox Christian might prefer Muslim rule; in the ninth century the Patriarch of Jerusalem could write of his overlords 'They are just and do us no wrong nor show us any violence'.[1] No minority in the West could have said the same.

If the Muslims had maintained the unity Mahomet had preached no Crusade could possibly have succeeded, but Islam had been no more successful than Christendom in preserving the unity of the faithful. As early as the middle of the eighth century the Muslims of Spain were virtually independent of their coreligionaries in the East. By the middle of the tenth century the split, which was in 969 finally to divide the Abbasid caliphs of Baghdad from the Fatimids of Cairo, was already evident. As in Christianity, doctrinal differences came to accentuate a division which was at root political, and 'western' and 'eastern' Muslims have no more love for each other than western and eastern Christians. The first prerequisite for a Christian counterattack had been fulfilled.

But it was not only from the West that a divided Muslim Empire stood in peril. A far more immediate peril came from the Turks, the savage peoples of central Asia who gave their name to Turkestan. One particular tribe, known as the Seljuk Turks, produced a prince of military genius in the person of Tughril Bey (†1063), and the Seljuks, by now Muslim converts, were able to take over the Abbasid half of the Muslim world. In 1055 the Caliph of Baghdad crowned Tughril king of the Muslim World, an appointment not recognized in Egypt, which remained loyal to its own Caliph.

In many ways the Seljuks recall those other recent converts to another religion, the Normans. They had the same fierce converts' zeal for their new religion and the same martial skill. Like the Normans, they were apt to prove bad neighbours and dangerous allies.

The rise of the Seljuks caused much consternation in the Christian East. For seven hundred years Byzantium had performed her historic function of preserving the Christian lands from invasion. She had survived the attacks of the Huns and the original wave of Muslim conquest, but for several centuries had not been called to face a major crisis of the kind the Seljuks now constituted. Moreover, Byzantium

---

[1] Patriarch Theodosius, quoted from S. Runciman, *History of the Crusades.* Cambridge U. P., 1951. Vol. i, p. 27.

was not in good shape to resist an immediate military peril. The peoples of the Byzantine Empire had none of the bellicose spirit which marked the less civilized Latins of the West; with a genuine dislike for violence, its emperors had always preferred diplomacy to battle, a characteristic for which they have been much censured by those who have seen decadence in a society which undertook no aggressive wars. There was none of the Western passion for fighting for its own sake; Byzantium was protected by a professional army of mercenaries some of whom were themselves Turks. During the ten-sixties Seljuk bands began to penetrate Byzantine territory in Asia Minor, and it seemed clear that they were only the forerunners of a major attack on Byzantium itself. The Byzantine leaders were not to know that the Seljuk commanders were more interested in the capture of Cairo than in that of Constantinople. In the apparent crisis the Emperor Romanus Diogenes (1067–1071) acted with a determination that deserved better results. At the head of a large army he not only cleared the Turks from Asia Minor, but began the invasion of Turkish-occupied Armenia. This was a fatal blunder; his Turkish mercenaries deserted to the enemy and at Manzikert (1071) the Byzantine army was destroyed; Romanus himself became a prisoner.

Manzikert at once made the position of Byzantium desperate. There was now no protection against Turkish invaders, who occupied much of the Byzantine empire. One Turkish prince, the Sultan of Rum, established his capital at Nicaea, only one hundred and twenty miles from Byzantium, and it seemed that any really determined effort would put an end to the eastern Rome. To make matters worse, the Empire showed every sign of disintegrating from within. Romanus returned from captivity only to find that his place had been taken by his stepson Michael VII, and his attempt to recapture the throne led to his death from a particularly callous blinding. For ten years Byzantium had no stable government, and while the generals were engaged in a greedy struggle for power the European provinces of the Empire in the Balkans also rose in revolt.

In 1081 Alexius Comnenus (1081–1118) gained control of the remnants of the Empire, and at last something of a revival began. Alexius was a capable soldier and realistic enough to see that Byzantium could not afford to be fussy about her allies. The Seljuks were the chief danger, and, however much he might dislike the crude barbarism of the Latin West, he could not ignore any possible source of aid. The past relationship between Byzantium and the West had not been a happy one; to the Byzantine government the Latins had appeared largely in the shape of the Normans attacking the Byzantine provinces in Italy and raiding deeply into the Balkans, while the eastern Church had no love for the insolence of Roman claims to papal control. The theological dispute with the western Church over the question of whether the Holy Ghost proceeded from the Father alone, or from the Father and the Son (*Filioque*), was only the pretext for disagreement, but it was capable of making co-operation very difficult. But the need for aid was now too great to allow such memories to stand in the way. Alexius renewed earlier appeals to the West for help; eastern representatives were present at the Diet of Piacenza (1095) to ask for military aid, and et the same time to do their best to smooth over the doctrinal difficulties with the Papacy.

From the beginning the Crusade thus suffered from a difference of opinion among its protagonists as to what it was really about. To Alexius it was a means of obtaining reinforcements to save Byzantium from possible future attack and to help in the process of recovering her lost eastern provinces. A decline in Seljuk fortunes since Manzikert gave him the hope that the time was ripe for counter-attack. But Palestine played no part in his ideas. But in the West the freeing of the Holy Places from a Seljuk domination which had made them virtually inaccessible to Christians was naturally the central interest; any aid this might give to the Byzantine emperor and his schismatic church would be very incidental. This confusion between East and West was to dog the whole operation.

The Crusade was proclaimed by Urban II in an address at the close of the Council of Clermont, on 27 November 1095. The war of Christian with Christian in the West would be at an end; God would lead them from the tribulations of their present life to the joys of those who lived in His service. If they should die, it would be in the certainty that their sins were forgiven and that they would enter the company of the blessed. As Urban spoke his words were interrupted by cries of *Deus le volt* from the huge congregation, and when he had finished crowds flocked forward to take up God's work at once; Adhemar, Bishop of Le Puy, was the first of many hundreds to vow themselves to the Crusade the same day.

The instantaneous reaction to Urban's words shows that the Christian West had been waiting for just such a call. Many indeed could not wait for their zeal to receive that organization without which it stood no chance of success, but inflamed by the oratory of popular preachers set off at once for Jerusalem. The People's Crusade, as it came to be called, was one of the most curious and pathetic manifestations of the religious emotion which was never far distant in the Middle Ages. It had none of the great lords who were the recognized military leaders of the age, and for the most part its ranks were made up from the most lowly classes of society. They included many old men, women and children, for God would surely make up what was lacking in the strength of His servants. Without either organization or any but the most rudimentary arms, the crusaders had only their faith to keep them on their way; it is not surprising that the wastage rate was high. Some lost heart when they gained some inkling of the difficulties which lay before them and returned home; many fell out on the journey and were massacred by the infuriated inhabitants of areas which had been pillaged to feed the main hosts. Others, again, turned from the prosecution of war against Muslims, who seemed very far distant, to the much easier task of taking vengeance on the people who had betrayed Christ and were yet in their midst; the summer of 1096 saw widespread attacks on Jewish communities throughout Germany, despite the efforts of various Church leaders, such as the archbishops of Worms and Cologne, to protect them. Religious ardour could combine with the hatred in which the people of a primitive economy will always hold the moneylender to provide this first big outbreak of anti-semitism in the Christian West.

Yet the bulk of the crusaders moved towards Jerusalem, kept to their task by the uncouth Peter the Hermit, a preacher whose words seemed to have supernatural authority. There were two main bodies of crusaders, led by Walter the Penniless and by Peter himself; by the end of June 1096 both parties were in Byzantine territory. Alexius had hoped for an army of reasonable size to take service under his orders. The appearance of this great rabble of famished fanatics was an unpleasant shock for him, and the news that the crusaders had destroyed Belgrade was a warning of the damage they might do. He reacted to the danger with good sense and promptitude; food supplies were improvised for the unwelcome visitors, and imperial escorts provided to see that they did not clash with the local population. By August 1st they had arrived outside Byzantium, and, lest the temptation of so great a city should prove too much for them, arrangements were at once made for their transport across the Bosphorus to Asia Minor. By now the crusaders had been reduced to more manageable numbers, and if they had been content to await the arrival of the main armies they might have formed a useful reinforcement for it. Alexius promised to continue supplying them, and Peter himself advised delay. But the crusaders had not come so far merely to delay; raiding parties went on into Seljuk territory in the direction of Nicaea, doing great havoc on the local population. As most of these were Christian, they became thoroughly biased against any future attempts to 'liberate' them. The Turks were forced to take energetic counter-measures; an army of highly trained soldiers was sent against the crusaders, and at the Battle of Civetot (October 1096) the inevitable happened; the entire crusading army, still numbering perhaps twenty thousand fighting men, was destroyed. The People's Crusade was over, and Peter survived almost alone to mourn those he had led to death or slavery.

While the People's Crusade was running its course, preparations had been going forward for the main expedition. The contrast with the chaotic enthusiasm of the earlier venture could not be more marked. The First Crusade was a highly organized operation acting on a well-thought-out plan; in this it differs also from most of the later crusades. A part of the reason for the contrast is to be found in the way the Church retained control of this crusade. Much of the credit for this should go to the papal representative, Adhemar, Bishop of Le Puy, who accompanied the expedition. The bishop possessed military skill, and what was even more important the tact necessary to run the various touchy crusading leaders as a team. But Adhemar's task would not have been possible if he had had to contend with the presence of kings on the crusade. No reigning monarch went on the First Crusade; the experience of later expeditions was to show that this was an unmixed advantage.

The crusaders came to Constantinople, the starting point for their operations, in three different ways. Those who came from the northeast took for the most part the same overland route that the People's Crusade had followed. Their leaders were Godfrey of Bouillon, the duke of Lower Lorraine, and his younger brother Baldwin. Godfrey seems to have been moved to make the journey largely by his difficulties at home; his support of Henry IV in the Investiture Contest had put him in difficulties with the Church, while his administration in Lorraine had been inefficient enough to make it probable that Henry might seek to deprive him of his duchy. Tall and fair, he looked the part of the crusading hero which tradition was later to give him, but in truth he had little initiative and was outshone by his younger brother. Baldwin took his wife and children with him. The West had little to offer him, and he had every intention of finding a permanent home in the East. Events were to show him a bold and ruthless leader. Their forces moved through Hungary, whose king Coloman, mindful of the destruction caused by Peter's following, wisely took hostages for their good behaviour. Alexius had made arrangements to shepherd them through his empire, and by the end of December 1096 they were outside Byzantium.

Meanwhile a party of French knights under Hugh of Vermandois had moved across France and Italy to embark from the Norman port of Bari. A storm during their sea passage to Durazzo wrecked all their ships and drowned many of their men, but the survivors reached Byzantium shortly before Godfrey. The Normans of south Italy had not at first responded to the crusading call, doubtless seeing little reason why they should aid their old enemy the Byzantine emperor, but the arrival of the French stirred their enthusiasm. They were quickly organized under Bohemond, a son of Robert Guiscard, and, following Hugh's route with more success, by April 1097 they too had arrived. The same crossing was made by the main bulk of the Norman crusaders from the north under Robert, Duke of Normandy, and the counts of Blois and Flanders; the few Englishmen who made the First Crusade were to be found in its ranks. They did not reach Byzantium till the beginning of May.

From southern France Raymond II, Count of Toulouse, with whom Adhemar travelled in company, led a force by a third and more difficult route round the head of the Adriatic and by land down the Dalmatian coast. The decision taken to avoid the peril and expense of a sea journey was unwise. The army had to march through very difficult country, and by the time it reached Byzantine territory north of Durazzo much of its discipline was gone. On the last leg of the journey through Thrace it got out of hand and forced Byzantine troops to attack and defeat it. It thus reached Byzantium in no very good heart. Nevertheless the entire crusade had reached its starting place more or less to time, a not inconsiderable achievement.

Alexius was anxious that no time should be wasted in attacking the Turks, and even more anxious that the Latin troops should be removed from the vicinity of his capital. Its riches put an almost irresistible temptation in the way of western knights, who had never seen anything approaching its wealth; already on Maundy Thursday 1097 there had been a serious clash between Godfrey's men and imperial troops. With difficulty all the western leaders were persuaded to take oaths of allegiance to Alexius, but the latter must have suspected that there would be difficulty in ensuring that the crusaders treated any conquests they might make as conquests made for Byzantium. Still, the first step was to clear a road through Asia Minor, and the crusaders were moved at once across the Bosphorus to start on this laudable task. Alexius cannot have expected them to reach Jerusalem, but they might well ease the situation on his frontiers.

The events of the next two years, until the fall of Jerusalem in 1099, form a very great military achievement. Against all probability the expedition succeeded. Nicaea was captured in October 1097, although the garrison cheated the crusaders of their expected pillage by surrendering to Alexius at the last minute (June 1097). The main Turkish army arrived too late to relieve Nicaea, but instead prepared an ambush at Dorylaeum as the crusaders advanced to the south-east. Bohemond's Normans were caught in the trap, but stood firm under a formidable barrage from the Muslim archers until the main host was able to relieve them. A fierce counter-attack then forced the enemy to withdraw so fast that his camp and treasure fell into Latin hands (1 July 1097). The victory acted as a fine stimulus for crusading morale, and conversely made the Muslims reluctant to risk other major engagements.

After Dorylaeum the crusaders passed through difficult times. The journey across the centre of Asia Minor was almost unbearably hot for heavily equipped troops, and suspicions were rife that their native Christian guides were misleading them. Moreover the latent hostility between the various leaders, ominous hints of which had already been seen at Byzantium, came into the open. Too many of them were hoping to establish themselves in the lands of their own, and were anxious lest their rivals might secure the plums for themselves. Baldwin indeed left the main body altogether, and moving far to the east across the Euphrates entered the county of Edessa. Thoros, its ruler, was an orthodox Christian who had started his career as a Byzantine official. When the Turks had appeared he had co-operated with them; now he was ready to be liberated by the Latins. Baldwin accepted his help to gain entry to Edessa, and then gave at least passive support to a revolution which deposed and murdered him. Baldwin took his place, the first of the crusaders to achieve his temporal goal.

In the meantime the main armies had reached the mighty fortress of Antioch. Any attempt to advance further towards Jerusalem leaving it unsubdued in their rear would have been foolhardy. The siege of Antioch (October 1097–June 1098) was the most critical engagement of the whole crusade. The town was well victualled, and the besiegers, with no regular lines of supply, suffered cruelly in the attempt to live off the countryside in winter. Their morale suffered; Peter the Hermit, a subdued figure since Civetot, had to be retrieved from an ignominious attempt at flight. All the time there was the anxiety of knowing that the Muslim world, divided as it was, would surely try to relieve the city. The crusaders indeed beat back attempts to bring aid from Damascus and Aleppo, but news came that a far more dangerous expedition had been mounted by Kerbogha of Mosul on the instructions of the Caliph of Baghdad. If it arrived before Antioch had been captured they would have no hope of avoiding obliteration. The danger was just avoided; on the third of June, with the help of Christian sympathizers within the town, Bohemond's men found a way through the walls; by nightfall a general massacre of the Turkish inhabitants had taken place. Four days later, while the remains of the Muslim garrison were still defending the citadel, Kerbogha arrived. Now it was the crusaders' turn to stand a siege in the city they had just taken.

At first it seemed that the end of the Crusade had only been post-poned. Alexius indeed believed a rumour that the crusaders had already been annihilated, and called off the attempt to rescue them which seemed their only hope of earthly salvation. Supplies of food ran desperately short, for many of the city's stocks had been prodigally destroyed in the orgy of loot and arson which had followed its capture. The defenders were only persuaded to continue resistance by a crop of visions promising celestial aid; these culminated in the discovery of the Holy Lance which had pierced Christ's side, by a humble peasant, Peter Bartholomew, who claimed to have been led to it by S. Andrew. The shrewd Adhemar doubted the authenticity of the find, but the effect on Christian morale was so good that it was not the moment to encourage doubts. But Kerbogha had his own troubles; his force was an uneasy alliance of different Muslim peoples, and once it was held up before Antioch the desertion rate became high. Moreover, the Seljuks were worried lest the Fatimids of Egypt should take the opportunity of the crusading diversion to extend their sway —no empty fear, for Palestine was in fact to be conquered by the Fatimids later in the same year. After a successful sally by the defenders on 28 June Kerbogha withdrew his army.

There was now no major Muslim army between the crusaders and Jerusalem. Some months were wasted in the unsuccessful siege of Acre as they advanced down the coast, but the army could now be supplied by Christian fleets operating in the eastern Mediterranean.

By June 1099 they were before Jerusalem, now occupied by a Fatimid garrison. As they had found at Antioch and Acre, they lacked the instruments of siege warfare to assault a strong walled town, but now they were so near their goal their enthusiasm was at high pitch. A wooden tower was erected to aid the attack, Peter the Hermit recovered his old eloquence, and after a general fast had been observed in the army the assault was launched from Mount Sion on the night of 13 July. All the next day there was savage fighting, and on the fifteenth a breach was made. Jerusalem was won, and the soldiers of the Prince of Peace celebrated the occasion with an indiscriminate massacre of the entire Muslim and Jewish population. This done they could fall to their knees in the Church of the Holy Sepulchre to thank God who had so manifestly aided His servants.

It now remained to organize the captured territory. Baldwin had already staked his claim to Edessa and Bohemond had been left behind as Prince of Antioch. The choice for Jerusalem, therefore, lay between the two surviving secular leaders of the crusade, Godfrey of Bouillon and Raymond of Toulouse; it was not made any easier by the sharp rivalry which already existed between them. Some form of election was held from which Godfrey emerged as the ruler of Jerusalem; in deference to his view that in Jerusalem there should be no king but He who had worn a crown of thorns, the title of *Advocatus Sancti Sepulchri* was created for him. A County of Tripoli was created to the north, between the lands of Jerusalem and Antioch, so that Raymond should not go without a prize, but this had yet to be conquered. When Godfrey died in the next year (1100), after having defeated at Ascalon (1099) the Fatimid attempt to win back Jerusalem, Raymond again had hopes of being summoned to the highest office. But Godfrey's knights saw to it that he should be succeeded by his own kin, and it was his brother Baldwin who gained the succession; once more there was a king upon the throne of David.

The four crusading states of Jerusalem, Antioch, Edessa, and Tripoli were known collectively as Outremer. For two hundred years Outremer was to preserve a precarious and fluctuating existence, perched like modern Israel on the edge of a Muslim continent. That it survived at all is surprising. The First Crusade had triumphed with invaluable aid given by Alexius in its early stages, but now that it had conquered, relations between the crusaders and Byzantium became very bad. The eastern emperors were resentful of the way the crusaders, unmindful of the homage they had paid Alexius, had filched Antioch for themselves instead of returning it to its rightful Byzantine ruler, while the Latins remembered only the way Alexius had seemed to desert them in their hour of greatest need at Antioch. Instead of presenting a united Christian front to the Muslims, both Greeks and Latins were prepared to ally with individual Muslim princes against the other. Strategically Outremer was difficult to hold. Edessa, reaching deep into Muslim territory, was dangerously exposed to attack. The other crusading states were much too long and thin to be easy to defend. Instead of extending to the edge of the Syrian desert, which would have acted as a natural defence, the crusaders were forced to try to hold a line of fortified castles along the line of the Jordan valley and the hills to the west of it. The crusading castles were finely constructed; Kerak and Krak des Chevaliers were two of the most formidable examples of medieval military architecture. Yet the hinterland behind them was dangerously thin; the sea was often less than forty miles away. Further advance was made impossible by sheer shortage of manpower. The kings of Jerusalem had to number their knights by hundreds rather than thousands even in moments of greatest emergency. There was barely enough military strength to hold the territory they already had.

Moreover much of the population of Outremer was Muslim and Jewish, and this too was a hazard; the massacre at Jerusalem was not easily forgotten, and loyalty to the Latin rulers was at best tepid. The country was organized for defence. Indeed there is no better example of organization of military feudalism than Outremer for, as in Norman England, feudalism was imposed as a system at one time. Yet this did not necessarily bring strength. The religious purpose of the states meant that the Church, in the shape of the two patriarchs of Jerusalem and Antioch, had a large part in directing policy, and its interests did not always coincide with those of the secular powers. In particular, after the creation of the two military orders of Knights Hospitaller and Knights Templar (1118–1120) these two big independent corporations of military monks came to have independent policies of their own, which often ran contrary to those of the lay crusaders. Such divisions were dangerous, and the dependence of all the states on the co-operation of the fleets of the Italian trading cities, such as Genoa, for new manpower and supplies added yet another separate interest.

Outremer's existence depended on two things, the lack of unity in the Muslim world and the ability of the Latin rulers to negotiate as well as fight with Muslim leaders. The original crusaders had come full of enthusiasm to slay all Muslims, but those who settled in the East soon came to modify their views. Later arrivals in the shape of pilgrims and crusaders from the West were often shocked to find how far their predecessors had gone in fraternizing with the Infidel. Many of the settlers had adopted eastern modes of dress, such as the turban; intermarriage with the Muslims was not uncommon; and there were even some shocking cases of conversion to Islam. From uncompromising hostility the attitude of the settlers gradually changed to one of some sympathy towards the Muslims, who for their part began to see some good in the western barbarians. In such an atmosphere, since the possession of Outremer was never a matter of life or death for the Muslim world, diplomacy became again a possibility.

During the years 1100–1144 Outremer on the whole prospered; the principality of Antioch, to which the Byzantine emperors had never become reconciled, seemed the only seriously threatened part of the crusading world. But the apparent security from Islam would last only so long as the Muslims lacked any leader of sufficient initiative to unite any considerable portion of it. In 1127 Zangi had become Emir of Mosul, and that condition was no longer fulfilled. At first his activities were directed against his immediate Muslim neighbours and caused no concern in Jerusalem, but soon he was threatening to unite all the Muslim emirates to the north-east of Outremer. In 1140 King Fulk of Jerusalem (1131–1143) brought aid to the Emir of Damascus when Zangi attacked his city. Thwarted there, Zangi moved further north to attack Christian Edessa, at once the most exposed and the worst governed of the crusading states. Choosing a moment when relations between Edessa and the neighbouring Antioch were at their worst, he suddenly attacked the county. No move was made to save it from Antioch, and the expedition organized from Jerusalem by Fulk's widow Melisande arrived too late. The first of the crusading states had fallen (1144).

In one sense the loss of Edessa was neither surprising nor from the strategical viewpoint particularly regrettable. It had been an exposed outpost which had been captured only to satisfy Baldwin's greed, and would not have been worth a prolonged struggle to retain. Yet this first defeat in the East, and even more the suggestion that it was caused as much by Christian bickering as by Muslim strength, was a great shock to the West; Jerusalem might easily follow Edessa. If this alone was not sufficient to provoke another crusade, the championing of the cause by S. Bernard made it inevitable. Bernard's spiritual prestige was enormous; he had long been interested in the Crusade and had already taken a large part in drawing up the rule of the Templars. He always brought unbounded vehemence to the causes he supported, and since the pope of the day, Eugenius III (1145–1153), was also a Cistercian and his fervent admirer, he was well placed to see that his views were followed. Eugenius himself determined to proclaim the crusade in 1145, and Bernard persuaded Louis VII of France to lead it; Louis's conscience, burdened with the memory of the massacre at Vitry-sur-Marne,[1] was in no condition to resist S. Bernard's exhortations. When the first reactions in France seemed tepid, a council was summoned at Vézelay (1146) to try the effect of S. Bernard's oratory. The issue was no longer in doubt: before he had finished speaking all available supplies of crosses had been exhausted, and in a dramatic gesture Bernard tore off his own habit to provide material so that more might be fashioned. It was in no idle boast that he could write to the pope a few days later: '*You ordered; I obeyed . . . I opened my mouth; I spoke; and at once the Crusaders have multiplied to infinity.*'[2]

From Vézelay Bernard moved on to deliver God's message in Lorraine and Flanders, amid like scenes of enthusiasm. The excitement spread to Germany, and here, as fifty years before, the first reactions came in the form of an ugly outbreak of anti-semitism. Bernard firmly checked this: '*God has punished the Jews by the dispersion; it is not for man to punish them by murder.*' German enthusiasm deserved a better outlet. Although Eugenius had originally intended the expedition to be limited to the French, Bernard determined to extend it to the Germans, so far more interested in their own Slavonic pagans than in the Muslims. Again his preaching had great effect; Conrad III put up more resistance than most, but in the end even his defences were broken down and he took the Cross.

The Second Crusade was launched with no less enthusiasm than the First, yet its outcome was abject failure. For this there are several reasons. The two leading participants were both kings, and although this was eloquent tribute to Bernard's oratory it considerably increased the difficulties of the Crusade. Co-operation between them proved to be impossible, and there was no equivalent of Adhemar on this crusade to exercise the unifying influence of the Church. Neither Conrad nor Louis were really of the stuff of which crusaders were made, and both had of necessity to concern themselves with the

---

[1] See Chapter 8.
[2] S. Bernard's Letters, quoted from S. Runciman, *History of the Crusades.* Cambridge U. P., 1952. Vol. 2, p. 254.

affairs of the kingdoms Bernard had persuaded them to leave, but to which they had every intention of returning. Louis's decision to take his queen Eleanor of Aquitaine on the expedition proved nearly as disastrous to the Crusade as it did to his marriage. Byzantine aid, whatever its shortcomings, had been essential to the success of the First Crusade; on this occasion the Byzantine emperor Manuel (1143–1180) deplored not only the form, but the very existence of an enterprise which looked likely to involve him in a major war on his Turkish frontier. The treaty he signed with the Turks in 1147 seemed the blackest treachery to the crusaders, but from the Byzantine viewpoint it was the only sensible arrangement. The Normans, who had taken so leading a part in the First Crusade, were now worse than neutral; the fear of the attacks Roger II was about to launch on Corfu and the Greek mainland (1147) was a principal reason for Manuel's neutrality. The Muslims now knew more of the tactics of the heavily armoured western knights, whose first attacks had surprised their more lightly armed troops. Finally it should be noted that whereas before the western leaders had been agreed that Jerusalem was the goal, now there was no such unanimity as to whether Edessa should be recaptured or merely revenged.

The two armies moved separately, but both elected to take the overland route to Byzantium. Conrad arrived there first, and after a fierce quarrel with Manuel left without waiting for Louis. Ignoring Manuel's advice to take the longer but safer coast road he tried to follow in the steps of the First Crusade. At Dorylaeum, very near the site of Bohemond's victory in 1097, his army was taken by surprise by a far larger Turkish force (October 1147). Conrad himself escaped, but by far the greater part of it was killed or captured. The emperor and the surviving Germans became an unimportant appendix to what was now a French expedition. Warned by Conrad's fate Louis took the coast road, where he thought his army would be safe in Byzantine territory. But progress was slow and food and fodder very scarce; the security from Muslim attacks proved to be an illusion. Finally Louis himself and most of the knights took ship from Attalia for the Principality of Antioch (March 1148). Of those who were left to continue the journey on foot, not many arrived. Conrad meanwhile, having returned to Byzantium, had gone direct to Palestine.

By now the crusade had been so much weakened that, even reinforced by the crusaders already in the East, it could not risk any very major operation. After much dispute it was decided to attack the Emirate of Damascus. Damascus indeed was rich, but since it was the one Muslim state which, being equally threatened by Zangi's son Nur-ed-Din, was anxious for Christian allies, it was an absurd decision. It only needed the crusaders to fail in their object (July 1148) for the whole crusade to disintegrate. A vision might show that in Heaven the places of the Fallen Angels had been taken by fallen crusaders, but on Earth the crusade had only weakened the Christian cause. The rift between the eastern and western Churches had been widened; the hostility between the crusading states and the West had grown; the French and German monarchies had both been seriously weakened; the crusaders' military reputation had been destroyed. The Second Crusade had benefited only its opponents.

For forty years after the Second Crusade there was no great effort made by the West. Individual crusaders still made the journey to the East, and pilgrims came in considerable numbers, but the leaders of western Christendom had other concerns. Even the Papacy, pre-occupied with the conflict with Barbarossa, had little regard for crusading. By far the most important developments in this period came in the Muslim world. Here the rift which had divided Fatimid Egypt from the Caliphate of Baghdad was ended. In 1169 Nur-ed-Din's general Shirkuh captured Egypt for his master; two years later the last Caliph of Cairo died. The enemies of Outremer were now united. No longer would the defence of the land by diplomacy be possible, for the crusaders' enemies in Syria in the north and Egypt in the south were now the same. When Shirkuh died, control in Egypt passed to his nephew Saladin. Shortly afterwards (1174) Nur-ed-Din himself died, and Saladin (1174–1193) was able to rule undisputed in both lands. For a space the Muslim opponents of the Latin kingdom were to have one ruler. Saladin stands out among the leaders of the crusading period as perhaps the greatest; certainly to twentieth-century eyes he seems the most attractive, and many even of his Christian contemporaries were able to recognize the charm of their opponent. A sincere Muslim, he yet respected the religious convictions of those who differed from him; many Christians not of the Roman faith preferred his rule to the intolerance of the Latins. A hard and resourceful soldier, he yet did not violate his word to gain a temporary advantage, and in the hour of victory he was to show himself just and merciful; his recapture of Jerusalem was to be marked by none of the disgraceful carnage which had been seen in 1099. If he drove the crusaders from the Holy City, they had only themselves to blame.

To face the threat of a united Islam Christian unity was the first essential. Yet it was not to be had; relations between the crusaders and the Byzantine Empire were made much worse by the scandalous conduct of the Prince of Antioch, Reynald of Châtillon. In 1156 he launched an unprovoked attack on peaceful and prosperous Cyprus, which was Byzantine territory. Great damage was done and the island's most prominent citizens were removed for ransom. Reynald had killed any desire left in Byzantium to aid the crusading states, and when in 1176 the Emperor Manuel suffered a crushing defeat at Muslim hands at Myriocephalum, the Byzantine emperors lost the power as well as the inclination to influence events further south.

Now if ever Outremer needed strong government, but it could not be provided by Baldwin IV (1174-1185) of Jerusalem. Only thirteen at his accession, Baldwin already suffered from leprosy, and while the disease was slowly blinding and then killing him he could not be expected to hold the ring among a greedy and quarrelsome nobility. Apart from the multitude of conflicting selfish interests, there existed a deep division as to the correct strategy to be followed. On the one hand, those whose families had been in the East for several generations and had lost their original pathological hatred for Islam desired coexistence; their chief spokesman was Raymond III of Tripoli. On the other hand stood the more recent arrivals, who against all the military evidence wished to win security by the sword; of these the chief representative was Baldwin's brother-in-law, Guy of Lusignan. The dying king realized the danger of the latter group coming to direct policy. In his will he directed that the regent for his successor, his young nephew Baldwin V (1185-1186), should be Raymond, and not the child's step-father Guy. Shortly after Baldwin IV's death Raymond arranged a four years' truce with Saladin.

The truce was not to last. Baldwin V died in the next year, and power in Jerusalem was siezed by Guy of Lusignan and his wife. Their coronation caused great disgust to many of the nobility and to one of the military orders, the Hospitallers. This disunity might have led even Guy to have second thoughts on the wisdom of ending the truce, but Reynald of Châtillon, now no longer Prince of Antioch, settled the issue for him. At the end of 1186 he attacked a large convoy moving from Cairo to Damascus, and removed the spoils to his castle at Kerak. It was Reynold's second great disservice to the crusaders. Guy refused to punish a royal vassal, and Saladin had every right to consider that this act of brigandage put an end to the truce.

When Saladin's host was known to be massing to cross the Jordan some semblance of unity at last began to appear in the Latin ranks. Raymond of Tripoli buried his differences with Guy, and Bohemond, the Prince of Antioch, sent a contingent. But it was too late, and even now there was no agreement on strategy. The cautious Raymond wanted to fight a wholly defensive campaign; in view of the greater numbers of the enemy and the strength of the crusading castles there is little doubt that he was right. But Guy allowed himself to be persuaded by Reynald and the Grand Master of the Templars to take the offensive. The crusading army moved out across the hills towards Tiberias. They suffered agonies from heat and thirst, since it was the hottest part of the summer. On 4 July 1187 Saladin brought them to battle at Hattin, in conditions of his own choosing. There could be only one end: the crusaders fought bravely, but by nightfall their army was destroyed, such of its leaders as survived were prisoners, and the precious Relic of the True Cross itself was in Muslim hands. No recovery from such a disaster was possible. Jerusalem capitulated at the end of October on Saladin's promise to spare the lives of its Christian inhabitants and to allow them the opportunity of purchasing their ransom. His promise was kept, but by the time Saladin abandoned the operation and dispatched his troops to their homes in the autumn of 1188, the port of Tyre was all that was left of the kingdom of Jerusalem. Further north little remained of the Principality of Antioch and the County of Tripoli except their capital cities.

The news of the disaster in Outremer was sufficient to shake the apathy of the West. When the archbishop of Tyre arrived with the first reliable news of the disaster, all Europe was aghast. It did not need papal intervention, although this was not lacking, to produce the Third Crusade. From Scandinavia to Sicily the fall of Jerusalem was seen as a reproach to Christendom. Many in the West had close relatives who had lost lands or lives there; only its recapture could satisfy the honour of Europe. The Third Crusade was to be the last time that the religious ardour of the West expressed itself in military terms, for although there were many in the subsequent crusades who went in answer to the call of religion, they were either to be swamped by those with more mundane motives, as in the Fourth Crusade, or limited to one European nation, as in S. Louis's ventures. As it was the last, so also the Third Crusade was to have most distinguished leaders of them all. The Second Crusade indeed had been led by kings, but there had been notable absentees from its ranks; few Englishmen had made the journey and the Normans of Sicily had been deliberately excluded. Now both omissions were rectified; William II of Sicily was the first to answer the appeal from Tyre, and the convenient death of Henry II of England in 1189 after taking the Cross left his obligations to be fulfilled by the young Richard I. With the addition of the Emperor Frederick Barbarossa, now keen to use in the service of the Church the armies which had so often been used against her, and of Philip Augustus, the first really powerful king of France, it seemed that the whole military might of the West was mobilized at last.

Yet this proliferation of the mightiest names of Europe, while adding to the impressive nature of the Crusade, also multiplied its difficulties. There was no trace of co-ordinated action. Sicilians and Germans acted quite independently, and if the English and French nominally formed one expedition, events were to show that they were far from being of one mind. Indeed the decision of Philip Augustus to take the Cross was certainly an obstacle to the success of the expedition. It was not merely that he lacked the necessary ardour, and went on the Crusade because of the unfavourable effect his refusal to do so might have had on his position in France; throughout its course his interest was centred on France and on the problem of whether events in the East could be turned to serve the French monarchy in its primary concern, the limitation of English power in France. It was not thus that the Muslims could be defeated.

The first aid to reach stricken Outremer after the disaster had been merely a lucky chance. Conrad of Montferrat with a company of western knights was peaceably bound on a pilgrimage to Jerusalem when he arrived off Acre ten days after Hattin; the arrival of a Muslim official alongside warned him of the disaster and that Acre was already in enemy hands. Hurriedly putting off he sailed to Tyre, where his reinforcements probably made the difference which allowed one port in the kingdom of Jerusalem to remain in Christian hands. Further seaborne help reached the beleaguered garrisons in Tyre and Tripoli in the form of a Sicilian expedition under William II. Although his death in the next year (1189) was to mean that the Sicilians were to take no more part in the Crusade, they had brought aid when it was most needed. In 1189 a Scandinavian fleet also appeared in the East, and for once the Italian cities were acting in concert; Outremer had been one of their best markets. These operations saved the remnant of Christian lands in the East, and made counter-attack possible. But it could not take place until the great land forces of the West had arrived.

The first to set out was the German emperor Frederick Barbarossa. As a young man he had accompanied Conrad III on the Second Crusade, and through all the vicissitudes of his later career he had retained an interest in the East. Although in his late sixties he at once took the Cross, and his reputation in Germany was such that he was assured of a large following. First he had to make arrangements for the government of the country in his absence; they included the exile of his most dangerous rival, Henry the Lion, to England. But by 1189 he was ready to start, and he led his great army by the overland route to Byzantium. The Byzantine Emperor Isaac II (1185–1195) was even less enthusiastic than his predecessors about having to act as host to a large army of uninvited crusaders. The Third Crusade nearly suffered the fate of the Fourth in being turned into an attack on the Eastern Empire. However, this danger was averted, and after wintering at Adrianople the army moved off to the south. But disaster awaited it; moving at first fairly near the coast until it reached Laodicea, it then struck inland, aiming to reach the coast again at Seleucia. It was harassed by local Muslim forces, but had nearly reached its goal when it lost its leader. Frederick was immersed in the River Calycadnus; it is not clear whether this was an accident or the consequence of a mistimed desire to bathe. But the consequences were fatal: the emperor's body continued to accompany the Crusade, but his soul was elsewhere. Deprived of its leader, the morale of the German expedition disintegrated. Some returned home at once; others refused to go farther than Antioch; only a remnant consented to go on with Barbarossa's son Frederick of Suabia towards the Holy Land.

Philip Augustus and Richard I were more tardy in setting out. The final touches had to be put to the peace settlement between England and France, and Richard's recent accession meant that numerous arrangements had to be made in England before he could depart. Philip meanwhile had no intention of leaving his ally any opportunities at home by preceding him to the East. But at last they were ready, and in the summer of 1190 both kings set out. They had wisely decided to use the Christian control of the sea to avoid the land route, and this should have enabled them to make the journey more quickly. But it was not until the next spring that they arrived in Outremer. On the way they had stopped in Sicily, and Richard had immediately embroiled himself in the dispute which had followed William II's death. Relations between him and Philip had become very strained. Even when they left Sicily Richard had not gone direct to Palestine; some of his ships, including the one which contained his sister Joanna and his fiancée, Berengaria of Navarre, got blown to Cyprus in a storm. Richard took the opportunity of capturing the island from the rebel Greek who controlled it. Instead of returning it to Byzantium he was later to sell it to Guy of Lusignan. Cyprus was later to prove the most valuable and much the longest lived of all the crusading captures, but at the time this independent English venture did nothing to improve Anglo-French relations.

When at last they were in Outremer the kings found the crusading forces engaged in the attempted recapture of Acre. In the operation against it Richard's military qualities showed at their best. Although seriously ill, probably from scurvy, he brought a new vigour to the attack; in July 1191 the town was captured. Some weeks later, in direct contravention of the surrender terms, Richard had the entire garrison butchered. Philip meanwhile had reckoned that he had done enough to qualify him as a crusader and left for home in the same month. He was no doubt delighted to leave the king of England behind him, although he cannot have known how long it would be before his rival returned home.

Philip's departure left Richard as the undisputed leader of the Third Crusade, but it did not stop dissension between the English and the French. Without it Richard might well have won Jerusalem; whether he could have held it is another matter. Saladin, now past his best as a general, was twice defeated in the field, but it became clear that the reconquest of the kingdom of Jerusalem was an impossibility. Richard, like Moses, had to be content with a galling and distant view of the land he had failed to win. In September 1192 he signed a treaty with Saladin, by which a thin coastal strip some one hundred miles long from Acre to Ascalon should remain in Christian hands as a relic of the kingdom of Jerusalem. Christian pilgrims were to be allowed to visit Jerusalem, but it was a small outcome from the greatest military expedition ever sent forth by Christendom. Richard's return to his own country might serve to explain why so much effort came to nothing; captured by one Christian prince and held to ransom by the Emperor of the West, he illustrates by his journey the disunion of the West which must have wrecked any combined venture.

The Third Crusade was not the end of Outremer; for nearly another century there were to be Latin states on the mainland of Asia; the final fall of Acre did not come till 1291. But after 1192 Outremer is no longer a central interest in the west. Jerusalem was lost, and only incurable enthusiasts could hope that it would be regained.

Viewed as a whole the crusading movement was a vast failure. Started as a demonstration of the unity of Christendom, the Third Crusade showed clearly enough how this unity was cracking; it was left to the Fourth Crusade to demonstrate to what depths the Holy War could sink.[1] Despite the great quantities of blood and treasure spent on the struggle to free Jerusalem, at the end the city remained more firmly than ever in Muslim hands. Europe indeed learnt much from the rich Muslim civilization in thought and architecture, medicine and mathematics. But this knowledge reached the West, not (with minor exceptions) through Outremer, but through more peaceful points in contact with Islam, such as the tolerant kingdom of Sicily in the twelfth and thirteenth centuries. Much more indeed was learnt from the secondary front against the Muslims in Spain, for here there were longer periods of peace. It is hard to learn much from a people who are held in contempt and hatred, but those in Outremer who began to feel sympathetic towards Islam soon found themselves regarded with scorn by those of their own religion. Certainly there were individual rulers in the West who used the Crusade skilfully to further their own interests at home: Philip Augustus is the most obvious example. Certainly also the Italian seafaring towns, such as Pisa, Genoa, and Venice, made a rich profit from carrying the Crusades and from supplying Outremer. But this was not vital to them. Philip Augustus would have been a great and successful monarch without the Third Crusade, and Venice and Genoa remained rich and powerful long after Outremer had passed into nothingness. The negative achievements of the Crusades, however, were greater. Two great civilizations were at least in part destroyed by them: Byzantium was fatally weakened by the Latin incursions, and the crusades had some responsibility for the weakness of the Muslim world before the Mongol attacks of the thirteenth century. The crusades had spread their own fanaticism and intolerance to religions other than their own. In the twentieth century, when the civilized world is again split by fiercely intolerant ideologies, it is for this that they deserve to be remembered.

[1] See Chapter 10.

8

France under the Early Capetians

The early history of the French monarchy is scanty indeed when compared with that of the German kings. During the three centuries which divide the reign of Charlemagne from the Investiture Contest the interest of historians has been focused on the story of the German kings. Nor is this surprising; the successors of Lewis the German alone could make something like the original Carolingian claim to dominion over Western Christendom. In the end, indeed, the claim made in some way by every German ruler from Otto I to Henry IV was to be rejected, but it was not absurd that it should be made by kings who were at the same time controllers of by far the strongest political machinery in western Europe and the military defenders of Christendom against the pagan world to the East. No other Christian kings (least of all the kings of France) could have dared to make such a claim.

The comparison between the kingdoms of the eastern and western Franks in the ninth, tenth, and eleventh centuries leaves no doubt about the superiority of the former in almost every respect; the surprising thing is not that the French kings failed to´challenge German hegemony in Europe, but that the French monarchy survived at all. In Germany the monarchy was supported until the Investiture Contest by the accumulated prestige and practical experience of the Church; the only two strong organizations of the age pursued common ends. In France the Church paid very little attention to the French king except when some moral lapse, such as Philip I's appropriation of a vassal's wife in 1092, seemed to call for excommunication. Certainly there is no trace of the appearance of anything analogous to the German *Reichskirche*. The Crown had little or no influence over the appointment of the most influential churchmen of the kingdom.

The most important other weapon in the armoury of the German kings was their possession of an extensive royal domain scattered throughout the country, so that no part of the kingdom was far distant from territory directly controlled by the Crown. There was

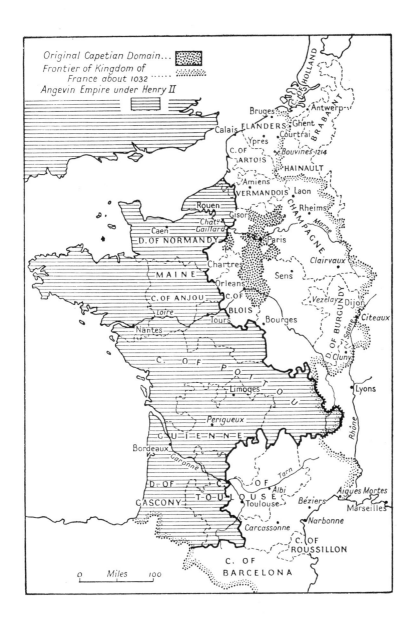

HOLLAND

Bruges
Antwerp
Calais FLANDERS Ghent
Ypres Courtrai
C. OF Bouvines 1214
ARTOIS HAINAULT
Amiens
VERMANDOIS Laon
Rouen Rheims
Gisors Marne
Chât. CHAMPAGNE
Gaillard
Caen Paris
D. OF NORMANDY Clairvaux
Chartres
M A I N E Sens
Orleans Vezelay Dijon
C. OF ANJOU C. OF
Loire BLOIS D. OF BURGUNDY Citeaux
Tours Bourges Saône
Nantes Cluny
C. O F Lyons
P O I Limoges O Rhône
U
Perigueux
G U I E N N E
Bordeaux Garonne Tarn
D. OF C. OF Albi Aigues Mortes
GASCONY T O U L O U S E Béziers Marseilles
Toulouse
Carcassonne Narbonne
C. OF
ROUSSILLON
C. OF
0   Miles   100   BARCELONA

THE KINGDOM OF FRANCE AND ANGEVIN POWER

thus no part of the country which was far from a potential royal base, and a vigorous king could make royal authority more than a name anywhere in the kingdom. In France there was none of this. The royal domain was far smaller in extent, and limited in area to the Ile de France, a small patch of territory roughly rectangular in shape which included Paris and, of greater importance in the tenth century, Orleans. Outside the domain the French kings had little prestige and no power to carry through any policy; the best they could hope for was to be allowed to continue unmolested in their obscurity. Nor was this all; even their control of the meagre domain was very limited. It was not the absolute property of the king; indeed the idea of absolute property was foreign to the medieval mind. Rather the domain was an area over which the Crown possessed a variety of rights; the systematic exploitation of these by an efficient and intelligent king might well lead to something not unlike absolute ownership, but conversely the failure through sloth or incompetence to assert rights might well extinguish them. The early Capetians were not without such faults: Philip I (1040–1108), for instance, was described by an admittedly hostile cleric as 'lazy and incompetent in war . . . dulled by his masses of flesh and too occupied in eating and sleeping to fight'.[1] Such failings were as harmful to the administration of the domain as they were on the battlefield.

The kings of France had other difficulties to face. Every medieval monarch was concerned with the problem of the overmighty subject, the great baron whose power approached or even exceeded that of the Crown itself. The wars of Robert II (996–1031) with the duchy of Burgundy are not different in kind from those waged by Otto II against Henry of Bavaria. But whereas in Germany the problem responded to the firm treatment of the Saxon kings, so that by the reign of Henry III the Crown seemed reasonably assured of the loyalty of its more important vassals, in France it became very much worse. From the middle of the eleventh century onwards the Norman duchy formed a problem which must have seemed insoluble to the Capetians. Normandy was not only far larger than the whole royal domain; it was far better administered. In the eleventh century Rouen was a far more real capital to Normandy than was Paris to France or even to the domain. Normandy lay in immediate proximity to the domain, and border territories such as the Vexin were bound to cause dispute. The Normans themselves had a formidable

---

[1] Quoted C. Petit-Dutaillis, *The Feudal Monarchy in France and England*, trans. E. D. Hunt. Routledge, 1936, p. 76.

reputation as fighters, deservedly inherited from their Norse ancestors; their dukes were both efficient and belligerent. The union of
Normandy with England in 1066, which Philip I was powerless
to prevent, redoubled the Norman threat, even if at the same time
it opened a new possibility of creating division within the duchy
itself.

William I of England was the first English king to hold a large
portion of France, but the problem did not die with him. In its later
form of the Angevin Empire it continued to provide the central
political problem for every French king, until Philip Augustus
contrived the ruin of John. It was not a problem of a foreign invader
seeking to occupy France, as it must seem to modern eyes. The
Norman and Angevin kings were after all French speaking and
accustomed to spend much of their time in France; most of their
French lands they held nominally as vassals of the French crown.
But there was every danger that the feeble monarchy of Paris might
simply cease to exist, as earlier the Merovingians had given place to
the equally Frankish but more dynamic Carolingians.

Such difficulties confronting the kings of France make the weakness
of the early Capetians far from surprising. Yet the Capetians had
certain advantages. Hugh Capet (987–996) and his successors did
succeed in inheriting something of the aura which had surrounded
Carolingian kingship. According to the legend the oil for the coronation of Clovis, first of the Christian Franks, had been brought to S.
Remy at Rheims by a dove; the Capetians too received the holy oil
of coronation, and from the mid-eleventh century they wisely
received it at Rheims so as to associate themselves with the legend.
The rite of coronation did not confer any specific powers upon the
recipient, but it gave to him a mark of divine approval which was not
erased by any temporal failure. This respect for the office of kingship
was compatible with active opposition to royal plans, but at least it
ensured that even the disobedient would ultimately seek some form of
reconciliation.

Moreover, there were advantages to be won from the very poverty
and insignificance of the Crown. The mighty German kings, claiming
to be more than kings, won for themselves the imperial title. Yet
with this title went the constant temptation to intervention in
Italian affairs, and ultimately to the dissipation of German resources
in Italy. This, admittedly, is a one-sided interpretation of imperial
policy in Italy, but it was not a temptation to which the Capetian
kings could be subject. Their frailty forced them to concern themselves

with the affairs of France alone, or even more narrowly of the domain itself.

In the same way the comparative coolness of relations between the early Capetians and the Church was not all to the former's disadvantage. It is true that the French kings could not, like the Ottos in Germany, make use of the prelates of the Church as the leading figures of their adminstration, and this was no doubt inconvenient for them. Yet when the wind of Gregorian change blew through the Church it could do but little damage to the French monarchy. The French kings had not been averse to simony; they had simply not been able to practise it on anything like the scale of the German emperors. The German monarchy was bereft in a few years of the major part of its administration; no such disaster occurred for the Capetians. Moreover, the Investiture Contest opened the way for an era of cordial relations between Rome and Paris at a time when the support of Rome was of increasing political importance. The Papacy was embroiled deeply enough in its recurrent struggle with the German kings; the kings of France gained a certain undeserved prestige simply by not being German. When Louis VII (1137–1180) gave succour to Alexander III, for three years an exile at Sens from the supporters of Barbarossa, or for seven years helped to shelter Becket in his struggle with Henry II of England, it is clear that the house of Capet has taken over the role of privileged ally of the Papacy.

Another important consequence followed from the early division between Crown and Church in France. Without any chance of being able to use the administration of the Church for its own ends, the French Crown was obliged to develop its own administrative machinery. Admittedly such civil service as it possessed was even by twelfth-century standards crude and primitive, but it did at least belong to the Crown. The German monarchy had been able to make use of a far more developed organization provided for it by the Church, but when the breach with Rome took place it was left bereft of any administration. In the twelfth century Barbarossa can be found struggling to improve the system of *ministeriales* to replace the vanished assistance of the Church. No such break with continuity can be seen in France, where from very small beginnings in a group of household servants concerned only with the royal domain there grew the highly specialized administration for the whole kingdom of France, which was to be the envy of other European rulers at the end of the thirteenth century.

One other characteristic of the Capetian kings calls for attention in this preliminary survey. In the one hundred and eighty-four years which separated the death of Hugh Capet in 996 from the accession of Philip Augustus in 1180 only five monarchs ruled over France, giving an average length of reign of nearly thirty-seven years; no reign was shorter than twenty-nine years. This longevity would be remarkable in any age; in the Middle Ages this power of survival is quite exceptional, particularly when it is remembered that the family had a hereditary trait of obesity which would certainly have deterred a modern life insurance company. Moreover none of them neglected their duty of begetting male heirs to succeed them. In this way the crises which inevitably accompanied the death of a sovereign were reduced to a minimum. The heir apparent was regularly associated by the reigning king with the business of government well before the end of the reign. In this way he could not only give needed assistance to the failing physical powers of the old king, but could also accustom the baronage to the idea of his own accession. An adult heir thus nominated and accepted in his father's lifetime stood little chance of not being 'elected' when the time came. In this way 'election' in France came to be a formality, and the idea that succession was a right of birth was generally accepted. The contrast with the German scene is clear enough; there the rulers were less fortunate or less prescient in their affairs, and by the twelfth century it was obvious that election had come to triumph over the hereditary principle. An emperor might be succeeded by his next of kin, but, as the elections of Lothar III and Conrad III showed, there was no certainty about it. Moreover, the electors might well be moved by consideration of their own interests rather than by the desire for a strong Crown. Undistinguished in many ways, the early Capetians deserve to be remembered for saving the French Crown from this fate.

The period which separates the cession of Normandy to Rollo in 911 from the election of Hugh Capet in 987 is one of considerable obscurity in French history. The throne was occupied by the last feeble representatives of the Carolingian line, Charles III (896–929), Louis IV (936–954), Lothar (954–986), and Louis V (986–987). But they were the merest puppets. Royal power had long been meaningless in the whole southern half of the country, known as Langue d'oc from its use of the Latin form of the affirmative, *hoc*. Now it was becoming equally meaningless in the northern Langue d'oil, the area where an approximation to the modern French affirmative 'oui' was used. The Carolingian domain had vanished; some of the more important vassals of the Crown, such as the dukes of Brittany or the counts of Flanders, had broken all contact with it; others, such as the newly enfeoffed dukes of Normandy, or the dukes of Burgundy, had far more real power than the kings themselves. Indeed, Raoul, duke of Burgundy had been crowned king of France at Sens, and from 929 to 936 he had been the only king in France. Probably only his failure to provide himself with an heir prevented the formation of a Burgundian dynasty of kings.

Among the powerful families which surrounded the throne were the marquises of Neustria, Robert of Neustria (†923), and Hugh the Great (†956). Their family lands included a large bloc in the centre of northern France, the counties of Maine, Anjou, Blois, and Paris, and this gave them far more real power than the Carolingians. If from sentiment they gave their support to the accessions of Louis IV and Lothar, they did not scruple to use their control over the Crown to try to further their own territorial ambitions. When Louis V died without leaving a son in 987 Hugh Capet, the son of Hugh the Great, was elected by the nobility with the full support of the Church. The Capetian line had begun.

Only in retrospect does the coronation of Hugh Capet seem of great significance. Others had claimed to be kings of France earlier in the century; both his grandfather Robert I of Neustria (922–923) and Raoul of Burgundy, who was his uncle, had made the claim. Only the future was to show that this time the greatest of the French dynasties had begun.

During the reigns of the first three Capetian monarchs, Hugh (987–996), Robert the Pious (996–1031), and Henry I (1031–1060), the continued survival of the house must have seemed very unlikely. True, their possession of a royal domain made them less pathetically inadequate than their Carolingian predecessors, yet their resources were dangerously small. Any attempt to assert royal authority throughout the kingdom was out of the question; the best that could be hoped for was formal recognition from the more important of their vassals. Certainly they seem to have cherished extravagant ideas of the role of the French monarchy in European affairs. Robert the Pious, for instance, became entangled in an extensive plot against the emperor Conrad II. But since they lacked the means to implement any of their European plans, they proved entirely ineffective. Even their control over the domain was very uncertain. The territories which had formed the March of Neustria began to break up even before Hugh Capet came to the throne. First Blois, then Maine, and finally Anjou broke away from the control of the Crown, though their rulers remained nominally its vassals. The royal domain contracted until it was reduced to the county of Paris, extending just far enough south to include Orleans. If the dukes of Normandy had not remained loyal to their overlords, nothing could have saved the Capetians.

Nor do the early members of the line seem to have met the challenge of their situation with any remarkable qualities. Information about them is hard to come by; the doings of the king of France were of no interest to the compilers of the monastic chronicles which form the main sources of information about the period, and very little record has survived of their political actions. Of Hugh Capet practically nothing is known. A dignified presence and an unusual preference for diplomacy as against war are the only attributes which can be at all confidently ascribed to him. There survives a highly laudatory account of his successor Robert the Pious by the monk Helgard, but this is more concerned to point out the Christian merits of the late king than to describe him as a statesman; in any case obituaries are rarely reliable. Robert may have died a saint, but his earlier career was marked by matrimonial disputes over both his wives, the first of which involved him in a quarrel with the Papacy. Like his father he seems to have been of an unmilitary disposition, a dangerous characteristic in the eleventh century. It may have been this lack which caused him to be so uniformly unsuccessful in his disputes with the dukes of Anjou, and the counts of Blois. The evidence is that the royal domain was further diminished during his reign, nor was the domain itself made more orderly.

Henry I, who succeeded Robert in 1031, had the military qualities his predecessors had lacked. In his campaign against the revolt launched against him on his accession by his mother and his brother, and later in the operations he carried on first against Anjou and then against Normandy, he showed that he had no clerkly reluctance to fight, but this ardour does not seem to have been balanced by any corresponding sagacity. The decision to end the Norman alliance was his; early in his reign (1035) he had fulfilled his promise to Duke Robert of Normandy by recognizing and investing his illegitimate son William the Bastard, later to be William the Conqueror of England. Henry had personally led an army to the assistance of the young duke when he was faced by a rebellion in 1047, and William in his turn had come to the aid of his overlord against the rebellious Geoffrey Martel, duke of Anjou, the most unruly of the vassals of the French Crown. Without warning Henry switched his allegiance and began an attack on the duchy which had done most to preserve his throne (1050). It is true that the power of Normandy and its geographical proximity to his domain did represent a threat to his independence; earlier in his reign he had ceded the Vexin, the county on the east bank of the Seine midway between Paris and Rouen, to the Normans as a recognition of their support in the troubles he had faced on his accession, and he may well have feared complete dependence on them. But if he had planned so formidable an operation as the destruction of Normandy it would have been wiser to have attempted it while William was still a child. As it was he lacked the necessary resources and skill, and his two invasions of the duchy (1054 and 1058) both came to grief. He had thus assured himself of the hostility of the most powerful of his vassals at a time when that vassal was shortly to add the power of the English monarchy to his own.

The fourth Capetian king, Philip I (the Fat, 1060–1108), has been harshly handled by historians. Certainly his gross sensuality and the physical corpulence which went with it are not endearing characteristics, even if they scarcely justify the description of him by Gregory VII, always a master of hyperbole, as a tyrant possessed by the Devil.[1] But it is by no means clear that the charges against his efficiency as a monarch are justified. He is accused of having allowed the union of England and Normandy to take place; serious as this was for the Capetians, it is not clear how he could have prevented it. The subsequent dispute between William the Conqueror and his eldest son Robert of Normandy owed something at least to the encouragement of the French king. In the same way he has been accused of feebleness in his relations with the Papacy. No friend of Gregorian reform himself, he saw it imposed throughout France without his co-operation, so that he lost that measure of control he had possessed over some of the French bishoprics. An inactive role is rarely glorious, and certainly there is no glamour about his inactivity. Later he was to be an excommunicate spectator when Urban II launched the First Crusade on French soil at Clermont; no excommunicate could take the Cross. Yet the monarchy would not have been aided if he had decided to emulate Henry IV or if he had set himself up as a crusading leader. Indolence may well have been aided by some element at least of masterly inactivity. Another count in the

[1] Quoted Fawtier, *The Capetian Kings of France*, (trans. Butler and Adam). Macmillan, 1960, p. 17.

accusation is that although he still styled himself *Rex Francorum*, he had an even more parochial view of his duties than that of his predecessors. Certainly it is true that during his reign the great nobles of the realm met the king in consultation less frequently; Philip's assemblies met in the domain and for the most part were attended only by the vassals of the domain. This was a natural enough reflection of his policy. Philip had no extravagant ideas of extending his power by diplomacy or war throughout Europe, and thus had no need to invoke the support of the great feudatories of France. He preferred to concern himself with the domestic but real problems of the domain. It is less clear that this policy was mistaken. Neither Robert nor Henry had gained anything from their more grandiose schemes; the monarchy had to be more firmly rooted in the domain before it could hope to make much impression in the rest of France or beyond her borders. Philip is recorded as having said to his son, the future Louis VI, 'Look, son, make sure you never let the Tower of Montlhéry out of your keeping. It has caused me untold trouble. Frankly, that tower has made me old before my time.'[1] He was right; the piecemeal reduction of particular trouble spots in or bordering the domain was the essential, if prosaic, task of the monarchy. His real failure was not in choosing the wrong ends, but in failing to achieve the security of the domain. Towards the end of his reign, beset by physical degeneration, he seems almost to have given up the attempt. It was as well that from 1100 onwards Louis VI was at hand to take over most of the active business of government. The first three Capetians had kept the dynasty alive when it might well have perished; there is not much more that can be said for them.

With the reign of Louis VI (1108–1137) a new vigour came into the royal house, and with it the first clear signs of a growth in monarchical power. The new king was not exempt from the physical failing of his family; he too was to be known as 'le Gros', and the chronicler Henry of Huntingdon brackets him with his father as having deified 'the belly, most baleful of gods'. But there was no torpor about his political actions. His first aim was to accomplish the task in which his father had failed, by asserting royal authority in the domain. Nobles who refused to accept their obligations to the Crown or who terrorized the countryside must be subdued. In a series of campaigns lasting for most of his reign Louis gradually subdued a turbulent baronage; early in the reign (1111) he succeeded in defeating and capturing Hugh of Le Puiset, thus avenging a

[1] Suger, *Life of S. Louis.* Quoted Fawtier, *op cit.*, p. 17.

humiliating defeat inflicted on his father more than thirty years before. In his struggle Louis was aided by the nature of his opponents, who seem to have resembled the bold bad barons of popular imagination. No great affection for the Crown was needed to support its cause against opponents like Thomas de Marle, who rejoiced in torture for its own sake. The royal cause thus gained not only popular sympathy from merchants and peasants, who saw the Crown as their safeguard against similar treatment in the future, but, what was more important, it gained the powerful aid of the Church. Philip I had seemed a sordid transgressor of the divine law; Louis VI began to associate the king with the idea of righteousness. The process of disciplining the domain was a long one, partly because his opponents were numerous, if fortunately disunited, but even more because of Louis's reluctance to take the ultimate measure of execution or degradation against his opponents. Time and again a defeated opponent was restored to his estates, only to rise in rebellion again; the continued trouble with Hugh of Le Puiset is a case in point. Yet in the end he was successful. By the end of the reign there was a peaceful acceptance of royal authority in the domain such as had not been known before.

But military force was only one side of Louis's achievements. He also brought a new efficiency to the civil administration. This too was largely a reflection of his energy. Feudal kingship consisted of a wide collection of ill-defined 'rights'. Adequate written accounts of what these rights were did not yet exist, and much, therefore, depended on the ability of the king to remember what these rights were and to assert them at the crucial moment when they became due, if necessary adding the stimulus of his own presence. A right once neglected by the Crown would soon cease to be anything of the sort; conversely the most tenuous claim could be converted into a firmly established custom by a judicious royal appearance on two consecutive occasions. This imposed on the king a duty of vigilance and a willingness to undertake continuous travel, a duty which Louis did not shirk. In the domain these rights largely took the form of *Champipart*, the royal claim to fixed portions of the produce of some of his vassals, or of the *Corvée*, the right in certain circumstances to demand labour services. *Censi*, money rents paid to the Crown, were also not unknown. In this way the resources behind the monarchy gradually grew. Nor were such rights entirely limited to the domain. Louis VI added but little new territory to the domain, less indeed than his predecessor, but the increased prestige he brought to the Crown led individual churches and towns outside the domain to seek his protection when they felt themselves threatened. In this way a network was established which his successors would be able to use to extend royal power.

Moreover, Louis introduced significant new changes into the royal methods of administration. The earlier Capetians had operated a system of government akin to that of the Carolingians. Occasional great councils of the nobility of the realm were held, but since the king possessed no control over his greater feudatories, who in their turn had little desire to serve the Crown, power within the domain itself had passed to the officers of the royal household with some obligation of serving the king's person. For instance the Chamberlain had the duty of safeguarding the king's wardrobe and treasury, the Chancellor that of preserving his correspondence, while the Seneschal and the Butler were charged with supervising his royal progresses and the domestic accommodation of his household. These became the men who most naturally and easily were his councillors on matters of state. They were men themselves of noble birth and more interested perhaps in the fortunes of their own families than in serving the Crown. Moreover, as was so often the case in the earlier Middle Ages, their offices had tended to become hereditary, so that they had become not a circle of councillors selected by the Crown, but a small group of men fated by birth to use office for their own profit. In Louis's reign one particular family, the de Garlandes, had come to enjoy an altogether disproportionate share of these high offices. One brother was Seneschal, another Butler, while Stephen, the youngest and ablest, was Chancellor. Nor were the de Garlandes likely to enhance the prestige of the Crown whose resources they were coming to control. Stephen certainly was able enough, but such crimes as the unpunished murders of Archambaud, sub-dean of S. Croix d'Orleans, and Thomas of S. Victor did not assist the growing reputation of the Crown for justice. It was only Stephen's attempt to nominate as his successor not a son, but a mere nephew by marriage, that moved Louis to action against them. This provoked the family to a revolt (1127), which the king was successful in putting down. Stephen was pardoned and even restored to office, but the incident seems to mark the beginning of a change in royal methods of government. The great offices of the household were not abolished, but they were filled at the royal will, while the habit of keeping them vacant at intervals prevented any one office from coming to exert a wholly preponderant influence. At the same time much more importance was given to a new type of royal servant, the clerk who had risen from a lowly post in the administration. Such a man had great advantages over the noble officers of the state. Wholly dependent on the favour of the Crown, he had no family resources to encourage him to personal ambitions. It was far more likely that his first loyalty would be to the monarchy. Long experience of the details of administration gave him a much better knowledge of what could and could not be attempted, so that the advice he gave the king was likely to be at once less prejudiced and more realistic than that tendered by more traditional councillors.

The prototype of these new ministers of the Crown was the Abbot Suger of S. Denis. Born in 1081 a native of the royal domain, Suger had entered the monastery of S. Denis as a boy; his ability in the practical field of administration of the monastic estates had soon been recognized. It was no doubt this ability which had recommended him to the service of the Crown even before the death of Philip I. During the early years of the next reign he was extensively used by the king on such business as a royal embassy to the papal court in 1112. Even his election to the abbacy of S. Denis in 1122 did not stop him being primarily concerned with the business of the kingdom, until the reproaches of S. Bernard, contrasting his readiness to serve 'Caesar' with his reluctance to serve God, recalled him to the service of his order. Less is heard of him in the last decade of Louis VI's reign, but there is no doubt that his influence with the king, fortified by a close personal friendship, remained strong. The administration of monastic lands was only a microcosm of the administration of a kingdom; in both there was the same need for uncorrupt officials, for the proper keeping of records and accounts; both suffered equally from the activity of rebellious lay vassals. His advice to the king must have been in favour of a less exalted but more efficient administration. Two other services he was to perform for the king: his *Life of Louis VI*, written in the next reign, was to be largely responsible for the very favourable view historians have taken of that king. Moreover, by putting his experience at the disposal of the king's son and successor Louis VII (1137–1180), he helped to provide that continuity of administration which is one of the greater benefits of a professional civil service.

The major political events of the reign were both concerned with marriage. Already on Louis's accession Henry I of England had re-established the link between England and the duchy of Normandy; Louis's attempts to separate the two by supporting William Clito, son of the deposed Duke Robert, who was Henry's prisoner, met with ignominious failure at the battle of Brémule (1119). Worse was to follow. The marriage between Matilda, Henry's daughter and proclaimed successor, and Geoffrey the heir to the county of Anjou (1128) was a most serious threat to the French royal house; an effective combination of England, Normandy, Maine and Anjou would prevent any further expansion of royal power in northern France. The harmful effects of this match were to be masked for many years by the anarchy in England, but it was one of the main foundations of later Angevin power.

If this marriage was a disaster for the Capetians, the other seemed a glorious diplomatic victory. The most powerful of the feudatories of the Crown in the south of France were the dukes of Aquitaine. They had had little contact with their overlords, whose problems were not their problems. Any attempt to extend royal authority by force over Aquitaine would have been totally misguided and doomed to failure. Yet when in 1137 Duke William X (1127-1137) died without leaving a male heir to his duchy, he entrusted the custody of his daughter Eleanor, and with it the arrangements of the marriage she would surely make, to his overlord the King of France. Under feudal custom the protection of a vassal's daughter after his death would naturally fall to his overlord, yet that William suggested this arrangement is striking testimony to the new reputation Louis VI had given to the Crown of France. It is now recognized not only as being powerful enough to give some protection at least even in the south, but also as being on the whole likely to use its power to defend the rights of its vassals. Louis, himself near death, did not hesitate to accept this last opportunity; his own son and heir apparent, the future Louis VII, was straightway nominated as the bridegroom and sent south to enter on his new inheritance. Without a blow he had extended royal power deep into the south of France and seemed to have opened up the possibility of a French kingdom which might extend in more than name from the Channel to the Mediterranean. The disastrous failure of the marriage, which was to end by giving Aquitaine into the hands of the Angevins, meant that the question of whether the Crown could possibly have ruled so large an expanse of territory cannot be answered. Certainly Louis VI would have been foolish to refuse so surprising and apparently glorious a gift, and he cannot be blamed for the subsequent failure of the marriage. When he died in the next year (1138), he left to his son a kingdom stronger in men, money and administration and, perhaps more important still, stronger in reputation than that which he had inherited. Suger's praises were not unearned.

With the reign of Louis VII (1137–1180) the throne came to be occupied by a ruler of a less constant purpose, who came to face a graver external danger than any of his predecessors. The clue to Louis VII's actions seems to be the extent to which he was influenced by other people. Respect for Suger, first love and then hatred for Eleanor of Aquitaine, dread of S. Bernard, these were sentiments which many men might have felt, but which in his case can be shown deeply to have influenced his policy. Of himself Louis seems to have been a peaceable man of simple tastes; Henry II's courtier Walter Map has a story of how the king, hearing an Englishman's boast of the extent of his master's dominions, replied 'Now in France we have only bread and wine and our heart's desire'.[1] But often he came under more dangerous and heady influences.

Early in his reign his love for the sensual and vivacious Eleanor of Aquitaine seems to influence his policy. Certainly the invasion of the County of Toulouse (1141) served little purpose for the Crown; invading Toulouse had been a traditional occupation of the dukes of Aquitaine. Failure in this operation was not the only blow Louis suffered in his early policies. An unnecessary and damaging dispute with the Church may also owe something to Eleanor's influence; resistance to and resentment of the reforming influences in the Church were common in southern France and seem to have been felt by the queen. The attempt to impose his own Chancellor Cadurc on the archbishopric of Bourges against the wishes of the cathedral canons, who had canonically elected another candidate, was unwise, as was his support of Ralph of Vermandois, who had bigamously married Eleanor's sister. On both issues Louis found himself opposed by Theobald, Count of Blois and of Champagne, a friend of the reformers. Theobald was among the strongest of his vassals, whose support against the Angevin kings would have been most valuable; instead he was turned into an opponent the more dangerous because he had right on his side. No longer was it a case of righteous king against evil barons. Louis's assault on his vassal was the occasion of the massacre at Vitry-sur-Marne, later to be the lever on his conscience which S. Bernard used to dispatch him on the Second Crusade. By 1144 the king owned himself wrong on both issues, evacuated Champagne and allowed the other candidate to be archbishop of Bourges. Probably the process of disillusionment with Eleanor had

[1] Walter Map, *De Nugis Curialium*. Quoted Fawtier, *op. cit.*, p. 22.

already begun; she had after all failed to provide him with the expected heir.

During the two years of Louis's absence on crusade (1147–1149)[1] a double responsibility rested on Suger; he had not only to carry on the ordinary administration of the kingdom but also to find additional revenue with which to finance the crusade. That both tasks were accomplished without undue strain says much for his efficiency, and underlines the loss the monarchy suffered in his death the following year. Meanwhile Eleanor's supposed infidelity to her husband in Antioch had turned his feelings for her to repulsion. She for her part was too spirited to accept the role of discarded wife. By the time they arrived back in France an open breach seemed likely. Like Henry VIII of England, though with less good ground, Louis may even come to believe that there was something in the claim he now made that the original marriage was invalid through the consanguinity of the contracting parties. At all events a brief reconciliation was followed in 1151 by an open break. Louis took his wife with him back to her family lands in the south, systematically destroyed all the castles he had had created there, and withdrew to the domain; a council of the French Church at Beaugency duly declared the marriage invalid (1152). The consequences of this renunciation might have been foreseen. Indeed since jealousy of the Prince Henry had been one cause of the final rupture it can be said that they were foreseen, but were disregarded by Louis in his hatred for his wife. Eleanor escaped from her husband, and within two months had married the future Henry II of England. The loss of Aquitaine was perhaps not in itself a serious matter for a French monarchy which had had difficulty in controlling it; its conjunction with the English Crown was an error all the more grave because it had been so easily avoidable. Henry indeed was prepared to do formal homage to the French king for his lands in France, and Louis had to rest content with that. At a meeting at Gisors in the Vexin in 1158 the two kings (Henry had acceded to the English throne in 1154) formed a regular alliance, cemented by a marriage alliance between Louis's daughter Margaret and Henry's infant eldest son; the disputed Vexin territory itself was given with Margaret as a dowry. The Gisors treaty can be seen as a further surrender by the Capetians to their most dangerous rivals. In the last decade of his reign the bitter family feuds among the Plantagenets gave Louis further opportunities to work against the Angevin power in France, but he seems to have been too frightened by the might of

[1] See Chapter 7.

the English king to make more than tentative gestures; it was left to his son to show how profitably these feuds could be exploited.

To set against this failure to face up to the outstanding political danger which faced the French Crown two successes can be assigned to the later years of Louis VII's reign. The relations between the monarchy and the Church became extremely cordial. Both pope Alexander III and Thomas Becket took refuge in the territory of the French king; the triumphal return of the former to Rome in 1165 and the posthumous triumph of the latter both redounded to Louis's credit. The favour of the Church was a valuable political asset. 1165 also saw an even more important success: in that year Louis's persistent efforts to provide himself with a son and heir were rewarded by his third wife, Adela of Blois. Giraldus Cambrensis, who was in Paris at the time of the birth of the future Philip Augustus, tells how an old woman, celebrating in the streets the birth of the prince, told him that the son would grow to be a king who would drive the English from France[1]; the story is not to be taken as literal truth, for the Welshman was not above embroidering a story, but it seems to represent a genuine growth of popular feeling for the monarchy. Certainly a bishop congratulating the king on the event could do so in the words 'God has given you a son and us a king'. No such words could have been used in similar circumstances in twelfth-century Germany, and they are a measure of the success achieved by the unspectacular methods of the early Capetian kings.

The story of the survival and growth of the monarchy is the central theme of French politics in the eleventh and twelfth centuries, but twelfth-century France saw another and more striking achievement in a field far removed from politics. Monasticism, which in the tenth century had received its great renewal from the French abbey of Cluny, received a second great renewal, again from a French abbey. The reasons for the rise of the Cistercians are curiously similar to those which had produced the Cluniacs in an earlier generation, even though Cîteaux itself was a largely conscious protest against Cluny. For the Cluniacs had succeeded only too well: seeking first the kingdom of Heaven, all other things had been added to them in such abundance that by the twelfth century Cluniac houses, often themselves great property-owning corporations, had become deeply involved in the things of the World from which the cloister had once been a refuge. Cluniac monks held many of the highest offices

---

[1] See *The Autobiography of Giraldus Cambrensis*, ed. and trans. H. E. Butler, Jonathan Cape, 1937, p. 38.

in the Church; their abbots were often the trusted servants of kings, and within their congregations were many who had chosen the religious life as a good way of pursuing an advantageous career. Yet, as the crusading movement was to show, the age was one in which men were easily and deeply stirred by religious emotions. A new monastic reform was the inevitable outcome.

That Cîteaux was not an isolated phenomenon, whose success was based only on the persuasive strength of S. Bernard's example, is shown by the number of similar monastic reforms which occurred at about the same time. As well as Cîteaux, the Camaldolese (1012), the Carthusians (1084), the Order of Fontevrault (1094) the Antonines (1095), and the Order of Grandmont (c. 1100) had all in different degrees sounded the call to a more ascetic form of the monastic life, and a concentration on the life of dedicated prayer which had been the original purpose of monasticism. But in their scope and vitality the Cistercians were far to outstrip these other reformers, so that the twelfth century, at any rate in its ecclesiastical aspect, can be seen as the Cistercian Century.

The spark which was to kindle the Cistercian fire started at the Burgundian abbey of Molesme, where the abbot Robert and a group of his monks led a movement away from the laxity which had characterized Molesme and so many other Benedictine houses towards a strict interpretation of the Benedictine Rule. The reformers failed to carry the majority of the monks with them, and a secession took place in 1098. They removed themselves to the hamlet of Cîteaux, not far from Dijon, but itself a wild and inhospitable place where they would not need to look far to find asceticism. There under Alberic (abbot 1099–1109) and the Englishman Stephen Harding (1109–1133) they lived a life of a simplicity and austerity which were in part their own choice, in part the necessary outcome of their poverty. Their buildings were rude and simple, with no decoration other than a plain wooden cross on the high altar. Their clothing was very plain: even the mass vestments were made only of wool, and of necessity much of their time had to be spent in hard manual labour trying to wring an existence from the forest around them.

In its early years Cîteaux came near to extinction. The original brethren began to die off, and new recruits did not come to replace them. The turning point came in 1112, when the young Burgundian knight who was to become S. Bernard arrived to ask for admittance. For Bernard did not come alone; with him were thirty followers including some of his own brothers, the first eloquent testimony of the extraordinary personal influence he was always to exercise, an influence which was to sweep almost his entire family, including his father and mother, into the cloister. It is said that when Bernard was asked by the doorkeeper at Cîteaux why he had come, he replied 'To be crucified with Christ'. There could be no better summary of the ideal of Christian asceticism.

With the arrival of S. Bernard the problem of recruitment was solved; only the next year Cîteaux was able to found the first of her daughter houses at La Ferté; by 1115 four such houses existed, including that at Clairvaux which had S. Bernard as its abbot. From then on recruits joined the order in almost embarrassing numbers. It was fortunate that the new order possessed in Stephen Harding an organizer of genius, whose skill sufficed to shape it to receive the new numbers which threatened to swamp it. The *Carta Caritatis* he produced in 1119 gave a constitution for the order, and he was also responsible for most of the detailed regulations first gathered together in 1134. Much of the emphasis lies on renunciation. The order is strictly forbidden to indulge in any form of luxury of food or clothing. For much of the year there was to be but one meal a day, and even when two were permitted, meat, fish, eggs, and butter were forbidden. Their clothing was to be of coarse undyed wool; hence the name of grey or white monks by which they were sometimes known. In their churches no form of ornamentation, carving, or rich mass vessels were to be allowed. In the early days Cistercian abbey churches must have been like great barns; the decoration which can be seen at, for instance, Fountains Abbey is always the product of a later period, when the strict observance of the rule was no longer maintained. Worldly goods were strictly renounced, not only by the monks themselves but by the order as a whole. Bakeries, mills, the holding of fairs, the possession of serfs, all the means by which Cluniac houses had profited from the gifts of the laity to make themselves important in society, were not to be permitted. Nor was it only secular goods that were set aside; the *Carta Caritatis* was equally opposed to contact with the 'secular' Church. The order was not to own parish churches, to draw tithes or to receive altar dues for services performed outside the monastery. A similar austerity marked the performance even of the *Opus Dei*. The liturgy of Cluniac houses had become very lengthy and complicated, with a proliferation of feast days and a growing complexity of the chants employed. At Cîteaux the whole stress was on simplicity, and feast days were cut to a bare minimum. One consequence of this was that the time spent on the liturgy, which at Cluny had become nearly a full time occupation, was very much reduced. This gave space for another essential feature of the Cistercian life, the stress it laid on hard manual work. The self-chosen poverty of the order and the deliberate policy of founding houses in remote and uninhabited areas would in any event have forced this on the brethren, but work was regarded as in itself a form of prayer. There was more time also for the monks to engage in private prayer and meditation, and in that prayerful reading of the Bible, Lectio Divina, of which S. Bernard himself was a chief exponent. His knowledge of the Bible was equal to that of any seventeenth-century Protestant, as can be seen from the extraordinary frequency with which consciously and unconsciously he quotes it in his books and letters. Moreover, as can be seen in his commentary on *The Song of Songs*, the Bible thus used could become a fertile inspiration for many themes apparently far removed from its text; the method was one which could lead alike to new depths of spiritual insight and in lesser hands to great absurdities; for good or ill it was a product of Cîteaux.

Stephen Harding also gave attention to the constitutional problems of governing a large order. Certain common abuses were checked: the novitiate was to be strictly kept, so that unsuitable entrants should not take their vows, and the practice of child oblation was to be stopped. More important were the arrangements made to check the inevitable danger of decay which popularity itself was bringing. Each year every abbey was to be inspected by the abbot of the house from which it had been founded; each year there was to be a general chapter of the order at Cîteaux, at which every house should be represented. In this way the order could retain its unity and every part of it except the mother house itself could be subject to regular inspection. For Cîteaux a special clause was necessary. She was to be inspected by the abbots of the four senior daughter houses.

It is a mistake to read too much importance outside monasticism into these constitutional developments. But within that limited field they wrought a decisive change; the day of the independent monastic house, on the pattern of Monte Cassino, was closing; its place was being taken by the unified international order responsible ultimately to the head of the order, who is responsible to the pope alone. Future religious orders were all to follow this general pattern.

The importance of manual work in the Cistercian way of life led to two other innovations of importance. The areas directly worked by the monks themselves were much larger than was the case with the older orders; often they required more labour than the monks themselves could provide. There grew up, therefore, a class of *conversi* or lay brethren, whose prime function it was to cultivate the monastic land. They were monks, in the sense that they had taken vows and were expected to start each day with prayer in the church and to consider themselves bound to silence while doing their work, but their lay status exempted them from the *Opus Dei*. Often they lived in outstations known as granges, at some distance from the abbey itself, where their work might be supervised by one or two members of the community. This growth of a species of second class monk may seem distasteful today, but the statutes of the order were in no doubt that the *conversi* were 'under our care, our brethren and sharers with us in all our spiritual and temporal goods'.[1] Wholly illiterate peasants could not be expected to train themselves for choir service, unless, indeed, they came to the life of religion very young, and the rapid increase of the *conversi* suggests that to contemporaries a life under Cistercian direction offered both a surer way to Heaven and perhaps greater security on Earth.

The extent and speed with which the Cistercian Order spread throughout western Christendom is astonishing. The general chapter of 1153, only forty years after Cîteaux had established its first daughter house, was attended by no less than three hundred abbots, and its influence was not limited only to itself. The Premonstratensians, founded in 1120 by Norbert of Magdeburg, a close friend of S. Bernard, owed much to the Cistercian example: their role in the conversion of Germany has been noted in another chapter.[2] Even existing Cluniac houses were compelled in some measure to follow the same pattern; Peter the Venerable, abbot of Cluny from 1122 to 1156, by no means agreed with all the criticisms S. Bernard directed at his abbey, yet under his wise and moderate rule an attempt was made to restore to the Cluniac Order some of the ascetic practices and discipline which had marked its earlier years. The work which the Cistercians undertook was not intended to open up new economic opportunities for the unconverted, yet the clearing of forests and the draining of marsh was not only of service to the religious. The white monks played a valuable if unwitting part in the general expansion of the economy and population of twelfth-century Europe. If S. Bernard had a good claim to be considered the greatest man of the twelfth century, the growth of the Cistercian Order is one of the more important achievements of twelfth-century France.

[1] *Statuta Ord. Cisterciensis.* 1134 C. VIII.   [2] See Chapter 6.

9

France Leads Christendom

In 1179 the fourteen-year-old son of Louis VII, the future Philip II (1180–1226), was formally associated with his father in the task of governing France. The future cannot have looked bright for the boy. The health of his father was rapidly failing under a series of strokes, and the problems which crowded on the young Philip might have daunted a much more experienced ruler. First there was the danger that he might become the puppet of his mother's family. Adela of Blois had four brothers in posts of importance around the Crown. Thibault and Henry were counts of Blois and Champagne respectively; William, who as archbishop of Rheims was to crown his nephew, had good reason to think himself the most influential churchman in France; and the fourth, Stephen, count of Sancerre, if less highly placed than his brothers, was a tough and effective military leader. To knit the web even more closely round the Crown, both Thibault and Henry had married half-sisters of the future king. The threat of domination by this family of overmighty subjects was a very real one.

Next there was danger to be feared from Philip of Alsace, who as count of Flanders and Vermandois was nominally the vassal of the king of France. The wealth of Flanders, so much greater than any similar area in northern Europe, was always sufficient to make the controller of the county a potentially dangerous man. Moreover, although politics linked Flanders to France, her economic ties were with England, the supplier of the major part of the wool she needed for her cloth industry; the danger that to the already existing Angevin menace would be added an Anglo–Flemish alliance was always present. Philip of Alsace himself was an ambitious man, whose hopes clearly rose to more than autonomy for his county. He had already secured a marriage between one niece and Henry of Champagne; now he planned to marry his niece Isabelle of Hainault to the heir-apparent. He would then be well placed to exercise his influence on the Crown, and no doubt to use the resources of the French monarchy in his own interests, remote from France though these might be.

Finally there was the Angevin menace. Relations between Louis VII and Henry II had improved of recent years as both men grew old; a visit made by Louis to Canterbury when Philip became seriously ill in 1179, tactless though it might seem, was a sign of this improvement. Yet the excessive power of a vassal, whose total lands on both sides of the Channel so far exceeded those of his overlord, was bound to remain a grave threat to any Capetian king.

Paradoxically the very multiplicity of these dangers was the chief hope of the new king, for there was no cohesion among his opponents. Even the Angevins did not present a unified front; it should not be difficult to split so notoriously cantankerous a family. Philip Augustus was to show supreme skill in playing off his different enemies against one another.

Philip determined to deal with his own relations first, as the most immediate of his problems. He consented to marry Isabelle of Hainault in 1180, but her subsequent coronation was performed in Paris by the archbishop of Sens. This was a deliberate insult to his uncle, the archbishop of Rheims, to whom belonged the traditional right of crowning the kings and queens of France. At the same time he seems to have given his mother and his uncles to understand that he did not need their assistance in governing.

Adela of Blois reacted immediately. Removing herself from the domain, she entered Normandy to ask Henry II to take action against her undutiful son. But the English king did not want to be drawn into another conflict; at Gisors in June 1180 Henry met the young Philip, whose father was still alive, and the promises of friendship were renewed. Philip had succeeded in neutralizing the most powerful of his potential enemies in the struggle with his vassals which clearly lay ahead.

War broke out in 1181 after the death of Louis VII, and Philip found himself faced by a coalition of his vassals headed by Philip of Alsace. It was to continue for four years, despite the intervention of several papal legates, who tried to persuade the combatants to settle their differences and make common cause against the Saracen. Although Philip won no outstanding victory, he was able to use diplomatic weapons to break up the coalition. Neither Thibault of Blois nor the archbishop of Rheims had much inclination for fighting; in return for a promise that they would be restored to their offices at court, they consented to make a separate peace. A more ingenious way was found of splitting the Flemish ranks. Philip let it be known that he was thinking of repudiating his wife. Her father, Baldwin, count of Hainault, was much agitated by the suggestion, and deserted his ally Philip of Alsace. The latter was so incensed by this conduct that he himself attacked Hainault. The inherent weakness of the coalition had been exploited by the French king's mixture of apparent good will and calculated fraud, qualities which were to remain characteristics of his diplomacy. At Boves (1185) a treaty was signed with Philip of Alsace, by which a considerable portion of his domain, including much of Vermandois, and the city of Amiens, passed to the French Crown. For a king who was only just twenty it had been a considerable achievement.

Philip II was now free to turn to the greater problem of the Angevins. On the face of it he would seem to stand little chance against so strong and experienced a king. But Henry was not to be fought alone; his sons had already shown how tenuous their loyalty was, and it might be possible to create difficulties for him with the Empire. While Philip had still been engaged further north, the English king's eldest son, Henry le Jeune, had made an attempt to raise Aquitaine in revolt against his father (1183). Young Henry's death (1183) had put an end to the rising, if at the same time it had come near to breaking his father's heart. But Richard, Geoffrey, and John still survived; the two older brothers had shown, as far back as 1173, that they had no objection to working against their father. Richard now stood heir to the whole inheritance, and it was natural for Philip to look to Geoffrey as an ally against his father. During the early part of 1186 Geoffrey was living at the French court, and it was widely rumoured that he would become seneschal of France, renouncing his allegiance to Henry and joining with his new lord in a combined attack on Normandy, from his own country of Brittany and from the Île de France. Geoffrey's sudden death in the late summer of 1186 was an unexpected setback to Philip's plans; now it would be necessary to cultivate yet another Plantagenet.

It is clear that by this time Philip was becoming increasingly confident of his position. His lands might be small, yet he had overcome the internal divisions which threatened them at the beginning of his reign, while Henry II faced increasing opposition. Nor were grievances lacking to give his operations the cloak of justice. In particular Henry was retaining the Vexin, the hotly disputed territory which lay between Normandy and the French royal domain. This had formed the dowry of Philip's step-sister Margaret, who had been married to the ill-fated Henry le Jeune, and it had not been returned on her husband's death. It was now arranged that it should be used as the dowry-of her sister Alice, whose marriage to the prince Richard had already been arranged. Certainly Henry II was in feudal law bound either to allow the new marriage to take place or to return the Vexin; his failure to do either raised dark stories of his own relationship with Alice, who was already at the Norman court; such stories could only aid Philip's cause.

In 1187 Philip felt strong enough to hasten matters by attacking the castle of Issoudun in Berry. The operation was completely successful; at the treaty of Chateauroux not only did Henry consent to the cession of Issoudun to Philip, but he was brought to the point of speeding Alice's marriage. But the plan was now to be changed: she was to be the bride, not of Richard, but of the king's youngest son, the future John of England. To celebrate the event the couple were to be invested with the duchy of Aquitaine and with all the other French possessions of the Angevin kings, Normandy alone excepted. Henry's decision may have rested on affection for his youngest child or on a merited suspicion of Richard; in either case it was unwise. Richard understandably felt deprived of a great part of his proper heritage, and fell an easy prey to the dangerous friendship of the French king. He too sought the French court and was received so warmly there by Philip that 'by day they ate at one table off one dish and at night they slept in one bed'.[1] At the same time Philip was strengthening his ties with the German emperor Barbarossa, who had long resented Henry's support for his rival Henry the Lion. A great coalition to overthrow the Angevin Empire seemed in the making.

It was at this moment that the news of the fall of Jerusalem summoned all European monarchs to forget their differences in the common service of the Cross. Philip and Henry met at Gisors (January 1188), and answered the exhortations of the Archbishop of Tyre by agreeing to abandon their quarrel and to go together on Crusade. Whether Philip even felt much genuine enthusiasm for the expedition may be doubted. More probably he merely realized the damage his prestige would suffer if he alone among the great kings refused to go. He may even have foreseen that the expedition might be turned to his own advantage in France. Henry II was old and ill; if ever he started for the Holy Land it was unlikely that he would return, while if the duty was delegated to his son Richard the latter's enthusiasm might well overreach itself.

The participants at Gisors showed no undue haste to leave for the

---

[1] Quoted from W. H. Hutton, *Philip Augustus*. Macmillan, 1896, p. 40.

East. While Barbarossa was speeding the preparations which were to lead him to his death in Cilicia in 1190, the two western kings remained preoccupied with their own affairs. In the summer of 1188 Richard, who had been raising troops in Aquitaine for the crusade, became involved in a war with another vassal of the French Crown, Raymond V of Toulouse. Philip intervened to put an end to the fighting, and at Bonmoulins (November 1188) the monarchs of France and England again met. Richard also was present, and when he received an indecisive answer to his public demand that his father should recognize his right to his whole inheritance, he melodramatically turned his back on his father and knelt in homage to the king of France. Certainly Philip had been aided in this diplomatic victory by Henry's unwise treatment of his son, which had combined with Richard's own instability to produce a pathological hatred by the son for his father. Nevertheless Philip's own achievement was remarkable. His most powerful rival in France now faced a hopeless situation; together Philip and Richard attacked the lands of the English king. Maine and Touraine were captured, while Henry seemed almost powerless to resist them. At length in July 1189 he capitulated; at the Treaty of Azai Henry recognized defeat. He handed over Auvergne and other territories to the French Crown, paid a sum in compensation for the war, and did homage to Philip for all English lands in France. Richard was promised that his marriage to Alice would shortly take place, and his right of succession to all his father's lands was recognized. This last was a blow to the hopes of John, earlier raised high by the dispute between his father and his elder brother; now it was his turn to conspire against a father who had loved him too well. This final blow proved too much for Henry. Learning of it he fell in a seizure, and within a few days he was dead (July 1189).

In nine years Philip had emerged triumphantly from the dangers which had surrounded him on his accession. By the treaty of Azai he had won a decisive victory against the gravest danger which had threatened the Capetian house, and he had won it by superior intelligence rather than by force. Yet the danger from England was not yet gone, and there still remained a discontented Plantagenet. Richard might well be suspicious of his fellow-soldier for Christ.

The events of the Third Crusade have been described elsewhere.[1] Philip cut an inglorious figure alongside the crusading hero Coeur de Lion, but from his own point of view the Crusade gave him a

[1] See Chapter 7.

great opportunity. By crusading at all he had fulfilled one of the main requirements of a Christian king in the twelfth century, while his early return enabled him to spread calumnies in France about the part Richard had played; the latter was made to appear as a man secretly in league with the infidel, a man who had not scrupled to attempt to poison Philip himself. The technique was worthy of later French kings with a more perfect command of the art of propaganda.[1] By it the ground was prepared for another blow against the English monarchy. The capture of Richard on his return journey was an unexpected stroke of fortune, for he had already been away from his lands too long for safety. Philip tried to exploit the opportunity. An embassy (1193) was sent from the French Crown to the Emperor Henry VI to try to persuade him to keep his royal captive as long as possible. Meanwhile Philip joined with John in an attack on Normandy. The Vexin was conquered, and the royal army laid siege to Rouen, but failed to take it. John proved to be of small value as an ally, and Henry VI's desire for a ransom proved stronger than his wish to keep England immobilized. With Richard's return, Philip's dispute with the Anglo–Norman monarchy became again a matter of straightforward military action, and here he was not the master. Four years of confused fighting (1194–1198) ended with a papal legate negotiating a peace, which restored the situation which had existed at the beginning of Richard's reign (Treaty of Vernon, 1199).

But Richard did not live to enjoy the fruits of victory; a few weeks after the treaty had been signed he was again in action, this time against a rebellious vassal in Aquitaine. At the siege of the castle of Chalus, a well-directed arrow again gave the French king the initiative. The tactics Philip used were very similar to those already employed against Henry II and Richard, but the personality of the new king of England made their success the more probable. Henry had been widely recognized as a great king, while Richard's military qualities made him a dangerous enemy; by contrast John's bad reputation, deserved or undeserved, and lethargy in moments of crisis did little to recommend him as a fit successor. Moreover, there was the inestimable advantage of a genuine doubt about the succession; against the claims of John, the sole surviving son of Henry II, could be set those of Arthur, Duke of Brittany, the child of John's elder brother Geoffrey of Brittany. As in so many cases feudal 'law' was a matter of uncertain precedents, and spoke with no clear voice for

[1] See, for instance, the exploits of Philip IV of France in Chapter 14.

either candidate. If England, Normandy, and Aquitaine, the major portion of the Angevin inheritance, accepted the claims of King John, Touraine, Maine, and Anjou itself declared for Arthur. These signs of disintegration could not but favour the French king. At first Philip seemed inclined to support John; his own resources had been strained by the prolonged war of the previous decade, and he was in the throes of a dispute with the Papacy over his attempted renunciation of his second wife, Ingeborg of Denmark. At the treaty of Goulet (1200), in return for John's cession of Evreux and his renunciation of any claim to the territories of Berry or Auvergne and for a substantial cash payment of twenty thousand marks, he consented to give no support to Arthur.

John proceeded to work his own destruction. His marriage to Isabella of Angoulême was a flagrant breach of feudal law; she was already betrothed to one of his own more important vassals, Hugh, Count de la Marche. Hugh registered his protest, first by armed resistance, then by an appeal to Philip as overlord of all France. Summoned to answer for his alleged offence to the royal court at Paris, John refused to come; the French king was well within his rights in declaring him contumacious and depriving him of all his fiefs (1202). All the fiefs thus made vacant were transferred to Arthur, with the single exception of Normandy, which Philip prepared to annex directly to the royal domain. Arthur, a youth of only fifteen, proved unsuccessful in the field, and was captured by his uncle at Mirebeau in the same year. There seems no doubt that he was murdered on John's orders at some time during the next two years; if the exact details of the crime remained unknown, the speculations, highly circumstantial if widely differing, which circulated through both countries served Philip's purposes well enough. Alive, Arthur might well have grown to be in his turn an overmighty subject; dead, not only did his memory disgrace the cause of John, but it served also to reinstate Philip in the favour of the Papacy. The horror of this greater offence obscured his own matrimonial indiscretion.

John proved quite incapable of rallying the Anglo–Norman baronage to the defence of his lands; many of them when asked replied like William the Marshal, that 'that would be evil for they were Philip's men'.[1] The loyalty of those who owed a double allegiance could not but be uncertain when their two lords were at war with one another; certainly it was not to be stimulated by a leader such as John, who varied intermittent bouts of activity with

[1] See Ernest Lavisse, ed. *Histoire de France*. 9 vols. Paris 1900–11. Tome III(i), p. 138·

periods when he sat in Rouen saying 'Let be; some day I will win all back.' The key to the defence of Normandy itself was the Chateau-Gaillard, the strongest castle in all France which commanded the vital crossing of the Seine. For eight months (September 1203–April 1204) it was besieged by Philip's troops; eventually it was taken by assault. By the end of June Rouen had fallen and all Normandy was in Philip's hands. Almost the entire Norman administration hastened to declare its loyalty to the conqueror, who wisely accepted their declarations. The whole duchy, which once had so dominated the puny Capetian kings, was incorporated in the royal domain. Nor was this all: Maine, Anjou, and Touraine had all been annexed to the domain, while the duchy of Brittany was securely held by a loyal vassal. The royal domain, the secret of strong government in the Middle Ages, had been nearly trebled; not for nothing was Philip styled Augustus, 'the increaser'.[1] There were no English possessions left north of the Loire, and if Philip was not so successful in establishing royal authority further south, this did not mean that John was any the more secure. The nobles of Aquitaine had learnt already to profit from the clash of differing authorities to conduct their own affairs in their own way, resisting any attempt at external control.

The Angevin Empire had ceased to exist, and although English intervention in French affairs was by no means over, from this time on it was increasingly seen as foreign intervention; the major obstacle to the development of national monarchies on both sides of the Channel was gone. Yet before the dust was allowed to settle Philip was to make an effort to reverse the previous situation. Now France would intervene in England; the Angevin Empire in France would be succeeded by a Capetian Empire in England: John, for his part, was to make the final attempt to restore his position in France that culminated in the disaster of Bouvines.

The quarrels of John with his English barons do not properly belong to the scope of this book, except in so far as they inevitably came to Philip in the guise of an opportunity. The idea of a possible intervention in England had long been present to him; the hope of obtaining Danish ships for such a purpose had been one motive behind his unfortunate marriage to Ingeborg of Denmark in 1193. By 1212 the situation seemed favourable for such a venture; England was under the papal interdict imposed by Innocent III, and a steady flow of exiles from England, such as Robert Fitzgautier, was arriving to ask for Philip's intervention. He could hope to surround an

[1] This explanation of the title is given by the chronicler Rigord.

entirely self-interested operation with all the spurious sanctity of a crusade. The rights of Holy Church, threatened by John's refusal to recognize Innocent's nomination of Stephen Langton to Canterbury, must be defended; if the operation should happen to end with the deposition of the Plantagenet line in favour of Philip or his heir, that would be only a fortunate by-product. In the spring of 1213 he summoned all his tenants-in-chief to Soissons to give them their instructions. Only Ferrand of Portugal, the new count of Flanders, failed to obey; no doubt he saw no reason to assist a king, whom he rightly suspected of wishing to extinguish the independence of his country, in an attack on his closest trading partner. A large army and fleet collected at Boulogne; one writer, with the wild exaggeration customary among medieval chroniclers when dealing with large numbers, says the latter consisted of 1,500 vessels. But it was not to be used. At the last moment John made his submission to the papal legate Pandulf. In the official story, as told by his chaplain William the Breton, the king claimed to be delighted that his preparations had moved John to penitence; unofficially he was furious with the pope who had so baulked him.

It was perhaps natural that Philip should wish to vent his anger on the count of Flanders, who alone had refused to serve. But there were more solid reasons. Control over Flanders, so rich in mercantile resources, would offer him a prospect of steady revenue far above that of the much wider lands of rural France. At the same time there were already signs that an alliance was forming in the area to the north-east of his domain, an alliance which might link the opponents of the expanding power of the French monarchy with those who, under the leadership of Otto IV, were opposing in Germany the imperial claims of the young Hohenstaufen emperor Frederick II.[1] Ferrand might be expected to join this; if so, it was logical to strike first.

Philip began the invasion of Flanders in May 1213; his first intention was to launch a joint land and sea operation, by which the count's forces might be encircled. But the French fleet was taken by surprise by the Flemings, assisted by an English squadron under William Longbow, Earl of Salisbury, and it was largely destroyed at anchor at Damme; from then on all the fighting was on land. While the French army promenaded through Flanders, wreaking Philip's vengeance on his vassal's subjects, the coalition against him took shape. The plan worked out by Otto IV and John was strategically

[1] See Chapter 13.

sound. The French king was to be forced to fight on two fronts. John was to raise an army in the south and west of France, where little encouragement was ever needed to stir the nobility of Aquitaine into revolt. While Philip was thus drawn off to protect his capital from attack from the south, the main army of the coalition under Otto would advance on Paris from the north-east. But the plan had one fatal defect. It depended for success on the ability of John. He had little difficulty in gaining support after he had landed at La Rochelle (February 1213), but as soon as Philip appeared in the area he retreated hurriedly towards the safety of Bordeaux. Philip was able to leave John covered by the lesser portion of the French forces under his son Louis, while he himself went north to face the greater danger. After a series of indeterminate manoeuvres, which did nothing to encourage the idea that here was a victorious general, John's army ended by being ignominiously routed by Louis's forces at La Roche-au-Maine (2 July 1214); one arm of the pincers had been broken.

The defeat of his allies caused natural consternation in Otto's camp, already somewhat disorganized by the strains inherent in a coalition of widely assorted feudal dignatories. Philip seized his chance; in a rapid advance Tournai was captured at the end of July, and a feigned retreat then brought the opposing army to battle in one of few firm open spaces among the surrounding marshes. Here the superior quality of the French cavalry could offset the larger numbers of his opponents. By nightfall on 27 July 1214 the battle of Bouvines was over. Otto escaped, to find his cause in Germany ruined, but Ferrand and Longbow were both prisoners and many of the other leaders were dead; the army had ceased to exist.

Bouvines deserves its place among the decisive battles of European history. It did more than complete the ruin of King John and set the final seal of military success on the endeavours of the Capetian kings. The defeat of Otto marked the clear end of the German Empire as the dominant political force of the Christian West. The Empire would continue to exist but in a changed and Mediterranean form; in the West the future lay with France.

Yet the military and diplomatic triumphs which culminated in Bouvines were only the more spectacular half of Philip's work. They would have been of little avail without the reshaping of an administration which had grown up to meet the needs of a small domain, and was now required to govern much of France. Throughout the reign a steady growth of professionalism in the methods of government can be observed. As the financial and military position of the Crown improved, so the king could afford increasingly to dispense with the great councils of the leading ecclesiastical and lay nobles of the realm, which had been the chief instrument of government under the earlier Capetians. Indeed, after Bouvines there was no military need large enough to demand a full feudal host, and the royal exchequer was well enough placed to raise such troops as it required. Some of the traditional great offices of the household, such as that of the Seneschal, Philip allowed to remain unfilled; others were filled by men of a new type. Gautier de Nemours as Chamberlain and Raoul as Constable were men who owed their importance entirely to their office; they had not been given office because of their previous importance. The process, already observable under his father and his grandfather, by which real power is exercised by a smaller and more intimate council of royal servants chosen by the king and dismissable by him at any time, was carried much further.

But, however efficiently government might be exercised in Paris or in the presence of the king, as the area of the domain grew the problem of how to get royal instructions obeyed in areas far distant from the court grew in size. The existing system of royal provosts was not very efficient; far from the king and often chosen because they were already powerful local magnates, the provosts could too easily choose to act independently of the Crown and seek to use royal powers to establish their own positions more firmly. Philip's answer lay in the institution of *baillis*. When the first *baillis* were appointed is uncertain, but the system was fully described when the king drew up the 'Testament' in 1190, which laid down how France was to be governed during his absence on crusade. The domain was divided up under the care of royal officials chosen by the king and receiving a salary from the exchequer. They were made responsible for both the administrative and the judicial supervision of the areas under their control, and they were especially charged with seeing that the king drew the full revenues to which he was entitled; thus, despite their initial expense, the *baillis* more than paid for themselves. Since they had no local ties and were always liable to be called to account for their actions by the king, and indeed had to render annual account, they were much more scrupulous than the provosts had been in doing the royal will. At first nine such *baillis* seem to have been appointed; at least two more were established when Normandy was added to the domain. This system of Crown appointments by the government to supervise administrations largely recruited locally recalls the system of colonial governors instituted by most successful colonial empires; that the French Crown was in a position to adopt it at the beginning of the twelfth century argues a greatly increased political maturity.

Nor did Philip neglect to cultivate the link between the Crown and that other class which had so strong an interest in the replacement of baronial warfare by firm central government,[1] the bourgeois population of the towns. By no means the first of the kings of France to issue charters, he did so on a far larger scale than any of his predecessors. His reasons were in part financial. The charters all lay down the payments due to the Crown in return for the privileges granted; the revenue thus gained could go to the financing of its professional army and bureaucracy. But there were also sound political reasons for favouring the establishment of new communes. Once the immediate struggle to gain new territories for the domain was over, there was bound to be baronial opposition to any royal attempt to exercise central control there. The creation of independent communes directly linked to the Crown in the middle of such territories could not but weaken the opposition, and at the same time give the king opportunities of extending his influence. So new charters were granted not only in the older parts of the domain, for example Chaumont and Pontoise, but also in the more recently acquired areas; Nonancourt in Normandy, Bapaume in Artois and Peronne in Picardy can serve as examples of the latter group. Moreover, the more the Crown came to be known as the protector of towns, the more easy it might be later to incorporate even the south into the domain, for there too the towns might need a defender; it was at once a policy of consolidation and of preparation for future expansion.

Financial success lay at the root of much of Philip's achievement, for it allowed him a far greater liberty of action than had been enjoyed by any of his predecessors. It is less easy to say precisely how it was obtained. His encouragement of a lucrative link with the towns has already been seen; similarly he did not neglect to encourage merchants from outside the kingdom, for trade could be made to mean additional revenue for the Crown. His support by privileges of the settlement of foreign merchants in Paris and his attempt to extend royal protection to the seasonal fairs in Champagne both show his realization of this. Nor did he neglect the more traditional sources of royal income. The profits of justice, the exploitation of wardships and the other feudal rights of the Crown all continued to be used for

[1] See Chapter 11.

revenue; more efficient administration now ensured that most of the money raised now actually reached the exchequer. The formation of an effective system of records in Paris was an important aid to securing that no royal rights were allowed to lapse.

A variety of expedients produced new sources of revenue. Just as landowners were becoming increasingly prepared to accept the commutation of labour services into cash rents, so now the Crown, the biggest landowners of them all, encouraged the process by which dues owed to it in service and produce should be paid instead in money. Paris, for instance, was allowed to pay a sum of 4,000 livres annually in settlement of its military obligations to the king, while in 1215 the inhabitants of Valois were relieved of their obligation to perform the *corvée* in return for annual payments. The widespread adoption of such commutations provided the Crown with a considerable increase in income to replace services which had often been inefficiently performed and difficult to enforce. Philip found another profitable source of income in the Jews. At the beginning of his reign (1182) he had attempted to expel them altogether; later he came to realize that licensed usury might well be turned to the profit of the Crown. Jews were allowed to carry on their usurious transactions only under special seals provided by the Crown. Two custodians were appointed for each of these seals; their duties were to see that the rates of interest charged were not outrageously high (forty-three per cent was the stipulated maximum), and that the king received his share of the immoral earnings. The result was all that could be desired: between 1202 and 1217 revenue from the Jews increased more than sixfold.

If Jews were thus milked, professional Christians could not hope to be ignored. The Church contained wealth enough to tempt any ruler, but its strength and independence made it difficult to lay hands on its riches without provoking a major conflict with a Rome by no means so vulnerable as she was later to become under Boniface VIII. However, the Third Crusade seemed to offer an opportunity; the Saladin Tithe (1188) was an attempt to extract from the clergy of France a tenth part of their revenues, ostensibly for crusading purposes alone. The operation was not a success, probably because the initial figure had been set too high. Determined resistance led by the archdeacon Pierre de Blois led to its temporary withdrawal. Nevertheless, later in the reign Philip was able to draw considerable sums from the Saladin Tithe on two different occasions (1213 and 1218), and the weapon remained for his successors. A further device by which the Crown could extract money for the treasury from clergy and laity alike was that of *pariage*. By this, groups of small ecclesiastical or lay landholders outside the domain could gain the protection of the Crown against local oppression by consenting to 'share' their ownership of their land with the King. The advantages to the Crown are clear enough; that the protection should have been thought worth having by those who lived far from the domain is a striking tribute to the new power and influence of the monarchy. That influence was built largely on the possession of an income greater than any other thirteenth-century ruler except the pope.

For the last nine years of his reign Philip Augustus found himself for the first time out of immediate danger. They were comparatively uneventful years, used rather for the consolidation of the gains he had already made than for new large acquisitions. The double defeat John had suffered in 1214 might seem to have given Philip a perfect opportunity to renew the attack on an English king now hopelessly entangled with his own subjects. But John was to perform two of the better calculated actions of an unsuccessful career. First (1215) he took the Cross, and declared that his whole kingdom was under the protection of a Papacy which had little desire to see the kingdom of France grow yet stronger; then (1216) he died. The expedition which the future Louis VIII disembarked in Thanet in the spring of 1216 had thus neither papal approval nor, after John's death, the hope of representing itself as the just dethronement of a tyrant; the child king Henry III of England had as yet no offences to his charge. After suffering defeat in battle near Lincoln and hearing of the destruction of part of his fleet at Calais, Louis wisely decided to make peace (1217). By the treaty of Lambeth the French forces were to be withdrawn and French claims dropped in return for an indemnity of ten thousand marks. The long war was over.

The other major event of the period, the Albigensian Crusade, has been described elsewhere.[1] Here Philip showed masterly inactivity. The French monarchy stood clear of a war which might well have dissipated its resources. The fighting was left to its vassals, and the moment when it was able to gather the proceeds did not come until the next reign. Philip himself fell ill in the autumn of 1222, and died the next year in the customary atmosphere of piety and panegyric. This aura cannot conceal that France had lost a king whose chief qualities lay in efficiency and tough realism; in another age he would have been described as a supreme Machiavellian.

[1] See Chapter 10.

The short reign of Louis VIII (1223–1226) is notable chiefly for the control over much of Languedoc which the royal house now gained for the first time. In reality this was a posthumous triumph for Philip Augustus; the careers of Louis VI and Louis VII had shown that until the monarchy was strongly rooted in the north it could not hope to assimilate large areas of new territory. The ease with which Louis VIII could move in triumph to Carcassonne in 1226 showed that the monarchy now possessed that strength, and the ease with which two portions of the extreme south of the country could be added to the royal domain, though separated from the rest of it by hundreds of miles, was a testimony of its new powers.

Yet the annexation also posed new problems. Now that the royal domain had a Mediterranean coastline, the kings of France would be compelled to have a policy towards the Mediterranean world. It was perhaps fortunate that the extreme weakness of England allowed the English problem to remain quiescent. The minority of Henry III indeed gave Louis the opportunity to annex to the domain the fief of Poitou with little difficulty.

Louis's reign then reads as a story of success, at least so far as the augmentation of the domain is concerned. But one administrative device he employed had less desirable consequences for the future. In an attempt at simplifying the government of the country he grouped large numbers of smaller fiefs into three great fiefs under his three younger sons, Robert, Alphonse, and Charles. Since the boys were only infants there could be no question of personal rule as yet, and the direct link to his own kin may have seemed a useful device for stimulating loyalty to the Crown, a parallel to Edward I's future treatment of Wales. Yet these children would not grow up to be kings. The very size of their fiefs might tempt them to aspire to some of the prerogatives of kingship, such as an independent foreign policy; the future career of Charles, to whom Anjou and Maine were given, illustrates most of the dangers.

Louis VIII committed the sin of dying young; the eldest of his young family, Louis IX (1226–1270), was only a boy of twelve on his father's death. The Capetian monarchy was called upon to face the crisis of a regency, at a time when its previous growth had made the threat it offered to baronial independence perfectly clear. Moreover it had to face it under the regency of the queen mother, Blanche of Castile, whom Louis had nominated on his deathbed. A little-known foreign woman seemed to have small chance of controlling a revolt which involved baronial leaders, some of them princes of the blood royal, from Boulogne to Toulouse and from Champagne to Brittany.

But Blanche was a remarkable woman. During the next eight years she systematically tackled the dangers which faced her son and triumphantly surmounted them. Certainly she was aided by various factors. There was little unity and co-ordination among her opponents; just because they represented a spirit of regionalism and of protest against the whole idea of 'France', it was difficult for them to combine. Then again Philip II's policy of favour towards the towns now paid off handsomely; the towns to which he had granted charters almost without exception remained loyal to his daughter-in-law. Paris in particular rallied to the cause of a monarchy which had shown it much favour. Blanche could thus control not merely a series of military strongholds throughout the country, for the walled town was hard to capture, but a supply of money on a scale quite beyond the command of her opponents. Moreover, even in the countryside the government of the Crown and its *baillis*, rapacious though they might sometimes be for the treasury, yet seemed preferable to a return to conditions of chronic baronial warfare. These assets Blanche used so skilfully that she was able to hand to her son an undiminished inheritance when he assumed personal responsibility for government in 1234. Even then her influence did not cease; she was closely associated with the government of her son for the rest of her life, to the understandable annoyance of his own queen Margaret of Provence, and during his prolonged absence on the first of his crusades it was again Blanche who exercised the regency. More important still, it was from her rather than from his Capetian ancestors that Louis inherited the quality of deep religious devotion which underlay the practical ability of both mother and son.

S. Louis of France, both in his own age and subsequently, has been taken to represent the ideal of medieval kingship. No man more fully represents the political ideals of the High Middle Ages; if some of those ideals were already perhaps growing scarce even in his own age, it is no uncommon experience to find an age admiring qualities which it lacks but believes its predecessors had. Today there are many who look back nostalgically to the industry and integrity of the Victorians.

To S. Louis kingship was a matter of applied Christian ethics; the supreme duty of the king was to show the quality known to Plato as διϰαοσυνη or to S. Augustine as *iustitia*. Thus, where Philip II had concentrated on the privileges of the Crown and had sought to extend them over his subjects wherever this might be possible, S. Louis concentrated rather on the duties he owed them. Certainly this brought a further increase in strength, for obedience to such a Crown became a habit, but it was as well for S. Louis that the initial foundations had been laid by his unscrupulous grandfather.

What seems to many modern historians the defects in S. Louis's rule appeared to his contemporaries often as but a necessary part of his righteousness, but there is much over which there need be no disagreement. In the field of administration he divided the body of permanent officials which had grown up in Paris under Philip II into two distinct bodies, later to be known as the *Parlement* and the *Chambre des Comptes*. The one was staffed by men with an expert knowledge of the law, and could exercise the king's justice to his subjects; the other was composed of financial advisers, and supervised the national finances. Undoubtedly the use of *Parlement* as a royal supreme court gave greater consistency and efficiency to the legal decisions of the Crown, and made royal justice clearly the best in the kingdom; and so, although the king showed himself scrupulous of the rights of baronial courts, the prestige of the royal courts was such that litigants made increasing use of them. Incidentally this also brought financial profit to the Crown. S. Louis was strong enough to abolish obsolete and obviously unjust legal processes, such as trial by battle or even the baronial warfare which had so often been the alternative to more formal legal processes, and to direct the parties into the royal courts. In the same way the king's moral principles forbade him to indulge in that debasement of the coinage by which so many local mints sought occasional profit. In consequence the royal coinage came to be known as the soundest in the kingdom, to the ultimate profit of the Crown.

But the greatest change wrought by S. Louis in the government of France lay in the institution of *enquêteurs*. Previous kings had commended their justice and their administration as offering a way of escape from baronial misrule; none had faced the possibility that monarchical institutions themselves might become oppressive. Indeed it is a mark of the greater order now prevailing that S. Louis could now concern himself with this practical application of his duty towards his subjects. The first *enquêteurs*, sent out in 1247, were charged 'to receive in writing and examine all pleas which any man may bring against us or our ancestors; and likewise all statements of injustice and exactions of which our *baillis*, provosts, foresters and serjeants and their subordinates are alleged to be guilty since the beginning of our reign'.[1] The device, curiously similar to that of the 'Ombudsman' in modern Scandinavia, became permanent; *enquêteurs* were sent out in pairs, of whom one was normally a cleric and the other a layman, and their wide terms of reference meant that there were few complaints that they could not investigate. That S. Louis frequently used Franciscan friars rather than regular royal officials for this purpose is additional evidence that his purpose was sincere, and this extra curb on the operation of local officials did much to restrain the misuse of their powers. At the same time the Crown was provided with a double check on its administration; future kings with less concern for establishing God's will on earth were provided with an instrument which could be used for very different purposes.

The king's relationship with the Church had a curiously two-edged nature. No man had more desire to live according to the rules of the Church, yet his success in doing this paradoxically made it easier for him and his successors on occasions successfully to oppose the Church. The roots of his ecclesiastical policy are to be found in his own personal religion. S. Louis's faith went far beyond the conventional piety which was so easily accredited to medieval rulers. When he told the Sire de Joinville that 'there is no leprosy so foul as being in mortal sin',[2] he really meant it. Throughout his reign he observed the full monastic regimen of seven daily offices, and he heard mass twice daily. Observing a strict moral code himself, he believed it to be his duty to make all France do likewise. Even a great prince of the royal house like Charles of Anjou could find himself strictly rebuked for dicing, and such offences as prostitution and drunkenness were sternly punished.

Yet, great as was his respect for Holy Church and her rights (he was even prepared to return tithes which Philip II had appropriated), S. Louis was far from being a mere creature of the Papacy. The very reputation for sanctity he had earned was of the greatest assistance to him when he felt he was standing up for what he believed to be right. The worldly popes of the thirteenth century were not in a position to lecture such a king on questions of right and wrong. When Innocent IV sought to raise special papal taxes in France for his struggle against the Emperor Frederick II, S. Louis refused to allow him to do so; Frederick in his turn was compelled to return the fine bag of a hundred prelates he had captured in 1241.[3] Both pope and

---

[1] Quoted from Fawtier, *op. cit.*, p. 33.
[2] Quoted from *History of St. Louis. Sire de Joinville*, trans. Evans, Oxford U. P., 1938. p 7
[3] See Chapter 13.

emperor received a severe reproof from the king who was so much more Christian than either of them, to the effect that they should be ashamed of their conflict and should make peace at once. Naturally such a king took the keenest interest in appointments in the French Church; he was genuinely concerned that it should be served by the best bishops, and, because this was his motive, questions of simony did not arise. Yet the precedent would be useful indeed to his less high-minded successors.

In his relations towards other states the king was governed by a desire to do justice and to preserve that peace which should exist among all Christians. A good example can be found in the Treaty of Corbeil (1258) with James I of Aragon. Now that French royal power had extended into the south the relationship of France and Aragon had become a difficult problem. James could put forward quite good claims to much of Languedoc, while Louis for his part could have pressed a claim to the county of Barcelona, south of the Pyrenees. The settlement arrived at in 1258 can be called the obvious and sensible one. The Pyrenees were to act as the boundary between the two countries, Roussillon alone excepted. Both monarchs consented to drop their claims to lands on the other side of the range. But how many rulers in a position as strong as that of S. Louis would have been prepared to agree to it? It was more difficult to negotiate with Henry III of England, who refused to give up his claim to Aquitaine, but the Treaty of Paris (1259) was the best that could be done in the circumstances. Henry abandoned all claim to Normandy, Anjou, Maine, Touraine, and Poitou, receiving in return formal recognition of his right to hold Guienne from the French Crown and some additional fiefs in the area of Perigueux and Limoges. Paris was not, like Corbeil, a complete settlement, but it provided at any rate a temporary peace in the tempestuous relationship of the two kingdoms.

Nothing more clearly shows the wide respect in which Louis IX was held than the frequency with which he was called in to arbitrate to prevent the danger of war, even outside his own country. The fierce family quarrel over the succession to Flanders and Hainault was submitted to him by all the parties concerned; it is hard to imagine a similar invitation being extended to Philip Augustus. In the *Dit de Péronne* (1256) Louis produced an ingenious settlement which certainly averted a prolonged war. Other examples of his ability as a conciliator can be found in Navarre, Burgundy, and Lorraine. He was even asked to mediate in the dispute between Henry III and his barons, and if his attempt to do so by the *Mise of Amiens* (1263) was not in the end accepted, the invitation itself is testimony enough to his international reputation.

But there was another side to this rosy picture. If many twentieth-century men react with distaste and incomprehension to the tale of ascetic practices which so impressed contemporaries, there are two charges in particular which can be pressed against him. On the one hand it was through S. Louis that the worst horrors of religious persecution reached France, on the other he was responsible, and not once only, for dissipating the best blood and treasure of France in futile crusades on the southern shores of the Mediterranean.

Certainly he cannot and would not wish to be acquitted of either charge, but both must be examined. The Papal Inquisition had evolved gradually during the earlier years of the thirteenth century as a central organization of the Church to replace the sporadic local heresy hunts of earlier times. It could not operate in any country without the co-operation of the secular authorities, who were in any case needed to give effect to its sentences. S. Louis not merely gave it every encouragement, but kept its operation largely under royal control; the goods of many convicted heretics found their way to the royal treasury. Moreover, it was during his reign and on French soil that some of the worst excesses of the Inquisition were committed. The zeal of the king for religious orthodoxy helped to allow an unbalanced sadist, Robert le Bougre, a converted Albigensian turned inquisitor, to consign one hundred and eight-three alleged heretics to the flames in one *auto-da-fé* at Mont-Aimé in Champagne in 1239. But, without seeking to belittle the suffering of the unfortunates caught in the inquisitorial net, it must be noted that S. Louis's attitude was the necessary complement of the devout religion which inspired his whole life; the good thirteenth-century Catholic inevitably wished the extirpation of heresy.

The same line of defence might be advanced for his crusading activities. To the king the whole point of his internal reforms, the whole justification of his endeavours to secure that Christians should live at peace among themselves, was that France might lead a united Christendom against the forces of the Infidel. The Holy Places had indeed been recovered for a time for the use of Christians by the Fifth Crusade, although by methods of which an old-fashioned crusader could scarcely approve,[1] but in 1244 an expedition from Egypt again drove the Christians from Jerusalem. S. Louis decided

[1] See Chapter 13.

to throw all the resources of France into an attempt to win back what was lost. The Sixth Crusade differs from any of its predecessors in that it was a French national expedition rather than a manifestation of the international Church; in this can be seen a sign not only of the growing power of nationalism, but also of the declining force of the crusading ideal except where a great and loved sovereign could rekindle it.

The king's plan was to strike at Egypt; a decisive victory here would carry with it the possession of Palestine. If any strategy could be sound, this may have been, but its execution was lamentable. The crusaders sailed from Aigues Mortes in the autumn of 1248. They wintered in Cyprus, and launched their attack on Egypt in the spring of 1249. The port of Damietta was captured, and the expedition remained there in dangerous inactivity for most of the rest of the year. It was then decided to make a direct attack on Cairo by a march across the desert, an operation for which the army was ill-equipped. The army was cut off from its base and exposed to terrible sufferings through shortage of supplies: 'The sickness of the host came upon us, which was such that the flesh of our legs altogether dried up, and the skin of our legs became blotched with black and earth-colour, like an old boot; and on us that had this sickness there grew rotten flesh upon our gums; nor did any man recover from this sickness but he must come near to dying thereof.'[1] Weakened by disease the army was smashed at Mansurah (1250) and compelled to surrender. Robert of Artois, the king's favourite brother, had been killed; S. Louis himself and the best of his knights were taken into captivity; those not considered worth a ransom were killed or sold as slaves. The payment of the vast sum demanded for the return of the prisoners was itself a considerable strain on the finances of France. Moreover, the prolonged absence of the king could not but have a harmful effect on his country. His personal popularity remained undimmed—it may even have been enhanced by his captivity—but the peasant revolt of 1251, known as the rising of the *Pastoureaux*, if it had as one of its impossible aims the liberation of the king, yet showed the damage his government had suffered. Eventually the money was raised, but even then the king only left the East with reluctance to return home in 1254, after an absence of nearly six years.

The first of S. Louis's crusades can perhaps be defended as the inevitable corollary of his merits; it is much less easy to offer this excuse for his second expedition, which lacked even the merit of wide

[1] *History of St. Louis*, Sire de Joinville, p. 87.

popular support. Many of those who remembered the earlier crusade, like de Joinville, had learnt their lesson. 'I held that they all did mortal sin that counselled his going because at the point at which France stood, all the realm was at good peace with itself and with all its neighbours; nor even after he had gone did the state of the realm do aught but worsen.'[1] Nor had the Seventh Crusade even the advantage of a sound strategy. The idea that the Emir of Tunis could be persuaded to change his faith and co-operate with the crusaders was itself unlikely; even if Tunis had been taken it would not have been of much value as a base for operations at the other end of the Mediterranean. Control of Tunis would indeed be of value in the furtherance of the Italian schemes of the king's brother, Charles of Anjou. It seems certain that he had succeeded in deceiving his brother into using crusading resources for an entirely secular aim. The preparations for the expedition were as extensive as before, and included the complete refortification of Aigues Mortes to act as base; once more France was drained for a cause in which few besides her king now believed.

S. Louis's participation in the Seventh Crusade was short. He was already a sick man when it started, having to be carried on board at Aigues Mortes in a litter; he had no resistance to the disease which struck the army soon after its arrival in Africa, and there before the walls of Tunis he died (25 August 1270).

The Sixth and Seventh Crusades certainly had but little success. In truth the whole crusading ideal was out of date; on the one hand the cynicism engendered by the Fourth and Fifth crusades had sapped it of vitality, on the other S. Francis had shown a better way with the infidels. Nevertheless a crusading death was what the king had always desired, and it formed a fitting conclusion to a life in which the desire for the service of Christ had always been strong. Nor, on balance, can the crusades be held to have robbed the reign of its chief glory. Philip Augustus had made the French monarchy strong. S. Louis left it both strong and popular.

The story of the French monarchy in the period between the beginning of the eleventh and the middle of the thirteenth centuries is thus one of great outward success. Its achievement was built upon a society which was itself vigorously expanding and developing. As might be expected, this development can be seen in a wide variety of fields. Two only can be touched on here, education and architecture. They are chosen because in them the France of the twelfth and

[1] *op. cit.*, p. 223.

thirteenth centuries produced some of the finest achievements of the whole of the European heritage.

The general awakening of European life in the eleventh century had increased the scale of the demand for educated men. A more organized Church and more organized royal courts needed more administrators, more lawyers, more theologians; more schools were needed to train them. The traditional centres of learning in the Dark Ages, the monasteries and cathedral schools, could do little to satisfy the new demand, for their schools were concerned with the education of novices for the religious life. It is true that abbots might sometimes be extracted from the cloister to act as bishops or royal servants; Anselm of Bec is a case in point. But something more was needed. South of the Alps in Italy the need was largely met by schools closely linked to the city communes. Here the tradition of urban life never died out; long moribund city schools could be revived and new schools created. The tradition of such schools was markedly utilitarian; once their pupils had mastered the basic techniques of learning they were directed towards the skills of which their society had immediate need. It was from them that universities such as Salerno and Bologna, famous for the study of medicine and law respectively, were to evolve.

North of the Alps a different pattern prevailed. Everywhere education remained much more closely a concern of the Church; there was no surviving tradition to make it a matter for town governments, which in any case developed much more slowly. Here the principal instrument of education in the eleventh century had been the cathedral schools which Charlemagne had once striven to perfect. Every bishop was supposed to maintain a school under the direction of his chancellor for the education of the future clergy of his diocese. Where a cathedral school possessed a bishop who was exceptionally interested in it, or masters of unusual merit, it might attract pupils from far beyond the diocese; among the cathedrals of northern France, Rheims and Chartres, which owed its fame to Fulbert, bishop of Chartres in the early eleventh century, were outstanding examples. The curriculum of the cathedral schools was based on the traditional seven liberal arts of the classical world, divided into the *trivium* of grammar, logic and rhetoric, and the *quadrivium* of geometry, arithmetic, astronomy and music. The main aims of the courses were to give students an acquaintance with some of the best of the literature of the past and a facility at expressing themselves in Latin; at the same time they were designed to give them a view of what seemed best in the classical world as interpreted by Christian tradition.

At their best the cathedral schools provided a broadly based humanistic education, incomparably superior to anything that had been found in northern Europe since Roman times; indeed many who had been brought up under their regimen, such as the twelfth-century Englishman John of Salisbury, who had spent several years at Chartres, continued to admire it long after newer forms of education had largely displaced them in general favour. Today those who were educated in the classics often show the same nostalgia in a scientific and technical world. But the new interest was philosophy, and this interest was further stimulated by the rediscovery of the works of Aristotle. Aristotle had always been somewhat vaguely honoured as a name among those ancient philosophers who were almost automatically considered as being greater in stature than any modern thinker, but since very few of his works were known in the Latin world he could exercise little practical influence. But from the first half of the twelfth century onwards an ever-growing corpus of the works of Aristotle, some genuine and some reputed, began to appear in the West. At once the two strongest intellectual beliefs of the medieval world found themselves in conflict; admiration for the classical past was now hard to combine with the honour due to the Christian faith. For if the true Aristotle had but little interest in theological problems, the spurious works which masqueraded under his name, which included a so-called 'Theology', and the commentaries on his genuine works by non-Christians such as Averroes, might make him a dangerous enemy to the Christian faith.

This was the central intellectual interest of northern Europe for three hundred years. Although the liberal arts continued to be taught in the schools, itinerant masters began to touch more and more on philosophical problems, and often to attract pupils away from the older disciplines. Of these Peter Abelard (†1142) is by far the best known, but he was only one of several masters who, by teaching in the vicinity of the cathedral school of Paris, helped to change the schools of the city imperceptibly into the first and greatest of the universities of northern Europe. In this process the university owed much to the steadily growing importance of the city as the capital of the Capetian domain, and to the favour shown to it by the Papacy; not until 1231 did a bull of Pope Gregory IX finally recognize it as an independent corporation of teaching masters, but at every stage the masters received support in their claim to establish their freedom from the interference of either the secular or the local ecclesiastical authorities.

The university was to repay the debt in full. Paris led the movement by which the Church was shown that even Aristotle, who had at first seemed so dangerous an enemy, could be used in the service of Christ. A patient task of translation carried out in Spain, Sicily, and Byzantium, where contacts existed with the Muslim world, was followed by a careful process of sifting the genuine writings of the philosopher from the various accretions they had acquired in over fifteen hundred years of wandering. In this process the leading roles were played by William of Moerbeke and Albertus Magnus, a German Dominican who was teaching at Paris from 1245 to 1254. This task once accomplished, it was left to others to show that a Christian Aristotelianism was possible; the *Summae* of S. Thomas Aquinas (†1274), again a Dominican who spent a part of his life lecturing at Paris, represent the most successful attempt ever made to produce a specifically Christian philosophy. In the twelfth century a grave danger had existed that the old religion and the new learning would part company, and two opposed cultures be produced, in much the same way that natural science and religion were to part company in the nineteenth century, to the great detriment of both. It was largely the work of the university of Paris that this did not happen and that theology became enthroned as the queen of the sciences. As Robert de Sorbon, founder of the college which bears his name, wrote in the thirteenth century, 'The sword of God's word is forged by grammar, sharpened by logic, and burnished by rhetoric, but only theology can use it.'[1]

Paris was the type of the universities of the North. Spreading quickly by spontaneous migrations of their masters throughout the thirteenth and fourteenth centuries, these universities were to reach such distant points as Cracow in Poland (1367) or S. Andrews in Scotland (1413). This is perhaps the greatest of all the achievements of medieval France.

The period from 1150–1250 also saw the great change which transformed the Romanesque architecture of an earlier period into the fully-fledged Gothic, which is one of the chief glories of the High Middle Ages, and here again it was in the lands of the royal domain in the *Île de France* that the most striking changes took place. As in England, the eleventh century had been a period of much

[1] Quoted from C. H. Haskins. *Studies in Medieval Culture.* Oxford. U. P. 1929. p. 46.

church building to match the general spiritual awakening of the age. The Romanesque architecture of France during this period has much in common with the style known as Norman in England. In both the central problem of how to support the massive weight of a stone roof could be answered only by making the whole building equally massive. Walls were thick and heavily buttressed, the round arches which had been typical of Roman building were built close together from ponderous blocks of masonry, and windows, inevitably flaws in the strength of the support, were kept as small as possible. Towers too, often playing an essential part as a central stabilizer for the whole building, had to be built very solidly. There is no denying the power and effect of many Romanesque buildings; particularly by contrast with much later medieval building, there is a strict order and stark simplicity about buildings like the abbey church at Vézelay or the *Abbaye aux Dames* at Caen, which is extraordinarily powerful.

The change of style into the developed Gothic architecture of the twelfth and thirteenth centuries came largely from the finding of technical solutions to the problem of how to carry the weight of the roof. The development of the fanned vault enabled all the pressure to be concentrated on certain points where it could be balanced by flying buttresses. Walls could be built much more lightly, pillars no longer needed to be so massive, and with the development of the pointed arch much greater height came to be possible. Moreover, with the whole structure of the walls no longer acting as the main support of the roof, large windows became a possibility and the way was open for the whole art of stained glass.

The architectural revolution was very sudden, and the number of new cathedrals built, and old ones largely destroyed to make place for the new style, suggests an age almost intoxicated with its sense of a new-found technical mastery expressing itself in the glorification of the old religion. The process has been often held to have started with the reconstruction of the abbey of S. Denis under Suger in the eleven-forties, and to have reached its culmination, again in Paris, with the completion of *Notre Dame* and the *Sainte Chapelle* a hundred years later. The intervening years had seen great cathedrals rising at Sens and Laon, Bourges and Chartres, Rheims and Amiens, and many others as well. Even the order of their construction unconsciously mirrors the growth of royal power in France; political and architectural change alike started in Paris and reached out to affect all France. The Gothic cathedrals reveal a society with faith in God, the monarchy, and itself.

10

The Church Triumphant

One hundred and twenty-five years had separated the accession of Gregory VII in 1073 from that of Innocent III in 1198. It had been a period of astonishing growth in the history of the Church. It had seen the triumph of Hildebrandine ideals in the Investiture Contest and their successful defence against Barbarossa, the birth and highest achievements of the crusading movement, at Cîteaux the last great flowering of monasticism before the Reformation, the formation of the first universities, a start to the building of the finest Gothic cathedrals. All these had been movements within the Church, and they had been accompanied by a corresponding growth in the moral prestige and authority of the Church as an institution. The Hildebrandine reformers had conquered because their cause really had been associated in men's minds with righteousness, and no man in history has been better able to speak for the conscience of Europe than S. Bernard in the twelfth century.

The Papacy had shared to the full in this growth. The process by which the moral authority of the Church had advanced, and that which extended the authority of the Papacy over the Church, had been largely one and the same. It had been aided by the attention which was paid in the twelfth century to the formulation of a code of law which should be one and the same for all parts of the Church. The most important development in this formulation of a Canon Law was the collection made about 1140 by a monk called Gratian at Bologna, the great centre for the study of law. The *Decretum*, as it was called, drew heavily on existing compilations of the laws and customs of the different parts of the Church, but Gratian also made use of the old imperial law. It was natural enough for a writer of the twelfth century to look back to Roman Law as the best law, but the effect of so doing was considerable. The Roman Empire had been an autocracy, and the *Decretum* was used as the basis for the development of the Canon Law over the next hundred years. Thus the law of the Church also came to point more and more to the Church as a centralized monarchy under the Pope. In exactly the same way Roman

Law was to assist the growth of strong secular monarchies. Innocent III himself, and the most powerful of his predecessors and successors, were all experienced lawyers.

The tendency to centralization would have made itself felt even without the aid of Gratian and the canonists. For 'righteousness' within the Church demanded some degree of centralization. The chief danger to the Church in an age when churchmen were extensively used by all kings and powerful landowners, was that it should come to be too much dominated by them. Kings indeed expected that 'their' churchmen would show a proper favour to their interests; the story of Henry II and Becket is a good illustrations of this. Only if there was an authority in Rome to which in the last resort disputes could be referred, could the Church hope to be independent and to do justice impartially. Time would reveal that centralization had its own dangers, but it was the answer to the particular problems of the twelfth century. An outward sign of the new unity in the Western Church was the series of three Lateran Councils (1123, 1139, 1179) held during the century. These councils were attended by delegates from every part of the Church, but they met in Rome and were presided over by the Pope, who determined who should be invited from each country. The decrees of the councils were accepted everywhere in the West. The Lateran Councils thus served a double purpose: they gave an impressive display of Catholic unity, and they enabled the Papacy to impose its policy on the rest of the Church. Nor were they only concerned with clerics. The Third Lateran Council in particular was equally concerned with the laity, and included among its decrees prohibitions of such secular occupations as usury and jousting.

The pontificate of Innocent III (1198–1216) saw the completion of this process. It is fair to regard it as the highest point reached by medieval papacy. Seen in retrospect everything before it seems to find its logical fulfilment there, while after it signs of decay are very soon evident. It must, therefore, be examined in some detail.

Cardinal Lothar became Pope Innocent III on the same day his predecessor Celestine III died. He had apparently everything to recommend him for his office; even his exceptional youth (he was thirty-seven at the time of his election) must have seemed a desirable contrast to Celestine, who had been ninety-two when he died. Innocent was a skilled canon lawyer, who had been in the papal court for some years. He was vigorous and intelligent, with a supple enough mind to be prepared to think out new methods to deal with new problems as they arose. His previous career had given him a good knowledge of the papal administration and the problems of European diplomacy. His qualities were perhaps those of the administrator rather than the saint; in a later age he might have made an excellent managing director of a large-scale industrial combine. But this was no criticism of his suitability as pope. The work of his predecessors had made the Church so large and complicated an organization that administrative ability was an essential for anybody who sought to control it. The disastrous consequences of making pope one who had only holiness to recommend him were shown in the next century by Celestine V, whose sanctity reduced the Papacy to chaos in one year (1294–1295). But if Innocent had an essentially practical ability, he had a genuine personal religion and a desire to benefit the Church as a whole rather than to exalt himself. Moreover, he had a rare gift for recognizing in others qualities he himself lacked; S. Francis was the administrator's nightmare, but Innocent recognized his real spiritual quality at their first meeting.

In the world of politics Innocent's policy had many great successes, some of which have been shown in other chapters. The young papal ward, Frederick II, was secured in the *Regno*, and when Otto IV showed signs of dominating the Italian scene Innocent took a prominent part in the diplomacy which preceded Bouvines and his utter ruin. When Frederick was installed as emperor he owed his throne very largely to the Papacy, though the future was to show that gratitude was not a part of his nature. The humiliation of King John of England in his conflict with the Papacy was a striking tribute to the new power of the Popes. Even Philip Augustus, the most powerful of European monarchs, was compelled to take back his queen Ingeborg rather than risk a papal interdict. Aragon, Portugal, and Hungary all became at least in name papal fiefs. Only in Norway was the papal headship of the Church not effective in practice as well as theory. The Papacy seemed in a fair way to becoming what since Gregory VII she had claimed to be, the moral guardian of Europe, capable of disciplining even the strongest rulers when they transgressed God's laws or violated His Church.

That this position was so nearly achieved can be put largely to the credit of Innocent himself. Of course he was aided by the stock of moral prestige which had been gradually accruing since the first Cluniac reforms in Rome, but the twentieth century has shown clearly enough that good intentions accompanied by political weakness cannot achieve much. So long as the Papacy remained politically unable to control even its own Italian lands, its position as an independent moral authority was bound to be uncertain. How, for instance, could the decrees of the Third Lateran Council which aimed at securing the impartial election of a new pope by the College of Cardinals be fulfilled, if there was nowhere the College could meet where they might not be subject to the direct pressure of a ruler anxious to secure a new pope favourable to himself? On his accession there was no part of the so-called papal territories that Innocent could really call his own. Rome itself and the various cities of the Campagna all had different governments and pursued independent policies. Innocent started with Rome, then under an anarchical constitution of fifty-six senators, all elected annually. By degrees he was able to replace this by a system over which he himself had full control. In place of the fifty-six he set up one senator chosen by a limited body of electors, known as *mediani*, over whom he established his influence. It was not easy; in 1203 he was forced to withdraw from Rome for a time to escape physical violence. But he was helped by the fact that not even the Romans wanted perpetual anarchy, and by the real threat he could make of withdrawing the Papacy from Rome and making it an insignificant city. The steadily increasing body of papal administrators, bringing wealth and prestige to Rome, gave the citizens a powerful vested interest in the Papacy, however much they might dislike its political control. Having established himself in Rome, Innocent went on to try to extend his control over the rest of what had been the papal lands, known as the Patrimony of S. Peter. He managed to do this, and then tried to establish papal control over the Duchy of Spoleto and the March of Ancona, so as to build up a thick belt of papal territory right across the centre of Italy. He did not succeed in getting either firmly under his control, but papal influence was made powerful in both. It is easy to condemn Innocent for these ventures in Italian politics, and certainly there was the danger that by forcing the Papacy to indulge more freely in them he might lead the Vicar of Christ to seem nothing but another Italian politician. But this is only a part of the truth. If he had not undertaken them the Papacy would have become a pawn in Italian politics or the puppet of whichever of the great powers came to dominate Rome. This would hardly have increased its spiritual prestige.

Innocent did much too to improve the working of the papal Curia, now the central judicial and administrative body of the whole Western Church. The success of such a body would depend on the quality of the men who could be got to serve in it; good men must receive an adequate reward. The expenses of the Curia thus became a serious problem, which Innocent sought to solve in two main ways. He taxed the clergy throughout Europe, and, since it would be unfair for the clergy to pay a double taxation to kings and popes, he forbade secular rulers to tax their clergy without papal permission. He also extended the system of Provisions, by which the Papacy claimed the right to fill a large number of offices throughout the Church with men of its own choice. Very frequently the man so 'provided' remained in Rome, and got a deputy to perform the duties of the office in return for a lower salary. Papal provisions in the reign of Innocent were normally used for excellent purposes, the proper staffing of the Curia or the encouragement of learning. It is not easy to see how else the Papacy could have financed these activities. But both Provisions and the immunities claimed for the clergy had dangerous possibilities for the future. As taxation grew in the kingdoms of the West, laymen were bound to ask why clerics should share in the security of the kingdom without paying for it, while no absentee bishop or rector was likely to be popular. The seeds of future anti-clericalism were being sown.

In the same way the extension of the Curia brought its own dangers. Innocent himself loved justice, and it is probably true to say that in his day the papal courts gave better justice than could have been obtained from any local courts. But even in his own day what later were to become the notorious defects of the papal court were visible. These were threefold—delay, corruption, and luxury. The sheer size of the organization the Papacy was creating helped to make it unmanageable. The distance of the courts from most of those who used them and the bulk of business they had to handle meant intolerable delays; it was possible for Giraldus Cambrensis, pleading for the rights of the archbishopric of S. Davids, to spend much of his life going to and from Rome, or waiting for a decision there. Honest as Innocent himself was, it must have been impossible for him to keep a check on the honesty of all his officials, and under a less efficient pope of less integrity the position might be much worse. It did not take long for the idea to get about that the best way to get things done was to grease the right palms. 'And the poor man went away and sold his cloak and his tunic and all that he had, and gave to the cardinals and the doorkeepers and the chamberlains. But they said, "And what is this among so many?" And they cast him out, and he going out wept bitterly and could not be comforted.' The 'Gospel of the Silver Mark' is a savage parody, but it seems to have been based on a bitter truth. Finally there was luxury. It was no doubt right that due respect should be shown to God's representative on Earth, but the danger was always present that he would forget that his task was to be the *Servus Servorum Dei* and concentrate instead on the outward trappings of power. This temptation was not to be resisted by many of Innocent's successors. Yet when all is said it is hard to blame Innocent for the failings of later popes. The system he brought to its peak was the answer to many of the earlier troubles of the Church, and as operated by him it served the Church well.

The Fourth Lateran Council summoned by the pope in 1215 saw a big step forward in the production of a reasonable Canon Law for laity and clergy alike. Many of its enactments were obviously sensible. Some imposed a stricter discipline: many Benedictine monasteries for instance stood in urgent need of reform, and they were now made subject to a system of mutual inspection copied from Cîteaux. Others relaxed harsh or unworkable laws. For example the laws of consanguinity, which laid down the degrees of relationship within which the Church would not permit marriage, had become an abuse. In some villages where everybody was distantly related to everybody else legal marriage had become almost impossible, and the laws had become merely an underhand way of raising revenue. The new laws did away with the more remote prohibitions, and could be seriously enforced. A basic minimum of religious observance was now to be demanded from the laity: they are, for instance, to go to confession and to receive Communion at least annually. Later the Canon Law was again to become an abuse; by the end of the thirteenth century, after later legally-minded popes such as Gregory IX and Innocent IV had finished with it, it had again become over complicated. But 'Abusus non tollit usum'; if a centralized Church was to exist at all it must have a code of laws, and Innocent III should not be blamed for the failings of his successors.

Innocent is frequently accused on two other scores. By his proclamation of the Fourth Crusade he is said to have brought about the ruin of the crusading movement, and by his treatment of heresy needlessly to have stained the history of the Church with cruelty and persecution. There is something in both accusations, but neither charge is as simple as it looks at first sight.

It is not surprising that Innocent should have wanted to renew the Crusade. For over a hundred years crusading had been *the* Christian activity. For all those who for one reason or another were not suited to the cloister it offered both the most direct way of serving God in this life and the surest hope of salvation in the next. Moreover, it was one activity in which Christians of different lands could unite. A successful Crusade controlled by the Papacy—for since the failure of the Third Crusade royal enthusiasm in this direction had waned—would be a most impressive demonstration of that spiritual unity transcending all temporal disunities which was nearest to Innocent's heart. Probably too even from the beginning he had in mind the Eastern Church, whose very existence defied the unity of the Church. The defeat of Muslim power after all was in its interest as well as his, even if until now Byzantium had shown more interest in the Muslims in Asia Minor than in regaining the Holy Places. If the West could perform this great service for the East, might not the Eastern Christians be led to accept papal leadership of the Church, so that there might in truth be one fold and one shepherd? Moreover, the strategic situation seemed not at all unfavourable to crusading. The death of Saladin in 1193 had removed at the same time by far the greatest Islamic commander and a powerful factor for unity in the Muslim world. When the pope heard in 1199 that the counts of Flanders and Champagne were thinking in terms of another crusade, he had no hesitation in encouraging them and putting the movement under his protection.

Yet the position was not really favourable for the renewal of crusading. The experience the West had gained through the Latin crusading kingdoms had done much to dampen the earlier fervour, by demonstrating that coexistence with Islam was perfectly possible and could be highly profitable. By the beginning of the thirteenth century Christian merchants were trading regularly with Muslim ports; the last thing they wanted to see was a renewal of the 'hot war'. It is clear too that the religious impulses behind the movement had been ebbing. The motives which had inspired the leaders of the First and Second Crusades had been largely religious; it is difficult to feel the same about Philip Augustus in the Third. From the beginning both religious zeal and the hope of gain had inspired the crusades, but by the end of the twelfth century the latter was dominant. In so far as it was, there was always a grave danger that crusades would be diverted from the Holy Land, far from the richest area of the Near East, to some more profitable field. Earlier crusaders had only with difficulty resisted the lure of Byzantium whose fabulous wealth was a grave temptation. It was not likely that this temptation would be resisted now if they came under its influence again.

The original strategy of the crusade would not have exposed

them to the danger. It was planned to make a direct attack by sea on Egypt, now the centre of Muslim power in the Near East. A decisive victory there should bring as one of its fruits Christian control of Palestine. This was sound strategy, but before it could be put into effect the crusaders had to get hold of a fleet from somewhere; neither Innocent nor the northern knights who made up the bulk of the crusaders could provide one from their own resources. Fortunately the Republic of Venice proved willing to hire out a fleet, and the aged doge Enrico Dandolo took the Cross. There was never a more improbable crusader. Dandolo was over the age of ninety, and completely blind. But his physical infirmities did not stop him having a very shrewd business head. Venice lived by her trade, and her commercial welfare was his only motive in crusading. The terms he drew up with Boniface of Montferrat, who had become the temporal leader of the expedition, were extremely harsh. The crusaders were to pay 85,000 marks before sailing. If they made any conquests Venice was to be entitled to half of them. It is unlikely that Dandolo ever had any intention of transporting the expedition to Egypt. The trade with Alexandria had already become the main route by which the spices, cinnamon, and indigo of the East reached western markets. It was a trade of great value both to the Muslim Egyptian merchants who transported the goods from the Red Sea, and to the western merchants who finally marketed them. Moreover, Venice had established a favoured position in the trade. She maintained a permanent embassy in Egypt, and handled most of the trade in her own ships. Dandolo was not the man to imperil so valuable an asset by any ill-conceived military exploit. As it happened he was provided with an excuse for altering the arrangements. The zeal of the crusaders had outrun their financial sense, and they were not able to produce more than about fifty thousand marks of the sum required. If Enrico was to be required to transport the crusade at a cut rate, might he not be able to have a say in where it went?

At the same time events elsewhere showed a far more desirable target. In 1195 the unfortunate and incompetent Eastern emperor Isaac II had been deposed in a palace revolution by his own brother, who now ruled as Alexius III. While Isaac had had his eyes put out and was kept a strict captive, his son, another Alexius, had escaped to the West. While the Fourth Crusade was in preparation he was touring western courts in an attempt to gain support for an attempt to restore his father to the throne. In return he was lavish in promises of rewards and of the crusading he might do in the future.

He received a particularly cordial reception from Philip of Suabia, his brother-in-law, who undertook to put a new idea to his cousin, Boniface of Montferrat. Why should the Crusade not sail to Byzantium, rather than Egypt, and restore Isaac? The financial pickings of the Eastern Empire would be richer than anything Egypt could offer, and if the Byzantines were not exactly Muslims, they were at any rate schismatic Christians who might by this means be induced to accept the rule of Rome. This revised itinerary received Dandolo's enthusiastic support. Relations between Byzantium and Venice had been very bad since 1171, when the Emperor Manuel had expelled the Venetian merchants and confiscated their property. Venice's rival Pisa now controlled most of the Byzantine trade, and the doge saw an opportunity of reversing this state of affairs. It was decided that the Crusade should have Byzantium as its first objective; only a small minority refused to agree and sailed direct for Palestine.

It will be seen that Innocent's responsibility for the diversion was small. He never agreed to it, and was fully aware that the Crusade was being twisted to strange purposes. In 1202, before its new destination had been made clear, the Crusade on its way down the Adriatic had stopped to destroy the port of Zara. Zara was a Christian town—but it was a trade rival to Venice. Innocent excommunicated those who had taken part in the operation; his action was ineffective, but does something to clear him of the responsibility for the outrage.

In July 1203 the Crusade reached Byzantium. Alexius III prudently withdrew, and what was left of the Emperor Isaac was reinstated to rule jointly with his son, Alexius IV. This restoration was only to last seven months. To the cultivated Greeks of the city these Latins seemed no less rude and uncouth than their predecessors of the first Crusade. They objected to the open contempt the crusaders showed for the Orthodox religion, often taking the form of mocking at their bearded priests. Not unnaturally they could not take the pretensions of these so-called crusaders seriously, and they resented having an emperor foisted upon them by the sheer force of western arms. From the Latin side there was growing resentment at the failure of Alexius IV to implement any of the promises he had made while he was persuading them to undertake his cause. They had been promised rich rewards, if they restored him; they had done so, but now he seemed to have lost interest in them. A period of great tension ended in complete disaster. In February 1204 a rising of the Greek population led to the murder of both Isaac and Alexius, and the installation of a new emperor (Alexius V) who was openly anti-Latin in his aims.

At this the Latin army lost patience and successfully stormed the city. Its capture was followed by a disgraceful orgy of looting, arson, and rapine. The crusading army, whose discipline had steadily deteriorated during the months of enforced idleness in the suburbs, lost all control and indulged themselves to the full.

The sack of Byzantium is the most shameful episode in the whole history of the Christian West. When the smoke had cleared it could be seen that these knights dedicated to the service of Christ had succeeded in destroying much of the most populous and cultivated city of Christendom. Byzantium had preserved intact many of the most precious riches of the classical world for nine hundred years; now the greater part of them were destroyed. Nor did it even achieve its purposes from the western point of view. It had been planned to replace the destroyed empire with a new Latin Empire of Constantinople. This was set up under Baldwin, Count of Flanders, but it was to have a short and unhappy existence. It never succeeded in winning the outlying provinces of the Empire or in commending itself in any way to the Greek population. It could only be maintained by constant help from the West, and none lamented its passing in 1261. It had been hoped that the destruction of the Byzantine Empire would lead to a reunion of the Eastern and Western Churches, for the new Patriarch of Constantinople was to be in communion with Rome. In practice it had exactly the reverse effect. What the Greeks had seen of Latin Christianity in action made the hope of reunion between the Churches far more distant. That a crusade could turn to this finally discredited the crusading movement; in the future it was only a man like S. Louis, living almost consciously in the past, who could recapture any of the old religious fervour for serving God with the sword. The Fourth Crusade weakened the defences of Europe in the East, defences which had stayed intact for a thousand years. That Constantinople fell to the Turks in 1453 must be blamed at least in part on the Fourth Crusade. On the other side of the balance Venice alone would seem to have profited, and that only in the comparatively short run. In the political arrangements made in 1204 Dandolo secured for his city the concession of a large portion of Constantinople and a variety of trading outposts in the eastern Mediterranean, so that her control of eastern trade was for the time secure. He at least emerges from the events of 1203–1204 having shown shrewd intelligence; the rest of the crusaders had been both wicked and stupid.

The Fourth Crusade was a catastrophe which disfigures Innocent's pontificate. But it was not a catastrophe for which he was in any direct way responsible. He had censured the attack on Zara and been horrified by the destruction of Byzantium. If subsequently he had welcomed the establishment of the Roman Church in the East, it was as one who sought to find a silver lining to the cloud. At worst he can be blamed for an error of judgement. A really far-sighted man might have foreseen some of the consequences which followed from the proclamation of another crusade so soon after the failure of the previous one. But the idea that crusades were beneficial was so embedded in the minds of the churchmen of his day that to have refused his blessing to a crusade that was already in the making would have required exceptional intelligence and determination. Judged by normal standards Innocent cannot be blamed for the Fourth Crusade.

The other accusation against him relates to his treatment of heretics, and can only be judged in the context of the attitude of the medieval Church as a whole to heresy. The Middle Ages are still sometimes referred to as the Age of Faith. The term is suspect; too often it is the preface to grossly unhistorical adulation. But if interpreted strictly, it is true. One of the characteristics of western Europe from 800 to 1500 is that at any period the vast majority of its inhabitants belonged to the same Roman Church and held, with very varying degrees of intensity, the same set of Christian beliefs. Yet it could not be expected that there should be no deviations from those beliefs. In areas such as reconquered Spain or Sicily, Muslims were often to be found, and Jewish communities were settled in many lands; detested by the local inhabitants as the murderers of Christ, they were often valued by rulers on economic grounds. But besides these there were always some at every period who, while being Christians, held different beliefs from those of the Roman Church. In the early years, before 1000, they were very few in number; the occasional heretic like Gottschalk is regarded with horror largely because he is such a peculiarity. The reason for this lack of heretics is clear. Heresy demands the formulation of new beliefs, and this in itself demands a certain level of education and intelligence. It was very difficult for doctrinal heresy to grow up in a society of illiterates; the main problem of the Church in such an age was to check the grosser superstitions surviving from paganism. In matters of belief men were content to accept the Church's beliefs more or less on trust. The reasons for them, or the possible objections to them, were alike beyond them.

But after 1000 heresy comes to be an ever-increasing problem to the Church. It is as well at the outset to draw a distinction between two main aspects of the problem. On the one hand there were the heresies which were of their very nature intellectual. Once active minds got to work on complicated Christian ideas such as the Trinity or the Atonement, they were almost bound to stray into heresy. Others were led into heresy by too close an attachment to pagan thinkers, such as Aristotle. Such heretics were treated with lenience by the Church. In extreme cases, when faced by an intractable spirit like Peter Abelard, the Church might burn heretical books, forbid their authors to write in future, or subject them to short periods of restraint. But such cases were rare, and there is in any case a considerable difference between burning a book and burning a man. On the whole the Church preferred to meet such heretics with their own methods of argument and persuasion. The universities, institutions where freedom of discussion was almost bound to lead to heresy, were themselves actively encouraged by the Church. Innocent III was perhaps the greatest of the patrons of the University of Paris. There were two reasons for this lenience. Firstly the Church needed the live and speculative minds which the academic life would breed; the theology of the Church itself was soon to reflect the results of discussions which could not have taken place had not somebody propounded heresy. Secondly the particular type of heresy thus produced could only appeal to a small minority of people; they were no more likely to corrupt ordinary people than today a mistaken view of thermodynamics would be likely to corrupt public morals.

It was far otherwise with the other type of heresy, which set out to exercise a popular appeal. Here the Church took a much sterner line, for the salvation of many souls might be at stake. There were two main varieties of such heresy current in the twelfth century: their followers were known respectively as the Waldenses and the Albigenses. In their origins the two movements were quite different but since they existed at the same time and largely in the same areas it is understandable that the Church was often confused between them.

The Waldenses took their name from a certain Peter Waldo, a merchant in Lyons in the twelfth century. Dissatisfied with the life of the Church around him, he had gathered together a group of like-minded men to lead a life of austerity, to read the scriptures, and to expound them to each other. Originally they had no intention of doing anything other than making themselves better Christians; certainly they had no conscious intention of separating from the

Church. But their very existence constituted a criticism of the genuine defects of the Church. Their austerity was a criticism of the luxury and opulence in which many prelates lived; their preaching to each other was a criticism of the fact that no one preached the Gospel to them. It is significant that the Waldenses, and similar groups found in Italy and Flanders, were all associated with towns. By the twelfth century the Church was confronted in the towns by a new problem, the problem of the educated layman. The simple methods of authority suitable enough for ignorant peasants were not sufficient for them, but the Church had not yet provided her own answer. The Waldenses could not hope to be popular with the clergy, any more than John Wesley could hope to be popular with the clergy of the eighteenth-century Church of England. But in both cases the wrong answer was applied. Persecution turned a potential asset into a heretical movement. Local diocesan bishops forbade the groups to meet, and under persecution the Waldenses naturally enough produced genuinely heretical ideas. Originally they had believed only in the desirability of godly poverty (did not the Church advocate this in the monasteries?) and in the value of a study of the Scriptures (could the Church deny this?). Under persecution from clerics they came to hold that the priesthood itself was wrong; all true believers must be priests. And from that they went on to an attack on the doctrines of the Mass. By the time that Innocent III proscribed them they were clearly heretical, but the Church itself had made them so.

The Albigenses, sometimes known as the Cathars, have a very much longer history behind them. They have been traced back through various Balkan sects, such as the Bogomils in the tenth century, to the eastern portions of the Roman Empire, and there seems little doubt that they go beyond it and find origin in the Zoroastrian religion, the state religion of Persia in the early centuries of the Christian era. Zoroastrianism was in strong contrast to Christianity. Where the Christian believed that there was one good God who had created the World and all that was in it, the Zoroastrian believed that there were two. The one was pure good and pure Spirit; the other was pure evil and wholly Matter. Man is a combination of the work of both gods, doomed to a conflict between his spirit and his body. There are great advantages in this theory of dualism. It gives, for instance, a much simpler explanation of the undoubted presence of Evil in the World than the difficult Christian doctrine of the Fall of Man. But it cannot really be combined with Christianity. To take only one example, the Christian believes that

'God was made flesh and dwelt among us'; to a dualist this is the equivalent of saying that the good God became bad, an impossible statement. Nevertheless the attempt had been widely made, and the early history of Christianity is riddled with such dualist sects.

The Albigenses were the descendants of these sects. Unlike the Waldenses, they were never within the Roman Church, and always sought to make converts from it to their own Church. This Church grew rapidly, particularly in the south of France; at the time of the Second Crusade Pope Eugenius III had been shocked at its wide spread, and had sent S. Bernard to preach in the area; the Albigenses, however, had withstood even this drastic remedy. Their success there seems to have two main causes. To judge from the letters of Innocent III the clergy of that part of the Church contained particularly bad examples of the prevailing faults of the Church. 'Blind men, dumb dogs who know not how to bark . . . hence is the insolence of the heretics . . . the Archbishop of Narbonne has a purse instead of a heart . . . in his diocese monks and canons cast habits aside and take wives.' Confronted by this, the appeal of a Church which could offer a class of '*perfecti*', living a life of the greatest asceticism, is clear. Moreover, the Albigenses could appeal to both types of religious temperament. The spiritual elite, the *perfecti*, were offered a most vigorous life of self-denial, even in some cases to the point of suicide by starvation. But the ordinary run of believers did not take the ceremony of initiation, the *Consolamentum*, until they were on their deathbeds. They could have the hope of salvation without the inconvenience of lifelong mortification. The second cause of their success was that in southern France they had found an area where the secular authorities were not actively hostile. The counts of Toulouse had long found it expedient to allow their subjects to follow very different faiths in peace. It already formed an area almost unique in medieval Europe, where synagogue and mosque stood unmolested alongside the church; the addition of another church did not raise any new issue.

Most of our knowledge of the Albigenses comes from Catholic, and, therefore, hostile, sources, but even allowing for this it does not seem that the Church can be blamed for wanting to do away with them. A belief which taught that the Christ of the gospels was an apparition, which hated the whole idea of the sacraments with their assumption that matter could be used for spiritual purposes,

---

[1] Quoted from A. Luchaire, *Innocent III. La Croisade de Albigeois*. Paris, 1911. pp. 23-24

which preferred abortion to birth and taught that marriage was a grave sin and which held the Roman Church to be a chief instrument of the Evil God, could not really expect acceptance Innocent III tried to deal with the problem in two ways, by force and by persuasion. The only question is whether he should have relied only on the latter.

In a sense Innocent's whole campaign to raise the standards of the Church by imposing a centralized discipline on it was an attack on heresy by removing one of its main causes. But the foundation of the Dominican Order and the Albigensian Crusade were more particularly aimed at Albigensian heresy. At first he had hoped to check heresy by reforming the Church in southern France, with the help of the preaching friars, without calling in the help of force. But results were slow, and repeated requests to Count Raymond VI of Toulouse to ban heresy in his domains had little effect. Raymond indeed was in an unenviable position: he could foresee the results which might follow if Innocent were to excommunicate him, but if he started to drive on heresy he would plunge his lands into civil war. A special legate, Pierre de Castelnau, was appointed to see to the extirpation of heresy in Provence. In 1207 on his advice Raymond was excommunicated and his lands put under a papal interdict. The immediate results were satisfactory. Raymond, conscious no doubt of greedy if orthodox Christians around his lands, submitted at once and promised to take all necessary measures against heresy. But in the next year Castelnau was murdered by a Provençal squire; there is no reason to suppose that Raymond had anything to do with it. Innocent immediately assumed his guilt, and most unwisely proclaimed the Albigensian Crusade. All those who took the Cross and took part in the deposition of the again excommunicated count were to have full spiritual benefits. The offer was taken up with enthusiasm by the land-hungry knights of northern and central France. It offered a far greater prospect of quick gain for much less risk than the old-fashioned type of crusade to the Holy Land. Nothing that Raymond could do could save Provence. He did penance for the crime he had not committed, he even tried to demonstrate his orthodoxy by taking the Cross himself, but to no avail. Innocent himself tried to stop the movement he had so rashly provoked; the French barons would not listen to him. The 'Holy War' turned into a series of particularly brutal massacres, such as the notorious massacre of Béziers in 1209. In these it was impossible to distinguish between Catholic and heretic. The only distinction was between northerner and southerner, and many

Catholics were butchered. Nor was it only the lands of the Count of Toulouse that were affected. The Kingdom of Aragon had fiefs north of the Pyrenees, and these too were attacked. When King Peter II tried to come to the aid of his vassals, he was killed at the battle of Muret in 1213. The Fourth Lateran Council in 1215 had to accept a *fait accompli*, and recognize Simon de Montfort, the leader of the barons from the North, as the new Count of Toulouse. Unfortunately even this was not the end of the fighting. Raymond's son was to attempt a comeback, and fighting was to drag on until 1229. In the end it was the French monarchy which alone profited from the Albigensian Crusade. Raymond VII was allowed to keep a much reduced county, but most of the lands of the south passed under the direct control of the French crown, which had wisely kept clear of the original venture. But by the time that happened one of the most precious of medieval cultures had been irreparably smashed.

It would not be true to say that the Albigensian Crusade ruined the crusading movement; that had already been done by the Fourth Crusade. But this turning of Christian on Christian in licensed butchery did great damage to the whole idea of Christendom, and to the Papacy which had started it. It is true that it solved the particular problem of the Albigensian heresy. By the time the crusaders and the inquisitors who came in their wake had finished, there were no Albigenses. But the damage which had been done to the moral authority of the Papacy made this too expensive an achievement. The Papacy's position depended in the last resort on its association with righteousness; episodes like Innocent's two crusades gravely threatened this association.

Yet it is less easy to be certain of Innocent's own responsibility for what had happened. As with the Fourth Crusade, his original motive had been to establish more firmly the unity of Christendom. Certainly in neither case had he intended anything like what in the end came of it, and when he discovered what was happening in both cases, he did his best to stop them. Here too he can only be convicted of a disastrous mistake.

The two 'crusades' were Innocent's main failures, but it would be wrong to end with them. During his reign two new religious Orders of a strikingly original kind were coming into existence. One, the Franciscans or Order of Friars Minor, was recognized by him in 1210; the other, the Dominicans or Order of Preachers, was not officially recognized as a separate order until just after his death in 1216, but was actively encouraged by him in the period when it was taking shape. Quite different in their original aims and organization, the two orders of friars were alike in representing a revolutionary change in their approach to religion. For eight hundred years the monk had stood as the pattern of the Christian life in its highest form. Whatever services the monasteries may have performed to the rest of society were quite subordinate to their main aim. The monastic life was dominated by the idea of withdrawal from the world in order to serve God in the cloister. The friar stood for a different ideal, the ideal of going out into the world in order to convert and heal it. Bound by the same triple vows of poverty, chastity, and obedience as the monk, the friar was yet far freer to undertake any sort of work which would lead men to God; the whole of the missionary and medical work of the modern Churches has come to reflect this ideal. It has so come to dominate men's minds that in Protestant countries at any rate the older monastic ideal seems largely unintelligible.

S. Francis (1182–1226) and S. Dominic (1170–1221) were sometimes represented by later painters as being in complete agreement in heaven; on earth they differed profoundly in their aims and personalities. S. Dominic has always tended to suffer from comparison with the one medieval saint whose appeal is almost universal. Even the legends told of him have little appeal to this age. S. Francis preaching to the birds has encouraged many an artist in stained glass, sometimes with unfortunate results; the legend of S. Dominic, interrupted in his sermon by the Devil in the form of a sparrow catching him and plucking him feather by feather with suitable execrations, has yet to be represented. Yet his order has performed perhaps even greater services for the Church.

The Dominicans grew directly out of the challenge of heresy in Languedoc. Dominic himself was a Spanish canon who in 1205 had occasion to travel with his bishop through southern France. What he saw there shocked him profoundly: the heretics, encouraged by the luxury and sloth of the Church itself, had all the initiative. Dominic saw that they must be fought with their own weapons. If the Albigensian *perfecti* were austere, then the Church must show that she too could be ascetic. If the heretical preachers were making converts, then the Church too must preach. If the learning of the heretics was showing up the ignorance of the Catholic priests, then the Church too must be learned. So he gathered around him a little body of men, trained to be learned preachers and to go out and meet the heretics on their own ground. At first they had no Rule of their own, but used the most flexible of the existing monastic rules, the Augustinian.

It is impossible to tell how successful they would have been in dealing with the Albigensian heresy; persuasion is necessarily slower than force, and the Albigensian Crusade was started before they had had an opportunity of showing results. But Innocent gave them every encouragement, and he and his successors found many uses for them. There was a grave danger that the Church might lose ground in the thirteenth century, particularly among townsmen and in the growing universities. Monasteries could provide no answer there, but the new order of preaching friars could regain the position for the Church. The penetration of the universities by the Dominicans was so successful that they came to dominate the intellectual life of the thirteenth century. Moreover, their example came to stimulate other branches of the Church. The learning of the Dominicans helped to raise the very low standards of ordinary secular priests; their preaching encouraged others to preach. They played an important part in helping the Church to meet the challenge of a more sophisticated age.

It is perhaps true that the Dominicans never reached the heights of inspired sanctity of the first generation of Franciscans, but it is only fair to add that once the first fervour had worn off they never deteriorated to anything like the same extent. Completely loyal to the Papacy, they remained an invaluable *corps d'élite* for successive popes.

The Franciscans reflect much more clearly the personality of their founder. The son of a wealthy cloth merchant in the Umbrian hill town of Assisi, the early career of Francesco Bernardone is curiously parallel to that of Peter Waldo. It is easy to see that he too was a potential heretic. There is the same revulsion against the materialist values of his class, leading to an exaltation of poverty as an ideal. To Dominic poverty was only a useful piece of strategy in the war against heresy; to Francis, an incurable romantic, it became My Lady Poverty, a fair maiden to be won, and the very centre of his ideals. His conversion to religion came from hearing at Mass the words 'If thou wilt be perfect, go and sell all that thou hast and come and follow Me.' It is only to rich young men that such a message may seem compelling; the poor know too much of poverty already. When this strange figure started gathering around him a small band of friends similarly dedicated to poverty, the Church might easily have condemned them and driven them into heresy. After all their exaltation of poverty could not but be a criticism of that wealthy corporation the Church. But instead at every stage of his career the

Church aided Francis. In his quarrel with his prosperous but incensed father in 1205 it was the bishop of Assisi who befriended him. Five years later, when his companions had reached the number of twelve, Francis had the idea of forming a new religious Order, and went to Rome to get Innocent's permission. It was of course a preposterous notion. It was the pope's declared policy to reduce rather than increase the number of religious Orders, and in any case this strange collection of vagrants were the last people likely to gain such permission. Yet Innocent gave it. In the upper church at Assisi Giotto, himself a Franciscan, has painted one explanation. The mighty pope, sleeping uncomfortably and improbably in his triple tiara, is shown dreaming that the Church itself is falling, and is being supported by the ragged figure at his gates. Perhaps Innocent had recognized in Francis that spark of Christ-likeness without which all his reform and organization would be without value, but it required a great man to back something apparently so alien from all his own organizational techniques.

Whatever his motives, Innocent's decision was one of genius. Backed with papal authority the brothers went out to convert the whole world. Within a few years they had reached every European country, and everywhere they went they made new converts, so that the movement grew like a huge snowball. It created new Orders for those who could not be Friars Minor themselves: in 1212 the 'Poor Clares' for women devoted to the service of plague houses, and later a Third Order for married people. Nor did it stop with Europe. As early as 1214 Francis had visited Morocco to preach to the Moors, and within a few years the friars had pressed deep into Asia. For hundreds of years the attitude of the Church to the non-Christian world had been that of the crusades. Now Francis had shown a new and better way of making the world Christian, at a time when the old policy had broken down finally. Whatever the later failures of the Order, they had given spiritual rebirth to much of Europe.

Francis's triumph was a triumph of the spirit; certainly it owed nothing to organization. The first Rule he drew up for his brethren was little more than a series of quotations from the Sermon on the Mount, and all his life he had a horror of organizing the spirit out of his Order. Yet even in his lifetime there were those who felt that some sort of organization was necessary, and it is hard not to sympathize with them. The vast flood of recruits into the Order brought many unsuited to it; should not something be done to control it? Could an Order now many thousands strong really practise the absolute poverty Francis had wanted? These and similar questions disturbed the Order even in the saint's life. When he returned from the East in 1220 it was to find that his Rule had been replaced by a much more detailed set of instructions and that in many places the friars now owned property. Unable to cope with the new situation he resigned the headship of his own Order. By the time of his death in 1226 the tensions which later were to tear the Order in two were clearly felt. It was perhaps bound to happen, yet it in no way detracts from the greatness of the founder. Two years before his death Francis is said to have received in his body the Stigmata, the wounds of the crucified Jesus. Certainly no man has more clearly shown forth Christ in his life.

The subsequent history of the Franciscans is a sad story. The quarrels between the Spirituals, those who wished to preserve the absolute poverty of the early days of the Order and the Observants who wished to observe the modified Rule, became very bitter. Less than a hundred years after Francis's death Spirituals were actually to be burnt at the stake for practising that very poverty their founder had insisted on. The founder had said that his brethren should not even touch money; it is difficult not to feel that something has gone wrong when arrangements are made for the issue of gloves so that those who handle money should not touch it. Some of the trouble came from the Order undertaking tasks which were no part of its original role. The preaching of the gospel or the tending of hospitals did not need property, but in imitation of the Dominicans the Franciscans had turned themselves into a learned order and sought to rival them in the universities. They were to have great success; some of the greatest names of the universities were to be Franciscans; Duns Scotus, Roger Bacon, and William of Ockham were all Grey Friars. Yet they had deserted their original purpose. Nor were the friars always welcome in the parishes. Quite apart from the fees they might divert into their own coffers from the parish priest, the very liberty of their Order made it difficult to deal with offenders. Chaucer's friar in the *Canterbury Tales* knew the taverns well in every town, and innkeepers better than lepers; there is no reason to think he was very exceptional.

The heights the Order reached at first only emphasize the depths to which it later sank, but it would be wrong to paint too black a picture. One side of their founder's vision at least they preserved. Throughout the thirteenth and fourteenth centuries a steady flow of Franciscan missionaries continued into Asia and Africa, many of them never to return. The Fleming William of Ruysbruk penetrated to the court of the Grand Khan himself, while John of Monte Corvino became first archbishop of Pekin and made a determined effort to convert China to Christianity. The Dominicans soon followed the Grey Friars into this missionary work, which must be counted one of the finest achievements of the mendicant movement. At home the very heavy casualties suffered by the Franciscans in the Black Death suggest that even at that late date the Order was still serving its original purpose in the slums and plague houses of the large towns, where the death rate was highest. On balance the Church gained heavily from these two great Orders of friars and their numerous imitators, and the recognition of their possibilities must be reckoned greatly to Innocent's credit.

A final verdict on Innocent's work must depend on the view that is taken of the desirability of a centralized Church. Possibly the defects which became clear in the course of the next hundred years were the inevitable result of such a system, but it is dangerously easy for the historian to use the word 'inevitable'. The mistakes of men like Innocent IV and Boniface VIII were not the responsibility of Innocent III. He strove to remedy the defects of the Church as he saw it in his day, and in this he was largely successful. The two crusades were disasters, but not disasters for which he was more than partly responsible. He is among the greatest of the medieval popes.

11

Feudalism and its Exceptions

That feudalism was the characteristic form of social organization throughout the Christian West from the time of the barbarian invasions to the Black Death is a historical platitude. But it is much less easy to give any precise summary of what this means. For 'feudal' is a word which is capable of carrying an embarrassingly large number of connotations. For the military historian the Feudal System is the method by which most medieval kings normally furnished themselves with armies, and by which, equally, a rebellious baron could furnish himself with the forces with which to conduct a war with some neighbouring lord, or indeed with his overlord the king himself. For the lawyer it is the general description applied to the nature of the legal relationship—in the last analysis neither that of free men nor that of slaves—which prevailed between man and man throughout medieval Europe. For the economic historian it carries again another meaning, being applied to the method by which by far the greater part of Europe was cultivated for most of the Middle Ages.

So wide a variety of meanings makes feudalism a word difficult to use with any precision, and the imprecise word can easily become meaningless. Yet there is a common factor in all those definitions— that of protection given in return for service. The origin of feudalism in the need for protection in the dark ages of barbarian invasion and internal disorder which followed the disintegration of the classical empire has already been discussed.[1] Here it need only be repeated that commendation was a bargain in which protection by the strong local chieftain was purchased with the military service of those whom he protected. As such it was to continue as the principal form of military organization until at least the thirteenth century. Appropriate symbols were found to express the relationship of lord and man which the bargain involved. By kneeling before his lord and by placing his hands within those of his master, the man could signify his submission to the other's superior power. The subsequent exchange of kisses between the two signified the lord's

[1] See Chapter 1.

acceptance of the new relationship which now prevailed between them; the man had now become the *homme de bouches et de mains* of his lord. On this original ceremony of Homage, wholly pagan in its origin, the Church, as early as the ninth century, imposed the Christian ceremony of Fealty, or faith-pledging, in which the new man, or Vassal, pledged his fidelity to his lord with an oath sworn on some holy relic or on the Gospels.

At first the ceremony of homage was held to confer only lifelong obligations on both sides, but it very soon developed into a hereditary system. Nor is this surprising. The particular circumstances of disorder which gave the most powerful impetus to the spread of feudal commendation disappeared partly with the end of the barbarian invasions, partly with the slower growth of organized monarchies. But a child king, a child lord, or a child vassal had every need of protection in any age, and recognition by all parties of the hereditary nature of vassallage gave some hope that this might be provided. Moreover, the system gave the expectation of stability, of changelessness, after which medieval men hankered in every field.

In a more ordered society the mere fact of physical protection was not always a sufficient inducement to win or retain the loyalty of vassals. Nor could monarchs or great lords hope or wish to support the large numbers of men who were now 'theirs' directly by keeping them at court. Instead there grew up a system of *beneficia* or, to use the commoner term in later periods, of fiefs (*fei*). By this the man received not only the pledge of his lord's protection, but also the grant of a portion of land to hold as his own from his lord. Thus the overlord received at one moment both the means by which he might raise an army, and the means by which he might control much larger areas of land than would be possible by any direct method. The vassal, for his part, received the pledge of enough land to guarantee his position in society in return for services whose extent was constantly being made more precise and limited.

So feudalism provided Europe with ready-made armies of vassal knights, instruments for the constant baronial wars which marked society, and instruments also by which strong suzerains might establish order throughout their lands. For the ordinary military needs of a society in which warfare, if fierce, was normally short, the system worked well. Baronial wars were generally short, often ended by a need common to the men of both sides to go and take in the harvest, and even the invasion of barbarian tribes on the move, such as the Saxons in tenth century Germany, produced crises as short as they were acute.

But feudal armies were not the answer for any warfare that, because of its length or because of its distance from the homeland, required prolonged periods of service. The Crusades cannot be said to have been fought by feudally enlisted armies, while the Hundred Years War required, from England at least, alternative methods of enlistment. Moreover, the growth of specialized branches of the military art, such as archery and, later, artillery, produced a need which a necessarily conservative feudalism could not satisfy. For that matter even infantry, as main line rather than support troops, did not normally find a place in feudal military organization. By the fourteenth century successful armies are tending to become more and more professional.

If a new scale of warfare was tending to render feudal armies out of date, scale was responsible in another way for hastening the end of feudalism. The simple picture by which a man held land from one lord alone did not for long represent the truth. Men might well come in course of time to enjoy widely scattered lands from different lords, and although the widespread use of the device of Liege Homage was an attempt to counteract the muddle arising from these conflicting loyalties by recognizing a superior sort of homage,[1] Liege Homage soon became as common and as liable to confusion as any other. The confusion arising from such events as the Norman conquest of England or the Aragonese incursions into southern France, when men might easily have conflicting loyalties to both of two warring kings, was such that the whole theory of homage came to seem unreal. Only by establishing one supreme loyalty, direct and by all men, to the Crown could the kings of the new nation states cut through the tangle, but in so doing they were killing feudalism. It was not to feudal laws, but to the clear and direct laws of the Roman Empire, that the effective monarchs of the thirteenth and fourteenth centuries turned.

But feudalism was not only a means of providing armies or of spinning a legal web to govern the relationships of lords and their men. It also governed the life of the country villages, the very stuff of which all medieval society was made. The textbook pattern of the medieval manor, with the lord's domain farmed by the labour

---

[1] 'However many lords a man may acknowledge, it is to the one whose liegeman he is that his chief duty lies.' Anglo–Norman customary, c. 1115. Quoted Marc Bloch, *Feudal Society* (English trans.), Routledge, 1961, p. 216.

services of those who held in return holdings in the two or three great fields surrounding the village, is familar enough. So too are the services performed by the lord of the manor through his court, and the various exactions, such as insisting that all corn must be ground in the manorial mill, with which the lord might compensate himself for his services. Great variety existed among the customs of medieval manors, as between different countries, and as between the different areas of the same country. But behind all the customs lay the same principle as animated feudalism in its military aspect. For the service of the plough, by which alone his lord could live, the peasant received his protection, protection in the physical sense from assault, and protection legally in the safe enjoyment of his own holdings. Strictly, of course there is no formal connection between the feudal organization of knight service and the like in the higher reaches of society and the system of dependent agriculture which prevailed at its roots, but the pattern of connection between man and man in both is so similar that in a looser sense both can be described as 'feudalism'.

It should not be thought that the peasant was necessarily the loser by this organization of society. Certainly he was not a free man, but then, in any modern sense, he did not wish to be free, and equally it is certain that he was not a slave, since he had rights both in law and in custom. Moreover, if his status was lowly, he was at least close to that ground from which life itself came. The great ones of the land who accompanied the king to court or on expeditions might well return to find themselves cheated by the unjust stewards they had left behind them. Chaucer's Reeve understood the art of appropriating his lord's goods painlessly to his own use,[1] and in the Middle Ages the landlord, whose position in society compelled him often to become an absentee, lacked the checks and devices of modern accounting to save him from fraud. The peasant lived a life which was full of restrictions, which in the hands of an oppressive lord might well become intolerable, but he did have a high degree of security in the tenancy of the land he cultivated. Often his family survived by centuries the great ones whose lives contained all the hazards of greatness.

Rural society, as might be expected, was not uniform in its characteristics in the different parts of Europe and in the different periods of the Middle Ages. In England, where the Norman Conquest had

---

[1] *Ful rich he was astored prively*
His lord wel coulde be plesen subtilly,
To yeve and lene him of his owne good,
And have a thank, and yet a cote and hood.
                    Chaucer, *Prologue to Canterbury Tales*, ll. 609–612.

imposed royal authority throughout the country as a reality, the Crown could exercise a check on local lords whose exploitation of their rights might mean less for the royal exchequer. In France, where royal authority outside the Île de France was something of a myth until the end of the twelfth century, the right of the local lord to *banalités* was much less questioned; the exclusive right to hire out his wine-press, the right to insist that his horses were used to tread out corn at harvest time, and that his mill was used to grind it, and even sometimes that his oven should be used to bake it into bread, all these and many others too were more frequently found in France than in England or Germany.

Banalités were a source of cash income to the lord. The very emphasis on raising them in the eleventh, twelfth, and thirteenth centuries showed a ruling class which had become intensely interested in money. The spread of the *taille* (tallage) during the twelfth century, a cash payment on land, in theory a 'gift', in practice often imposed in place of discontinued labour services, revealed a similar interest. A perfect Feudal System would have nurtured no such interest.

But if the Feudal System had ever been as systematic as the name implies, this chapter would not need to be written. There is some truth, particularly for the period before 1100, in the idea that feudalism, interpreted in its loosest sense, was an all-embracing system covering the whole of medieval Europe. The vast majority of Europeans were countrymen engaged either in war, the traditional pursuit of the upper classes, or in agriculture and those trades such as milling which are directly dependent on agriculture. But medieval farming differed in one very important respect from its modern counterpart. Today, except in very backward areas, agriculture is directed towards producing goods for a market; for the sake of efficiency production is centred on those crops or stock which the climate and soil of each area favours most, and with the money gained in exchange for their sale the farmer buys not only industrial products he could not hope to make for himself, but also the agricultural products of other areas. This is not the normal medieval pattern. The large medieval estate or manor was self-sufficient to a great degree. The aim of production was to ensure that each area produced enough food to ensure that its own people did not suffer want. Small surpluses might be disposed of and local shortages remedied in small local markets, but there was no thought of the regular import and export of goods in bulk; the very fact that other areas were aiming at self-sufficiency would mean that they had neither the need nor the capital to buy them. Very similar conditions exist today in many parts of India. To a large extent the system was the inevitable result of the conditions which had prevailed during the period of the barbarian invasions. The decline of the Roman system of communications had made the movement of goods in bulk very difficult; the disappearance of towns meant also the disappearance of the most profitable markets; the fall in population had meant that, natural or man-made disasters apart, there was little difficulty in most areas in producing enough to feed the local population, for there was always waste which could be brought under the plough. Just as in law the manor was one unit depending on one manorial court, or in times of disturbance it depended on its own feudal lord for protection, so also in economic matters it was a self-contained unit.

This then is the general picture. Even in the earliest times it is an over-simplification of what was always a more varied reality. Some money rents, pointing to regular production for sale, existed even in the darkest of the Dark Ages; in Italy the urban civilization of Rome, weakened though it was, never disappeared, and the existence of towns is a certain indication of the existence of trade. Even in the north first the Frisians and then some at least of the Vikings, who besides the long boats of war had the broader-beamed craft of trade, lived largely by exchanging the products of one area with those of another.

But, especially from about the beginning of the eleventh century these exceptions gradually became more numerous. Trading systems multiplied; existing towns grew in size and many new towns were founded; a new mercantile Europe comes into being alongside the old world of self-contained rural communities. In terms of numbers the new world was much smaller than the old; probably at no stage of the Middle Ages did more than ten per cent of the whole population live in towns or by trade, and for long manorial economy in many areas could continue almost unchanged by it. But in the end the new was to destroy the old. Some of the reasons for this new growth are clear. More settled conditions removed some of the obstacles to trade; brigandage and piracy remained serious occupational risks, but they were no longer prohibitive. The rising power of the new monarchies supported a trend which, by giving them more money, might further increase their power. The decline of Muslim power in the Mediterranean opened up the possibility of using once more the central trade route of the ancient world. A steady rise in the population meant that in many areas there was no longer an excess of land over people. On the one hand this led to the process of expansion of which the German colonial movement is the best example, on the other it led to a search for means of livelihood which were not dependent on land. The towns which were the result of this search could not be fed by subsistence agriculture, and areas of more specialized and, therefore, more efficient farming came into being producing food for an urban market. With their most vital problem thus solved, the cities could expand even further.

Medieval trade was conditioned largely by the great difficulty of moving heavy goods by land. Paved roads were almost unknown outside the larger towns, and goods had thus to be transported by pack horses or by light two-wheeled carts. Moreover, the multiplication of different feudal authorities, none of them sympathetic to the peculiar needs of the trader, meant that constant internal customs and dues might have to be paid. The cost of moving goods was thus so high that in practice, except in emergencies, only relatively light and expensive goods were worth moving in this way over more than short distances. Furs and spices and high-quality cloth might repay the cost of transport; grain and timber would not. Water transport was much cheaper, but here again there were limiting factors. Until the thirteenth century sea captains did not have the use of the compass; without it and without accurate charts they showed an understandable preference for keeping reasonably near a known coastline. It was for instance not until the fourteenth century that Venice and Genoa, the queens of the Mediterranean trade, thought the hazard of regular voyages to northern ports worth undertaking. The ideal medieval trade route was one that passed for most of its way by sea, yet near a friendly coast, and terminated in a port which gave access to a system of navigable rivers by which goods could be distributed to inland markets.

The commerce of northern Europe was dominated by the trade in cloth which centred on Flanders. Woollen cloth manufacture was *the* industry of the Middle Ages, for it was the only form of manufacture for which there was an almost universal demand. In the absence of cotton and synthetic fabrics its only serious rival was the highly expensive linen. Originally each area made its own cloth; the weaving of cloth was a useful occupation for the women. Even at the height of the Middle Ages, Flanders was far from engrossing all the northern cloth industry; it was still cheaper to make the coarser and less expensive cloths, such as the Suffolk Kerseys, in their own countries. But Flanders became the centre for the manufacture, finishing and sale of the more expensive varieties, and its goods were re-exported to every part of northern Europe and beyond. Many factors account for the rise of the Flemish cloth industry. Flanders provided rich grazing lands on which the sheep which supplied the industry in early days could be raised; there were good deposits of fuller's earth, which was used in the whitening of the wool, and the soil was suited to the cultivation of teasels for raising the cloth and of woad and madder, the standard medieval dyes. There was plenty of water for the washing of the wool. But probably the most important part of the explanation of the rise of Flanders is to be found in the accessibility of the area. It was admirably placed in the centre of its potential market, so that French, English, and German ports were all equally accessible, Bruges itself was an ex-cellently sheltered port, and the flat countryside made it possible for communications within the area to be by water. England came to be the chief supplier of wool to the growing industry when it outran local supplies, and the Anglo–Flemish wool trade was the busiest of all northern trades. Wool was also imported from other sources, even from distant Spain, whose high quality Merino wool was in great demand. Until the trade was interrupted by political causes in the fourteenth century Flanders had no serious rival in the cloth market; it was to continue to be a trade of major importance until the second half of the sixteenth century.

Commerce on this scale had to be supported by industry on an equal scale. During the eleventh and twelfth centuries Flanders became unique in northern Europe as a predominantly urban area. Elsewhere towns were rising as the exceptions in a social scene which remained predominantly rural; here the towns came to predominate and the countryside had the function of supplying food for the towns. Moreover, industry on this scale demanded specialization; as the number of processes to which the wool had to be subjected before it emerged as fashioned cloth grew, so the industry drew further and further away from the original simplicity in which it could be carried on in the cottage homes of people who might well combine it with some other occupation. Now instead of being merely cloth workers, those employed in the industry became dyers or weavers, fullers or spinners as the case might be. Since the various branches of the complete process had to be carried on in close con-nection with each other, it became necessary for large numbers of workers to work in close proximity to each other; the factory system is clearly foreshadowed. Moreover, the growing complexity of many of the processes demanded the use of more expensive machinery, which the small working master with two or three assistants could not afford. They could only be bought by those with capital, and the control of the industry passed into the hands of a small band of rich men. The increasingly complicated task of securing raw materials and arranging the sale of the completed products to distant customers also needed men who possessed not only a close knowledge of foreign markets, but plenty of capital to finance ventures which might not be immediately rewarding. Such a one in the second half of the thirteenth century was Jean Boinebroke of Douai; a man of great substance, he not only owned his own dye-house and tenter-ground, but arranged for the purchase of his own raw materials of wool, madder and woad, going as far away as Northumberland in the search, and used the other members of his own family to act as his agents in overseas sales.[1] He is strangely reminiscent of some Victorian head of a prosperous family business.

Those who did not belong to this charmed circle of wealth found their condition depressed to that of mere wage earners, a proletariat in the Marxian sense of a class who did not own the means by which they produced. There might be considerable differences of status within such a class between the more and less skilled members, but all shared a common insecurity. Fluctuations of trade or interference with the source of their raw materials might deprive them of their jobs overnight. The villein, for all his disadvantages, faced no such danger, and it is scarcely surprising to find that the 'bluenails' of Flanders formed an unstable and potentially revolutionary element in society. Here, if anywhere in the Middle Ages, a genuine class conflict can be seen developing.

If the Flemish cloth trade was the most valuable individual trade of the North, it also did much to encourage several others. Bruges, Ghent, Ypres and the rest had to be fed, and if the largest of them were quite small by modern standards, perhaps not greatly exceeding twenty thousand inhabitants, yet the area as a whole had a total population which could not possibly be supplied by the neighbouring farm lands. Those who farmed in Flanders or near to it were in a highly profitable situation, in which there was a ready market for anything they produced; they were thus able to concentrate on what seemed to be the most profitable lines. By the thirteenth century

---

[1] Quoted from *Cambridge Economic History*, Cambridge U.P., Vol. 2, 1952, p. 381.

Dutch agriculture had already begun to specialize on the dairy produce which has remained its chief export. This tendency increased the need for other sources to supply Flanders with grain and meat. The growth of the Flemish towns and the development of the trade from colonial lands to the East were indeed closely linked; without the markets provided by Flanders the colonial movement could not have gone ahead so fast; without the food the new lands produced the Flemish towns could not have grown so quickly. To add to the connection, much of the manpower to people the East seems to have come as an overflow from Flanders. The methods of farming adopted in the East in the period from 1100 to the Black Death differ markedly from the subsistence agriculture which was normal in the West. The holdings of the settlers were much larger than the normal villein holdings of France or western Germany; labour services were rare, for those who had invested large sums in opening up these lands wished to be repaid in money; the settlers, therefore, had to produce with sales in mind, and they soon found that it paid to concentrate on one or two crops rather than on mixed farming. As in North America until fairly recent times, there was no shortage of land, and the impoverishment of the soil which is the long term disadvantage of single crop agriculture mattered less. Grain, in the form of wheat or the coarser rye, was the chief product of the East, but other areas concentrated on cattle and exported large quantities of salted meat and hides for leather to the West. As the forests were cleared so also large quantities of timber became available, and this too could find a market in the more heavily settled western lands, where forest land was becoming scarce in some places.

All these were bulky goods and difficult to transport, but here geography came to the settlers' aid. The rivers of Germany run from south to north and give easy access to the Baltic and the North Sea. The Elbe and the Oder and their tributaries, and further east still the Niemen and the Vistula, allowed the western settlers, and in the interior those Slavs who had the intelligence to imitate German methods of agriculture, to get their goods to the West at reasonable cost. At or near the mouths of these rivers grew up the largest of the group of trading towns which were later to form the Hanseatic League. Lubeck, for long the greatest of them, was being built in 1158, and was closely allied with the older Hamburg at the mouth of the Elbe. Rostock, Stralsund and Danzig were all founded early in the thirteenth century, and a settlement was even maintained at distant Novgorod, at the eastern end of the Baltic. But the way in which the Baltic trade was linked to Flanders is revealed by the establishment of the western centres of the Hanse towns at the *Kontors* in Bruges and London.

Northern Europe had other important trades, though none to rival the Flanders cloth trade in value or that from the Baltic in bulk. Salt, as the only cheap preservative, had great importance in medieval life; the simplest way of producing it was by the evaporation of sea water, and while much could often be produced locally by mining or in salt pans, German and Dutch fleets regularly went to the natural and artificial pans at the Bay of Bourgneuf on the French Atlantic coast. The difficulty of keeping stock alive over the winter months meant that meat was always rather scarce in the Middle Ages and gave to fish an added importance, increased yet more by the number of fasts, such as Lent, in which the Church forbade the eating of meat. Herrings, preserved by salting or smoking, were exported in large numbers from their shoaling grounds in the Baltic and the North Sea. Wine too became an important trade; it was a common drink of all but the poorest classes, for it was not until towards the end of the period that German beers began to give it serious competition. At first there does not seem to have been much movement of wine, each district for the most part consuming the products of its own vineyards, although the Vikings were occasional traders in French wines. Vines were grown much further north than they are today; it is clear for instance that there were a large number of vineyards in southern England. But wine was not the drink of the poverty-stricken, and while many local vintages continued to be drunk, certain areas established a reputation for quality which justified the extra cost of importing their wines; such were the Rhine and the Moselle, Poitou and Burgundy and Gascony; only in their regard for the sweet wines of Cyprus did the men of the thirteenth century differ from modern tastes. The great expansion of the Gascon wine trade in the twelfth and thirteenth centuries was one sign that Europe was becoming a more affluent society, for only from Bordeaux were wines of high quality available in sufficient quantity for a rapidly expanding market. In the Bordeaux trade English, French, and Bretons all took a part, but they were soon joined by Germans from the Hanseatic towns, so that the wines of Gascony reached the furthest outposts of the Baltic.

Potash and wax from eastern Germany, iron ore from Sweden for the nascent metal industry of Liège and Dinant, lead from the

Mendips and Cornwall—it would be possible to multiply examples of trades in northern Europe which by the thirteenth century were already flourishing. The general pattern of these trades, whether they are concerned with foodstuffs or with the raw materials for industry, is the same. They deal not in exotic goods, but in the essentials of industry and life itself; with the dubious exception of wine, none of them can be considered a luxury. But to this general rule there was one striking exception, the most romantic trade route of them all. As early as the ninth and tenth centuries Scandinavian traders had reached Byzantium by way of the great Russian rivers. This route was possible because the rivers which flow into the Baltic, such as the Memel, the Dvina or the Volkhov, rise comparatively near the Dnieper and the Volga, which empty into the Black Sea and the Caspian. Only a short land haul was necessary; for the rest the journey could be made by water. It was of course very long, and subject to political as well as climatic interruptions; only goods which showed a high profit on their weight were worth transporting in this manner. Originally evolved as an alternative method of reaching Byzantium when the direct approach through the Mediterranean was difficult, this so-called Varangian route gave access also to the Far East. From the Caspian caravan routes led to the Oxus and Samarkand, and by them costly eastern goods could start their journey to the West. The Varangian route brought to Europe the wax and furs of Russia; sable and mink were success symbols in the Middle Ages as today. But it brought also cinnamon and pepper and other spices to the West, where demand always far exceeded supply, with the silks and calicoes which could not be made there, and gold and precious stones. Such goods more than justified the expense and hazards of the journey.

The trade of southern Europe is inevitably linked to the Mediterranean; the decline of Mediterranean trade which had been going on since the third century had been accentuated by the Muslim conquests of the seventh and eighth centuries. Trade between East and West did not entirely cease, but the trickle of coastal traffic moving in fear of Saracen pirates was of little significance to the economies of either region. The trade of southern France and Italy had to be conducted by land and for the most part remained merely local. But by the tenth century the volume of trade was already probably increasing, and by the eleventh Christian control of the Mediterranean had been re-established and more extensive trading systems could be established.

Byzantium had always lived by trade and had never been deterred from trading with her neighbours by religious scruples. Now the Italian ports could share with her in the profitable trade with the Muslim world. The first beneficiaries were the nominally Byzantine cities of southern Italy, such as Naples and Taranto; Venice, also in name Byzantine territory, but with all the practical advantages of independence, came early to share in the trade. In return for the spices and textiles of the East the Italians could export timber and iron goods, which were in short supply in Fāṭimid Egypt; despite ecclesiastical censures the Italians also handled the considerable traffic in Christian slaves, from whom many of the Muslim armies were built. Later the Normans of Sicily came to take an important part in trade, and Palermo became one of the main points of contact between East and West.

During the eleventh and twelfth centuries other Italian cities came to join in the trade with the East, notably Genoa and Pisa. The Crusades certainly helped the process; not only was the carriage of crusaders a profitable business, but Outremer had to use western shipping to export its products. Moreover, by operating in the eastern Mediterranean, the Italian cities came to discover new opportunities. Colonies of Italian merchants appeared in both Christian and Muslim eastern ports, and the trade expanded rapidly in volume. It was the desire of the Doge of Venice to avoid upsetting the lucrative trade with Alexandria and to secure advantageous trading ports in the Empire which led to the disastrous diversion of the Fourth Crusade to Byzantium. The goods handled included valuable spices but they soon covered a wide range; high quality eastern fabrics were imported, some of which carried their names into western vocabularies; gauze for instance came from Gaza, muslin from Mosul and damask from Damascus. Cotton and sugar reached the West by the same route, and dried fruits were imported from the Levant and Palestine in considerable quantities. All these contributed to the rising standard of living of the more prosperous classes in the West.

While Venice, Genoa and Pisa were making themselves rich on the proceeds of the eastern trade a similar expansion was taking place in the industries of Lombardy and, to a lesser extent, Tuscany. Italian manufacturers did something to balance what was probably in terms of bullion always an unfavourable trade. The Lombard towns never concentrated on one industry to the same extent as those of Flanders, but here too cloth was the largest single item. Originally the Italian industry was little more than a finishing industry for cloth which had been woven in Flanders; from the eleventh century Italian merchants were the agents for the resale of Flemish cloth in the Mediterranean countries and further to the east. The Italian cloth towns, however, came increasingly to make their own cloth, and for this purpose native wool was augmented by imports from France and Spain. By the thirteenth century it was even thought profitable to import wool from England and Scotland to Lombardy, eloquent testimony to the high regard in which British wool was held. If the Italian industry never reached the productive size of that of Flanders, the markets it served were even more widespread and the commercial transactions involved of corresponding greater complexity. It is not surprising that Italian bankers became the acknowledged masters of bills of exchange, credit facilities, and the other monetary needs of international trade; Lombard Street in London still recalls this reputation.

Southern Europe knew other industries besides cloth. Venice had a prosperous glass industry from quite early times; metal was worked in Genoa and a number of other towns; Castile exported leather goods in increasing quantities as the reconquest of Spain advanced, and there were many others. The South saw also, as in the North, the development of regions of specialized agriculture where concentration on the production of grain or olives or grapes upset the balance of the old feudal agriculture. Except in backward areas subsistence agriculture was something of a myth in southern Europe well before the Black Death.

It has been convenient to treat the economics of northern and southern Europe separately, but clearly in fact neither was self-contained. Communication between the two was certainly difficult. The passes of the Alps were impenetrable in winter, and the only major river to avoid them and run for much of its course from north to south, the Rhône, was too fast flowing to be easily navigable. The journey by sea through the Straits of Gibraltar and the Bay of Biscay was long and hazardous; Genoese galleys did not regularly attempt it until the second half of the thirteenth century. Before then goods had to travel by land, the Brenner Pass and the Rhône valley being the two most popular routes. Merchants undertaking the journey preferred to seek the security of a convoy, and some half-way meeting place where goods could be exchanged and future orders made was an obvious convenience. This function was performed in the twelfth and thirteenth centuries by the fairs of Champagne. Towns of no great size, such as Troyes with its 'Hot' and

'Cold' fairs and Bar-sur-Aube, gained an importance out of all proportion to their size by holding regular fairs at which the merchants of north and south could meet and transact business. Champagne seems to have been selected for this purpose partly because its central position in Europe made it not too far distant from any of the main markets or centres of production, but partly also for political reasons. It was an area of reasonable order, which was yet distant enough to be outside the effective control of either the French king or the German emperor. The counts of Champagne were sensibly content to let the fairs flourish and bring custom to their lands without seeking to enrich themselves by imposing too heavy tariffs at their expense. Monarchs, with their ever-increasing need of revenue, might not have been so far-sighted; indeed the decline of the Champagne fairs dates from the political annexation of Champagne by Philip the Fair of France at the end of the thirteenth century, and from the Franco–Flemish wars of the succeeding decades.

Enough has now been said to show that medieval trade and the towns which fostered it were no mere unimportant appendage of medieval life. Large communities lived solely by industry and commerce, and there was no part of Europe which did not play its part in a trading system which extended well beyond Europe. Nevertheless it must be remembered that even the greatest cities of the West were small, not only by modern standards but also in comparison with medieval Byzantium, which had perhaps about a million inhabitants. Neither Milan nor Venice, the largest two cities of the West, had as many as two hundred thousand inhabitants even at the peak of their prosperity in the early fourteenth century; that is to say they were rather smaller than modern Plymouth. Palermo may not have come far behind them during the short zenith of it prosperity, but in the north only Paris ever exceeded the hundred thousand mark; the greatest city of Flanders probably never numbered more than sixty thousand even at its zenith. This does not diminish their importance, but it is well to remember that the Middle Ages saw nothing remotely equivalent to the urbanization of life brought by the Industrial Revolution of the eighteenth and nineteenth centuries; medieval towns remained exceptions in a society which was still in the main rural.

The speed with which new towns grew up all over western Europe in the period between 1000 and 1300 remains something of a mystery. Certainly the renaissance of international trade and industry already described has something to do with it. It has been seen that a really large-scale industry, such as was growing up in Flanders, demands a degree of specialization among its workers. To require one man to perform all the processes required to turn raw wool into finished cloth would be hopelessly uneconomic. This in its turn requires that the workers should be congregated close to each other, so that time is not wasted and expense incurred in shifting the uncompleted goods from place to place. Again the very existence of an international trade of any size will tend to create towns at certain key points, such as sea ports or the junctions of navigable rivers; no great understanding is needed to account for the growth of Calais, or of Coblenz at the junction of the Moselle and the Rhine. But there were very few areas in the least like Flanders, and towns were being founded all over western Europe, often far away from the great arteries of commerce.

A variety of explanations have been put forward for the problem, which admits of no one simple answer. An American professor, Carl Stephenson, has argued that the origin of towns is to be sought in the needs of defence: the original meaning of the suffix *burg*, *bourg*, *burgh* attached to so many German, French, or British towns is a stronghold, and very many medieval towns were in fact near sites already occupied by castles. Constructed on positions of defensive strength in the troublous ninth and tenth centuries, such castles could give protection to some at least of the local population in the event of attack. It was, therefore, a wise precaution to build houses near the castle. With the more peaceful conditions which followed a rise in the population took place and *faubourgs* grew up, outside the original *bourg* yet still near to it. There is much to be said for this explanation, which seems to describe the history of many towns. Cambridge is a good example: the oldest part of the town seems to have been on what passes for a strong defensive position in the flat Cambridgeshire countryside, the mound of Castle Hill. This early settlement must have been very small, scarcely meriting the description of a town. From the eleventh century onwards the *faubourg* began to grow on the opposite side of the river, and it was here that most of medieval Cambridge was built and here also that the university later came to find its home. Yet if the theory holds good for Cambridge, it is far from providing an explanation for the growth of all medieval towns; in particular it does not explain why it was precisely in the period when defence was becoming less necessary that the most new towns were founded, for very many of them were genuinely new and not extensions of existing *bourgs*. Nor does it

235

explain why the inhabitants of such towns were so insistent that their status as towns should be recognized. This indeed is at first one of the most puzzling aspects of the problem. If the origins of the towns were purely military or economic, it is hard to see why this was of such importance; few people today would worry much whether their neighbourhood was more properly described as a small town or a large village. Yet in the twelfth century it was a matter of vital importance. The official recognition of a town which was conferred by a charter was the common demand of the townsmen of the period. What they wanted were specific rights of a sort the town charters conferred, and for them they were prepared to pay good money to king, Church or feudal magnate as the case might be.

These charters, expressing as they do the rights townsmen felt they most needed, are the best indication both of why towns came into existence at all and of why their inhabitants were impelled to seek official recognition. Granted by different authorities and coming from different periods and from very different parts of Europe, there is of course no uniformity about them. Some were towns in the modern sense, others merely areas of countryside which for one reason or another sought freedom from feudal jurisdiction. Sometimes a charter whose form was thought to be particularly apt would be frequently copied: that of Beaumont in Argonne (1182) was given to over five hundred different communities in Champagne, Burgundy and Luxembourg, many of these 'villes neuves' being rural areas. The charter of Liège, a more obviously 'urban' community, was also widely imitated. Purely local needs and conditions are often reflected in them, yet certain demands remain sufficiently constant to indicate that they were the essentials of town life.

Almost always the charter included a clause stipulating that after a townsman had been present unchallenged in the town for a 'year and a day' his status as a free man should not afterwards be questioned. The importance of this is obvious. In ordinary feudal society free men were comparative rarities. Men had obligations to their lord; only God was entirely without obligation. Nor could these duties be escaped merely by withdrawing from the lord's land; such a withdrawal without permission was itself an offence against him. They could not even be escaped by death, for a son inherited his father's obligations. They could be incurred by marriage; a free man marrying a woman of villein status could himself become villein. Almost all the inhabitants of a town must have been either renegades from a lord themselves or at least descended from such. Even if free themselves they might marry unwittingly a girl whose lord subsequently appeared to claim her. Nor were the prospects of doing business with men who might be able to take cover under the protection of a lord encouraging, for the possibility of a bourgeois citizen being able to extract a bad debt from a feudal lord was remote. The desire of townsmen to establish their own liberty and that of their customers was no empty whim.

Similarly a clause granting the town the right to hold a court doing justice according to its own laws is standard form. This too is revealing; the manorial courts of feudalism administering the immemorial common law and the customs of the manor were well suited to their original purpose, the protection of life and limb and the settlement of local disputes about land in which local knowledge was of the first importance. But they were much less suitable for the needs of a trading community. Punishment tended to be in the form of some form of personal mutilation, hanging or branding or the deprivation of the offending limb. It may have been an effective deterrent against the simple crimes of a fairly primitive society, such as murder, rape or straightforward theft, but this is not the justice needed by a commercial community. A merchant who has been sold goods of inferior quality or under the specified weight does not need bloody retribution; he wants his money back. In other words he needs a system of punishment based on fines or in the last resort exclusion from the market. Urban justice could at times be cruel enough, but in general it was this mercantile justice that town courts supplied. Moreover, while feudal justice might be adequate for disputes between tenant and tenant, it was much less effective when one of the parties came from elsewhere; it was the duty of the lord to protect his own men. Nor could it be relied upon to give satisfaction to the tenant when the lord himself was a party to the dispute, since he was unlikely to give judgement against himself. Yet feudal lords with a natural hostility towards these strange new men in their midst might well become involved in proceedings against them; they would certainly feel the urge to protect their own tenants in any dispute. In short, feudal courts would probably be biased against townsmen; even if they were not they were ill-fitted to give the sort of justice townsmen needed. Moreover, feudal justice was often excessively slow, and townsmen needed a much quicker form of justice, which their courts could supply. Manorial law took little cognisance of the realities of business and trade, which by long experience came to be incorporated in the law of towns.

The towns, therefore, had to have their own courts, having jurisdiction both over their own citizens and over those who came to trade with them from elsewhere. They bore a variety of titles: sometimes they were known as courts of piepowder, an expressive corruption of *pieds poudrés*, the courts of those with dusty feet from their travels. Some even survive to the present. In Bristol the Tolzey Court still bears witness of the need of medieval Bristolians for a commercial court.

The right to hold a market and to decide on the regulations proper for it is also contained in most charters. This too is an obvious need. Nothing would divert trade elsewhere more quickly than the accumulation of excessive market dues and impositions; internal trade was made difficult enough in any case by the number of different authorities who might impose charges on goods passing through their territories. At the end of the fourteenth century there were nearly fifty different sets of customs to be paid in the course of a passage down the Rhine. Merchants could only survive by keeping their trade flexible, and a small market in particular could easily be killed if it raised its charges too high. A rather similar danger threatens British industries today, which may see their customers going elsewhere to avoid the high prices resulting from high taxation. Feudal lords were very likely to try to impose such dues; without themselves understanding what was necessary for the welfare of the market and without contributing anything to its wellbeing, they were only too likely to see in it an opportunity of gaining the money without which they could not share in a rising standard of living.

Personal freedom, their own jurisdiction, and the right to conduct their own markets, these then were the rights of which on the evidence of the charters townsmen stood in greatest need. To them must be added one further object pursued by townsmen. The greater order prevailing after the year 1000 was very relative; the feudal world remained a military world, and outbreaks of civil war were still liable to occur. The anarchy of Stephen's reign in England, the conflicts of the German monarchy with the Welfs in the twelfth century, the prolonged struggle between the French monarchy and the Angevin Empire, such disputes were of little concern to townsmen but their consequences might well be disastrous. At such times the town walls could give at least a measure of security; they were difficult to assault and a baronial army was rarely equipped to conduct a long siege. With their help towns could often preserve neutrality in feudal wars.

The smaller the town the greater was its need of some form of official recognition. Great cities like Milan or Bruges were capable of defending their own interests and stood in no need of protection. They might indeed in their turn become predators; some of the smaller Lombard towns, such as Pavia, stood in fear of domination by Milan. But a small town had little hope of preserving its rights unless it could find a champion. Hence their desire to gain charters; the only real essential from their point of view was that the authority granting the charter should be reasonably permanent and strong enough to give protection. A great lay noble or an ecclesiastical prince might often fill the bill, and many charters were granted by such. But the baronial class as a whole had interests which too often ran contrary to those of the towns, and the Church was never particularly skilful in its handling of urban communities. It was in the towns that the problem of heresy loomed largest, and at most periods of the Middle Ages the teaching of the Church on usury lagged behind actual commercial practice, so that it seemed scarcely possible to make a living from trade without offending against Church law. The commonest alliance, at least in France and England, was that between the monarchy and the towns. Here there was a real community of interest, for kings too had a direct interest in the suppression of noble disorder and the establishment of internal peace. Their chief requirement for this was money, and the towns could supply it. Hence the great spate of royal charters. The growth of royal power and of urban prosperity went together.

This process is of great importance. Revenue was not the only benefit which monarchies could gain from their association with towns. Less tangible but equally important was the advantage gained by association with urban methods of administration. A merchant class had of necessity to develop habits of financial accuracy and the proper keeping of accounts; it had also to employ lawyers trained in the law of that other commercial society, the Roman Empire. Such methods were equally valuable in the administration of a kingdom. When Philip Augustus appointed six burgesses of Paris to supervise the royal accounts or when the English Crown later came to associate the bourgeois members of the House of Commons with their government, they were paying tribute not only to the increasing importance of towns in their kingdoms but also to the superiority of urban administration. Again the regulation of trade and the raising of dues which town governments undertook formed in miniature a pattern for the systems of national customs which gradually accompanied the growth of modern states. The development of town life in the high Middle Ages was on a sufficiently large scale for no one single explanation to fit all the examples. There were, for instance, towns other than Rome which owed their existence largely to their importance as ecclesiastical centres or places of pilgrimage. Chartres, justly famous for its cathedral school in the eleventh century, or Compostella, where the shrine of S. James was the most popular goal of western pilgrims, come to mind. But the towns of northern Italy provide the most striking contrast to the description already given. Elsewhere, except in Flanders, the towns can be seen as non-feudal oases in a feudal desert. They are the exceptions, and it is just because this is so that they have to seek external aid. In Lombardy from as early as the eleventh century this is not the case; here the countryside was dependent on the towns, and the normal economic unit is not the manorial estate, but the town and so much of the surrounding countryside as was necessary for its maintenance in food and raw materials. The reasons for this were not purely economic, although trade certainly revived earlier in the south than further north. The area had been a heavily populated portion of the classical empire, and Rome had been an urban civilization. Aided by a more friendly climate, the actual fabric of the towns had largely survived, and despite a drastic fall in their populations they remained inhabited; urban life had not died. The level of population in northern Italy was always much higher than in the North. Early in the fourteenth century, before the Black Death and the Hundred Years War had come to take their toll, the density of population throughout the relatively fertile land of France has been calculated at rather over one hundred per square mile; this was certainly a higher figure than existed in any other northern country except Flanders. Yet the corresponding figure for the lands of the city state of Florence was about twice that figure, and in all probability the density was even higher in central Lombardy.[1] Such a population did not encourage feudal methods of agriculture, at their best never very productive; more intensive methods were needed. In the north the aristocracy always remained a class somewhat insulated from social change, wedded to traditional methods of agriculture and taking little part in commerce. None of this was true in Italy, where from early times the prolific noble families had no scruples about participating fully in the

[1] See *Cambridge Economic History*, vol. ii. ed. Postan and Rich, 1952 p. 303.

commercial life of the cities. Families like the Doria of Genoa came to play a role in commerce which overshadowed their original importance as landed nobles. This fluidity in a society, so that power and prestige based on land and wealth based on commerce can mingle easily, is generally a sign of economic well-being; a parallel can be found in the history of England in post-medieval times.

The conflict between feudal nobility and urban bourgeoisie was, therefore, largely absent from medieval Italy. The towns had no need to seek royal help, nor, since the Crown was held by distant German kings, would such help have been effective. Instead the struggle against alien German rule tended to unite the classes. Yet such unity when it appeared was very transitory and did not often link city with city. For the various city states were often deadly rivals. Venice and Genoa, Milan and Pavia, Perugia and Assisi, Italian history is full of these rivalries of city states both large and small, and always they are based on economic rivalry. As in the classical world, the city states could bring prosperity but they could not bring peace.

Medieval Europe then was not the series of closed economies which has often been imagined. Trade existed on both the local and the international scale from early times, and by the twelfth century this had reached considerable proportions. Economic convenience and the need for defence against the hostility of a feudal society led to the establishment of towns to act as centres for this trade and homes for those engaged in it or in the industries which supplied it. Only in Flanders and northern Italy did the cities become so large that they dominated the countryside in which they were set. But if urban life remained exceptional elsewhere, that is not to say that it was unimportant. It was conducted on very different principles from those which characterized the rural and feudal society in which it grew up; that the individual citizen should be free in the eyes of an imperial law, that the proper relationship between employer and employed is based on a cash payment rather than on an obligation of personal service, that government is and should be largely concerned with the balancing of national accounts, these were not feudal ideas. If they and others like them came to be widely accepted in many European societies long before the fifteenth century, this is proof positive of the extent to which feudal Europe was already damaged beyond repair by the urban civilization growing in its midst.

12

Barbarossa and Henry VI

The Empire at the death of Conrad III seemed in sorry plight, in no fit condition to support either the Carolingian universal ideal or the more limited role of an exclusively German monarchy. No longer had it the assistance of a German Church ready to help it in the task of administration; indeed the subservience shown by Lothar II to the Papacy suggested that the roles might come to be reversed. The last two vacancies had demonstrated that the hereditary principle, triumphant in France, had been defeated in Germany; Conrad indeed had recognized this by making no attempt to nominate his infant son as his successor. Yet the elective system carried with it the threat that the resources of the Crown would be whittled away to nothingness as each successful candidate purchased his way to the throne by new concessions to the princes. These princes indeed had greatly increased their strength relative to that of the Empire itself. In the east it was they, and not the Crown, who had benefited from colonial expansion, while to the west the Burgundian territories which had once formed a part of the German kingdom were now either virtually independent or, which was worse, formed an area in which other powers, such as Aragon or the French monarchy itself, were seeking to intervene.

South of the Alps the situation was no more helpful. The Lombard towns had profited from the weakness of the previous reigns to accustom themselves to independence. Any attempt to remove it from them now would be correspondingly more difficult. Nor was the picture any brighter further south in the peninsula. The Papacy was still enjoying the fruits of its victory in the Investiture Contest; to the south again the Norman kingdom had replaced the confusion of earlier times, and was now a strong and apparently permanent part of the European scene. For all these the Empire would need to have a policy; in no case was it clear what that policy should be.

Yet there were certain assets which the young Frederick I (1152–1190) could count on in his difficulties. In Germany the princes themselves had come to realize, at least in theory, that the only result of the continued dissipation of royal lands and royal prerogatives might be a state of anarchy which would harm them all. Conrad III had shown his understanding of this when he had nominated, not his young son, but his nephew, Frederick of Hohenstaufen, to the Crown;

THE EMPIRE OF BARBAROSSA

a more striking testimony to it is found in the latter's unanimous election by the princes. There was at any rate some feeling for unity left. Similarly in Lombardy the disappearance of imperial authority was not welcome in all quarters; not only did it remove a check which had prevented trading rivalries ending in war, but it exposed the smaller cities to the danger of oppression by Milan, the self-appointed leader of Lombardy.

The Papacy under Eugenius III (1145–1153) was, temporarily at least, in a less bellicose mood than of late. Throughout the Church the Cistercian movement had sounded a call to contempt of this world and to concern for the life of the Spirit alone. The practical effects of this should not ḅe exaggerated; the career of S. Bernard shows that the definition of spiritual concerns could be stretched very widely. Yet under a Cistercian abbot as pope there was at least the hope of a pope who might be prepared to render rather more freely to Caesar the things that were his. Finally the growth of the study of Roman Law in Italy, if its effects are sometimes exaggerated, should not be ignored. For 'Roman Law' was the law of the classical empire; it spoke of a strong and centralized authority, and would give theoretical support to any attempt to create such an authority; from Bologna and the other Italian law schools the personnel for such government might be recruited.

Frederick had also the advantage of his own personality. About thirty years old at the time of his election, the new ruler, with his fine physique and the red hair and beard which were to give him the name of Barbarossa, looked like a ruler, no negligible advantage. His character matched his appearance; he combined physical energy and the martial interests, so necessary to maintain his position, with a high sense of his rights and duties. At the same time he did not neglect the truth that effective government could rest only on force. While he was the first of the emperors to use the terms *sanctum* and *sanctissimum* of the Empire, his speech to the nobility of Rome who had 'offered' him the imperial throne in 1155 showed clearly enough that he recognized that his claim rested on the surest divine right of them all, that of conquest.[1]

Something of this realism is shown in his initial approach to the problem of governing Germany. The extensive dissipation of the old royal domain which had taken place during and since the Investiture Contest meant that the old system of governing the kingdom through the domain was no longer possible. But if he no longer had a far-flung royal domain, his own family lands formed a relatively cohesive bloc in south-west Germany; they could be made to act as the basis of an attempt to build up a new conception of imperial power. The possession of these Hohenstaufen lands led him to try to extend his effective power over the territories which adjoined them. If he could control Burgundy, Switzerland, and Lombardy, none of which was under the protection of any great power, he would have

[1] See Barraclough, *The Origins of Modern Germany*, Blackwell, 1947, p. 170.

a solid mass of territory right in the middle of the lands to which the Empire laid formal claim; from there a much wider extension of his influence might be attempted. Of course it is possible to hold that this plan was unsound, that the Empire to be real had to be based on Germany, and that Frederick was avoiding the real problem of governing Germany and squandering German resources outside the country. Yet the traditional method of governing Germany was no longer possible, and Professor Barraclough is probably right in arguing that Frederick was consciously trying to exalt the authority of the Empire, now newly established on lands over which he could exercise control, over the authority of any of its constituent kingdoms.[1] His marriage to Beatrice of Burgundy in 1156 brought him effective control over Provence and the lands of the old kingdom of Burgundy; at the Diet of Besançon in the next year he was able to receive the homage of the lay and ecclesiastical princes of the Empire, many of them from 'lands long alienated from the Empire'.

This policy left unanswered the problem of how he was to control the more distant parts of the Empire. Here direct action was impossible, and Frederick had to play off various constituent parts against each other by diplomatic means. Papal power could be balanced by the power of the Welf duchy of Tuscany to the north of Rome; the dangerous strength of Henry the Lion in Saxony and Bavaria could be checked by supporting Albert the Bear in Brandenburg to the east, and by the creation of the new duchy of Austria (1156) in the south. Such methods could not give the Crown real control, yet they were not entirely ineffective. The threat of giving imperial support to his opponents could keep a prince well-disposed. Such a threat was not necessarily empty; Henry the Lion received imperial support in putting down a revolt in Saxony in 1166, but twelve years later, after he had quarrelled with Frederick, a similar revolt broke his power. But so long as they were content to recognize that they held their fiefs 'of our munificence', Frederick was content to allow his feudatories very considerable rights of independence; on three occasions during the reign, 1156, 1168, and 1180, he deliberately increased these rights. The general picture is one of a controlled monarchy growing up in a limited area as the core of a much larger feudal whole. The fact that in the end a national monarchy did not develop from this beginning does not necessarily condemn the policy; the much-praised Capetian kings of France solved their problem by a very similar formula.

[1] Barraclough, *op. cit.*, p. 174.

If the Hohenstaufen central bloc was to be effective the resources of Lombardy would have to be added to it. To obtain this the co-operation of the Papacy was essential. At first it seemed to be readily available. Eugenius III was not a militant personality, and with the Papacy threatened from the south by William the Bad of Sicily (†1166), and from within by Arnold of Brescia's attempt to revive the ancient regime of the Roman Republic, he was in no mind to collect an even mightier enemy. At the Treaty of Constance (1153) Eugenius III agreed to crown Frederick emperor, if in return German troops were provided to reinstate the pope securely in Rome. Both sides agreed to have no dealings with the eastern emperor, who was showing signs of wishing to regain the lost Byzantine provinces in Italy. Unfortunately, by the time Frederick was ready to come south (1154), both Eugenius and his successor were dead; the papal throne was now occupied by Nicholas Breakspeare, who as Hadrian IV (1154–1159) was to be the only English pope. He was soon to show himself of much less conciliatory temper.

To begin with Frederick's first Italian expedition (1154–1155) went well. Although the appearance of a German army in Lombardy provoked an immediate revolt it was noticeable that there were cities which took no part in it and were gratified to see Milan at last in difficulties. The siege of Tortona took longer than Frederick had expected, but it ended in the capture and obliteration of the city as an object lesson to the others. Arnold of Brescia, whom Hadrian had managed to expel from Rome, fell into German hands. Frederick agreed to the pope's request that he should be punished, and his incineration for heresy provided a cordial start to the relations between the two. It was not to be maintained. Hadrian's sense of papal rights made him consider Frederick as a papal vassal, a view Frederick could not be expected to share. Much bickering over points of precedence surrounded the ceremony of coronation (July 1155).

Soon after he was crowned Frederick started back for Germany. His desire to return is understandable enough; he had already been away too long, and he could not risk being forced to spend another winter in Italy by the closing of the Alpine passes. Yet it was unfortunate, leaving Hadrian with the impression that the Emperor had not fulfilled his side of the bargain by securing the pope more firmly in Rome. On his return journey Frederick was unexpectedly approached by the Byzantine emperor Manuel Comnenus with the suggestion that he should co-operate in a joint attack on the Norman kingdom. The Treaty of Constance and his own desire to get back to Germany alike demanded that he should decline the offer. Manuel then decided to approach the Papacy, showing that he was in earnest by seizing the port of Ancona on the Adriatic coast. Hadrian, feeling himself deserted by Frederick, came to an agreement with the Byzantine government, in direct contravention to the terms of Constance, for a joint attack on the Normans. After some initial successes this venture met with complete defeat at Brindisi (1156); the Byzantine expedition withdrew, and Hadrian was left alone to face the victorious Normans. The only alternative to his own expulsion from Rome was to reach a settlement with them. In the same year the Treaty of Benevento was concluded. Considering his situation the terms Hadrian received were not unfavourable, for the Normans agreed to recognize that they held their Italian lands as a papal fiefs only insisting on royal control of the Church in Sicily. But that there should be any agreement at all ruined any hope of friendship between the Papacy and the Empire; the old alliance of Gregory VII between the Papacy and the Normans against the Empire was once more in existence.

The opposition from Milan had been far from overcome in 1155, when Rome had been the main object of Frederick's expedition. Yet the subjection of Lombardy was essential if the plan of attaching it to his German and Burgundian domains was to succeed, and in 1158 conditions in the North were settled enough to allow him to lead the largest German army yet across the Alps. Frederick's failure to carry out this apparently simple plan was caused by two main factors, the many-headed nature of the opposition and the support it could receive from the Papacy further south. Any particular city he could reduce, although the operation might take many months, but he had not the men to garrison it permanently, and while he moved on to another its power would tend to revive. Moreover, the Papacy, once more in an attitude of hostility to the Empire, was prepared to use all its influence to prevent its enemy gaining control of Lombardy.

In 1158 Frederick moved first against Milan, which was taken by surprise unprepared for a siege and compelled to surrender. He then attempted to dictate a permanent settlement for his Italian lands at the Diet of Roncaglia (1158). The various communes were to recognize imperial overlordship and to agree to pay various feudal dues to the Crown, for instance *fodrum*, the payment made in lieu of provisioning royal armies. In return Frederick was prepared to cater for the strong feelings of urban independence, which were one of the features of the Italian scene, by allowing the communes the right to choose their own magistrates, the central figures of urban administration. At first this right was not allowed to all, those which had opposed him being put under an imperial *podesta*, but he was very ready to extend it after a period of probation to any which had shown their loyalty.

The system sketched at Roncaglia seems a sensible attempt to combine imperial control with local independence; if the Emperor had been able to include the Papacy in the system as he had originally intended, it might even have made the basis of a general Italian settlement. Hadrian, however, saw it only as an attempt to subjugate the Papacy and refused to allow imperial legates even to enter Rome. The next year (1159) Hadrian died, as a result, apparently, of swallowing a wasp, and it was a matter of great importance to Frederick that the next pope should have imperial sympathies. The cardinals were unable to agree, and the proceedings concluded with a free-for-all in which each faction fought to gain possession of the papal mantle for its candidate. But in the schism which resulted there was never any real doubt as to who was the legal pope. The papalist Cardinal Roland Bandinelli, Pope Alexander III (1159–1181), received the support of twenty-three cardinals, whereas only five persisted in supporting the imperialist Victor IV; a council summoned by Frederick at Pavia to consider the rival claims only showed that there was no support for Victor elsewhere in the western Church. The schism damaged both the military strength and the moral status of Frederick's cause.

The papal schism led to a renewal of trouble in Lombardy. For four consecutive summers (1159–1162) the Emperor was occupied with the Hydra of revolt in Lombardy, but although he was again able to capture Milan (1162), this time with much more difficulty, and to raze its walls, there was no guarantee that the peace would be continued once the Emperor was gone. Physical control of the pope himself might have been more useful, but Alexander did not allow Frederick to have the chance. A month after the fall of Milan the pope took the dramatic step of removing himself from Italy to the safety of France. Installed at Sens, he proceeded to demonstrate that his universal authority was in no way damaged by the move, while his opponent bore the responsibility for driving the shepherd from his Roman flock.

Frederick's prolonged absence from a Germany which had to provide the resources for his Italian wars had understandably provoked reactions there. The most serious was a revolt by the much-taxed citizens of Mainz, who signified their displeasure by the murder of Arnold, their archbishop. In the autumn of 1162 the Emperor returned to Germany, leaving the government of Italy in the hands of his chancellor Rainald of Dessel. Frederick himself might claim to be so exalted that he was above national differences, but this was clearly foreign rule and extremely unpopular. During the years 1162–1166, in which he paid only one short visit to Italy, the imperial cause certainly lost ground; the substitution of a new anti-pope, Paschal III, when Victor died in 1164 made a settlement with Alexander III even more unlikely. Alexander indeed felt sufficiently secure to return to Rome in 1165, with his prestige enhanced by his absence.

In 1166 Frederick attempted a final blow to shatter the coalition of the Papacy and the Normans. He moved down on the eastern side of the Apennines, taking hostages for the good behaviour of the cities he left behind him. Ancona was retaken from the Byzantines, and Rainald in command of the vanguard defeated the papal forces covering Rome. Alexander was forced to emulate Gregory VII, and withdrew to Norman territory at Benevento; his rival was duly installed in Rome. If Frederick had stopped there he would only have won another indecisive victory of a sort to which he was now accustomed. Instead he determined to try to make it decisive, and in so doing lost his whole expedition.

The late summer was not a good time of year to attack southern Italy. His German commanders may not have been aware of the dangers of malaria, and his army was defeated by mosquitoes rather than by the enemy. Within a few weeks most of his leaders were dead from a disease to which they had no immunity, and the army had disintegrated. Lombardy chose the favourable opportunity to rise again in revolt, and the closing of the Alpine passes by the winter snow made escape impossible. During the winter months Frederick moved from castle to castle with an ever-dwindling retinue of followers, and the next spring he was lucky to be able to bribe the Duke of Savoy to allow him to pass as a fugitive through the Mont Cenis to his own lands (1168). He was one of the very few survivors of the whole mighty army he had led to Italy.

The blow he had suffered, and the troubles it brought with it in Germany, prevented Frederick making another attempt on Italy for six years. During this time the Lombard cities formed themselves into a regular Lombard League for defensive purposes; even those cities which had had imperial sympathies found themselves coerced into joining. The city of Alessandria, named in honour of the pope, was especially constructed as a great fortified base to guard Lombardy from any attack from the north-west. But in the autumn of 1174 Frederick made his last crossing of the Alps as a would-be conqueror of the Lombard plain. He had enough initial successes to gain some support, but Alessandria by successfully enduring a siege of six months showed the weakness of his position. It became clear that unless Frederick could obtain reinforcements from Germany he was in grave danger of another major defeat. During a truce in 1175 he appealed to his rival and alleged vassal in Germany, Henry the Lion, for help, but it was not forthcoming. In May 1176 his army was totally shattered at Legnano; he himself was lucky to escape with his life.

Legnano marks the final end of Frederick's attempt to incorporate Lombardy in a central bloc; over twenty years of endeavour had come to nothing. Yet the terms he received after the battle were surprisingly favourable, and suggest that his reputation was still formidable. Traces of this reputation can still be found throughout northern Italy. The little town of Gubbio in the Apennines has as its venerated shrine that of S. Ubaldo, whose chief claim to canonization seems to have been his ability to negotiate the safety of his city with Barbarossa. Even in defeat such a leader appeared formidable. The terms the emperor negotiated in the Truce of Venice (1177) were made permanent by a definitive peace treaty at Constance before the truce expired. By then the Italian problem was divided into two. Lombardy, whose cities had throughout provided the mainspring of resistance to Frederick, gained a large measure of independence. The cities were to have their right to elect their own magistrates recognized, and gained the right to exercise all royal rights (regalia) within their walls. The exercises of such rights constituted a big apparent loss to the imperial treasury, but since it had always been difficult to collect revenue in Lombardy the loss seemed greater than it really was. In return the emperor was to retain regalia in the surrounding countryside, to receive a large lump sum in compensation for his loss of rights, and a lesser sum annually in the form of a tribute which the cities would pay him in recognition of his somewhat shadowy overlordship. The Lombard League was prepared to pay quite heavily for the guarantee of the effective self-government for which they had been fighting.

But there were other benefits for Frederick in the Peace of

Constance. If control of Lombardy was lost to him, he gained instead a much larger measure of control further south. In Tuscany and the other lands of the south of Lombardy the cities, possessing the same urge for self-government, had developed economically and politically much less far; only in the stress of war had they occasionally been able to win independence. Now the Lombard cities were willing to assist Frederick in establishing imperial control over an area whose economic interests might well be in conflict with their own and whose communes were *extra societatem* (outside the Lombard League). With Lombard aid Frederick established two consuls as imperial officials in the larger towns; in two large areas, the eastern coastal area centred on Ancona, and the Romagna, he was able to establish complete control, dividing the regions up into administrative districts under German counts. Here he was able to get the full benefits of all tolls and duties imposed on trade, and of various other forms of taxation, such as a hearth tax, which were widely applied to the benefit of the imperial treasury.

Frederick's new policy of attempting to gain control of central Italy was aided by his long-standing claim to the lands of the Countess Matilda.[1] Without papal co-operation, this claim had not been of much practical value, but here again fortune favoured Frederick after Legnano. The death of the belligerent Pope Alexander III (1181) led to the election of the more pacific Lucius III (1181–1185). He proved to have a real desire to work with the emperor, and gave active support to the marriage of Frederick's heir, the future Henry VI (1190–1197), with the heiress to the Norman kingdom, Constance of Sicily. By this marriage, arranged in 1184, the old hostility between the Empire and the Norman kingdom was at last ended; future emperors could, if they wished, use Sicily as a base for much wider Mediterranean schemes.

Frederick's military operations in Italy had ended in decisive defeat, yet he had emerged from the wreckage of Legnano with an Italian policy which was workable, even if very different from that which he had at first attempted. Before he departed on the Third Crusade his son Henry VI had already been crowned king of Italy; his general acceptance through the peninsula seemed to promise future tranquillity. Imperial diplomacy had succeeded where the German armies had failed.

The long years of conflict in Italy had created grave problems in Germany. Frederick never attempted centralized government there,

[1] See p. 114.

but if even a feudal administration was to be made to work it was essential that he should gain the co-operation of both the Church and of the most powerful feudal princes. The two aims were connected, a failure to secure the second might mean that the princes themselves would come to dominate the Church in their own lands. The prolonged dispute with the Papacy naturally put a great strain on his relationship with the Church, but in general the German Church remained much more loyal to him than it had to his Salian predecessor Henry IV. A combination of tact and the discreet replacement of the more ardent papalists among the higher clergy kept the German Church loyal to him. Indeed there was considerable resentment of Alexander III's attempts to stir up revolt in Germany; the papal cause was not necessarily strengthened by association with political intrigue. Nothing could restore the happy days before the Investiture Contest when the Church had been the loyal servant of the German Crown in all things, but Frederick had reason to be satisfied with the general loyalty of the Church.

The control of his lay vassals was a more difficult problem. He had not the resources to impose his will by force, while his repeated and prolonged absences in Italy provided frequent opportunities for revolt. Frederick was aided by chance. The death in 1167 of Conrad III's son not only removed the possessor of the strongest hereditary claim to his throne, but, since there was no heir, allowed the emperor to gain control of his lands. The possession of Suabia gave Frederick overwhelming power in the south, while eastern Franconia allowed him to strengthen the footing of the Crown in the rapidly expanding east.

But it was in the north that his problems were most difficult. The almost complete erosion there of royal lands and rights over the previous seventy-five years had left him with no basis for royal power. Henry the Lion of Saxony (†1195) the head of the Welf family, seemed the pattern of the overmighty subject. He controlled the most powerful of the German duchies; his control over north German ports such as Hamburg and Lübeck gave him the possibility of extracting handsome revenue; his house had profited to the full from the Wendish Crusade of 1147. Allied to these opportunities was an ambitious and forceful nature which aimed at nothing less than control of the whole kingdom. At first Frederick tried a policy of appeasement; his situation allowed him little choice, but the restoration to Henry at the beginning of the reign of the duchy of Bavaria gave him a massive block of territory. Any imperial expansion in the east would be at the will of the duke of Saxony. But this initial generosity did not lead to sympathy between the two men, and gradually their relations worsened. There were various occasions of dispute. The marriage between Henry and Matilda, daughter of Henry II of England (1168), gave ground to the suspicion that the vassal was seeking to operate an independent foreign policy. In the same year Frederick had insisted on the return to the Crown of Goslar, the Saxon city designated by Henry IV as his capital, as his price for the aid given to Henry the Lion against a rebellion of his own tenants. In 1169 Henry's uncle, Welf VI of Tuscany, had sold his Italian lands to Frederick; his nephew had expected to obtain the inheritance. Again, in 1172 Henry had gone on pilgrimage to the Holy Land, and he believed that during his absence his nominal overlord had cheated him out of some of his lands.

But the crisis in the relationship between the two men came with Legnano. Henry's refusal to send reinforcements to his overlord seemed to Frederick the direct cause of the disaster. After Legnano the new imperial policy in Italy no longer required a major military effort there, and the emperor was no longer faced with the danger of war on two fronts; he could look for an opportunity of settling his score with Henry the Lion.

The royal resources were not sufficient for a direct attack on Saxony, but fortunately Frederick was not alone in his resentment of Henry. The latter's imperious conduct had offended many. His own vassals had already shown in 1167 that their loyalty was uncertain; he had offended prominent churchmen, such as the Archbishop of Cologne and the Bishop of Halberstadt, by his attempts to appropriate Church lands; while his unconcealed intention to win for Saxony pre-eminence on the eastern frontier antagonized those who already saw themselves exercising leadership there. The Margrave of Brandenburg, son of that Albert the Bear who had already proved such a hammer of the Slavs, had particular reason to feel suspicious of Henry's schemes. With so much simmering discontent against Henry the Lion Frederick had no need to institute action himself; he could wait until the inevitable strife broke out among his vassals. The dispute then became one in which the overlord had a duty as well as an interest to intervene. An imperial Diet was summoned at Worms at the beginning of 1179, to which Henry along with the other contesting parties was summoned. Henry suspected, no doubt rightly, that the Diet was intended to break the power of the Welfs as much as to settle the particular points at issue.

He refused to come, and gave the Emperor the chance to declare him a contumacious vassal and to sentence him to the deprivation of both Saxony and Bavaria.

The sentence could only be carried out by force of arms, but there was little doubt of the issue of the fighting. Henry had been a real threat to the existence of many of the princes; Frederick by contrast had made few demands on them. They, therefore, sided with their overlord against their fellow-vassal. The foreign aid for which Henry had negotiated proved a delusion; neither Henry II of England nor the king of Denmark had any inclination to allow themselves to be involved in a German civil war. By 1181 the war was over. Henry had been stripped of all the lands he held of Frederick and had departed into foreign exile under sentence of three years banishment.

The breaking of Welf power was Frederick's supreme achievement in Germany. Apparently impossible at the beginning of the reign, it had been brought about by an astute combination of diplomatic and military skill. The victory made possible a large-scale rearrangement of the German map, since there was now no prince so powerful that he could obstruct the process. The general principle followed was to split the kingdom up into smaller units all possessing a direct link with the Crown, so that in place of a small number of very powerful duchies the Crown had as its tenants-in-chief a larger number of princes, none of whom alone was likely to rival it in power. The duchy of Saxony, for instance, continued to exist under its new duke, Bernard of Anhalt, but in a much reduced form, having been stripped of many of its appendages, which in turn became new fiefs. Frederick has indeed been criticised by some historians for his failure to use the opportunity he had won to establish a more direct form of rule, such as the Norman kings in England had imposed. But the criticism seems scarcely fair; not only did he not have the machinery necessary to operate such a system of government, but the situations were not parallel. The victory he had won had not been over the combined forces of a whole nobility but against one particular overmighty subject, and it had been won only through the good offices of the nobility themselves. It is easy to be too much influenced by knowledge of the future difficulties into which royal government in Germany was to run, but this should not detract from the reality of the victory Frederick had won or from the good sense he showed in the arrangements he subsequently made. When he publicly associated his son Henry VI with his rule in 1184, Germany seemed to be entering at last on an era of peace.

Frederick's death on crusade lies outside the scope of this chapter. If it was to allow Henry the Lion to attempt to stage a comeback, it provided also the appropriate romantic death which ensured that this tough and realistic ruler should pass into German legend; seven hundred and fifty years later Hitler could still make play with the idea that Barbarossa might come again in a last attempt to stimulate German resistance in 1945. Frederick was not only a great ruler; he was also in a real sense the last great unquestionably German emperor.

The reign of his son Henry VI (1190–1197) can be seen as a transitional period between this German empire and the quite different Mediterranean concept to be pursued by Barbarossa's grandson Frederick II. Henry VI's reign inevitably recalls that of a much earlier predecessor, Otto III, and, as with the earlier reign, its very brevity has prevented any final judgment being passed on it. To some, such as the chronicler Otto of S. Blasien, only an untimely death prevented him from restoring again the western empire in its fullness, and some modern historians have shown sympathy for this view;[1] others have considered that, having squandered the assets his father had left him, he was fortunate to die young enough to avoid the worst consequences of his own folly.[2] Henry's concern for the Mediterranean did not spring only from the optimistic temperament of a young man fully conscious of the possible implications of his Roman title; his father must carry a share of the responsibility, for Henry's marriage to Constance of Sicily had made him heir not only of the Norman lands to the south but also of traditional Norman interests, such as the desire to dominate the Mediterranean and the hostility towards the Byzantine Empire which went with that aim. It was not surprising that Henry should have been enthusiastic about his Sicilian inheritance. It offered him not merely an end to the constant hindrance to imperial schemes which Sicily had for so long constituted, but also the prospect of rich supplies of money on a scale never before enjoyed by German emperors. But Sicily was a prize which needed careful handling if its possession was not to involve a rupture of those better relationships with the Papacy which had marked the later years of Barbarossa's reign, for, nominally at least, it was a papal fief. It would have been wiser as well as more tactful if Henry had consented to do homage for this portion of his lands, but this would not have squared with his exalted conception of the Empire. His refusal to do

[1] See, for instance, A. L. Poole in the *Cambridge Medieval History*, Vol. iii, ch. 9, Cambridge U.P., 1922.
[2] See C. W. Previte-Orton, *Outlines of Medieval History*. 2nd edn. Cambridge, 1930.

so, and his creation of an imperial March of Ancona, running right down the east coast of Italy from Ravenna to the Abruzzi and under the control of his best general Markward of Anweiler, roused understandable papal fears of encirclement; henceforth Henry could count on the opposition of Celestine III (1191–1197).

In Germany Henry VI was aided by several strokes of fortune. The chance capture of Richard I on his return from crusade was one; admittedly the homage he had to do to the Emperor to secure his release was of no more than prestige value, being immediately renounced when Richard returned home, but his confinement had removed the chief external support of the Welf opposition in Germany. The death of Henry the Lion in 1195 further assisted the royal cause. But in his policy there, shaped as it was by his wish to pacify the country so as to allow him to pursue Mediterranean schemes, he is open to the criticism of having missed opportunities of strengthening the royal power. For instance, in 1191 the failure of the direct line of the Landgraves of Thuringia gave him the chance of securing Thuringia for the royal domain; instead he allowed it to pass to the last Landgrave's brother, thus creating a precedent for collateral descent which would plague his successors. Similarly, the grant in 1192 of the duchy of Styria to Leopold, who was already Duke of Austria, was calculated to produce overmighty subjects in the future.

In 1194 a son, Frederick, was born to Constance of Sicily, an unexpected event, and one which carried with it the hope of the survival of the Hohenstaufen line. Yet it by no means followed that the infant, if he survived, would inherit all his father's domains. The Sicilian Crown might be hereditary, but the German was elective; the German princes might well refuse to elect this half-Italian child, who had been born at Jesi in the Italian March. Indeed in 1195, led by the Archbishop of Cologne, they specifically refused to do this. At a Diet at Würzburg in 1196 Henry tried to persuade the German princes to abandon for all time their right of election to the Empire, if he on his part allowed them the full rights of succession through female or collateral lines to their own fiefs. At the same time he was trying to gain papal baptism and coronation for his son in return for his offer of a crusade, which he had in mind in any case, and of a steady income to the Papacy from his Italian lands. Celestine, however, was thoroughly suspicious of these advances, and was in close contact with the German princes. After much negotiation in both Italy and Germany all Henry was able to obtain was the normal election of his son as king by the German princes; no past experience suggested that there was any guarantee that the princes would feel bound by this if his father should die before the boy reached maturity.

Meanwhile Henry was assembling a mighty force in his southern kingdom to go on Crusade. His exact objects in this expedition are not altogether clear; certainly they extended further than the mere recapture of Jerusalem, and probably included the establishment of a Latin Empire in Byzantium. Celestine, however, was far from welcoming the crusade, and when in the spring of 1197 its departure was delayed by a widespread revolt in Sicily, he was widely thought to be responsible. Henry succeeded in putting down the revolt, and punished the rebels with the indiscriminate use of torture and crucifixion. But the postponed crusade was never to take place. In the autumn of the same year he contracted a fever which, aggravated by dysentery, proved fatal within the month.

As he lay dying in Messina Henry must have been very conscious that his son Frederick Roger, named after his two grandfathers, was only three years old. His prospects of succeeding to either of his grandfather's possessions must have seemed slight indeed. On his deathbed Henry dictated a testament which reveals that he realized the dangers to which the boy was exposed. In it he recommended widespread concessions to the Papacy, in an attempt to gain papal support and protection. Homage should be done on the child's behalf for Sicily and for the March of Ancona, and all papal territory which had been occupied should be at once evacuated. By this alone could something perhaps be salvaged for the child from the disaster of Henry's death. That Henry should have died when he did was unfortunate, but it is hard to feel that his policy as a whole was not mistaken. Too obviously he had been provoking the hostility of a Papacy whose capability of causing trouble for him in his German lands was only too great. Henry had failed to learn from the experience of his father.

13

Frederick II

The unexpected death of Henry VI led to a disintegration of imperial authority in both Germany and Sicily. There was little real expectation that his son Frederick II (1197–1250) would inherit all his domains; indeed it seemed unlikely that Henry's vaunted *unio regni ad imperium* would survive his death. The boy was promptly sent south to join his mother in the island of Sicily, while further north the imperial March of Ancona collapsed, and the Lombard towns celebrated Henry's death as a victory for their own independence. Markward of Anweiler, who had ruled the March for Henry, moved south to claim the *Regno* for the Empire. When he got there it was to find that this in no way agreed with the schemes of Constance of Sicily. Her relations with Henry had never been particularly cordial. Almost certainly she had been involved in the revolt against him, and there were not lacking those who accused her of poisoning him. Now that he was dead she chose to pose as the champion of Sicilian independence from German control, a cause which the brutal handling the Sicilian leaders had received from Henry after the revolt of 1197 made the more popular. Her son should be ruler of Sicily, true heir of her own Norman line, and for this purpose he had no need of Markward's German troops. These aims agreed very well with those of the new pope, Innocent III, for he too wished at any price to break the link between Germany and Sicily. He was delighted when Constance sought to make him the guardian both of her possessions and of her son; that at the same time she was prepared to recognize papal overlordship of the *Regno* and control over the Sicilian Church only made the arrangement better.

No sooner had Constance come to this agreement with the Papacy than she died (1198). A fierce civil war broke out between the supporters of German rule led by Markward and those of the Papacy, whose chief champion was the Frenchman Walter of Brienne. Frederick himself was not old enough to take a side, but possession of him would have been valuable to either faction. Some, indeed, hoped that the child's death would ease their own rise to power.

258

Nothing is more surprising than that at the end of ten years of confused civil war the boy emerged, not only unharmed, but as undisputed ruler of the kingdom (1208). Innocent had performed his duties of guardian well, and Frederick could enter into at least one part of his inheritance.

The situation in Germany was even more confused. Those who supported the Hohenstaufen cause found their champion in Philip of Suabia, Henry VI's youngest brother; it was never quite clear whether Philip's claims were being put forward in his own right or on behalf of his brother's distant and largely forgotten child. Those who opposed the Hohenstaufens were able to find a champion in an accustomed quarter. Otto IV was the younger son of that old enemy of the house, Henry the Lion. Both 'emperors' hastened to get themselves crowned, and the ensuing muddle merely convinced the supporters of each of the essential rightness of their candidate's claims. Philip was crowned with the genuine regalia of the German royal house, but in the wrong cathedral (Mainz) and by the wrong pair of archi-episcopal hands, those of the Archbishop of Tarentaise. Otto IV had to make do with spurious regalia, but his coronation took place at the proper place (Aix-la-Chapelle) and was performed, as was the tradition, by the Archbishop of Cologne. Neither in fact could be seen to be 'right', and the expected civil war followed. In the course of it the chief sufferer, inevitably, was the power of the monarchy itself, irrespective of who might come to possess it. The bribes each was forced to offer to attract support, and the activities of many of the baronage who saw in the dispute only an opportunity for self-help, made it only too probable that the crown, once it had been decided who should wear it, would not be worth wearing.

Both contestants were understandably anxious to gain the papal support which would do so much to fortify their claims. Innocent III was open-minded about the rival claimants; for either to accept the crown at the hands of the pope would clearly be a victory for papal prestige. But for this to happen it was necessary for him rightly to appraise the struggle and to back the winner; this most markedly he failed to do. By the *Deliberatio* of 1200 he gave his support to the anti-Hohenstaufen cause. Philip was declared to be an infidel and thus unworthy to be emperor, and as Leo III had conferred the Empire upon Charlemagne, so now Innocent conferred it upon Otto. He for his part formally abandoned any claim on any Italian territory. Innocent saw the vision of an emperor dependent on the Papacy for his position and making no claims on Italy.

The result was a trifle disappointing; Otto proceeded to lose the civil war, for all his papal support. By 1208 he was in exile in England, and Innocent was preparing to absolve his rival, and make the best terms he could with him. But this change of sides was not to be necessary. The murder of Philip in 1208 made a reconciliation between the two sides possible. Philip's daughter Beatrice was married to Otto, who was now recognized alike by supporters of Guelphs and Hohenstaufens.

For some months Otto seemed desirous of retaining the support of his old ally Innocent. The Concession of Speyer (1209) announced that the new emperor renounced any claim to interfere in the ecclesiastical jurisdiction of Germany or in the election of her bishops, and that he would not seek to control the revenues of vacant bishoprics. But, having pacified Germany, Otto proceeded to take possession of what he saw as the rest of his imperial territories. A German army appeared in the plains of northern Italy in the autumn of 1209, and Innocent noted with alarm that there was no longer a strong Norman *Regno* to call to his aid. Otto occupied Lombardy and what had been the March Territory, and did not hesitate to enter territories such as the Duchy of Spoleto which had since passed into papal control. By 1210 Otto controlled the whole of mainland Italy except the Patrimony of Peter, and the successful invasion of the island of Sicily waited only upon the arrival of the Pisan fleet which was to carry Otto's army there. Frederick meanwhile realistically kept a galley at anchor off Palermo ready to secure his flight to Africa if Sicily should fall.

Innocent was now confronted with exactly the same menace which had originally caused him to support Otto; a German ruler was likely to control an unbroken stretch of territory from Palermo to the Baltic. The protection Innocent had given to the Hohenstaufen child in the past from good will now became of vital interest for the Papacy. There seemed to be much less danger in recognizing Frederick, now in the gravest danger of losing even the *Regno*, as emperor, than in persisting with the recognition of a ruler now quite beyond papal control. Philip Augustus showed equal alarm; a strong German Empire would be a grave hindrance to his plans for control over Flanders. Frederick's position was sufficiently parlous to enable Innocent to insist on various precautions before he consented to support him. Frederick had to give his assent to the Concession of Speyer, to renew his homage for Sicily, and to give an undertaking that under no circumstances would the *Regno* and the Empire be treated as one; as a pledge of this his infant son Henry was crowned king of the *Regno* when Frederick accepted the imperial crown.

But in the summer of 1211 it looked very much as if Otto was on the point of victory. Indeed he might have done well to have ignored the stirrings of revolt in Germany and to have carried out his attack on Sicily; certainly he was never to be so near victory again. Instead he hastened back to Germany, where his cause became merged in the much wider conflict which was to culminate on the field of Bouvines. Loyalty to the Hohenstaufen joined with French gold and fidelity to papal instructions to produce the coalition which there triumphed over Otto and his allies. By the time of his death in 1218 Otto had lost all support except in his duchy of Saxony, and Guelph pretensions to the imperial crown had evaporated. Yet Frederick had had to pay for his victory. By the Golden Bull of Eger (1213) he formally confirmed all the concessions made by Otto and himself to the Church, while the successful outcome of Bouvines made it possible for the Fourth Lateran Council (1215) to claim that the Emperor held office only so long as he retained papal favour.[1]

It is now time to consider the character of the young emperor. By any reckoning Frederick II, *Stupor Mundi* to his contemporaries, is one of the outstanding personalities of the thirteenth century. Men who catch the imagination of a whole age do so either by embodying the ideals of that age uniquely well or by flouting it equally conspicuously; S. Louis stands as an example of the first method, Frederick II of the second. The multitude of legends which came to surround his name, although in part a tribute to the fertility of papal propaganda, are largely explainable only by the genuine amazement of an age confronted by the explicit denial of all its inherited values. This is not to deny that he had many partial imitators; in a later age Machiavelli stands as a reminder that teachings loudly attacked may yet be silently followed. Yet there is something extraordinary about the spectacle of a Christian Emperor of the thirteenth century who, in that age in which the minds of most men were acutely affected by religious belief, seems to have been entirely uninfluenced by it. Frederick may not have been the author of the book *De Tribus Impostoribus*, in which Moses, Mohammed, and Christ were alike held up as charlatans imposing themselves on the world; the important point is that there was nothing unlikely in so representing him. Jew, Muslim, and Christian alike were permitted to worship openly in

[1] See Chapter 9.

261

the *Regno*, that part of his lands which most clearly carried the print of his personality, and Frederick's acceptance of this state of affairs seems to have been based on a profound scepticism about the merits of all three religions. Certainly he was prepared to persecute savagely, but his grounds for doing so were always political. Heretics might be burnt, but only to establish a temporary reputation for orthodoxy or because their views might endanger public order. Muslims in Sicily, close to their allies in Africa, were a political menace to be exterminated; when transferred to Lucera on the mainland they became favoured subjects, particularly valued as soldiers entirely immune to the papal artillery of anathemas. Such 'breadth of mind' might win him the favour of future liberal imaginations. It may be doubted if it was a source of strength in his own age.

His morals, too, were a cause of much fascinated gossip among his contemporaries. Sexual immorality among princes was common, but the splendours of the harem tended by eunuchs which Frederick maintained in Sicily, and to which his various wives were confined when they had served their purpose by giving him offspring, had about them an exotic flavour; report much exaggerated the oriental splendour of the establishment. The menagerie of wild animals, some of them such as the giraffe totally unknown in Europe, helped to strengthen the impression that here was an oriental despot, and by taking it round with him throughout the *Regno* he spread the image more widely. Stories spread widely of Frederick's cruelty, and certainly those who resisted him unsuccessfully could expect much more than mere execution for their pains. Some of the unsuccessful rebels of the Sicilian town of Capaccio were to be tied up alive in sacks with poisonous snakes and thrown into the sea. Stories came to abound of his ruthless pursuit of knowledge; one told of the two men bidden to dine with the emperor, who, having fed them, ordered one to be strangled immediately after dinner while the other was preserved alive for two or three hours. An autopsy on both of them might enlighten the emperor on the functions of the human digestion. Another story told how the emperor, wishing to find out which was the original human language, kept a number of children born from parents of assorted races under the charge of nurses bound to remain strictly silent in their presence; when they began to talk he hoped that their words would turn out to be in whichever was the first language. This experiment failed. All the children incontinently died before their infant lips had had time to lisp anything.

How much fact lies buried in these fables is impossible to say, but they make clear that Frederick seemed to his contemporaries both fearful and wonderful in his disregard of all accepted canons of behaviour. Much in them recalls stories of eastern potentates, and it is clear that the Hohenstaufen emperor was aware of the awe which such conduct would inspire in his more parochial western subjects. Sicily was a meeting place of East and West, and the western emperor was to look to the East for instruction on how to cast fear into the hearts of his western subjects.

The *Regno* must be regarded as the base of Frederick's power; half Sicilian by birth, it had been here that all his childhood had been spent, and it was as the *Puer Apuliae* that he first appeared on the wider European stage. There can be no question of the remarkable scope of his achievement there. In 1208 the Norman kingdom lay in ruins. Civil war had eroded royal rights everywhere; the Muslim subjects of the Crown were in revolt; the treasury was empty; such profit as was still to be made from the much reduced trade through Sicilian ports went entirely to Pisa or Genoa, under whose flags it was carried. The measures Frederick took restored order to the *Regno* and established there a firm state. The Muslims controlled much of the interior of the island of Sicily, and their proximity to their co-religionists in North Africa made them here a political danger. In 1222 he began a war against the Muslim Emir Ibn Abbad, and after two years' fighting the Muslims were at his mercy. As many as possible were removed to the mainland, and replanted at the largely deserted township of Lucera, near Foggia. Here, safely distant from Africa, they were given every encouragement to build their own mosques, and within a few years they had become among the emperor's most loyal and productive subjects. It was a solution at once entirely novel in the age which saw the inquisitorial excesses of Conrad of Marburg, and highly successful.

Different methods were required for his Christian subjects. At three royal Diets, at Capua in 1220 and 1223, and at Messina in 1221, every effort was made to establish the lapsed feudal rights of the Crown. For instance, the right of the Crown alone to build castles was reasserted and existing castles were confiscated or destroyed. But Frederick was aiming at much more than the recreation of a feudal monarchy. His knowledge of Roman Law, and perhaps some acquaintance with the despotic systems of government in the East, alike pointed him to attempt an altogether more centralized form of administration than any secular society in the West had yet known. Justice, taxation, administration, all were made the concern of the central government alone. Feudal courts were allowed to lapse, and their functions passed to royal justiciaries, professional judges who were employees of the Crown; in all important cases a right of appeal lay to the royal courts at Palermo. The process of replacing a legal system that was feudal and religious with one that was centralized and secular was not to be accomplished in a day, but by 1231 Frederick was in a position to issue the Constitution of Melfi, the first attempt by a secular ruler since Justinian to codify the complete laws of a society. The Constitutions of Melfi are perhaps the first description in medieval Europe of the secular state. They did not mark the end of Frederick's activities as a lawmaker. At intervals for the rest of the reign *Novellae* were issued, further implementing the powers of the newly born state.

Money, like justice, became a prerogative of the Crown. The issue of coinage was strictly confined to the royal mint, which proceeded to strike coins in imitation of those of Augustus and bearing, like his, the inscription IMP/ROM/CESAR/AUG. These coins, known as *augustales*, were of gold at a time when no other coins in the West were so made; they were the outward sign of a society which had achieved financial stability.

Modern states and the efficient bureaucracy needed to run them are expensive; the *Regno* was no exception. If the bureaucracy was to be impartial it must be well paid. The sporadic and piecemeal collection of dues by a host of different authorities, so characteristic of most western societies, was abolished. Customs became a prerogative of the Crown, and a professional customs service known as the *Doana* (cf. Arabic *Diwan*) was introduced in imitation of the methods which had long been in use at Alexandria and other Muslim ports. By this means Frederick found it possible to reduce the nominal level of taxation while at the same time getting more from it, and a general rise in the trade passing through the ports of the *Regno* is evidence that the *Doana* had no inhibiting effect on trade, and other measures taken by the Crown, such as the standardization of weights and measures, were positively beneficial.

Nevertheless customs alone did not satisfy the financial needs of the *Regno*; probably it would not have done so even if incessant war had not come to upset all financial calculations. The sale of monopolies, such as that to the Jews of Trani for the silk trade, brought in some revenue, but the major part of the gap had to be bridged by direct taxation. A variety of such taxes were applied, most notably the *Collecta*, a form of hearth tax the great merit of which was ease of assessment.

The government of the *Regno* under Frederick II gives the impression of an efficient, and on the whole benevolent, despotism. The *Regno* came to know the benefits of good government; in particular that northern half of it which lay on the mainland of Italy enjoyed a period of prosperity it was never to know again. Frederick spent more time on the mainland than in Sicily proper, and Naples became at least the equal of Palermo. The foundation of the University of Naples was, most uncharacteristically among the medieval universities, the result of deliberate royal action, and it demonstrates not only Frederick's concern for the supply of trained officials to serve him and desire to spite the Papacy, but also a genuine intellectual interest. The court circle, most notable among them the Chancellor Piero della Vigna, attracted scholars widely from the rest of Europe, and teachers such as Arnaldus of Catalonia and Peter of Ireland came to enjoy the royal favour. There were few medieval courts with as lively a concern for the things of the mind as that of the *Regno*. In two respects it was unique; alone among European courts it gave shelter to some of the Provençal poets who escaped from the wreck of their homeland, and here alone an awakening interest in classical Greek could find a living Greek tradition, a relic of the days of Byzantine occupation. One poet, Georgios of Gallipoli in Calabria, wrote the praises of the emperor in a lengthy poem in Greek.

It was not to last. Before the end of the reign the taxation of the *Regno* had changed from efficiency to the most flagrant oppression, and the vaunted gold augustales were being coined in leather. Discontent at last grew to open rebellion, and even the trusted Della Vigna was to plot against his master and, like Judas, to go and hang himself. But none of this sprang from any inherent defect in the machinery Frederick had established in the *Regno*. It was inadequate only for the immense load laid on it of supporting a whole empire engaged in war throughout the length of Europe. Understandably it cracked under the strain, but, if Frederick is to be blamed, it can only be for pursuing outside the *Regno* aims which could only lead to the destruction of this, his first love and finest achievement.

In Germany the starting point of any consideration of Frederick's independent policy must come with Bouvines. At that battle Otto's golden imperial eagle had fallen into the hands of the victors, and the incident is symbolical. The Crown of Germany was now indisputably Frederick's. Yet its resources were much diminished. Lands had been squandered and all vestige of control over the Church had been surrendered. Worse still the imperial *ministeriales*, the small body of professional administrators on whom Barbarossa and Henry VI had lavished attention, had largely passed from the service of a distant and powerless leader to the task of accumulating lands for themselves. This state of affairs combined with Frederick's own inclinations to make him decide not to attempt the restoration of the German monarchy as such. The *Regno* to him was always his homeland, 'a haven amidst the floods and a pleasure garden amidst a waste of thorns',[1] while Germany by contrast was a land of 'sombre forests', 'muddy towns', and 'rugged castles'.[2] It is arguable that his view of his northern kingdom was unduly pessimistic, and that a society with enough energy to produce the colonial movement and enough cultural vigour to produce Cologne cathedral was worth striving to control. The German situation was no more unpromising than it had been on the accession of Barbarossa, and certainly there were Germans such as Eike von Repgau who during Frederick's reign hoped for decisive royal action to restore order to their society. But Barbarossa had not had to think of the *Regno*. Granted Frederick's Italian birth and upbringing, and the strength of his 'Roman' leanings, his decision to regard Germany as a possible source of men, prestige, and money rather than as an area he controlled directly was probably inevitable. He could not be in the *Regno* and in Germany at the same time, but the one from which he was absent would necessarily witness some degree of erosion of royal authority. Frederick was present at Aix for his coronation in the manner of Charlemagne in 1215, and for five years after that he was in his northern kingdom. But there followed a period of fifteen years (1220–1235) before he again visited Germany.

From this decision sprang the policy of appeasement towards the princes of Germany, lay and ecclesiastical alike, a policy operated by the regents Frederick left to represent him, Archbishop Englebert of Cologne and Lewis of Bavaria. The Golden Bull of Eger had already represented the first step in Frederick's abandonment of any pretension to control the German Church; the *Privilegium in Favorem Principum Ecclesiasticorum* (1220) allowed the princes of the Church complete rights to dispose of fiefs on Church lands how they willed, and abandoned the royal claim to raise taxation in emergency or to build castles on them. This apparent act of favour towards the Church seems to have worsened the long-term relations between it

---

[1] Quoted from Kantorowicz, *Frederick the Second*, English trans., E. O. Lorimer. Constable, 1958, p. 220.

[2] Quoted from Barraclough, *Origins of Modern Germany*, Blackwell, 1947, p. 220.

and the Crown, for now the German Church had little to look for from its alliance with the Crown; since real power was coming to rest with the princes, realistic churchmen would increasingly look to them for temporal support.

The one person who came strongly to object to Frederick's German policy was his own eldest son, the Prince Henry. In return for the *Privilegium* the princes had recognized him as 'co-regent' of the Empire, and the boy had been brought up in Germany. In 1228 he took over as regent in his own right, and it would seem that he was alarmed at the speed with which the powers of the German Crown were disappearing. Knowing little of the *Regno*, where indeed he might well not be accepted, he did not wish to inherit a merely nominal throne. He began to use the surviving powers of the Crown to rally those forces which might resent the domination of the country by feudal princes behind the Crown's regent; in particular he appealed to those regular opponents of the feudal baronage, the towns. Individual towns, such as Bern or Ulm, or leagues of towns received charters in his name, guaranteeing their rights against the princes. This is of course the policy which had long been pursued with happy results by monarchs elsewhere in Europe; if Frederick had been aiming at the control of Germany it would have been the right policy for him. But it was regarded by the princes as a direct threat to their power, and they appealed to Frederick to protect their rights. His response was the *Statutum in Favorem Principum* (1232) by which the same rights already granted to the ecclesiastical princes in 1220 were extended also to the laity.

This seems to have broken Henry's loyalty to a father he did not know. He continued to work with the towns against the princes and his father, and at the same time entered into negotiations with the much more powerful Lombard League. Logical as it might be to unite the urban forces, this was an act of open hostility towards his father, since the League was among his most implacable opponents. In 1234 open fighting broke out in a Germany in which public order had been gradually disintegrating since 1228.

The alliance between Lombard and German towns could never be very effective unless control of the Alpine passes was assured. In the next year Frederick was able to move through Lombardy against his son in Germany. His reputation was such that though he arrived in Germany without an army, the revolt collapsed almost as soon as he arrived. Henry threw himself on his father's mercy, and Frederick sat in judgement on his own son. For the moment his life was spared;

but he was removed to a distant castle in Apulia; there seven years later he died. Some said that, crazed by the prospect of perpetual surveillance, he had ridden his horse over a cliff, but there were not lacking those who believed that Frederick had killed his own son. The sermon at the funeral, where the preacher took as his text 'And Abraham stretched forth his hand and took the knife to slay his son', may have strengthened their suspicions.

Henry was succeeded in Germany by Frederick's second son, Conrad IV (1250–1254). The princes had no objection to electing an infant who could not threaten their power for many years. In fact Henry's revolt in 1234 was the last serious attempt made by the Hohenstaufens to control the German kingdom. After that year the increasing severity of the struggle with the Papacy prevented Frederick from having any second thoughts as to his German policy. But even the limited aims he had set himself were not achieved. Germany was not insulated from the rest of Europe, and the effects of the conflict in the south were felt in a series of uprisings engineered by the Church to distract the emperor. In 1241 the ingratitude of the German Church towards its excommunicate emperor was shown by the defection of the three powerful archbishops of the Rhineland, Mainz, Cologne, and Trèves. From that time on there were constant attempts to dethrone Frederick, and Innocent IV sent a special legate, Philip of Ferrara, to Germany with instructions to create as much difficulty for the Crown as possible. Attempts were made to set up anti-emperors against Frederick: in 1246 Henry Raspe was elected by the Church leaders to replace the excommunicate and deposed emperor. Raspe died within a year, but he was replaced by William of Holland. It cannot be said that either of these anti-emperors gained very wide recognition, but in Innocent's view their purpose was not to re-establish the German throne but to add to Frederick's difficulties, and in this they were wholly successful.

The last decade of Frederick's reign in Germany then was one of constant warfare. In the course of it the imperial cause received its best support from the very towns against which Frederick had taken up arms in 1234. Nor is this surprising. After the *Privilegium* of 1220 Frederick had put it beyond his power to render further services to the German Church; it could scarcely be expected to follow an excommunicate from gratitude alone. The towns by contrast, with no reason for gratitude to the Crown, could yet see in it a possible safeguard against noble persecution. Frederick must have wondered in those years whether perhaps his dead eldest son had not after all understood German realities better than himself.

To understand the last great clash of Empire and Papacy, which, as has been shown, ultimately settled the fate of both Germany and the *Regno*, it is necessary to have an understanding of the aims of the three main contestants for power in the Italian peninsula, Frederick himself, the Papacy, and the communal governments of northern Italy. Frederick himself aimed at the creation of a real Roman Empire, and for this purpose he needed more than the *Regno* to act as a base. Well-established there, he hoped to extend his control also over Lombardy, to do which he needed to forge some firm link between the two territories. Once this had been done he would have at his disposal the combined wealth of Lombardy and the *Regno*, and his position in Italy would be invincible.

The Papacy, by contrast, was the most considerable landholder in central Italy. If the Empire in Italy was weak the Papacy itself was the most natural leader of the peninsula; conversely an Empire which really controlled both the *Regno* and Lombardy would produce a Papacy in grave danger of becoming an imperial puppet. There had been troubles enough between Papacy and Empire when the latter had been a primarily German institution; now that it had become Italian, a conflict could scarcely be avoided. Deplorable as it may have been, the implacable hostility of the Papacy towards its ex-ward is scarcely surprising; Frederick's unsavoury reputation even gave it some moral justification.

The motives of the third party were less clearly defined. The north Italian towns, their fortunes firmly founded on manufactures and trade, had their own mercantile rivalries. The products of Milan competed with those of Brescia, Asti and Alessandria competed for the valuable transit trade from Genoa to the Alpine passes, and so on. Further south in Tuscany the struggle between 'Guelph' and 'Ghibelline' cities marked a whole series of economic disputes, setting Pisa against Lucca, and Florence against Siena. Yet all the cities had a common interest in resisting any external threat to their right to conduct their own anarchy in their own way; in Lombardy at least tradition and common sense alike indicated the Empire as being a much more likely source of such a danger than the Papacy.

A struggle for power could therefore be expected in Italy. Nevertheless it was some time before fighting began. The Papacy had, after all, been forced to maintain the right of Frederick to the Empire, while the Emperor's necessary absence in Germany from 1212 to

1220 made him unlikely to undertake any major ventures in Italy; after his return the organization of the *Regno* was to occupy him for some years. Moreover, Honorius III, pope from 1216 to 1227, was a quiet and pacific man anxious to avoid trouble if possible. His main interest was in reviving the crusading movement from the disrepute into which the Fourth Crusade had brought it, and he spent much time in trying to persuade Frederick to fulfil an early vow he had made to go on crusade. To this end he lent his offices to securing his second marriage (1225) to Yolande de Brienne, through whom he secured the titular claim to the throne of Jerusalem. Frederick proved a reluctant crusader, and turned first to the problem of Lombardy. In 1226 he summoned all the cities of the Empire to attend an imperial Diet at Cremona. The Lombard towns were quick to see in this a threat to their independence, and the immediate result was the rebirth of the Lombard League. At once Frederick found the communications between the *Regno* and the rest of his empire severed; short of a large-scale war he had no means of restraining the League, and for the present he was not ready for this ultimate test. He accepted the mediation of Honorius, and the Diet was not held.

Shortly after this Honorius died, and as so often in the history of the Papacy a new pope brought an entirely new tone to papal policy. Cardinal Ugolini of Ostia, who became Pope Gregory IX (1227-1241), was already elderly on his accession; he brought to his new office strongly held opinions, which at this stage of his life he was not prepared to modify, and much of the irascibility which often goes with old age. It is worth noting that his earlier training in papal diplomacy had come at the court of Innocent III, at a time when there was no effective imperial challenge to papal *plenitudo potestatis*. He held that all Christ's power on Earth belonged to the Papacy; that the pope was indeed *verus imperator*, a phrase used by Gervase of Tilbury of Innocent III. The imperial dignity would normally be conferred on a temporal ruler, but it would be held strictly on terms of good behaviour; it was always open to Peter to resume his own.

At first he had no hostility to Frederick, terming him 'the Church's beloved sapling'. But since the Emperor certainly did not see himself in this light, a collision between the two could not be long postponed. It came through Gregory's insistence that Frederick should at once fulfil the crusading vow he had made. The Crusade indeed was already gathering in the *Regno* during the summer months of 1227, and a start was projected for August. During July a sickness struck the army, causing numerous casualties and infecting the Emperor

himself—or so Frederick said. Some of the troops went east, and
Frederick himself set sail, only to return again a week later to Otranto
saying that he was not well enough to make the journey. It is difficult
to be sure of the truth. Gregory saw fit to consider the incident as
another prevarication by one who had already tarried far too long,
and promptly excommunicated him. It may well be that suspicion of
Gregory's intentions during his absence played a large part in
Frederick's reluctance to go.

The Emperor had not been absolved when in the next year he left
for the east, and the excommunication already in force against him
was specifically renewed, for the impenitent had no right to take the
Cross. The Fifth Crusade thus started under the curious handicap of
a doubly excommunicated leader. In every way it turned out to be
a quite exceptional crusade. No serious fighting against the Infidel
was done, perhaps because the pope's action made it very doubtful
whether that part of the army which did not come from the *Regno*
would follow Frederick into battle; many of the crusaders were
shocked by the spectacle of their leader fraternizing with the Sultan
Al Kamil, and even, so it is said, going to visit the dreaded sect of the
Assassins in their mountain fastness. Yet the diplomatic method was
far more likely to be effective than the military. The Muslims had
their own domestic reasons for not wishing war, and Al Kamil,
himself a notably westernized sultan, was much struck with the
personality of the emperor. A treaty was concluded between the two
men in February 1229 by which the Christians were to be allowed
possession of the more important Christian Holy Places, including
most of Jerusalem itself, on the conditions that they did not fortify
them, and that they allowed free access to the Muslim population.
They were also allowed to occupy a narrow coastal strip by which
they could have access to the city. A crusade in which the only
fighting had been the seizure of Cyprus from its Christian ruler, had
accomplished more than its three predecessors, which had strained
the military might of the entire western world. The Middle Ages
have few more curious sights than that of the excommunicate emperor
crowning himself in the Church where Godfrey of Bouillon had
refused to allow himself to be crowned where only He who wore a
crown of thorns had the right to reign (1229).

The same autumn Frederick was back in the *Regno*, incurring a
further renewal of the excommunication *en route*. He found his
return was none too early. During his absence Gregory had attacked
the *Regno*, having first formally loosed its subjects from their duty

of obedience to their king. The resources of the Church were used to hire mercenaries for this task; as Frederick complained 'with the moneys which he has received to aid the Crusaders in Christ's work, this Romish priest entertains mercenaries to molest us in every way'. Gregory hoped not only to depose·the sinful king, but also to obtain full control over the Church of the *Regno*. The point was of some importance; the area was grossly over-endowed with prelates, having twenty-one archbishops and one hundred and twenty-four bishops; at the Fourth Lateran Council nearly a quarter of the assembled clergy had come from the *Regno*.

The attack had been a disappointment to the pope. Frederick's lieutenant, Reginald of Spoleto, had put up an unexpectedly effective resistance, and there had been none of the expected risings elsewhere in the Emperor's domains. With the return of the Emperor, Gregory realized his inability to win a decisive victory, and a peace was patched up at San Germano (1230).

It did nothing to solve the problem of the Lombard League, which refused to dissolve, and continued to obstruct Frederick's policy in many ways. In 1231 it rendered sterile an attempted imperial diet at Ravenna by refusing to allow any German delegates to reach it, and in 1234 the League had sided with Henry in his revolt against his father. In 1236, after the collapse of the revolt, Frederick felt strongly enough to move on Lombardy. The defeat inflicted on the army of the League at Cortenuova (1237) seemed likely to be decisive; after it many of the lesser cities of the League submitted to him, and even Milan sought to negotiate a peace. Frederick refused to grant it; more than ever he was dominated by the idea of himself as the incarnation of Ancient Rome, whose duty it was to destroy this new Carthage. The war continued, and the successful defence of Brescia in the next year showed that Frederick could be resisted.

In retrospect Cortenuova appears as the Emperor's greatest opportunity of success. Having failed to make use of it, it was not long before the Papacy was again numbered among his opponents. To the other grounds of conflict could now be added Frederick's marriage of his bastard son Enzio to a Sardinian heiress, and the claim he made through her to the control of what had earlier been recognized as a papal fief. In the conflict which followed, a conflict to last for the rest of the reign, the immediate balance of military strength within Italy seemed to favour Frederick, yet Gregory and his allies had very real assets. The world-wide resources of the Church gave them an advantage in finance and in propaganda which the

Emperor could not challenge, while the alliance negotiated by the pope between Venice and Genoa enabled the coalition to challenge Frederick at sea.

In the early years of the fighting Frederick did well; his forces made progress in central Italy, capturing Spoleto and a great part of the papal states in 1239 and 1240. At the same time the papal counterstroke, a combined invasion of Sicily itself, came to nothing. The efficiency of Frederick's fleet, with its Pisan allies, was even more strikingly demonstrated in 1241. In that year Gregory summoned to Rome a council of all the leaders of the Church, and it was no secret that further measures against the Emperor, who now openly accused his adversary of heresy, were to be discussed there. The Genoese convoy carrying the main body of French delegates was intercepted when it was near its destination, the port of Civitavecchia. Twenty-two ships were taken, and an almost embarrassingly heavy haul of four thousand prisoners, among them no less than a hundred prelates, including the abbots of Cluny, Cîteaux, Clairvaux, and Prémontré, fell into Frederick's hands. This stroke, much as it annoyed S. Louis, who at once demanded the release of the French prisoners, seemed to complete the ruin of the papal cause, and the death of Gregory in the same year gave an opportunity of settling the war.

The period between the death of Gregory in August 1241 and the election of Innocent IV (1243–1254) in June 1243 was one of intense diplomatic activity. Frederick's aim was to secure the election of a pope who would be willing not only to lift his excommunication, but to make peace on his terms. The small number of cardinals available, ten, made it unusually easy to put pressure on them in one direction or the other. The first conclave, held under terrible conditions in a Roman August, with sewage dripping through a leaky roof on to the cardinals locked into a small room below, produced an imperialist pope in Celestine IV after two months of agonized deliberation. His pontificate lasted only a few days before he succumbed, like two of his former colleagues, to the rigours of his election. Understandably it proved exceedingly difficult to get the surviving cardinals to go into conclave again; when they were at length persuaded to do so their choice fell on the Genoese Cardinal Sinibaldo Fieschi.

Frederick had supported the election of Innocent IV under the impression that the new pope was 'one of the noble sons of the Empire and has ever been well-disposed towards us in word and deed'.[1] He had made a bad mistake. The new pope, a noted canon

<hr>

[1] Quoted from Kantorowicz, *op. cit.*, p. 578.

lawyer, was to show in office that he held the most extensive views on the prerogatives of the Church and remarkably few scruples about how to exercise them. At the beginning of his reign he opened negotiations with Frederick, but they were only intended to act as a blind for his real purpose. In 1244 he suddenly transferred himself and the whole papal court to Lyons. Here there was no hindrance to his summoning a council to depose the Emperor. From Lyons he was able to mobilize the entire resources of the Church in his efforts to work his adversary's downfall. Philip of Ferrara was hard at work in Germany, Cardinal Gregory of Montelongo kept the papal flag flying in central Italy, and in 1246 papal encouragement was given to a revolt in a Sicily now over-burdened with taxation to pay for the expenses of the war. Frederick's generals, among them Enzio and the dreaded tyrant of Verona, Ezzelino of Romano, could win local successes, but always the Alps stood between him and any final solution of his problem. In 1247 he decided on the desperate expedient of a direct attack on Lyons. While he was at Turin and the bulk of his forces were already crossing the Alpine passes the news reached him that the city of Parma, the key to his communications with the south, had risen in revolt behind him. At once he turned back to reduce it, but while the army was blockading the city it was heavily defeated by an unexpected sortie (battle of Victoria, 1248); in this, the most serious defeat of his career and one which involved the loss of his whole treasury and regalia, the Emperor had been taken unawares; he had been hawking in the neighbouring marshes. After Victoria, Frederick suffered a series of reverses. His closest councillor della Vigna, engaged in treachery against him, and Enzio, always his favourite son, fell into the hands of the enemy, to die after two years of captivity. Finally, in December 1250, when it seemed that he was restoring his power in Italy, the Emperor himself fell victim of fever, and died in Apulia, the heart of the *Regno* which itself he had made the centre of his power.

Innocent at once burst into a paean of thanksgiving for the death of Antichrist. 'Let the heavens rejoice,' he wrote to the Faithful of Sicily, 'Let the earth be filled with gladness. For the fall of the tyrant has changed the thunderbolts and tempests that God Almighty held over your heads into gentle zephyrs and fecund dews.'[1] And in truth the death of Frederick with his empire unaccomplished was a signal victory for the Papacy; where this man had failed none would

---

[1] Quoted from S. Runciman, *The Sicilian Vespers*. Cambridge, 1958, p. 16 (Penguin, 1960).

succeed in challenging the empire of God's Vicar with a restored Roman Empire. The Pope could be indeed *verus imperator*. Yet the victory had been bought at a cost. To gain it Gregory and Innocent IV had used his own weapons against Antichrist: political intrigue, false witness, financial extortion, the indiscriminate use of excommunication, these were not the fruits of the Spirit, and the reputation of the Papacy, by which alone in the last resort it stood, had been much damaged by their use.

Nothing had shown more clearly the total failure of emperor and popes alike to face up to their responsibilities as rulers of the Christian West than the crisis precipitated by the Mongol invasions. From the wastes of central Asia had come periodic surges of savage fighters whenever the population had risen above the very low level allowed by a nomadic way of life. Fortunately for Europe, not all these surges came towards her; China, South-east Asia and India had all suffered from similar attacks. One such wave had been indirectly responsible for the collapse of the classical Roman Empire; now in the middle of the thirteenth century the West was suddenly confronted by a like danger.

The great expansion had started some time about the beginning of the thirteenth century, when a collection of tribes in the area north of the Gobi Desert had grouped themselves under one leader, Genghis Khan, the redoubtable 'Scourge of God'. Under his leadership the Mongols commenced the most remarkable career of conquest in the annals of the world. One group attacked eastwards towards China; before the end of the century the China of the Sung Dynasty would be overthrown. Others moved west to attack both Christian and Muslim lands. The Muslims suffered even more severely than the Christians; Persia had already been penetrated by the time of the death of Genghis Khan in 1227, and under the rule of his successors Ogodai and Kuyuk much of the Muslim world was overrun. Its spiritual capital Baghdad was to be sacked by the Mongols in 1258. Only the Mameluk Sultanate of Egypt, North Africa, and Spain were to remain untouched.

But Christian Europe was in no position to congratulate itself on the fate that was befalling its fellow monotheists. During the twelve-thirties the Mongol hordes moved through southern Russia. The great city of Kiev was destroyed, and by 1240 the Mongols were at the edge of the Catholic West. In 1241 the Mongol army divided into two prongs; the first kept moving west through Poland, the second turned south-west through Hungary. Both were entirely successful. The northern army destroyed Cracow, and shattered the resistance of the Poles and their Silesian German allies at Liegnitz (9 April 1241). Further south the Hungarian army was annihilated at Mohi only two days later. The armies then united and to all appearance their next move would be south into the plains of Italy itself. The danger did not go unrecognized. Far away in his cloister at St. Albans, Matthew Paris trembled at this clear sign that the end of the world was at hand. But even at this juncture Frederick and Gregory IX had been unable to compose their differences. Each was ready enough to accuse the other of preventing a common effort being made, but neither was capable of the gesture needed to unite Christendom. Europe was saved, but by no merit of its nominal leaders. The death of Ogodai Khan summoned the Mongol leaders back to central Asia, and the new Khan, Kuyuk, discontinued the attack on the West. In 1242 the main Mongol armies withdrew, destroying much of the Balkans on their way. Frederick and Innocent IV had revealed the moral and physical weakness to which that struggle had already reduced the Christian West.

By his will Frederick had designated his son Conrad IV (1250–1254) as his successor as emperor, and had decreed that Manfred, one of his surviving bastards, should rule under Conrad in the *Regno*. Conrad could do little to restore imperial power in Germany, but at least the anti-emperor, William of Holland, gained little recognition there. By 1252 Conrad was ready to move south to claim his inheritance. Meanwhile Innocent had felt it safe to leave Lyons and return as far as Perugia; he did not yet trust the turbulent population of Rome. Prolonged negotiations took place between the two men, for Conrad had no wish to court the opposition of the Papacy. But Conrad was not willing to abandon any claim to Italy outside the *Regno*, while Innocent did not waver in his fear of encirclement by Hohenstaufen territory; the struggle must be renewed. The pope's first plan was to split the family itself by offering the crown of the *Regno* to Henry of Hohenstaufen, Conrad's younger half-brother, at the same time securing Henry's support by marrying him to one of his own nieces. This plan failed when Henry died in 1253—poisoned by his brother, Innocent charitably conjectured—and by the next year the situation had reverted to normal, with Conrad answering papal excommunication and deposition with counter-charges of heresy. For once excommunication proved really effective. The mosquitoes of Sicily co-operated with the Holy Father, and before the year was out Conrad too was dead, at the early age of twenty-six. Like his grandfather in a similar predicament, Conrad attempted to save his house by a deathbed appeal to the pope; in a will drawn up in his last days he commended his two-year-old son Conradin to the protection of the Papacy, at the same time nominating him as King of the *Regno*. The German military commander in the south, Berthold of Hohenburg was designated as regent for the child.

But Innocent IV was not Innocent III; he had no desire to perpetuate the accursed family, while the claims of Conradin, a child remote in Bavaria, had no appeal in the *Regno*. Berthold found himself unable to control the *Regno*, where German troops were by now thoroughly disliked, and abdicated his office to Manfred, who had been brought up there. Innocent dealt directly with Manfred, who consented to be regarded as '*balio*', or regent, for the Papacy (1254). Neither party took much account of a vague promise to review Conradin's claims if the child should ever come of age.

This settlement gave a real hope that Innocent might come to control the *Regno* at last; it was frustrated by his own greedy impetuosity. Papal troops at once began to enter the *Regno*, and it became clear that the recognition of Manfred was likely to be but transitory. Manfred understandably decided to resist them. Taking possession of the royal treasury at Lucera, he raised an army largely composed of Muslims, who could not regard the prospect of papal government with favour. The papal army, incompetently commanded by one of Innocent's over-large body of relations, Cardinal William Fieschi, was routed by Manfred at the battle of Foggia. The news reached Innocent at Naples, which he had recently entered in triumph. The news killed him (1254); it is appropriate enough that he, like Frederick, should die confronted by the ruin of his plans.

Manfred was now in secure control of the *Regno*. Innocent's successor, Alexander IV (1254–1261), was a man of different calibre, who, if it had been possible, would have wished to restore a more spiritual note to the papal office. In any case the same indecision which made him denude the Sacred College through his inability to make up his mind who should be cardinals made him a somewhat ineffective political figure. For ten years Manfred struggled to extend his control outside the *Regno*, by making alliances with various rulers in Tuscany and Lombardy, and by intervening in the tangled affairs of south-east Europe, where the Latin Empire of Constantinople was moving towards the close of its ill-starred career. After the recapture of Byzantium by the Greek emperor Michael Palaeologus in 1261, Manfred seems to have nurtured the hope that he might regain favour by recapturing the city for the dispossessed Latin emperor Baldwin II.

But the Papacy was much more concerned with the *Regno* than with Byzantium. Some champion must be found to dethrone Manfred and restore the *Regno* to friendly, if not directly papal, control. Long negotiations with the English court failed in their rather improbable purpose of getting Henry III's younger son Edmund to accept the title of King of Sicily. Meanwhile Manfred was building up his power in the Mediterranean through marriage alliances. His own second marriage, to Helena of Epirus, strengthened his foothold in the East; while Constance, the daughter of his first marriage, by becoming the wife of Peter, the heir to the Aragonese throne, increased the prospect of Spanish aid for his schemes; he was becoming a danger to Rome itself. When the Frenchman Urban IV (1261-1264) succeeded Alexander, he turned to his native country for support. S. Louis, who had earlier declined the offer of the throne himself, now allowed it to be made to his brother Charles of Anjou; probably the king already had in mind the strategy of the Seventh Crusade, and foresaw that Manfred would be an obstacle to it.

Charles accepted with alacrity. Able, energetic and intensely ambitious, already he had added Provence by marriage to the duchies of Anjou and Maine his brother had granted him. But he had little chance of succeeding to the French throne, and was anxious to find some sphere in which to expand his family fortunes. He had already succeeded in securing a base for operations in Italy by gaining control of the county of Piedmont; now a much greater prize offered itself. A treaty (1263) was finally concluded with the next pope, Clement IV (1265-1268), another Frenchman, by which Charles agreed to hold the *Regno*, once won, as a fief of the Papacy, and to pay to his overlord a large annual tribute. In return Clement conferred on the expedition the status of a 'crusade'; not only were the participants to enjoy the full spiritual benefits of crusading, but Charles was empowered to raise levies on the French Church for his expenses.

The operations begun in 1265 went well for the Angevin. Leaving the main body of his forces to make the customary slow advance down the peninsula, Charles daringly took a small vanguard directly to Rome from Marseilles, avoiding Manfred's fleet on the way. On hearing of his rival's move Manfred had remarked complacently 'The bird is in the cage', but he seems to have taken no measures to close the cage. The two Angevin forces were allowed to reunite, while these first Angevin successes led to the stirrings of revolt in

Apulia. The two armies did not meet until the February of the next year (1266), and then at Benevento Manfred, deserted by many of his own barons, was killed in the complete defeat of his army. His death marks the end of the *Regno* as an independent power, and with it perished the Norman and Sicilian culture which had grown up there over the last two hundred years. Italy lay at the mercy of the Angevin–Papal alliance—for so long as it might persist.

Charles had no intention of playing the tyrant in his new domains. He was not vindictive towards his former enemies, and he did his best by his lights to provide good government for the area. But nothing could prevent his government seeming to be that of aliens in an area so long accustomed to its own rulers, nor could he prevent many of the Frenchmen who had come with him from fulfilling their intention of enriching themselves at the expense of the territory they had won. With Manfred dead, there was no surviving figure in the south on whom the loyalty of the Sicilians could focus. Their minds naturally turned to Conradin, the grandson of their greatest ruler and the last survivor of the Hohenstaufen line. Gradually refugees from the *Regno*, such as Peter of Prezze and Conrad of Antioch, began to filter north to Germany to make contact with Conradin. The burden of their message to him was always the same: the Hohenstaufen should come south and claim his own.

Conradin was only fifteen. Living under the tutelage of his uncles, Lewis and Henry of Bavaria, he was quite ignorant of conditions in Italy, but his imagination was naturally kindled by the thought of the rich prize which awaited him. His mother Elizabeth discouraged his schemes, realizing only too well what might come of them, but his childhood friend, his cousin Frederick of Baden, encouraged him to risk all. In the autumn of 1267 the two boys left Germany at the head of a pathetically small army to make their fortunes in the south.

At first things went well for them. Some of the old Ghibelline strongholds in northern Italy, such as Verona, opened their gates to him; the Muslims of the *Regno* conveniently rose in revolt, creating a diversion in the rear for Charles. But the two boys could not be expected to be a match for so old and experienced a leader as Charles. At Tagliacozzo (1268), one of the fiercest battles of the Middle Ages, their forces were deceived by apparent victory into scattering, and a violent counter-attack by the Angevins eventually led to the capture of the youths. The subsequent execution of both in Naples, while it shocked much of Europe, did not surprise the pope; Clement is said to have given his advice in callous but realistic phrase: 'Vita

Conradini, mors Caroli. Vita Caroli, mors Conradini.'[1] The legitimate Hohenstaufen line was extinct.

Charles was now free to pursue his more ambitious schemes of
restoring the Latin Empire in the East and of building up Angevin
power on the southern shores of the Mediterranean. S. Louis's second
crusade[2] was designed by Charles to serve this second purpose; in
that it ended by making the Emir of Tunis an Angevin tributary it
could be said to have succeeded in its purpose, despite the unfortunate
loss of much of the Angevin fleet through a storm at Trapani on the
return journey. But it was the hope of gaining control of Byzantium
that proved the richest lure. For this purpose papal co-operation
might be expected; an expedition against the schismatics might be
made to seem a crusade. Unfortunately the Papacy was no longer in
the hands of Frenchmen, who would realize the sacred nature of
Angevin expansion. The present incumbent Gregory X (1271-1276)
had been on a crusade in the East at the time of his election; neither
of his two main objects, the restoration of genuine crusading and the
negotiation of union with the Eastern Church, fitted well with
Charles's schemes. The nominal restoration of unity with the East
which Gregory succeeded in establishing at Lyons in 1275, unreal as
it might prove to be, was nevertheless inconvenient; it removed his
main pretext for attacking Byzantium. Charles was compelled to
bide his time, but the project was postponed rather than abandoned.
In the meantime the *Regno* came to know the full weight of taxation
necessary for the upkeep of an army and navy which would be
sufficient for the venture. At length in 1281 came the opportunity
for which he had been waiting; after a succession of short-lived popes
another Frenchman, Simon de Brie, was elected as Martin IV
(1281-1285). He did everything Charles could require; denouncing
the 'union' of 1274 he gave him every encouragement in his plan to
force the errant sheep back into the fold.

It was not to be expected that the eastern emperor Michael
Palaeologus (1259-1282) would passively await his own destruction.
An energetic and unscrupulous soldier who had regained Byzantium
for the dynasty he had founded, he was well aware against whom the
armada being collected in the ports of Sicily was intended. Besides
his own somewhat battered military forces he had two assets on which
to count. The simmering discontent against French rule in the
Regno might easily be made to boil into open revolt. Moreover,

---

[1] Quoted from Runciman, *op. cit.*, p. 115.
[2] See Chapter 9.

Michael was prepared to produce a 'legitimate' alternative to the rule of Charles of Anjou. Manfred's sole surviving child, Constance, had been married to Peter the Great of Aragon (1276–1285); through her he could put forward a claim to the throne of the *Regno*, a claim which would go well with the expansionist mood of the kingdom of the Spanish eastern seaboard. Peter had as his chancellor in Barcelona John of Procida, a native of the *Regno* who was well-suited to weave these three components into a conspiracy to thwart the Angevins.

But the outbreak when it came appears to have been spontaneous. During the festivities in Palermo on Easter Monday 1282 a French sergeant named Drouet appears to have offered some sort of insult to the wife of a Sicilian, in front of the Church of the Holy Spirit just before Vespers; the incident is not unparalleled among the records of armies of occupation. The enraged husband promptly knifed Drouet, and from this isolated incident sprang the wholesale massacre of Frenchmen throughout the island known as the Sicilian Vespers. Everywhere suspected Frenchmen were seized and, if their accents betrayed their origin, murdered; the survivors counted themselves lucky to reach the safety of the mainland. At first the rebels sought to put themselves under the protection of the Papacy, but when their delegation arrived before Martin chanting 'Lamb of God, Who bearest the sins of the world, have mercy upon us' the only reply the pope would give them was 'Hail, King of the Jews—and they smote Him'.[1] Frustrated in this attempt, they turned instead to the court of Aragon, which gladly espoused their cause.

The war which started with the Vespers was to drag on until 1302, despite various expedients to end it; the most well-known is the much-bruited duel at Bordeaux, by which the war was to be decided by a conflict between an hundred champions of each king. Each arrived at Bordeaux by the appointed day in 1283, and each solemnly announced by heralds that he was ready to fight. Since they had chosen to do so at different times, each was able to claim that his adversary had ignored the challenge. The war long outlasted its original participants, and was prolonged solely by the inflexible determination of a series of popes to prevent the Sicilians having the kings they wanted. In this they failed. The final Angevin attempt to invade the island was shattered at Falconaria (1299), and at length the urgent necessities of the struggle with the French monarchy led Boniface VIII to consent to the Peace of Caltabellotta (1302). By it

[1] Runciman, *op. cit.*, p. 221.

the *Regno* was split, the island of Sicily itself becoming a new kingdom of Trinacria under Frederick, the youngest son of Peter of Aragon, with the stipulation that Aragon and Sicily should not be united. Various clauses attempted to conceal that this was a defeat for the Angevins and for the Papacy, but in effect Sicily had won its own king. It was to gain little from the effort. Exhausted by the prolonged war and severed from the *Regno* it was never to regain its former prosperity. The mainland territory with its capital at Naples remained under the rule of Charles II (†1309), but alone it was not large enough to rank as a powerful state and its resources had been dissipated in the war. In the future it would offer easy access to foreign intervention in Italy. The Papacy too could look only on financial exhaustion and on the failure of its temporal aims. To achieve them it had incurred not only financial but moral bankruptcy; in 1303 at Anagni this bankruptcy would be published to the world.

14

Philip the Fair and Boniface VIII

The stability given to the French monarchy by Philip Augustus and S. Louis was well shown in the reign of Philip III, the Bold (1270–1285). Medieval government was so personal that a weak or incompetent king could rarely fail to do great damage, particularly if he reigned for a considerable period. The son of S. Louis was such a king. In the early years of his reign he was notoriously swayed by the influence of a favourite, Pierre de la Broce, who brought to the office of chancellor great personal ambition as well as some statesmanlike qualities. Yet after his second marriage, in 1274 to Mary of Brabant, he lacked the strength to defend his favourite against an attack launched on him by his wife's friends, and consented to the execution of de la Broce to favour the interests of this new faction. In the same way his uncle Charles of Anjou, the cause of trouble enough in his father's day, exercised a continuous influence over the new king. French resources were again wasted in pursuit of the aims of the House of Anjou; indeed, it was to be on a 'crusade' in Aragon, purely Angevin in intention, that Philip was to die.

Yet this apparently weak and vacillating king seems to have done little harm to the cause of the monarchy. Indeed, outwardly at least, Philip the Fair inherited a crown even more securely established than at the time of S. Louis's death. This apparent contradiction is to be explained in two ways. Philip III's two great predecessors had provided the monarchy with institutions, such as that of the *enquêteurs*, which were capable of functioning smoothly for a time without the personal support of an able king; even more important was the prestige given to the institution of monarchy itself by S. Louis, a prestige strong enough to withstand an individual king who was unworthy of it.

Philip's reign saw two considerable achievements in furthering the territorial expansion of the French Crown. The first was a mere gift of chance. In 1271 his uncle Alphonse of Poitiers died on his way home from the abortive Seventh Crusade. Since his wife had predeceased him, their combined lands, which included the greater part of

283

Languedoc as well as Poitiers itself, could be considered as reverting to the royal domain. Other claimants naturally appeared for so rich an inheritance; they included the kings of England and Aragon. But none was in so good a position to make good their claim as Philip. Using the disobedience of a vassal, the Count of Foix, as a pretext, in 1272 Philip was able to lead a French army throughout the south, displaying as a chronicler says 'the justice and the majesty' of the French king.[1]

Shortly before the end of his reign Philip was to achieve a similar triumph. In 1274 king Henry III of Navarre died, leaving as his sole heiress his young daughter, Joanna. Navarre itself, a Pyrenean kingdom with more than half its lands on the Spanish side, was of no great importance to the French Crown. Indeed, in that it constituted a temptation to disregard S. Louis's Treaty of the Pyrenees and to intervene in Spanish affairs, it might well be considered a hindrance. But besides being queen of Navarre Joanna was also heiress to the county of Champagne, a county which would make an obvious and rich contribution to the lands of France. The child's mother and guardian, the French Blanche of Artois, was very ready to accept the protection of Philip in her defenceless position, and by the Treaty of Orleans in 1275 the French king undertook the duties of wardship. At the same time a marriage was arranged for the future between Joanna and Philip's own infant son, later to be Philip the Fair. The solemnization of this marriage in 1284 was to be the occasion of the second territorial *coup* of Philip's reign.

These two achievements apart, the story of Philip's reign is one of failure in aims where success might have been even more damaging than failure. Charles of Anjou believed that it would be useful to his own Italian schemes to have his nephew as Holy Roman Emperor, and tried hard to secure his election in 1273. There can be little doubt that victory in the election would have led only to the profitless expenditure of French money on German and Italian schemes irrelevant to France; the victory of Rudolf of Habsburg was a blessing in disguise. In the same way little good could have come of the expedition to Aragon with which the reign ended. Its sole purpose was to restore the position of the Angevin house in Italy. Even if Philip had succeeded in his aim of establishing his younger son Charles of Valois on the throne of Aragon, to have kept him there would inevitably have led France into a series of expensive

---

[1] Guillaume de Puilaurens, quoted from Lavisse, *Histoire de France*, Tome III (pt. ii), Paris, 1911, p. 108.

Spanish wars. It was perhaps fortunate that the Sicilian admiral, Roger Loria, rendered the whole expedition hopeless by destroying the French fleet in September 1285. Philip himself became ill, and had only just strength enough to lead his army back to the north side of the Pyrenees before his death. His one great external adventure had ended in ruin.

The accession of Philip the Fair (1285–1314) heralds the last incontrovertibly great reign by a Capetian king of France. Yet there is much dispute as to the part played by Philip himself in the reign, dispute of a sort not to be found in the reigns of Philip Augustus or S. Louis. To some he has seemed the wise directing mind at the centre of a governmental organization of unequalled power and efficiency, to others a nonentity who chanced to be served by ministers of unusual ability. Nor is there agreement about the success of his reign as a whole. Certainly during it the governmental organization reached a more developed form than ever before, so that the royal will could be put into action more certainly in any part of France. Abroad too, the striking triumph over the international power of the Papacy, fresh from its victory over the Empire, seems to mark the reign out as a period of great strength. But, real as these triumphs were, they were gained by a France which before the end of the reign would be torn by internal revolt caused by the taxation demanded by a disastrously unsuccessful policy in Flanders. Whatever the strength of the edifice built by Philip IV, it was not durable; apparently supreme over Europe at the beginning of the fourteenth century, the French monarchy by the middle of the century was to have lost most of its control over France itself. Many other factors may explain this rapid decline, but it casts at least a suspicion on the reality of Philip's own achievement.

Philip himself remains a curiously elusive figure. That he was tall and handsome is generally accepted, but beyond that there is as little agreement among historians as there was among his contemporaries. To some this destroyer of the Papacy has seemed the very type of the anti-clerical, areligious ruler, concerned only with the magnification of his own power, a French version of the Emperor Frederick II. Yet, even if the contemporary accounts of his piety are discounted as propaganda, the king who on his deathbed refused the food which might have saved him must be allowed at least a formal piety. He seems to have cultivated deliberately a distant and inscrutable air with all but the closest of his own subjects. The bishop of Pamiers, who had more cause than most to know the strong reality of his policy, was to say of him 'He is not a man, not a beast; he is a graven image'.[1] The sphinx-like ruler will always pose the question of whether he really has a secret, but the definite trend of the actions of Philip's ministers and their apparent unity of purpose seem to justify the assumption that behind the ministers lay the controlling intelligence of the king.

The administrative changes worked under Philip the Fair were far-reaching without being revolutionary. His predecessors had already moved some way in the direction of a centralized administration staffed by professional bureaucrats dependent only on the Crown; Philip took the process much further. At least five separate institutions can be identified in Philip's administration. To the *Parlement* more and more judicial business was coming even from the remotest parts of the kingdom, so that by now it was in nearly continuous session—to the great profit of royal finances. The financial machinery of the Crown was divided between two bodies, the *Chambre des Comptes* and the *Chambre aux Deniers*; the latter had the more specific job of supervising the expenses of the royal household. These permanent departments necessarily remained in Paris, but the king himself was still required to travel constantly throughout his kingdom, and with him travelled the *Hôtel du Roi* and the *Conseil du Roi*. The former was concerned with the internal administration of the kingdom, and included such sub-departments as a Chancery, whose function it was to keep a register of all royal correspondence. The latter was the king's advisory council on all matters of foreign policy. These various bodies were all in a sense sub-divisions of what had once been a simple King's Council, and they should not be thought of as entirely self-contained. There was a considerable degree of cross-fertilization between the various departments; Pierre Flôte, for instance, who as Keeper of the Seal had charge of the Chancery and was a prominent member of the *Hôtel du Roi*, was also a frequent voice in the *Conseil du Roi*. But each department would have its core of expert officials who had been trained in that particular work. At the same time a much larger number of petty government employees, sergeants, foresters, and the like, were coming into being gradually throughout France to make royal government more than a name.

Greater efficiency then the royal administration was certainly coming to have. But it seems likely that this was being purchased at

[1] Bernard Saisset, quoted from Fawtier, *The Capetian Kings of France*, Macmillan, 1960, p. 39.

the price of some of its popularity. The outstanding characteristic of the higher ranks in Philip's administration was the preponderance of men trained in the traditions of Roman Law. There was nothing unique about this; a very similar development can be seen in the thirteenth-century papal *curia*, and the widespread interest in the Roman Law can be seen as a cause as well as a symptom of the growing tendency towards centralization in all the large organizations of the period. But the Roman Law was much more concerned with the rights of the ruler over his subjects than with the reverse process, and the activities of men like Flôte and de Marigny, the last of Philip's chamberlains, contrasted sharply with S. Louis's concern for the rights of his subjects. Moreover, such a body of professional administrators had to be paid, and the expenses of the system were one cause of the increasing concentration on revenue which helped to make Philip the Fair unpopular in his later years.

The one innovation of Philip's government was found in the States General, and even here there are parallels in other European countries; the rise of Parliament in England is only one. In France the periodic meetings of great councils of the baronage had been an irregular feature for many years. In 1213, for instance, Philip Augustus had consulted with his barons at Soissons to secure their support for the possible attack on England. Similar assemblies were sometimes held for judicial purposes; one, of which the record survives, shows how in 1230 an assembly at Ancenis deprived Pierre Mauclerc of his rights as regent of Brittany on account of his crimes. The document is sealed by thirty great lay and ecclesiastical lords, but it is mentioned that 'other barons and knights have taken part in the judgment'.[1] But the three estates, clergy, nobility, and bourgeoisie, as such were not summoned to meet the king in France until they were called to show national support for royal policy in the dispute with the Papacy. This dispute led to the more formal gathering of 1302, which is sometimes dignified with the name of first States General. In 1308 the attack on the Templars led to a similar meeting, and in 1314 the need for fresh revenue for the Flemish war produced a third.

The circumstances in which these early States General were called give some hint as to their purposes. Legislation was no part of their purpose; even in England the idea of Parliament as a place where new laws are made was only to emerge slowly in the course of the sixteenth and seventeenth centuries. But the judicial element was there; the session called over the Templars, essentially a criminal trial, showed

[1] See Petit-Dutaillis, *The Feudal Monarchy in France and England*, Routledge, 1936, p.240.

that like Parliament these meetings could be regarded as the meetings of a very high court. But even more important was their role as an instrument of royal policy. By them the king could hope to give an impressive display of national unity by which foreign rulers such as the Pope might be impressed. At the same time they could be a useful way of winning support for his policies at home. The king had no more effective way of shaping opinion at home than by getting the more influential laymen and clerics of the kingdom together and subjecting them to the intensive propaganda of his ministers. When they returned to their own areas they would take with them the royal view of the issues which had been put to them; in this way opinion could be prepared for actions which by themselves might seem dangerously revolutionary. At the same time a States General could act for the Crown as a useful gauge of opinion in the country. By allowing considerable freedom of expression there, the king could gain a fair idea of what policies would be popular or possible. In all this Philip's use of the States General was not very far distant from the use of Parliament by Henry VIII at the time of the Reformation.

As with so much of his policy, financial need also came to play a part. In the dispute against the Templars the Estates were used to mobilize 'national' opinion against a rich and already unpopular corporation; it was the more easy to do since the alternative to annexing the wealth of the Templars would no doubt be wider taxation. But at length he came in 1314 to using the States General for direct taxation itself, and, if it had its disadvantages for this purpose, much more being promised than was to be received, the presence in one place of so many of the main holders of wealth in France gave the king a good opportunity of extracting at any rate promises to pay.

The States General then were a creation of Philip the Fair, even if he may well have had no deliberate intention of adding to the French constitution. They were to prove a useful addition to the machinery available to the Crown without ever coming to threaten it. There is a variety of reasons for this. The three estates sat separately, and each one of them thought more of the interests of its own order than of any 'national' well-being. Quarrels between the estates were to be frequent, and this allowed the initiative to remain with the Crown. The estates could be used both for revenue and as a court, but they never became the indispensable source of either money or justice. Parliament in England or the *Cortes* in Spain both became capable of challenging the power of the Crowns they served; the States General acted only as an additional prop of royal power.

On his accession in 1285 Philip can have had no thought of the clash with the Papacy which provided the most dramatic moments of his reign. Rather he was concerned with two traditional problems of the house of Capet, the power of the English kings in France and the possibility that Flanders might come to be allied with his enemies. Since the time of the victories of Philip Augustus there had been little danger that the English kings would control France, yet England retained considerable lands in Guienne. The more powerful the French monarchy became, the more loyalty to the king of France came to express itself in an embryonic spirit of nationalism, so much the more had resentment grown against this foreign occupation of France; Edward I might hold his lands nominally as a vassal of the French crown, but increasingly he seemed in Paris only an English king occupying a part of France. Edward had already shown himself an active and efficient ruler in Guienne. S. Louis might perhaps have been able to expel Henry III from France without a major war if he had not had so much concern for the feudal rights of his vassal, but war would certainly be necessary if Philip was to be rid of Edward. The situation seemed propitious for such a move, for Edward had troubles enough at home. Wales was far from pacified, and the resistance of the king of Scotland, Balliol, offered Philip the opportunity of creating that Franco-Scottish alliance which was to become so recurrent a part of the European scene. With this alliance (1295) any English operations in France would be gravely hindered. There was no lack of pretexts to put Philip into the position of an aggrieved overlord. A sea battle between Gascon and French seamen in 1293 was used to summon Edward before the Paris *Parlement* to answer for the misdoings of his men. He seems to have been genuinely anxious to avoid war, sending Edmund of Lancaster to answer on his behalf, and being prepared to hand over six border fortresses as a surety of his good faith during the examination. This was at least as much as feudal custom, if not the letter of the law, required. To Philip, no doubt, that Edward was prepared to do so much was evidence of the weakness of his position. In 1294 he was declared to be contumacious and Guienne to be forfeit to the French Crown. The military occupation of Guienne began, and by 1296 most of it was in Philip's hands, in so far as that turbulent duchy could ever be said to be controlled by anyone.

By 1296, then, Edward of England was faced with the prospect that only a major war could save the English possessions in France; his victory against Balliol in that year made him the more ready to undertake it. But in such a war he would need allies, and he set himself to trying to build up a coalition against France from among her north-eastern neighbours; for all its tragic failure at Bouvines it was the only possible policy for an English king wishing to stir up trouble for France. Flanders was the most obvious centre for such an alliance. Its count, Guy de Dampierre, had the most justifiable suspicions that the king of France, already seriously worried by his lack of revenue, wished to avail himself of the wealth which might be made to come from the Flemish cloth industry. Moreover, that industry was largely dependent on supplies of raw wool from England; an interruption of these supplies would very soon spell destitution for an industrial proletariat who could only feed on what they could buy. The internal policies of the county were complicated, with a small class of merchant princes who resented the control of the county, and who looked to the king of France to protect them alike from the count and from the possibility of armed uprising by the very proletariat their own capitalism had produced. These princes were to take as their symbol the *fleur-de-lys* of France, and came to be known as *Leliaerts*; their opponents in turn ranged behind the count and had as their badge the clawed foot of the Lion of Flanders; hence they came to be known as *Clauwaerts*.

Count Guy had little desire for a war which was only too likely to end in the loss of his own county, but if Edward and Philip came to it he was likely to side with England; an English victory would at any rate give him a chance of survival. As early as 1294 he had accepted the English offer of alliance by arranging the marriage of his daughter to Edward's eldest son. Such a match would technically require the agreement of his overlord, and Philip was very far from being willing to give this. French troops entered Flanders to occupy the main industrial centres, and Guy himself was imprisoned until the match was called off. Philip now had apparent control over the county; too soon he began to explore the possibility of increasing royal revenue by taxing it. This led Guy, now released, to take the risk of repudiating his allegiance, and, summoning English aid, to lead all the anti-French forces in his county in revolt (1297).

The war which now started was to last with only short intermissions until the final French victory at Cassel in 1328. On the face of it this is very surprising. It was only the prospect of substantial English aid which had led Guy to risk his small and divided county in open war with the French kingdom, but the English alliance was to prove a broken reed. In the early months of the war Guy's army was defeated at Furnes (1297) by Robert of Artois, and this defeat caused the king of England and the other possible members of the coalition against France to have second thoughts. In the next year (1298) a separate peace was signed between England and France, and this was subsequently confirmed by two marriages linking the two royal houses. Philip the Fair evidently considered Flanders a more pressing problem than Guienne, and in 1303 at the Treaty of Paris he formally restored the latter to its English duke. The main cause of war between England and France was now gone, nor was Edward II, who was to succeed in 1307, in any position to renew aid even if he had wished to do so.

But the reduction of Flanders proved to be much more than the subjection of one not over-powerful feudal vassal. Defeated in battle, the ordinary feudal vassal was accustomed to regard this much in the light of a judicial decision which had gone against him; it was up to him to make the best settlement possible with the victor, who for his part was unlikely to wish utterly to ruin him. But the Flemings who opposed Philip were a new kind of opponent. The count was only their figurehead; the real motive power behind their resistance was a bitter hatred alike of Frenchmen and of the pro-French capitalists who had reduced them to wage slaves. Their quarrel was no mere feudal dispute about sovereignty, but the outcome of bitter racial and class hatred. They could expect no mercy in defeat, and for their part were not prepared to abide by the customs of feudal warfare. The early stages of the war fulfilled all Philip's hopes. A French army moved smoothly into Flanders in 1300, occupied the whole county, and once more imprisoned the count. A French governor, Jacques de Chatillon, was installed, and Philip could expect the much needed Flemish revenue to enrich the exchequer. But in 1302 the Matins of Bruges saw the first rising of an urban proletariat against its oppressors, and the revolt spread rapidly to engulf the entire merchant aristocracy of its French allies.

Philip was quick to react. The whole feudal might of France was quickly mobilized and dispatched to wreak vengeance. At the battle of Courtrai (1302) this host was smashed in a series of cavalry charges against the prepared trench works of a mass of infantry armed with pikes and bows—and their own sense of desperation. At the close of the battle the French army was completely broken; among the numerous dead were Robert of Artois, who had commanded it, and Pierre Flôte, the most able of Philip's ministers.

Courtrai is a landmark in both social and military history. For the first time the industrial proletariat, newcomers on the scene of northern Europe, revealed that they must be taken into account even in the world of power politics. Their victory at Courtrai showed that the long dominance of the mounted knight in warfare, a dominance which had begun with the Slavonic invasions of the ninth and tenth centuries, might be challenged. If the French court had been able to appreciate the lessons of Courtrai the military disasters of the Hundred Years War might have been avoided; it had now been shown that determined and well-handled infantry could defeat the cavalry of the mightiest European king.

However, Philip preferred to regard the result as an unfortunate upset in nature which would not be repeated. Courtrai was a grievous blow both to his prestige and to his resources; it was to play a vital part in convincing Boniface VIII that he too could withstand France. But a new army was quickly raised, and the attempt to re-establish control over Flanders was renewed. A partial military victory in 1304 was followed by a long period of negotiation, in which Philip tried to make use of Count Guy's son, Robert of Béthune, who had succeeded his father in 1304, to regain control for France. But the weavers of Flanders had not been fighting for the count, but for their own lives. Engagements made for them were not kept, sporadic uprisings continued to take place, and by 1314 he was again engaged in open and fruitless war. At the time of his death he was no nearer control of the county than he had been twenty years before, and the failure had cost him dearly in money and popularity at home.

The French effort to control Flanders did not end with Philip the Fair. His successors Louis X (1314–1316), Philip V (1316–1322), and Charles IV (1322–1328) all continued to pursue the same aim by alternating diplomacy and war, with no more success than their father. It was left to Philip VI (1328–1350) to avenge Courtrai by winning the battle of Cassel (1328) at the beginning of his reign. Here the Flemish army was unwise enough to leave its position and to attempt an attack on the French cavalry instead of waiting to be attacked. In such circumstances the French could fight in a position of their own choosing, and a general slaughter of the Flemings ensued. Yet Cassel was not a really decisive victory. The opening of the Hundred Years War was now not far distant, and the disasters which were then to fall on the French monarchy would give Flanders another opportunity of pursuing an independent course.

The main effect of Philip the Fair's long and ultimately unsuccessful struggle to gain control of Flanders was to be found in the financial strain it placed on the monarchy. The extending bureaucracy Philip employed, efficient though it was, inevitably cost money, but to this was added the constant drain of incessant war and preparations for war. This cardinal fact explains much of the history of the reign. To a large extent it was the reason for the conflict with the Papacy, the attack on the Templars, and those on the Italian merchants and the Jews. Wherever Philip could see a reserve of capital he wished to transfer it to the royal exchequer; if that capital was controlled by some minority group which was not popular with most Frenchmen, then it became all the more desirable, for it could be taken with popular approval. But, successful as he was in many of his money-making ventures, he could not hope to provide himself by this means alone with a regular increase of income sufficient to sustain the national finances during incessant war. Long before the end of the reign the Crown had had recourse to financial measures which were as damaging to its prestige as they were morally questionable. Debasement of the coinage has always offered itself as a quick remedy for financially embarrassed rulers. Nothing is more simple for a strongly established monarchy than to compel the exchange of existing coinage for new coins of the same face value but less bullion content, and the profit is sure. Yet invariably this profit has to be paid for in terms of a general but erratic rise in prices affecting the Crown with everyone else, and, more seriously, by a general loss of confidence in the financial honesty of the monarchy. S. Louis had given the Crown an enviable reputation in this respect; his grandson came to be known as 'the False Coiner', a title only too merited by the debasements of 1295, 1303, and 1311. Nor was this all. The existence of two separate currencies in France, the one of *écus* and *gros tournois* which consisted of coins in circulation, the other of *livres* and *sous* which, like the modern guinea, existed only as a banker's and sales-man's fiction, gave further opportunity to the ingenuity of his ministers. By altering artificially the relationship between the two the Crown could be enabled to pay off some of its debts at less than their previous value in coinage. But the device was one which gained solvency rather than popularity.

No amount of financial sharp dealing could avert the necessity for new taxation, drastic as this measure was in an age which was not accustomed like our own to heavy and fluctuating government taxation. Indirect taxation, always less painful if less fair than direct levies, was made to carry as much as possible of the load, and a series of *maltôtes*, a form of sales tax, was applied; in so doing the Crown was putting the first real strain on the well-established alliance between itself and the bourgeoisie of the towns. But from 1294 subsidies, direct taxes on income or property, became increasingly common. By the fourteenth century almost every year saw subsidies proclaimed by the Crown and reluctantly accepted by local assemblies. The nominal size of these subsidies, which on income sometimes rose as high as a fifth, bore little relation to the revenue actually forthcoming; there was simply not the machinery necessary to extract such large sums from a recalcitrant public. But the sums that were gathered made the Crown highly unpopular, and, as was so often the case with medieval taxation, they were gathered largely from those who were too weak and uninfluential to avoid them—in other words from the classes who could least afford to pay them. The subsidy Philip attempted to raise for his last campaign against Flanders in 1314 provoked something like a general strike against payment; in many different parts of France local leagues came into existence to resist payment. Against this kind of collective disobedience medieval rulers were powerless, and Philip had no alternative to cancelling the subsidy and curtailing the operation. But that it took place is an indication of how far royal popularity had become a victim to the financial needs of the Flemish adventure.

The conflict between Philip the Fair and Boniface VIII must not be seen as the chance quarrel of two determined men. As in that other conflict to which it forms an obvious parallel, the Investiture Contest, personalities played an important part in determining that the clash came when and how it did, but that there would be such a clash was inevitable. Just as the reformed Papacy of the eleventh century could not but challenge the power of an Empire which had come to use the Church as the major part of its civil administration, so the rising power of the monarchies at the end of the thirteenth century must soon have clashed with a Papacy which was becoming ever more insistent on its duty to stand over the nations and to judge them. The unified nation states which were coming into being round such kings as the king of France would not for ever acquiesce even in theory to a system which put ultimate authority beyond their reach.

When Philip the Fair came to the French throne in 1285 he

inherited a tradition of some two hundred years of steady growth in the prestige and extent of French royal power. From its humble beginnings in the Île de France the monarchy had by now come to control the great majority of what was geographically France. Yet the power of the Crown was limited in two important respects. Churchmen were citizens not of the Earthly City which was France, but of the Heavenly City whose representative on Earth was the Pope; all men, lay and ecclesiastic alike, stood under the ultimate judgment of the Church in that they were sinners. This too was an ancient tradition and not without its records of conflict, but under Innocent III the theory of papalism had come near fulfilment. That this had been possible can be attributed to three main causes. Under Innocent the Papacy had come to have the machinery it had lacked in earlier generations through which it could exercise an authority which was actual as well as merely moral. Yet at the same time it retained the reputation for righteousness which had been built up for it by papalists such as S. Peter Damian and S. Bernard over the centuries; no glaring inconsistency was involved in the view that the cause of God and the cause of the Papacy were one and the same. Finally the national monarchies of Europe were not yet so firmly established that they either could, or in general wished to, challenge papal claims. If they did, the career of John of England illustrates the dangers they faced; wiser rulers preferred to seek the co-operation of a Church whose favour was so valuable an asset to them.

The period between the death of Innocent III and the accession of Boniface VIII had seen this papalist position increasingly weakened, and it is not hard to see the reasons for this. The popes of the thirteenth century were not for the most part inconsiderable men, but their talents were those of practical men rather than of saints. Perhaps this was inevitable; the Western Church was by now a sufficiently complicated structure to need considerable administrative ability at its head, and, even if this had not been so, the preservation intact of the papal lands in central Italy, always the most immediate problem confronting any pope, demanded strength and guile. Innocence alone would be but poor equipment for the dirty game of Italian politics. Gregory IX (1227–1241) and Innocent IV (1243–1254), the two outstanding popes of the period, were both canon lawyers and administrators of great ability whose main interest had been in politics, the internal politics of the Church and the external politics which concerned the relationship of the Church with the powers of Europe. They had led the Papacy to its resounding victory

over the Hohenstaufen Empire, but in so doing they had been forced
to use methods which could not but damage its spiritual prestige.
Such things as the savage persecution of the Spiritual Franciscans for
their sympathy with the emperor or the indiscriminate use of excommunication against political opponents, to say nothing of the
attempted use of assassination as a political weapon, could not fail
to weaken the image of the Papacy as an institution concerned above
all with righteousness. Moreover, prolonged warfare had proved
desperately expensive, and the Papacy, like the national monarchies
against which it was shortly to be ranged, had of necessity become
ever more concerned with problems of finance. Understandable as
this was, it had led to a situation in which the Papacy had lost its
unique position as *the* Christian authority on Earth; it was not
Frenchmen alone who saw in S. Louis rather than in Innocent IV
the Christian conscience incarnate.

The story of the clash between Boniface and Philip can be taken
to start with the election of Pietro di Morrone as pope in 1294, with
the title of Celestine V. The election, coming at the end of a deadlock
prolonged for two years at the papal conclave, can be seen as in part a
recognition within the Church itself of the need for holiness. For the
new pope had no other qualification than personal holiness for his
office; after his election he had to be extracted from the hermit's cell
in the Abruzzi to which he had retired from the government of a
small religious order. But it was also intended as a compromise
between the disagreeing factions at the conclave, between those who
supported and those who opposed the Angevin influence in Italy,
and between the Orsini and the Colonna. Morrone was thought to
have no political affiliations.

Celestine's short pontificate proved to be disastrous. Within a
few months he had reduced the delicate administrative machinery
of the Church to chaos. High offices of the Church were distributed
'against all custom, at anyone's suggestion and the dictates of his own
untutored simplicity'.[1] A native of the Neapolitan kingdom himself,
he never left Neapolitan territory, installing the Papacy at Aquila and
showing in all his actions that he favoured the Angevin rule of
Charles of Naples; on one occasion twelve new cardinals were
created at a single unexpected session, almost all of them nominations
of Charles. It was soon apparent that sanctity was not enough.

No one was more miserable about the state of affairs than Celestine

---

[1] Jacopone de Varagine, Archbishop of Genoa, quoted from Boase, *Boniface VIII*,
Constable, 1933, p. 45.

himself, unhappily striving to control an organization he did not understand, and there would be no surprise in his sudden abdication after only five months of rule were it not for the totally unprecedented nature of the action. It was even doubtful whether a pope had the power to abdicate. Later French propaganda was able to gain wide acceptance for the legend that when the simple old man fell to his knees at evening to seek the guidance of the Holy Spirit he gained clearer reception than usual: 'Resign, Resign, Resign' came the words of his successor, speaking through a carefully concealed speaking tube.

The conclave which followed (December 1294) had little difficulty in choosing Cardinal Benedict Gaetani to succeed him. The new pope, who took the title of Boniface VIII, was a complete contrast to his predecessor. A member of a gentle family with connections with at least three earlier thirteenth-century popes, he had already a distinguished career in papal diplomacy and administration behind him. Already elderly at the time of his election, he was resolved to waste no time in restoring order to the papal administration. Almost his first action was to revoke all the acts of his predecessor. But Boniface had two great disadvantages for his new office: his age and his temperament alike rendered him unlikely to be able to make the adjustments in papal theory which would be necessary if a satisfactory relationship were to be arrived at with the new nation states, and his health was far from good. He suffered from painful attacks of the stone; recent history has examples enough of the judgment of a statesman being upset by severe physical pain.

At the time of his accession Boniface was not thought of as being anti-French; all that was clear was that he had a most exalted view of papal power. In the opening years of his pontificate he concerned himself largely with a necessary revision of the canon law, which was to bear fruit in 1298 in the *Sext*, a codification of all the recent additions to canon law. With this task, with a fierce internal quarrel with the Colonna family, and a papal war with Sicily on his hands, he might have seemed to be fully occupied. But by 1294 the French and English monarchies were drifting towards a major war; both kings badly needed additional revenue for the conflict, and both were disinclined to allow their clergy to contract out of what seemed a national obligation. Early in 1296 an assembly of French prelates, acting no doubt under royal pressure, voted a subsidy to be raised from all clerics. On receiving a complaint from the Cistercian Order Boniface reacted swiftly; the decretal *Clericis Laicos*, issued in

February 1296, forbade any king to raise money from his clergy except with the express permission of the Holy See. The instruction was not new; a similar ruling had been made by the Fourth Lateran Council, but what had been appropriate to the age of Innocent III might be quite unworkable a hundred years later.

Both kings resisted *Clericis Laicos* immediately. Edward replied by outlawing all clerics who accepted the bull, giving them the choice of apostacy or treason; Philip's answer was more subtle but no less damaging to the pope. A decree of August 1296 forbade the export of any bullion from France and ordered all foreign merchants to leave the kingdom. At one blow this would prevent any Church revenues reaching Rome and would be a grave blow at the fortunes of Lombard business houses, like the Pulci and the Rimberti, which had extensive interests in France. Since these same houses played a vital part in supporting the tottering papal finances, it was an action well calculated to bring pressure on Boniface to surrender his position. The papal bull *Ineffabilis* in September was an attempt to justify the papal action in theological terms, while at the same time suggesting that kings would not necessarily be refused permission to raise revenue from the church. Meanwhile Pierre Flôte in France was organizing propaganda as a political weapon in a series of pamphlets suggesting, among other things, that Boniface wanted the money for his own relations.

In Italy Boniface was deeply embroiled with the Colonna family. If he was to break their power he must have the revenue of the Church at his disposal. In 1297 the bulls *Romana Mater* and *Etsi de Statu* mark his surrender. A face-saving formula was found. Kings must not tax their clergy except in emergency, but the monarchs, and not the Pope, are to be the judges of when such an emergency exists. The canonization of S. Louis which followed shortly was intended as a future gesture of reconciliation.

The period from 1297 to 1301 saw a lull in the struggle. During it Boniface was able apparently to put an end to the opposition of the Colonna family; their stronghold at Palestrina was razed to the ground in 1298 in a papal 'crusade', a word now stripped of all its original meaning. In 1300 Boniface celebrated a papal jubilee, a spurious antique custom by which the faithful were promised full remission of Purgatory if they visited the seven basilicas in Rome. It was a great success. The crowds of pilgrims flocked to Rome from all the Christian world; even converts from Asia knelt before the Holy Father to receive his blessing. Preachers such as Cardinal

Matthew of Acquasparta dilated on the theme of the superiority of the papal to all earthly powers. Boniface would have been more than human if the Jubilee had not filled him with indignation that he, the direct representative of God on Earth, had been forced to surrender before a more earthly king.

But the renewal of the struggle when it came was not the result of any papal action. Among the problems which confronted the French kings in the thirteenth century, the complete assimilation of that most recent acquisition of the Crown, Languedoc, must have ranked high. Inevitably the loyalty of an area so different in language and customs from northern France must be suspect. Within Languedoc lay the town of Pamiers, recently made into a bishopric by Boniface. Its bishop, Bernard Saisset, himself came from the South and was a personal friend of the pope. He also seems to have been a man of intemperate speech, given to criticisms of the Crown. Philip determined to make a test case out of him. He was suddenly summoned to attend before the king at a special assembly at Senlis (1301), and charged there with a fantastic variety of offences, the fertile imaginations of Philip's councillors Flôte and de Nogaret having embellished his real opposition to the French Crown with a wide variety of largely obscene inventions. The technique is now well known from Russian treason trials; political opponents must be made to seem also morally despicable. Philip demanded that he should be degraded from his orders so that as a layman he might suffer the penalties his offences demanded.

If Boniface had acceded to this demand he would have been guilty of a fatal surrender to the secular power, as well as of a grave act of injustice to Saisset. That he refused to allow Philip's demand, and referred the whole matter to Rome for investigation there, was neither surprising nor unwise. What was much more questionable, and typical of a tendency to be seen throughout his career, was his readiness to invoke general principles to support his action in a particular case, thus extending the whole range of the conflict. Weak as he was in prestige and material resources, Boniface's real interests demanded that he should do everything to avoid a direct collision with the kingdom of France. Instead, his actions deliberately provoked one. In the bull *Salvator Mundi* at the end of 1301 Boniface formally removed all the concessions he had made in *Romana Mater* and *Etsi de Statu*, and shortly afterwards *Ausculta, Fili* was a stern warning to the king of France to mend his ways. Claiming that 'his throat was already dry' with the complaints he had already had to make against him, Boniface announced that he was summoning representatives of the whole French Church to meet him in Rome in November 1302. Philip could attend if he wished, but the implication is clear that if he did not submit to papal judgment he would be both dethroned and damned.

The issue had now passed well beyond the matter of the guilt or innocence of Saisset, who in fact was able to make his way to Rome. Philip retaliated by summoning a general assembly of his nation, including the clergy, to Paris in the spring. It was noticeable that about two-thirds of the French Church put their loyalty to the king above that to the pope, and chose to go to Paris rather than Rome. At the States General Pierre Flôte turned the full force of his propaganda on the pope. Not only was he of vile life, but he was not pope. The abdication into which he had tricked Celestine could not possibly be valid. The assembly greeted this presentation of the royal case with enthusiasm.

Boniface himself had just enough French support at his council to encourage him to continue the struggle, and the French defeat at Courtrai must have given him encouragement. The bull *Unam Sanctam* issued at the close of the council is the most extreme statement of medieval papalism.[1] Nowhere is the unity of the Church more fully stressed; the Church is one body and has one head, 'not two heads like a monster', and this head is none other than Peter, and Peter's successor. The Gelasian theory is overthrown. Two swords there are indeed, but 'Both are in the power of the Church, the spiritual sword and the material. But the latter is to be used for the Church, the former by her'. If he who wields the temporal sword errs, he must stand under the correction of the spiritual power, but none can correct the spiritual power save God alone. And so the bull moves to its majestic conclusions. 'Furthermore we declare, state, define and pronounce that it is altogether necessary to salvation for every human creature to be subject to the Roman pontiff.'

It is easy to exaggerate the novelty of *Unam Sanctam*. There is nothing in it which had not been said already by the papalist writers of the eleventh and twelfth centuries, and its teaching had been implicit in the whole development of the canon law. What was new was that this teaching was now proclaimed officially in singularly uncompromising language at a time when the moral and physical powers of the Papacy were equally low. Innocent III could have

[1] For text see *Documents of the Christian Church*, ed. Bettenson. Oxford U. P., World's Classics, 1943, pp. 159–161.

issued *Unam Sanctam* with impunity; for Boniface it spelt ruin.
His fall fits closely to the pattern of Greek tragedy. Certainly he
was a man many of whose qualities demand respect, but who seems
infected with the fatal flaw of Hubris. Manifesting itself in *Unam
Sanctam*, this soon provoked Nemesis. During the summer of 1303
Nogaret was sent to Italy with sinister instructions 'to secure the
peace and unity of the Church'. The pope meanwhile was spending
the summer months at his summer palace at Anagni; he was widely
thought to be preparing the final excommunication of the king of
France. Nogaret found no difficulty in recruiting among the supporters of the Colonna men to help him on a desperate venture. On
7 September 1303 Nogaret's band suddenly appeared before Anagni.
The townsfolk aided them, those members of the papal court who
were there fled, and the old man was left alone to face his enemies.
Even now he had the chance of victory. 'Here is my head, here is
my breast' he is reported to have said to his captors, offering himself
for martyrdom. But his was not to be the happy fate of Becket.
After much debate between Nogaret and Sciarra Colonna they
decided not to kill him; to remove him to France was impossible,
and after sacking the papal treasury and removing everything of
value from the palace, his attackers withdrew.

It would have been better for Boniface if he had died. Martyrs
rule from the tomb; he had only succeeded in appearing absurd. The
contrast between the proud sentences of *Unam Sanctam* and the
reality of an impotent old man unable to protect even his own palace
made the whole doctrine seem absurd. Boniface himself did not long
survive the shame. Five weeks later he died, tearing the flesh from his
hands and battering his head against the wall in his rage, his enemies
said. Medieval papalism had within two years received both its
fullest expression and the demonstration that it was no longer possible.

The lesson was not lost on the surviving members of the Curia.
The next pope Benedict XI (1303–1304) had been an eyewitness of
the outrage at Anagni, but he had learnt from the scene the impossibility of opposing France, as well as the wickedness of Nogaret.
He did not live long enough to show if his attempt to conciliate
France by ignoring Philip's, as opposed to Nogaret's, responsibility
for it was feasible. The conclave which followed Benedict's death
was a long one, opinion among the cardinals being much divided
between those who still wished to avenge Anagni and those who felt
that there was no alternative to surrender to Philip. The election of
Bertrand de Got, Archbishop of Bordeaux, as Clement V (1305–1314)

may have been intended as another compromise. If he was a Frenchman, he at any rate came from the south of the country and was known to have been on good terms with Boniface.

In the event Clement's election proved to be something like a surrender to France. Clement was a man of weak will and nervous disposition, who never even attempted to enter the turbulent land of Italy. After his election he arranged for his coronation to take place at Lyons; the event was marred by the collapse of a wall, thronged with spectators, on top of the pope and his immediate attendants, an incident which acted both as an evil augury for the new pontificate and as a further strain on Clement's debilitated constitution. For four years he kept the *Curia* wandering in France, until in 1309 he finally settled at Avignon, close to the isolated papal county of Venaissin. The Babylonish Captivity of the Church had begun.

For Philip the Fair the presence of the Papacy within France was victory indeed. The College of Cardinals gradually became more and more French, while Clement himself lived in the constant fear that he would be forced to rule that Boniface had been no pope, a decision which would have cast grave doubts on his own position. A long judicial process did indeed drag on at the papal court until 1313 at which varied accusations of unlawful election, heresy, and unnatural vice were freely bandied around the memory of the dead pope. It was to end in a compromise. Celestine was enrolled among the saints, Philip and Nogaret were proclaimed to have acted from the best motives, but Boniface was allowed to have been a legitimate pope.

For Philip the 'trial' of Boniface had been only a means to an end. Money had been for long his main problem, and his covetous eye had rested on the Order of Knights Templar. Now that the era of crusading in the East was over the original purpose of this military Order had largely disappeared, but it remained a rich corporation holding more property in France than in any other country. At the beginning of the fourteenth century the Order in France seems to have consisted of some two thousand knights, most of them elderly gentlemen living inoffensive if somewhat futile lives, and perhaps ten thousand sergeants and other dependents. The rules of the Order contained a strict vow of secrecy, and as with many secret societies this had led many outside the order to suspect that secrecy must cloak something disreputable, but there is no sound evidence to suggest that they were either grossly corrupt or a menace to the peace of the kingdom. Nogaret was given charge of a propaganda campaign against the order, a task he performed with even greater zeal than Thomas Cromwell two hundred years later in very similar circumstances. They were accused of secretly betraying the Holy Land, of spitting upon the Cross, of practising gross sexual perversions learnt from the Infidel, or worshipping the Devil in the form of cats or of a graven image known as Baphomet (who must, one feels, have had the Prophet in his parentage). Then suddenly, on one night in 1307, the entire Order in France, including its recently arrived Grand Master, Jacques de Molay, was arrested. Under torture most of them confessed satisfactorily to whatever was put to them, and Clement found himself faced with a demand for the dissolution of the Order. The examination of the Templars, as Churchmen, was strictly no business for the Crown, and when on Clement's insistence they were brought before papal representatives many of them retracted their earlier confessions. This was unwise. They remained in the custody of the Crown, and they could now be handled as relapsed heretics. In May 1310 no less than sixty-three were burnt, an action which effectually terrorized most of the remainder. Nor could Clement protect them. Terrified lest the full force of Nogaret's machinery might be turned on himself, after the Council of Vienne he decreed the Order's dissolution (1312), even though investigations outside France had revealed none of the depravity found by Philip's ministers. Officially its goods were to pass to the parallel order of the Knights Hospitaller, but in France most had already gone to the Crown. Only Jacques de Molay and three companions were left three years later to protest the innocence of their Order when brought out of prison to testify publicly to its guilt, and their brave action cost them their lives. Otherwise the State had conquered all resistance.

The dissolution of the Templars makes a fit ending to the story of Philip IV, for no incident, not even Anagni itself, so clearly shows the great strength of the French monarchy. Well served by ruthless servants of great efficiency, it was now supremely master of its own house and the most feared power in Europe. Yet the methods Philip used made him a monarch more to be feared than loved. If a weak king came to rule the apparent strength might soon crumble. Like the Papacy itself fifty years before, the monarchy had purchased victory only at the price of much of its own prestige.

15

The Black Death and After

Thirteenth-century Europe presented all the outward characteristics of a robust and self-confident society. In most European countries all the evidence, scanty as it may be, agrees that the population had been rising, at least from the beginning of the eleventh century. Territorially the settled area of the continent was growing all the time, as the remaining supplies of wasteland in each country were colonized and as the boundaries of Christian settlement were pushed even further to the East in Germany or to the South of Spain. Within those boundaries the general impression is of ever-increasing efficiency. Stimulated by the lure of the markets for all saleable commodities which the growth of towns had offered, there had grown up areas, such as Gascony with its vines or eastern Germany with its wide corn fields, where specialization and the high productivity associated with it had become the rule. Even where this was not so and where the more old-fashioned methods of feudal agriculture remained the rule, the hope of easy markets for any surplus that might be produced, and the pressure for any tenancies that might become vacant, could not but act as forces towards better farming.

The towns themselves, small as they may seem by modern standards, had everywhere become an accepted part of the social scene. Aided by royal favour, they had expanded fast in population and influence; the two primarily urban areas, Flanders and Lombardy, were now exporting their goods far beyond the borders of Europe, so that they were not unknown in India or Samarkand, while internal trade within Europe itself grew steadily in bulk and value.

Economic growth had been accompanied by a similar growth in the institutions through which society was governed. The Church had at last achieved in the age of Innocent III the unity of outward organization it had long desired, together with the steady supply of officials needful if that unity was to be maintained. Nor were the secular organizations lagging far behind. In every country the growth of royal *curias* was bringing government of a kind which was at once far more efficient and far more expensive than the cruder methods which had necessarily prevailed in earlier ages. Different in many things, the kingdoms of Frederick II and S. Louis had this at least in common. Europe was growing in size and efficiency; at the same time society was growing much more capable of self-expression. The codifications of both the civil and the canon law, the constant foundation of new universities, the tendency to define what had been vague in precise terms in charters, all were symptoms of a society in which vigorous intellectual activity accompanied economic well-being. In literature too a kindred development can be seen. Medieval society had always been bilingual in the sense that Latin had existed as the language of the learned and of the Church alongside the various vernaculars, but broadly speaking the latter had remained spoken tongues alone. The literature of the Carolingian period or of the eleventh century is, for example, almost exclusively Latin. But now the vernaculars themselves were becoming literary languages. The twelfth century, in particular in France, saw the development of whole cycles of long narrative poems in which the epic deeds of the great heroes of the past, which had long been the substance of minstrels' lays in court and castle, were now for the first time recorded in written form. These *Chansons de Geste* dealt with the deeds of the warriors of ancient days; some of them, like the *Chanson de Roland*, were concerned with the earliest champions of their own society, with the exploits of Charlemagne and his knights who had saved Christendom from the Infidel. Others recounted the scarcely more remote achievements of the legendary King Arthur and the Knights of his Round Table, or the doings of Alexander, that greatest fighter of them all. But medieval Europe by now was no simple Homeric society in which the virtues of the man of war alone were recognized. The Arthurian cycle itself was given a deeper Christian significance by the addition to it of the theme of the Holy Grail.

At the same time other and different themes were explored. The *Chansons de Toile* were written from the viewpoint, not of the knights who went out to fight, but of their ladies who stayed behind, wondering if ever their loves would return; some have even suspected for them a feminine authorship. This interest in the phenomena of human love culminated in the thirteenth century with the *Roman de la Rose*, the lengthy allegory on love which remained in high favour for the rest of the Middle Ages. An entirely different approach is that of the *fabliaux*, where animal fables, like that of Reynard the Fox, are used in the manner of Aesop to point satiric lessons on human behaviour. Satire is a form of literary expression only associated with developed societies capable of reflection on their own experience and customs. Another sign of the development of the common tongues was the much greater bulk of prose which was being written, even on subjects which called for imaginative writing. The straight chronicles of events were now supplemented by accounts in the vernacular which sought to express the views of the authors themselves, and to give for events the explanations which they believed to be valid. In the thirteenth century Geoffrey of Ville-hardouin's account of the Fourth Crusade and de Joinville's life of S. Louis both give a clear picture of their authors as well as of the events they are seeking to describe, while in the fourteenth Froissart's *Chronicles* bear clearly the stamp of his own attitudes.

Nor was French the only vernacular language to show such development. Indeed by far the greatest single literary achievement of the Middle Ages was in Italian. One of the most remarkable facts about the *Divine Comedy* is that its author chose to write it not in Latin, but in Italian; indeed he is said to have started the poem in Latin before discarding it and choosing instead the vernacular. For Dante Alighieri (1265–1321) was no stranger to Latin, and chose it for the *De Monarchia*, that best account of the theory of the Christian Empire, written at a time when imperialist ideas were already obsolete. Nor was the *Divine Comedy* concerned primarily with entertainment, for which the native tongue might have been deemed more appropriate; in it the Florentine political exile sought to express through an extended allegory the totality of human existence and of the divine plan which God had made for it. The love of Dante for Beatrice was made the means by which the poet could investigate the very nature of Love, and therefore of that God who Himself is Love. In the course of the investigation Dante is also faced of necessity with all those deviations from love of which human sin is made. In its attempt to see the whole of the known moral world the *Divine Comedy* challenges comparison with the attempt of S. Thomas Aquinas to survey the whole range of human knowledge. Both were the products of a society uniquely confident of its ability to understand and make known its own experience. The *Divine Comedy* also stands as a reminder of the heights to which the vernacular languages of the Middle Ages could rise. With Petrarch (†1374) and Boccaccio (†1375) medieval Italian achieved a complete maturity of expression; its subsequent decline in the face of the enthusiasm of the Italian Renaissance, which held that only through the classical languages could real civilization be attained, is a reminder of how much was to be lost as well as gained in the Renaissance.

It is easy to attribute the very general decline which is observable in so many branches of medieval life in the later fourteenth and fifteenth centuries to the natural catastrophe of the Black Death. Certainly this was to play a big part, yet there is not lacking evidence to show that in many fields decline had set in even before 1348. Population is always difficult to assess in a society which does not keep accurate statistics of births and deaths, but it is becoming increasingly evident that at the very least the steady rise in population which Europe had experienced during the last two or three centuries had been halted before the Black Death; in several areas it would seem already to have declined. The colonial expansion to the East halted about 1290, and in some areas there was even some contraction. Further west the pressure of would-be tenants on available holdings, which had sometimes caused holdings to be sub-divided into units of barely economic size, eased somewhat, and operations such as land drainage in the Netherlands, which can only be accounted for by acute land shortage, were no longer found to be profitable. The reasons for this change, as for many changes in population, are exceedingly obscure. Possibly for some unknown reason the infant death rate rose; possibly the fertility rate among adults fell, perhaps as a result of some new dietetic factor. But, whatever the cause, the momentum of growth in Europe seems to have been checked.

But if some of the processes attributed to it had in fact begun to operate somewhat earlier, there can be no doubt of the impact of the Black Death. Something of the hopeless terror which it inspired can be felt from the passage at the beginning of the *Decameron* in which Boccaccio tells of its earliest appearance, 'I say, then, that the years of the era of the fruitful Incarnation of the Son of God had attained to the number of one thousand three hundred and forty-eight, when into the notable city of Florence, fair over every other of Italy, there came the death-dealing pestilence which, through the operation of heavenly bodies or of our own iniquitous dealings, being sent down upon mankind for our correction by the just wrath of God, had some years before appeared in the parts of the East . . . And there against no wisdom availing nor human foresight . . . nor yet humble supplications . . . made unto God by devout persons—about the coming in of the Spring of the aforesaid year it began on horrible and miraculous wise to show forth its dolorous effects. Yet not as it had done in the East, where, if any bled at the nose, it was a manifest sign of inevitable death; nay, but in men and women alike there appeared, at the beginning of the malady, certain swellings, either on the groin or under the armpits, whereof some waxed of the bigness of a common apple, others like unto an egg, some more and some less, and these the vulgar named plague-boils. From these two parts the aforesaid death-bearing plague-boils proceeded, in brief space, to appear and come indifferently in every part of the body; wherefrom, after awhile, the fashion of the contagion began to change into black or livid blotches which showed themselves in many (first) on the arms and about the thighs and (after spread to) every other part of the person, in some large and sparse and in others small and thick-sown; and like as the plague-boils had been first (and yet were) a very certain token of coming death even so were these for every one to whom they came.'[1]

There is little doubt that the disease which first appeared in the Yangtse Valley in China during 1334 was the bubonic plague. Even today plague remains a potent danger in those countries in which it remains endemic, and recurrent pandemics, of which the most recent was in 1911, have made it a lasting threat to world population. But, as with most diseases, the passage of time has made it rather less virulent as the population of affected areas build up something of a resistance to it; a comparison might be drawn with scarlet fever, regarded with good cause as a dangerous killer in the early nineteenth century. It would seem that the outbreak of 1348 often took on the pneumonic form of the plague, even today a most deadly disease.

Existing medical knowledge was completely incompetent to treat a disease, the unexpected cause of which was only to be discovered at the end of the nineteenth century. The bubonic plague was then discovered to be carried by means of a disease of the parasites carried by the black rat, the animal which boasts the charming zoological name of *Rattus rattus*. Incidentally the disappearance of plague from Europe probably owes more to the supplanting of *Rattus rattus* by that newcomer which we now think of as the common brown rat than to the improved sanitary conditions which so often get the praise. The disease was fatal alike to the fleas which first developed it, to the rats which acted as their hosts, and to humans who came into contact with it.

With no knowledge of the cause of the outbreak, any adequate treatment, let alone the unknown process of inoculation, was impossible. Some, like the story-tellers of the *Decameron*, by chance

---

[1] *The Decameron*, trans. John Payne. Chapman and Hall. Day the First.

hit on a strict isolation as giving the best prospect of survival, but the more popular remedies, such as the avoidance of moist foods, the consumption of quantities of vinegar, and the observance of strict sexual abstinence, can have had little effect. In any case there were only doctors for a minute fraction of the population. Guy de Chauliac, physician to Pope Clement VI at Avignon, told how even the normal family care of the sick broke down: 'In Avignon the contagion was so great that not only by remaining with the sick, but even by looking at them people seemed to take it; so much so that many died without anyone to serve them, and they were buried without priests to pray over their graves. A father did not visit his son, nor a son his father. Charity was dead. The mortality was so great that it left hardly a fourth part of the population. Even the doctors did not dare visit the sick from fear of infection . . . As for me, to avoid infamy, I did not dare to absent myself, but still I was in continual fear.'[1]

To arrive at any exact estimate of the extent of the catastrophe is not possible. Conjectures such as that the death rate was higher among urban communities than in the country or that the lower orders suffered more heavily than their betters, though probable enough, rest on little evidence. Accurate statistics were rarely kept, and normally reliable sources, such as diocesan registers of parochial clergy, often broke down in the face of an emergency which must have made the day to day tasks of administration seem irrelevant. All that can be said is that the disease first appeared in the West in the seaports of Sicily and in Venice in 1347, carried no doubt by the rats of ships calling there from the East; that by 1348 it was well established in France and England; that by the next year it had reached Scandinavia; and that by 1351 it had completed its circuit through Europe and was affecting the inhabitants of Northern Russia. Most modern estimates of the casualties put the death role at some-where in the region of a third of the total population; contemporaries naturally tended to magnify the number.

The first outbreak was very far from being the end of the Black Death. Just as the plague of 1665 has gone down in English history as the Plague for no other reason than that it was the last notable English outbreak in the terrible series, so the Black Death of 1348 gains a part of its notoriety from the fact that it was the first. For the rest of the Middle Ages plague remained a familiar enemy, the worst of the many natural hazards men faced. Every country knew

<hr />

[1] Quoted from J. W. Thompson, *Economic and Social History of Europe in the Late Middle Ages*, Constable, 1960, p. 379.

sporadic outbreaks only less terrible than the first. Like atomic energy in our own age, but with fewer obvious beneficent possibilities, it had come to stay.

The whole picture of economic life was transformed by the Black Death. In the country the chronic complaint of the last century had been of a surplus of manpower for the available land; now there was more than enough land for the available men. The colonial lands in the East found that many of their most profitable western markets had disappeared, and that there was no longer anything to be gained by producing intensively for a much reduced market. The abandonment of land there was paralleled by similar abandonment of land in the West. Now that there was land to spare there was no point in cultivating those marginal lands which, by the poorness of their soil, were only just capable of supporting their population. In both England and France traces of villages abandoned in the latter part of the fourteenth century are common. Only rarely was this caused by the extinction of the whole population; more often the survivors had migrated to easier lands left vacant elsewhere. The Black Death struck everywhere at the position of landowners who had been accustomed to work their own lands through the labour services of their tenants. Not only were there now rarely enough tenants left to keep the same amount of land under cultivation, but the tenants themselves came to realize that their services had a scarcity value. If their present holdings were encumbered with onerous duties they could remove themselves to areas where their tenancies would carry no such obligations. Even those classes of day labourers who had not before held any tenancies, but had hired their services for an exiguous daily wage, were now in a much improved bargaining position if they could sell their labour on an open market.

The immediate reaction of the landowning classes was to try to use their political control of the institutions of monarchy to prevent this new economic situation affecting their position. In England the Statute of Labourers of 1349 attempted to impose a 'wage freeze' on all the working classes, and in France John II issued an ordinance in 1351 which was designed to produce a similar effect in the neighbourhood of Paris. The next thirty years were a period of great social tension, aggravated in France and Italy by the effects of war. But no amount of political pressure could change the facts of a situation in which labour had acquired a new value; the more active the attempts made to conceal that this had happened, the more violent was the reaction. The Peasants' Revolt in England in 1381, the *Jacquerie* in

France in 1358, the French revolts in 1382, the revolt in Florence in 1378, and many other similar risings, all owed much to this attempt by the ruling classes to stabilize wages at a pre-Black Death level; in the end such an attempt was proved hopeless.

Landowners were brought eventually to face the reality that their personal economic crises could only be surmounted by economic methods. If there were not the men to work the lords' own holdings, then they must abandon the attempt to cultivate their own domains. Commutation of labour services for cash rents had already gone far in western Europe before the Black Death; now it became the common rule. Abandoning the attempt to go on producing surpluses from their own domains for a largely vanished market, landlords were happy to abandon responsibility for them by compounding with their tenants for a fixed money rent, to give themselves a steady income. From the landowners' point of view this might be a satisfactory arrangement for the present, but it gave little protection against a possible future fall in the value of money, which might drastically reduce their real incomes. However, it was to be a hundred and fifty years before any general inflation again struck European prices. Alternatively, if the peasant tenants were wealthy enough— or the landowner desperate enough—he might seek to sell out his estates altogether and seek the comparative security of some town where he might live in comfort on the proceeds. The third possibility, that of turning to some form of farming which might require less labour and would therefore mean lower costs, was of less importance in the rest of Europe than in England. North of the Channel the decline of the cloth towns in Flanders was balanced by a growth in the manufacture of native English cloth, but such growth seems to have been rarer elsewhere.

In general it can be said that feudalism as a system of rural organization had been much weakened before the Black Death; the decades after it saw its final dissolution. From the angle of efficiency there was little to be said for the change; ownership tended now to be vested either in a class of absentee town-dwelling *rentiers*, much commoner on the Continent than in England, or in a class of peasant owners. The former lacked the inclination to exert themselves to improve what was no longer vital to their existence, the latter have usually shown themselves to be the most old-fashioned of farmers, lacking either the inclination or the capital to indulge in improvements. But efficiency was no longer of the first importance, since there would have been no steady market for the extra produce it might bring. A more serious disadvantage was that while feudalism had died as a vital system, it had no more been formally abolished than if had ever been formally founded; in consequence many of the feudal obligations, to pay market dues, to use particular mills, to obey forest laws, and the like, remained in force. They were to remain in France as an irritating reminder of past subserviences right up to the time of the Revolution.

The consequences of the Black Death on industry and commerce were no less marked. Here again it was to start no new process, but it greatly accentuated changes that were already visible before 1348. In both northern and southern Europe the eleventh, twelfth and thirteenth centuries had been periods of very rapid economic growth. It is a characteristic of such periods that fortunes are to be had for the making by those who possess the necessary qualities of initiative and good fortune, and the guilds merchant, the free associations of the merchants of particular towns, were the appropriate expression of this expansionist age; the functions of the guild merchant were to provide the services which were common to all who traded. In an era of expanding markets entry to the guilds merchant was not difficult; the more members they had, the less the share of the expenses which would fall on individual members. Parallel to the guilds merchant, but slightly later in their inception, came the craft guilds, and it was these which became the characteristic organizations of the later period. In their origin the craft guilds were simply associations of the working masters of any one particular craft; by organizing systems of apprenticeship they could insure both that only those qualified to practise that craft did so and that some restriction was placed on the numbers of producers. A stipulated length of apprenticeship and a demand for a masterpiece as a proof of ability from candidates for the status of working master served both ends, while trademarks helped to give guarantees of quality to the finished goods. By the middle of the twelfth century there is documentary evidence for the existence of craft guilds among the tanners of Rouen, the coverlet weavers of Cologne, and many similar bodies,[1] and it is fair to assume that the system had become widespread.

But during the fourteenth century a change occurred. The motive of exclusion and restriction of output, which had always been present, came to be dominant. Masterpieces were made increasingly difficult, and the requirement of cash payments from otherwise qualified

[1] See H. Pirenne, *Economic and Social History of Medieval Europe*, trans. I. E. Clegg. Kegan Paul, 1936, p. 182.

apprentices often excluded them from the rank of masters. It is easy to see in this a realization that the market was not unlimited, and that the admission of each new member constituted a threat to the existing masters. Often one craft guild of substantial masters would come to dominate the whole local government of a town, and regulations which had been designed to serve the interests of the whole community, or at least those of the whole wide circle of producers, were now used to perpetuate the control of this narrow commercial patriciate. Urban society, which had grown up to serve the needs of men who were free not only before the law but in their economic condition, now tended to become increasingly set in a firm economic mould in which it was much more difficult for new men to make their fortunes; the symptom is a normal one of a static or declining economy.

These are generalizations in a field in which the generalization is never more than a very partial truth. They are broadly true of the Flemish cloth industry, where the social conflicts which had already arisen in the early fourteenth century were aggravated by the constant interruptions to the steady flow of wool caused by the Hundred Years War. Bruges, for instance, was by the end of the fourteenth century well on the way to becoming the picturesque antique it has remained. In France the evils of the Black Death were accentuated by the multitude of troubles brought by the constant depredations of the English armies and the free companies, troubles which affected the towns only less grievously than the countryside, But if war brought to most a lessening of opportunity, to some it came as a godsend. The market for arms had never been so good, and the iron industry of Dinant entered on a new period of prosperity, while other towns both inside and outside France hastened to make good this opportunity. Milan, for instance, was able to recoup from armaments some of the profits it was losing from the decline of its trade in cloth. Moreover, the very financial embarrassments which were the common fate of governments in the fourteenth and early fifteenth centuries created their own opportunities for those who had money and were prepared to lend it. Some part of the great profits made by Jacques Coeur (†1456), the merchant of Bourges who became the richest man in France during the first half of the fifteenth century, came from this source. Incidentally his activities, which ranged from counterfeiting the royal coinage to carrying out, under papal licence, a prosperous traffic in arms with the Turks, show clearly enough that financial success was still possible for a man with intelligence, daring, and a complete absence of principle; but it is perhaps significant that Coeur had inherited some wealth. The prospects for a genuine *novus homo* were not encouraging.

Similarly the disasters which struck some areas could not fail to benefit others, even on a generally declining market. The combined effects of the over-taxation of the fairs of Champagne since the time of Philip the Fair and of the war itself made the established trade link between north and south, by way of the western Alpine passes and Champagne, no longer a good risk. Yet the trade had to go on, and the long sea route through the Bay of Biscay was not a suitable alternative for all goods. The alternative was to move the route further east, making use of the Brenner Pass and avoiding any contact with lands affected by the Hundred Years War. The obvious beneficiaries were the cities of southern Germany. For Nuremburg, Augsburg, Basle, and many others the fifteenth century was a period of considerable prosperity, while on the southern side of the Alps the towns of north-east Italy, such as Verona and Bolzano, benefited from the same cause. The capital available from their profits as towns of transit enabled these areas to build up their own industries, and goods such as the linen of Ulm began to appear widely on European markets.

In the same way, the general expenses of war coupled with the unfavourable balance of trade with the East were sufficient to create a European shortage of precious metals. Here again the opportunity came to the East rather than to what had been the more prosperous areas of the West, for the best known sources of mineral ores lay in southern Germany, Austria and Hungary. The full exploitation of these resources did not take place until the second half of the fifteenth century, for this area too was beset by political difficulties. Great damage for instance was done to the Bohemian mines at Kuttenberg and Eyle during the Hussite wars. But since the demand existed, and until the discovery of the New World could only be satisfied from central Europe, as soon as peaceful conditions returned the expansion would begin.

Exceptionally, then, the fifteenth century can show prosperity in some areas, but the general picture was one of decline in both industry and agriculture. The forms of economic organization also came to reflect this. The supplanting of the guilds merchant by the craft guilds, with their insistence on the avoidance of over-production, can be paralleled by the growth of exclusionist tendencies in other organizations. The Hanseatic League, that body of north European cities with a common interest in the Baltic trade, was in its earlier days a very loose organization to which it was easy for new applicants to gain admission. But in its later years, after the Black Death had drastically reduced its markets, it became more concerned with excluding possible competitors than with anything else. In the same way some cities tried to insist that their own citizens alone should profit from commerce carried on with them; for instance Bruges was insisting in the fifteenth century that no commercial transaction carried on within the city should be valid unless it had been done through a local broker, a step incidentally which only further discouraged potential customers from using the city. This exclusionist attitude, which is found so generally in the later Middle Ages, was not adopted in conscious acceptance of any economic theory; rather it was the instinctive reaction which any society will show to the realization that it is no longer expanding. In the same way the confident *laisser-faire* liberalism of the high Victorian period was gradually replaced, first by the demand for protection, and ultimately by the acceptance of a wide measure of state control, at just the time when the economic situation of Britain as against her rivals on both sides of the Atlantic was deteriorating.

In all this the Black Death played a big, though by no means exclusive, part. But it was not in economics alone that its influence was felt. Less tangible but no less striking were its effects on the whole morale of the age. They can be seen perhaps most clearly in the forms in which religion came to express itself. Death is necessarily a concern of the Christian religion at any time, but the obsessive preoccupation with it which marked the religion of the fifteenth century can only have sprung from the catastrophe itself and from the abiding fear of the plague; always much closer than in more recent centuries, Death had now become a visitant to be expected at any moment of life. The monasteries and churches, the building of which in earlier ages had formed the outward expression of the piety of the laity, were now largely replaced by chantries, institutions whose sole purpose was to succour the souls of those who, having died, now endured the pains of Purgatory. Doctrine, too, was much concerned with speculation on the fate of the departed, and whatever the merits of the doctrine of Purgatory, it can safely be said that a Church which came to concentrate on it, to the exclusion of those doctrines more immediately relevant to life in this world, was in a diseased condition. The form of the characteristic tombs of the fifteenth century, with the deceased represented not only as he was in life but also as he is now that physical decay is at work in his corrupted flesh, is evidence of the part played by physical death in the imagination of the age; it was a morbid imagination. The same theme inspired the whole Dance of Death motif which was so very potent in the art and literature of what has often been considered the last medieval century. In it Death, the partner whose offer cannot be refused, presents himself to all alike at the times when so often they least expect him. In its simplest form no more than the *Memento Mori* which any society aware of the fact of human mortality may produce, the theme could easily revert to the prevailing obsession with physical decay, in itself a subject of despair. An allied theme, portrayed strikingly in the frescoes of the Campo Santo of Pisa, was that of the three young noblemen who were suddenly confronted by three corpses, a reminder that for all their finery this is what life comes to in the end. In externals, perhaps, the message of this is not far distant from Alcuin in the ninth century, ending his epitaph with the message to the passer-by 'What I am now soon shalt thou be', but the insistence on the physical realities of dissolution detach it from any period but its own.[1]

The prevalence of extravagant exhibitions of popular penitence also bears witness to a psychological malaise. The most well-known of these were the flagellant movements which occurred at intervals in the late fourteenth and fifteenth centuries. The Church rightly looked askance at these great processions of penitents scourging each others' backs in expiation of their sins, and indeed it is not difficult to discern that perverted sexual excitement must have played its part in stimulating these mass demonstrations. Penitence again is a necessary part of the Christian belief, but there is a gulf of a difference between the penitence demanded by S. Francis in the thirteenth century, a call for penitence backed by a demand for subsequent constructive action, and that of the Flagellants of south Germany in 1350 who showed their penitence by sadistic attacks on the Jews.

These changes in the form of religious expressions can be seen by the historian, wise as usual after the event, as throwing much light on the origins of the Protestant Reformation of the next century. But they were also evidence of a disease which did not stop short at religion. The intellectual world of the thirteenth century had equally fallen into decay by the end of the fourteenth century. It is too easy to talk glibly of the obscurantism of medieval scholasticism, and

[1] For a discussion of this theme see J. S. Huizinga, *The Waning of the Middle Ages*, E. Arnold. 1924. Ch. XI.

many such accusations are merely faint replicas of criticisms first made by Renaissance scholars, who were at once totally out of sympathy with what they criticized and contemptuous of it because its authors had neglected to write in Ciceronian Latin. Many of the criticisms made of medieval thought rest on the grossest misapprehensions; for instance the familiar gibe that medieval scholars spent their time arguing about how many angels (beings of form without substance) could repose on a pin (a point without area) rests on no firmer foundation than a deliberately humorous Wycliffite exaggeration; it would be as fair to judge our own western society on the strength of one cartoon in the Russian magazine *Krokodil*. The great thinkers who were teaching in the universities of the thirteenth century were engaged on exploiting one particular form of apprehending truth, that of deduction. Granted that certain postulates were true, they were out to show what logically could be deduced to follow from them, and in so doing an edifice of thought was constructed which has had few equals in the history of the world. Purely as abstract thinkers the great scholastics from Aquinas and Bonaventura (†1274) to Duns Scotus (†1308) must rank very highly indeed. But the form of their thinking had certain limitations, as indeed is the case with any form of thinking. In the first place, deductive thinking is appropriate only to certain branches of human knowledge. In our own day the mode of thought of the historian, concerned as he is with such insubstantial realities as the role of pure chance and influenced as he inevitably is by the factor of moral judgment, differs from that of the chemist. In the same way deduction, while an appropriate method of thought for philosophy and theology, which by their nature allow of no recourse to verifiable facts, is a much less suitable instrument for subjects such as the natural sciences where such recourse can be had. Moreover, it is a method of thought which can be self-exhausting, and which can reach the stage at which all the justifiable conclusions from the original premises have been made.

There is little doubt that medieval thought by the fourteenth century was approaching this condition of satiety. The deductive method had reached something of a dead end within the terms of reference laid down for it by its original assumptions, and much time was spent on the discussion of the same '*quaestiones*' which had engaged attention for over a hundred years. Such criticism as there was, most notably by William of Ockham (†1349), tended to cast doubt on the original premises rather than to suggest new fields of study. Moreover, with an acute shortage of books before the era of printing, and with a curious blockage in the rediscovery of new works of significance from the classical world between the early thirteenth and the fifteenth centuries, the tradition of medieval scholasticism was degenerating into a somewhat repetitive and finicky discussion of accustomed topics. Of course there are the exceptions. The Conciliar Movement gave rise to some fruitful political thinking in the effort to find a new answer to what was essentially a new political problem; in Gerson the university of Paris at the beginning of the fifteenth century had a chancellor who possessed a genuine originality of mind; even in religion the Brethren of the Common Life in the fifteenth century showed that the Church was not quite without answer to the problem of how to produce new forms to make the old religion appropriate to a new age. But the general picture of the medieval world after the Black Death is one of a world grown old; the Renaissance when it came would not be a renaissance of medieval ideals and ways.

16

The Hundred Years War

'The Hundred Years War' has long been one of the sacrosanct periods into which history has been divided. Such divisions, however inaccurate they may be, are of the greatest convenience; it would, for instance, be a deprivation to lose 'the Elizabethan Age', even though the final Elizabethan victory in politics was achieved in 1588, while the greater part of Elizabethan culture belongs to the seventeenth century and the reign of her successor. In the same way 'The Hundred Years War', deeply enmeshed as it has become in the traditions of both participating countries, will continue to dominate the histories of France and England in the fourteenth and fifteenth centuries, whatever mathematical and historical objections may be brought against it. There would be good grounds for reckoning it to have lasted either much more or much less than a hundred years. Even the dates normally given to it, 1337–1453, show it to have lasted much more than the stipulated hundred years, but one hundred and sixteen years could be considered a bad under-estimate. For increasingly the war is seen as only one phase in the intermittent conflict which had begun when the Norman Conquest first established an English monarchy with roots on both sides of the Channel; in this sense the Hundred Years War began in 1066, and was not to end until the final loss of Calais in 1558 confined the powers of the English Crown to the northern of the two kingdoms it claimed. Equally it would be possible to argue that the 'war' itself was only a loose term for a period of intermittent hostilities during which there were long intervals, for example after the Peace of Brétigny or after the Truce of Tours, in which no operations were being carried on. If the existence of fighting is the test of war, the Hundred Years War lasted for much less than a hundred years.

Nevertheless a Hundred Years it has become and will remain. In its origin it can be seen as an aggression by the English monarchy against France, and before the causes of this attack are examined it is necessary to explain how it is that such a venture was at all possible. There is no question as to which of the two countries was the larger, the richer, and the more powerful. France at the end of the thirteenth century is estimated to have contained perhaps as many as twelve million inhabitants, giving it a density of population greater than that of any other European kingdom. This high density is to be explained, not only by the existence of more numerous and more prosperous towns than were to be found elsewhere in northern Europe, but by a general level of agricultural prosperity which was the envy of less fortunate lands. By contrast England and Wales cannot have contained many more than three million people, and London alone was a city of European importance. Moreover during the thirteenth century France had achieved an enviably good reputation for political stability. The ruling Capetian dynasty had produced no fewer than three kings of first class ability in one century. At their disposal the kings had had, and had perfected, an administration with a high reputation for efficiency and impartiality; in Paris the monarchy possessed a capital, well-fitted geographically and in the prestige it commanded, to act as a centre of the kingdom. The decline of the Holy Roman Empire, which, to all but the most convinced imperialists such as Dante, had long been an accomplished fact, had left France with clear political hegemony in Europe; the presence of the Papacy at Avignon seemed to confer on this leadership the mark of clerical approval.

The recent history of England seemed to suggest much less political stability. It is true that in producing a unified administration England was second to none; the Norman kings had achieved this while the earlier Capetians had still been wondering how to survive in the Île de France alone. But in some important respects the kings of England had been less successful than their French counterparts. They had failed utterly to extend their kingdom to what seemed its logical limits; little serious attempt had been made to reduce Ireland, Bannockburn stood as a recent reminder of how completely they had failed to attach Scotland to its southern neighbour, and even Wales was still capable of revolt at any moment. This failure did more than reduce seriously the amount of territory subject to the English Crown. It provided its enemies with an excellent opportunity to create distractions in England. Just as in earlier centuries the rulers of the Angevin Empire had always had it in their power to bring the most pressing difficulties to bear on the French kings, so now any king of France could hope that, if the need arose, he might be able to find potent allies in the Celtic fringes of Britain. Moreover, if the English administration itself was sound, there had in England been much more question than had been the case in France as to who was to control that administration. Whereas in France the problem for long had been how to restrain the virtual independence of the greater baronage, in England the monarchy had been faced with the reverse problem of a baronage which, far from dissociating itself from the actions of the Crown, had sought to control them. During the thirteenth century various personal factors, such as the incompetence of King John and the long minority of Henry III, had made this danger more acute; the reign of Edward II at the beginning of the fourteenth century hardly seemed likely to offer an escape from such troubles.

The sudden weakness which afflicted the Capetian monarchy in the twenty-five years which followed the death of Philip the Fair was not the cause of the Hundred Years War, but it provided the occasion for it. No small part in the success story of the French monarchy had been played by the combination of good fortune and sapient marriage which had produced an unbroken male succession to the Crown. Now, most unexpectedly, that good fortune was to come to an end. Philip IV can scarcely be blamed for this. He had done his best by leaving behind him three sons, each of whom in turn was to reign over France, but none of whom was to leave behind him any lasting male heir. Against such an unlikely chance no foresight could have prevailed.

Yet, if Philip the Fair cannot be blamed for this, he must shoulder some of the responsibility for the unpromising situation which confronted Louis X (1314–1316) on his accession. The financial demands made by the late king on his subjects had created violent opposition, if not to the Crown, at least to the ministers who were most closely associated with royal policy. During his short reign Louis showed signs of wishing to restore the popularity of the Crown by a policy of concession. De Marigny, the minister most actively concerned with the financial demands of Philip IV, was executed at the beginning of the new reign, thus performing the final ministerial service of acting as a scapegoat for the failures of the king. The local leagues which had sprung up in opposition to Philip's demands were appeased by the grant of charters recognizing local rights and privileges. Not important in themselves, these charters are significant in that they represent the first conscious retreat by the central government since Philip Augustus had come to the throne. The wisdom of this new policy cannot be judged on the strength of a reign of a mere two years, but of his indiscretion in dying as early as 1316 there can be no question. He left behind him only a young daughter and a pregnant wife; whatever sex the new child might prove to be, it was necessary to solve at once the question of who should exercise power —as king or regent as the case might be. The child was a boy, but since he lived only a matter of days, his 'reign' as John I was the shortest in French history. Meanwhile the second son of Philip the Fair had already assumed the duties of regent, and on John's death had himself proclaimed Philip V (1316–1322). The fortune of the House of Capet had meant that French lawyers had never before had to consider the rival claims of a daughter as against a brother of the last king, a question which most monarchies had already had occasion to debate, often not without bloodshed. But the extreme youth of Louis's daughter Joanna made this particular case not hard to decide, and incidentally produced a precedent for the view that France could not have a queen regnant.

Philip seems to have shared some of his father's administrative ability, but he too was not to reign long enough for a sound judgment on his work. His chief legacy to France was a crop of three daughters. The succession issue in 1322 was exactly the same as it had been in 1316, and once more the throne passed to the surviving brother Charles IV (1322–1328). That he too should die after a comparatively short reign leaving behind him only daughters and, once more, an unborn child only emphasizes the good fortune which had attended the earlier Capetians. On this occasion the awaited birth produced only another girl, who could not affect the succession issue.

There were now no surviving children of Philip the Fair, and the succession rested between Philip of Valois, the son of Philip the Fair's younger brother Charles of Valois, and Edward III, the youth who had just inherited the English throne; the latter's claim came to him through his mother Isabelle, the daughter of Philip the Fair. Into the legal rights and wrongs of the issue it is unnecessary to go, for it was not to be decided on legal rights and wrongs. The so-called Salic law, by which the lawyers of the House of Valois later claimed that any argument in favour of the English claim was nullified, was a mere ingenious piece of antiquarian research; in so far as the law of succession to fiefs was consulted it seems clear that female succession was recognized in default of the direct male line—which would give Edward the better claim. But legally it would have been possible to make out quite good cases for other candidates, such as Louis X's daughter Joanna of Navarre, or Philip of Evreux, who had direct male descent from Philip III of France. The problem was insoluble in terms of the public law of the State, for no public law of succession to the Crown had as yet been formulated; the present situation itself would produce one for the future.

As it was the Great Council of the nobility, which Philip of Valois as regent summoned in April 1328, did not concern itself so much with the legal argument as with the practical question of power. Joanna and Philip of Evreux, for different reasons, were unfitted to exercise power, while Edward III for his part not only had the disadvantage of being the over-youthful son of a notorious and generally detested mother, but as king of England had the disadvantage of being descended from the family which had always striven to confound the revered Capetian kings of France. All this indicated Philip of Valois as the Council's choice, and to these arguments could be added one yet more powerful. As regent he was already partially possessed of power; the selection of any other king might well involve a civil war. This must have been a factor which played a large part in their decision in his favour. In May 1328 Philip VI (1328-1350) was crowned at Rheims.

If the Hundred Years War had really been about who should be king of France, Edward's reluctant acceptance in the next year of the verdict of the French barons and his promise of homage would have been a disastrous confession of the weakness of his own case. But increasingly it has become clear that the succession issue was only a suitable pretext for the war; its causes went far further back and are rooted in the whole situation of an English monarchy with lands in France. It would be wrong to regard this as an early example of conflicting nationalism. Edward III was, after all, half French by birth and French-speaking by inclination; the Gascon barons who supported him certainly did not so do from any desire to further the cause of England, an abstraction which they would neither have understood nor supported if they had understood it. Their support for their overlord in England was made up partly from a genuine belief that this was their feudal duty, partly from the natural idea that they would suffer less interference from the distant and perhaps ineffective control of the English court than from the much closer control of Paris.

Moreover, the very question of who owed allegiance to whom was very confused, even allowing for the confirmation of the English possession of Guienne by the Treaty of Paris (1259). Since then both Philip the Fair and Charles IV had attempted to confiscate the duchy, and although neither attempt (1294 and 1324) had in the end succeeded, the resulting settlements had left the question of allegiance very obscure. Not only were the precise boundaries of the duchy in question uncertain, but within them there were various enclaves where the king of France could claim jurisdiction. Also the Paris government had not relied on military means alone to extend its control over Guienne; from the thirteenth century it had been increasingly ready to entertain appeals from disputes in Guienne in its own courts in Paris, a source of constant irritation and financial loss to the English Crown. It was even alleged in some of the English complaints that sergeants of the French Crown had penetrated the duchy to pose to its inhabitants the vital question of where their allegiance lay, and that those who had answered, perfectly correctly in the English view, that it lay to the king of England had found themselves prosecuted for treason in the courts of the French Crown.

Guienne was the primary cause of conflict between the two kingdoms, but to it must be added various economic disputes. To see the war as springing primarily from economic causes would be to attribute to Edward III a much more mercantile outlook than is at all probable in one who saw himself as a great traditional king; his attempts to take direct economic action, such as the suspension of English wool exports to Flanders, were always calculated to secure political advantages, even at the cost of economic loss, and testify to his subordination of economic to political ends. Yet the dependence of the Flemish cloth towns on supplies of English wool remained a political factor of the greatest importance, even after Philip VI had apparently avenged the shame of Courtrai by his overwhelming defeat of the anti-French forces of the county in the battle of Cassel (1328). The possibility that this economic lever might be used to create difficulties for France on a second front could not be absent from Edward's calculations.

The flourishing trade in Gascon wines from Bordeaux and the trade in salt from the Bay of Bourgneuf both played a not unimportant part in the English economy; both were subject not only to the natural hazards of the rounding of Ushant, but to periodic attacks from Breton seamen. If the English Crown were to gain political control over Brittany these might be stopped, but in any event they added their quota to the hostility which existed between the inhabitants of Guienne and those of the rest of France.

In the early thirteen-thirties there seemed no reason to suspect that relations between the two kings were about to reach a final breaking point. Philip, having apparently settled Flanders, was actively if unrealistically engaged in the preparation of a great crusade to regain for the Cross control of the eastern Mediterranean, a project in which he received every encouragement from Pope John XXII at Avignon. Edward meanwhile was attempting to wipe out the memory of Bannockburn by campaigning against King David of Scotland. Both projects came to nothing, and in their own ways contributed to the greater war. When Pope Benedict XII succeeded John XXII in 1334, he soon realized that the crusade was impractical in a Europe so politically divided, but the indefinite postponement of the operation led Edward to suspect that the forces must have been raised for some more sinister purpose, such as the assistance of King David or an attack on Guienne. In his operations in Scotland Edward had already come across clear proof that the Franco–Scottish alliance was still a reality.

In 1336 Edward took the decision for war by renouncing formally his homage to Philip and himself laying claim to the French Crown. It seems very unlikely that he expected to make good his claim; in his most optimistic moments he could not have foreseen the series of events which were to lead to the coronation of Henry VI in Paris nearly a hundred years later. It is much more likely that the action was a gesture intended to be followed by sufficient military victory to compel Philip to recognize his absolute right to Guienne and perhaps to cede him other territories. It was a gesture, too, well calculated to enthuse his own nobility with a real zest for the war which lay ahead. In the past English kings who had engaged in operations in France had often done so with only the most lukewarm support from their own baronage; Edward succeeded in convincing his barons that the venture offered them the same bright prospects that it carried for the Crown, and there were no dissentients to the formal declaration of war he sent to Philip in 1337.

To carry out his discomfiture of the French Crown Edward relied on the traditional English policy for working against France. English money and promises would be used to build up a coalition to the north-east of France; it could then be used in conjunction with direct operations from Guienne. Despite the somewhat depressing precedent of Bouvines, there was nothing radically unsound about this strategy which would enable English financial strength to be put to military advantage. His agents in the Low Countries had informed Edward that the peace which had reigned since Cassel in Flanders cloaked a smouldering discontent in Ghent and Ypres; the complete embargo on the export of English wool decreed by Edward in 1336 produced the required effect within a few months. A widespread revolt among the industrial proletariat of the cities was given purpose and order by a wealthy merchant, Jacob van Artevelde, who espoused the popular cause; by 1339 the whole county was in the rebels' hands, and its count, Louis of Nevers, was a refugee at the French court.

Despite this first diplomatic victory, the policy of favouring the coalition was not destined to success. It laboured under two serious disadvantages. One, common to many coalitions, was that the interests of its members were often in conflict with each other. The more favour shown by Edward to the cities of Flanders, the less enthusiasm was felt by the cities of Brabant, such as Brussels, which had regarded the troubles of their old rivals with complete equanimity. The other, even more serious, was that none of the members of the coalition except England had any real interest in fighting a major war against France. The princes of Brabant, Gelderland and Hainault, and many of the German princes, including even the Emperor Ludwig of Bavaria himself, were ready enough to accept the subsidies Edward raised with difficulty, but when it came to sending troops in return it was another story. Even Van Artevelde proved an ally of dubious value. In return for his recognition of the Plantaganet claim to the French throne and an ill-defined promise of military aid, an agreement with Edward, signed in 1339, stipulated the resumption of English wool supplies and the transference of the English wool Staple, by which alone English wool could reach the Continent, to Bruges, a step far from popular in neighbouring Brabant. Subsidies amounting to £140,000 were to be paid to Van Artevelde, who also gained the promise of the reversion to Flanders of some of the towns of north-eastern France. For the amount of fighting actually carried out these were generous terms.

In consequence the early years of the war proved that if the English were to win any decisive military successes they could only do so by exerting the major effort themselves. In 1339 Edward led an expeditionary force to Flanders, but the tentative move it made into France accomplished nothing. Philip wisely refused to engage it, and the refusal of Edward's allies to send more than nominal support prevented him from moving further into France.

The year 1339 saw the effective end of the coalition, and if Edward could still hope for profit from the alliance with Artevelde, even this hope was soon to be destroyed. Artevelde's victory over Louis of Nevers had done nothing to right the permanent griefs of the Flemish working class, and, as the symbol of the 'haves' of the country, he was soon subject to the same deep hostilities which had overthrown the count before him. Conscious of his weakness, he was ready to clutch at the hope of an even closer alliance with England; in 1345 he had just offered the county to the Black Prince when he himself was murdered. Henceforth Flanders disappeared as an effective belligerent, and with it the hope of an easy access to northern France.

These preliminary moves over, the first great phase of the war began, a phase which was to last until the Treaty of Brétigny and which was to be a period of repeated English success. In many English school history books this period alone is covered in any detail. The rest of the war is hastily sketched—apart from a brief revival of interest about the time of the Agincourt campaign. Certainly the English successes were surprising, to none more so perhaps than to their authors; it must be remembered that both at Crécy and Poitiers the English commanders desperately tried to avoid an action to which only their own tardiness had brought them. But if luck played its part in the English successes, other more tangible factors were also at work. Among them should be reckoned the factor of personal leadership. For all their failings as men and as strategists, Edward III and the Black Prince did provide tough and effective command to the troops under their control. Much as they hankered after all the formalities of cavalry warfare, conducted in accordance with the traditional code of fighting which rendered it little more than an extension of the joust, they were forced to think beyond the limits of such fighting. Faced always with a numerical disadvantage in armed knights, and compelled to move their troops long distances through a hostile countryside, so that their cavalry when brought to an engagement were seldom fresh, they faced inevitable defeat if forced to fight battles consisting of a straight series of cavalry charges. Reluctantly they were compelled to recognize the value of infantry, an arm generally despised. Nor had they any scruples about the methods they used against the civilian population in a war which was, after all, being fought well away from their own homeland. The *chévauchées*, the campaigns of pure destruction in which the Black Prince took so prominent a part, make this war criminal a curious subject for so many stained glass windows, but there is no denying their efficacy.

By contrast Philip VI presents the picture of a man unable or uninclined to adapt himself to the conditions of either the warfare or the politics of the fourteenth century. His interest in crusading was symptomatic of a general failure to realize the nature of the tasks with which he was confronted; in a court in which aristocratic birth and chivalric observance predominated over administrative ability, he remained totally unaware either of the depth of suffering in which the war involved the people over whom he ruled or of the possibility of enlisting their total strength in the struggle. The complete disregard he showed for any but the traditional methods of waging war was of a piece with this general myopia, and ill-fitted him to wage war with the Plantaganets.

The very fact that the war was to be fought to the south of the Channel prevented the English commanders from thinking in terms of raising an old style feudal host. Such an army would have completed its obligation to serve before ever it had come to grips with the enemy; instead they were compelled to think in terms of a smaller body of men serving for a greater period of time. The contrast was felt not so much among the armed knights, whose methods and equipment varied very little from country to country, as among the supporting infantry. Here the men raised in England by Commissions of Array to man the infantry were of better quality than their French opposite numbers. Many of them had already seen service in Scotland or Wales, and had learnt there how to move for long distances while retaining their fitness for action, and how to use the weapons of infantry warfare. The long bow did not perhaps exercise quite the decisive effect on the fighting which tradition has assigned to it, yet there is no doubt that its use on concentrations of cavalry could cause many casualties and more confusion, and that it was a much more effective weapon than the heavier crossbow wielded by the Genoese mercenaries patronized by the French Crown. With better range and a much quicker rate of fire, it was only slightly more inaccurate. Moreover, it was a national weapon; it scarcely needed royal exhortations to ensure that there was a constant supply of men trained in its use, while the bowmen in the French service cost money.

As in most wars, finance played an important part, and here the advantage clearly lay with England, despite her poverty in comparison with her opponent. For the war was being fought in France, and it was Frenchmen who suffered by its continuance. Even under Philip the Fair it had proved extremely difficult to get enough money to maintain an army constantly in the field against Flanders. Now the fiscal machinery was being asked to provide much larger sums for a much longer war, while most of the money-owning classes asked for nothing better than a negotiated peace. In the early years of the war the belief was widespread that diplomacy would prevent the need for any really large scale military operations; after Crécy the lack of confidence in the leadership bred an equal reluctance to pour good money after bad. The French monarchy did not of course entirely fail to remedy this situation. New taxes such as a hearth tax first levied in 1342 and the *gabelle*, a compulsory tax on salt first applied to the whole kingdom in 1341, did something to meet its needs, but their collection from a population which widely regarded them as extortionate was not easy. In England, at least until the Peace of Brétigny, the war was popular. The loot won from France enriched many English houses of both the knightly and more lowly classes, while cloth merchants could hope that an indirect fruit of success would be complete control over Flanders. In consequence the English Parliament showed a readiness to vote supply for the war never equalled by the French Estates.

If the English could rest secure in the knowledge that this was a war in France, it was only because for the greater part of the war the general control of the Channel was in English hands. At the outset of the war it was not at all clear that this was to be so; in its early months French raids on the Isle of Wight had suggested the possibility of a French invasion of England. But in 1340 the Anglo–Flemish joint operations, abortive in their main purpose of invading France, had led to the much more valuable byproduct of the battle of Sluys. Caught at a disadvantage off the Flemish port by the main English invasion fleet, almost the entire French fleet was destroyed. Vigorous action in the form of building or impressing new ships might have made good the loss in a few years, but in fact no serious attempt was made to rebuild the lost fleet for thirty years. The great strategic advantage of being able to descend at any time on any part of the French coast was thus surrendered to England.

Finally the cause of the Valois kings was hampered by the inclination of its greatest feudatories to pursue independent policies, which might at times be actively hostile to that of the ruling house, a reminder of how recent in comparison with that of her opponent was the unification of France. Flanders, Burgundy, Brittany, even Guienne itself, none of them can really be described as pro-English, but equally none of them was consistently loyal in its support of the king in Paris. For their rulers the war was above all an opportunity to reassert forgotten local privileges, and by the same token each could provide English armies with a promising gateway into France.

After the collapse of the coalition the next opportunity of profitable intervention came to Edward III in the form of a dispute over the succession to the Duchy of Brittany, an area whose Celtic population and customs made it resistant to central government in much the same way as the Celtic fringes of Britain resisted English control. Its Duke John III died in 1341, and, in the absence of any direct heirs, the succession came to be disputed between the youngest half-brother of the late duke and the child of an elder brother who was himself dead. The former, by name John of Montfort, seized much of the duchy by force and, anticipating that Philip VI would rule against him, switched his allegiance to the Plantaganets. No better opportunity for English intervention could have been asked for, and things turned out better than Edward can have hoped. By 1345 not only were English troops in possession of most of Brittany, but John of Montfort was dead, his wife was mad, and their child, the new duke John IV, was firmly under English control.

The possession of Brittany with its ports enabled Edward once more to think of forcing Philip to fight on two fronts, this time threatening him from the north-west rather than the north-east. In 1345 the Earl of Derby led the first of the infamous *chévauchées*, leaving a trail of destruction through Poitou. Such an operation was popular enough with the English army, which returned heavily loaded with loot, while the inhabitants of Poitou, if no doubt confirmed in their worst views of the invader, were also moved to dislike the king who had done so little to protect them.

The Crécy campaign of the next year, led by Edward in person, was intended to be just such another *chévauchée*, this time taking the whole sweep of northern France as its target. The opportunity for it had been provided by the rash sentence of confiscation passed by Philip on Geoffrey of Harcourt, a Norman baron with lands in the Cotentin peninsula. The defendant, rather than see his whole position in society ruined, had appealed to the English king, thus giving Edward the unexpected chance of leading an army to what had for so long been English territory. The extravagant statements of chroniclers who were always ready to speak of armies of a hundred thousand or more, give no indication of the probable size of the army which landed no great distance from the invasion beaches of 1944. Certainly it cannot have consisted of more than twenty thousand men in all; twelve or thirteen thousand men is perhaps nearer the mark. The original landing took place on 11 July, and Edward's intention was to complete the whole operation and re-embark his army from Flanders or north-eastern France before the ponderous mobilization of the

French feudal host was complete. But too much time was wasted. After capturing Caen, Edward made a feint in the direction of Paris, and then wasted precious days in trying to find a bridge over the Somme which had not been destroyed in expectation of his coming. When he was at length brought to action at Crécy, a few miles north of Abbeville, by the full French army, his dilatory strategy seemed to have led his entire army into a trap.

In the event the circumstances which led up to the battle may well account for the extent of the English victory. In so desperate a situation Edward could not risk fighting a battle of cavalry charge against cavalry charge. He was forced to adopt entirely defensive tactics, to await the enemy's charges in a defensive position he had selected and strengthened, and to give a full role to his infantry firing rapidly from behind hedges and fences. It is equally true, of course, that Philip showed a singular lack of imagination in not adapting his own tactics to those of his enemy; Edward could not have remained permanently entrenched in the middle of Ponthieu. Whatever their cause, the results of Edward's tactics could not have been more decisive. Philip himself was lucky enough to escape from the battlefield with his life, but he left behind him among the dead the Count of Flanders, the blind King John of Bohemia, and many of the best of the French nobility. Others had fallen into the hands of their victors, and the business of ransoming them was to occupy many family exchequers in the years ahead.

Great as was the French defeat at Crécy, it was far from finishing the war; it did not even extricate the English army from a situation which remained dangerous. From Crécy Edward marched on Calais, but the town refused to surrender to an enemy poorly equipped to attack a strongly held town. For the whole winter of 1346–7 he laid siege to the town without success, and if Philip had shown rather more daring in the next spring, he might well have succeeded in trapping the English army. But, haunted by the memory of Crécy, Philip refused to risk another such defeat. The host he raised in 1347 was withdrawn, after some indecisive manoeuvring, to the south of Calais. Deserted by its king, the town surrendered. Although it escaped the complete destruction Edward was said to have contemplated, it was partly occupied by new English colonists. For it had a double purpose and would not be lightly relinquished. In time of war it could serve as yet another base from which to attack the Valois, while its position as the nearest port on the mainland of Europe to England fitted it to be a chief channel for English exports to the Continent; in 1363 the wool Staple was to be transferred there.

Meanwhile Philip had returned to Paris to summon his Estates. As so often after a military defeat, they were full of criticisms, not stopping short of suggesting royal incompetence as one reason for the disaster. The argument recalls the arguments of the early Stuarts with the English parliaments after the failure of their ventures on the Continent, and Philip might with the same justice have claimed that the failures had been due, at least in part, to the failure of the Estates to give him adequate supply in the first place.

Philip seemed to have little chance of obtaining the supply needed if he were to avenge Crécy, but by 1348 the Black Death had given both countries a subject for concern even more serious than the war. That this disaster did not lead to the immediate abandonment of all thought of war is only more evidence of how little the economic welfare of their peoples moved either of the chief adversaries. In 1350 Philip himself died. The presence of a son John II (le Bon) (1350–1364) prevented the succession issue from becoming further confused, but if ever a great ruler was needed, it was needed by a France carrying the burden of military defeat and grave social distress. John the Good utterly failed to match the situation he had inherited. Innocent of the viler insinuations later heaped on him in defeat, John's 'goodness' consisted of little more than a scrupulosity, amounting to an obsession, about the proper observation of the ritual which should surround knightly warfare. Certainly his father had had little enough conception of what the war meant to most of his people, but even he would have found it difficult to pen the letters in which John was to commiserate with his subjects after his defeat at Poitiers. His people had lost their father now languishing in captivity in England; his heart bled for them in their distress. That their homes were being burned by the invader, their lives destroyed by famine and disease, their fortunes ruined by crushing taxation, never seems to have occurred to him. The obvious sincerity of his grief only makes his inadequacy the more obvious.

The weakness of the Crown on John's accession invited a renewal of baronial opposition; it found a leader in Charles of Navarre (1349–1387). King of Navarre in his own right, Charles could put forward something of a claim to the French throne by virtue of his descent from Louis X. Believing his family to have been cheated out of their rightful succession to Champagne, this strong and evil man was perfectly prepared to negotiate with the King of England or anyone else who might be used to further his own schemes; for nearly forty years he was to prove a centre of disaffection to a Crown which was never strong enough to control him. John's efforts in this direction were singularly futile. Early in his reign he had given the post of Constable of France to Charles of Castile. Although Charles had been a favourite of the last king and was himself descended from S. Louis, the appointment was not a wise one, and John proceeded to provoke Charles of Navarre further by bestowing on the new Constable the county of Angoulême, to which the house of Navarre had itself a claim. Charles of Navarre made no secret of the fact that he was responsible for the brutal murder of the Constable in 1354. 'Know that it was I, who, with the help of God, had Charles of Spain killed'[1] he boasted to Henry of Lancaster when seeking English aid against John. The Treaty of Mantes (1354), by which Charles of Navarre was not only forgiven his crime but bribed to be of good behaviour in the future by the gift of new lands in the north, must have seemed a free invitation to raise his claims in the future.

Having missed an opportunity to show himself firm, two years later John tried to reverse his policy by a sudden show of determination. Understandably alarmed by the growing friendship between Charles and the heir to the throne, the future Charles V, John suddenly threw them both into prison. But the imprisonment of Charles of Navarre only aggravated the Navarrese faction in the country, and John shrank from the ultimate step of execution. The foreseeable consequence was the renewal of fighting by English troops with the aid and approval of the Navarrese faction elsewhere in the country. Henry of Lancaster from Brittany and the Black Prince from Guienne both proceeded to carry out thorough *chévauchées* of western France. A union between the two armies seemed likely, and for once John acted with decision in mobilizing his host. Henry regained Brittany safely, but the Black Prince was caught near Poitiers while still some fifty miles from the security of Guienne. Before a battle which he sought to avoid as desperately as his father had tried to escape Crécy ten years earlier, the English commander negotiated for a safe conduct to Guienne, being prepared to offer the promise of a seven years' truce. But John insisted on fighting, and battle was duly joined.

Poitiers lasted three days, in contrast to the one day affair at Crécy, but in other respects the two battles were very similar. Once

---

[1] Quoted from E. Perroy, *The Hundred Years War*, Eng. Trans. Eyre and Spottiswoode, 1951, p. 128.

more the French cavalry cut itself to pieces against a numerically smaller English force fighting from prepared defensive positions. But this time the defeated king ensured that his country should avoid none of the political consequences of defeat. Firmly imprisoned in the cage of his own obsolete conventions, John rejected any question of flight. By the beginning of October 1356 John had reached Bordeaux as a prisoner; the following May he was moved to his enemy's capital in London.

A child king was always a disaster; a permanently absentee monarch was, if anything, worse. It is no surprise that the unfortunate Dauphin found himself faced not only by military defeat, but by a grave domestic crisis. The forces which controlled Paris by the end of 1356, and seemed in a position to dictate their terms to the Dauphin, were made up of an alliance of various discontented factions. Chief amongst them were the burgesses of Paris itself, led by their mayor Etienne Marcel, a rich cloth merchant. Marcel could be taken as the symbol of the whole bourgeois class of France, pacifist in sentiment towards a war which caused them nothing but loss, and contemptuous of the administrative chaos which seemed to have replaced government. With them were aligned all those who supported the cause of Charles of Navarre, whether through a conviction that he was the true leader of France or through motives of pure self-advancement. Charles himself was still in prison, but this faction found its leader in Robert le Coq, bishop of Laon, a prelate ambitious of political power and possessed of a dangerous gift for inflaming the mob. Behind this uneasy alliance of two political groups thrown together by circumstances stood a third force of which both might reasonably be afraid. It was the power of the dispossessed, the power of all those in town and country alike who had suffered grievously from the war and its attendant evils and who were filled with bitter anger against all those in authority whom they held responsible for their misery. For so long as Marcel or Le Coq seemed to be the opposition they might count on this dangerous support, but if ever they came to be associated with government they ran the risk of being destroyed by their recent allies.

The first demands made by the reformers in 1356 were predictable enough; to the demands for the release of Charles of Navarre and for the elimination of 'evil councillors' was added the demand that the administration of the country should be purged of all wasteful expenditure, a demand common to all opposition groups in every country and age. To secure this end Marcel demanded in the Estates of Langue d'oïl, meeting in Paris, that the Dauphin should be pledged to take the advice of a permanent council of twenty-eight, no less than twelve of whom should be burgesses.

In effect this was a drastic reform programme directed towards establishing an oligarchical government heavily weighted in favour of the bourgeoisie. Yet the Dauphin, much as he no doubt disliked its revolutionary implications, could not afford to reject it out of hand, for if its sponsors were to make common cause with the Plantagenet, the house of Valois was lost indeed. During 1357 much of the substance of the demands was granted by an ordinance, by which six representatives of the Estates were to sit with the royal council. Meanwhile a special commission was set up to purge the whole administration of wasteful and unpopular officials. As a further check on governmental waste the regular auditing of the royal accounts was to be carried out by representatives of the Estates, which were themselves made reponsible for any future taxation which might be necessary. Finally, if Charles of Navarre was not exactly set at liberty, in the autumn of 1357 he escaped from prison and reached safety.

It can only be conjectured how far these measures might have led to a stable and more broadly based governmett; probably the difference between those who had forced them on the Dauphin were too wide for them to have had much hope of permanency. As it was, events soon rendered the ordinance of 1357 of merely academic interest. Early in the next year (1358) Charles of Navarre reappeared in Paris, where the Dauphin was still struggling to carry on the king's government. In a city where passions were already dangerously inflamed, his arrival helped to provoke riots. In the course of them the rioters broke into the court, murdered the marshals of Normandy and Champagne, two of the Dauphin's closest friends, and forced the Dauphin himself to wear the red and blue hood which Marcel's followers had adopted as their badge. The parallel with Louis XVI and the tricoleur is close, but the Dauphin had not been reduced to quite the same extremity as Citizen Louis Capet. Ten days later he made good his escape from Paris to the provinces, the figure of order escaping from anarchy.

At the end of May this interpretation received striking confirmation. The *Jacquerie* of 1358 was one of the most violent of all the peasant risings which marked the later Middle Ages. Its exact causes are not clear, but the sufferings inflicted by the war must have played a large part, and doubtless rumours of the political crisis in Paris helped to make the opportunity seem good. Starting as it did in the neighbourhood of Beauvais, the *Jacquerie* was too near Paris to be ignored either by the Dauphin or by his opponents. To the latter, indeed, the rising proved a fatally disruptive force. Charles of Navarre proved true to the traditions of his class. Whatever his differences with the Dauphin, they were as nothing compared with their common interest in laying the spectre of social anarchy, and he co-operated enthusiastically in the measures taken against the rebels. Marcel by contrast was by now lost in Messianic dreams in which he saw himself as the leader of the whole French nation, and interpreted the *Jacquerie* as the nation seeking its leader. Nothing could have been more dangerous for himself or his cause. Not only was he split without hope of reconciliation from his noble allies, but many of his own bourgeois class mistrusted the *Jacquerie* even more than they mistrusted the Crown. Moreover, the cause he championed could not but lose; the nobility of France might not show to advantage against the English army, but they were perfectly capable of cutting to pieces an ill-armed and led peasant rabble. The murder of Marcel at the end of July was only the chance prelude to the inevitable recapture of Paris by the Dauphin in the autumn. The Dauphin had ridden the storm, and from it the monarchy emerged with some of its prestige regained.

The monarchy—but not the king, for during these years King John remained a prisoner in London. At first he had been happy to abide by the fortunes of war; he had been the loser, and in due time no doubt a satisfactory ransom would be arranged to allow him to return to his people. Perhaps then he would be able to lead them on crusade. Edward, however, was set on making the maximum profit out of his lucky capture, and was not above helping matters along by worsening the conditions in which he held his royal prisoner. When John showed himself ready to agree to his original terms, Edward promptly raised them; by the Second Treaty of London (1359) John placidly agreed to the surrender of half of his kingdom as well as to the payment of an impossibly high ransom. But John was not France. The Estates refused to ratify the treaty, and a savage *chévauchée* in the summer of 1359 failed to move them.

The eventual Treaty of Brétigny (1360) was humiliating enough. By it the English right to possess their lands in the Calais enclave and the lands of a greatly enlarged Aquitaine, in all about a third of the kingdom, was recognized. The ransom for the return of John was fixed at the very large sum of three million gold *écus*, of which six hundred thousand were to be paid at once, while the rest were to follow in six annual instalments of four hundred thousand each. John himself might return on the payment of the first instalment, but he was to provide three hostages of the blood royal as a guarantee for the payment of the remainder.

The story of how Louis of Anjou, John's second son, tired of a captivity which might have lasted for decades and which was separating him from his young wife, and broke his parole, is well known. John's surrender of himself in place of his defaulting son, and his subsequent death in captivity (1364), formed an appropriate end to the life of this splendidly ineffective ruler.

Charles V (1364–1380), who succeeded his father, did so as no inexperienced ruler; as Dauphin he had already had experience enough of government. In character and temperament he had little in common with his father. John had at least won the reputation of a most gallant and chivalrous loser; Charles by contrast refused to fight. Himself physically weak and a prey to constant disease, not only did he not go into battle himself, preferring to leave that side of life to competent professionals, but he also pressed upon his commanders the absolute necessity of avoiding major engagements on the pattern of Crécy and Poitiers. In a moment of understandable irritation Edward III once referred to him as 'that lawyer' and the insult had in it more truth than he knew. Charles had much of the caution and good sense, as well as the guile, often associated with that profession. For his advisers Charles chose men qualified by proved ability in administration rather than by exalted birth, men such as John de la Grange, abbot of Fécamp, or Hugh Aubriot, the provost of Paris. While they were restoring some order to the civilian administration, John of Vienne, an admiral in the best tradition of *H.M.S. Pinafore*, since he never went to sea, at last reorganized the French navy to challenge English control of the Channel. From a well-equipped base at Rouen French squadrons would be able to raid Winchelsea and the other ports from which English forces embarked for France. Meanwhile, on land the Breton Duguesclin, a mercenary turned to the royal service, followed the policy of fortifying as many castles as possible to act as strong points in an entirely defensive strategy. His only considerable victory was at Cocherel in 1364, at the expense of Charles of Navarre, but when the uneasy peace which had followed Brétigny came to an end in 1369 the policy was to be vindicated.

By that year the English administration in Aquitaine was itself in difficulties. The nobility of Guienne had preferred English rule to French in the first place largely because in practice it was less effective and left them more independence. The Black Prince had striven to introduce English standards of efficiency to the duchy; in so doing he lost the allegiance of a great part of the local nobility. He was to feel the effects of this when war started again. The *chévauchées* continued as before; John of Gaunt in 1369 and 1373 and Sir Robert Knowles in 1370 were able to lead large armies into the heart of France, but against an enemy who refused to do battle they could accomplish nothing decisive. In the intervals in a series of minor engagements the French monarchy won back most of what it had lost at Brétigny; by 1374 the French had even penetrated deeply into Guienne. The French revival seemed complete.

The heroic period of the war had now ended; the deaths of the Black Prince (1376) and of Edward himself (1377) left England a prey to internal disorders which were to render any vigorous offensive strategy impossible. Even after Henry IV had seized the crown from Richard II, he was to be occupied with defending what he had won and with his attempts to reduce the Welsh and the Scots to subjection. Not until 1413 was the English throne again to be occupied by a king with the taste and the opportunity for conquest in France.

Such weakness in England might have given the Valois a chance, if not to expel the English from France entirely, at least to negotiate the lasting settlement that Brétigny had failed to be. It was not to be. The 'recovery' of France under Charles V had been of very limited extent; free companies of mercenaries continued to ravage the country, and the very tactics which had brought the Crown its military success had imposed even greater griefs on the shoulders of many of its subjects. Even before Charles's death there had been risings of his subjects, particularly in Languedoc, against the constant taxation for an apparently endless war. When his death in 1380 brought to the throne a child king in Charles VI (1380–1422), the revival was clearly over.

Under Charles VI the fortunes of France reached their lowest ebb, the damage being done less by English armies than by her own fatal disunity. The boy king was at once surrounded by relatives greedy to control the Crown and to use its diminished resources for their own purposes. In some cases these purposes were directed at territories well outside France: Louis of Anjou, for instance, was bent on continuing the Italian tradition of his duchy; while Philip the Bold of Burgundy, having used French arms to win him the battle of Roosebeke (1382), continued to work for the expansion of Burgundian power in the Germanic lands to the east of Flanders. Brilliantly successful as he was in this, his triumphs were in no sense victories for France.

Charles VI might have seen what was happening earlier, but his not over-gifted personality for long remained under the control of his uncles and of Isabella of Bavaria, the highly-sexed German princess to whom they married him in the hope that nuptial bliss would dim his political ambitions. Had he not possessed a younger brother, Louis of Orleans, to goad him to action he might have been content to remain under their sway. As it was, in 1388 he made an attempt to assert his personal authority. To their indignation the uncles found themselves dismissed; their impudent attempt to claim expenses for services rendered, services which had largely consisted of enriching themselves at the Crown's expense, was rejected, and Charles attempted the experiment of ruling by himself with the assistance of a body of councillors, popularly known as the Marmosets, many of whom had seen service under Charles V.

Whether the Marmosets would have been able to counteract the extravagance and lack of initiative of the king cannot be told. On 5 August 1392 an attempt at assassination near Le Mans threw Charles into the first of his fits of madness; next year a narrow escape from ignition, when a court masque with lighted torches went wrong, precipitated another outbreak, and for the remainder of his life the king was subject to recurrent fits of violent mania, interspersed with intervals of lucidity which grew ever shorter.

A child king was a disaster, but childhood is at least a self-curing disease. The madness of Charles VI was to last for thirty years, and it is not surprising that it nearly destroyed the French monarchy. At first the princes, having dismissed the Marmosets, were happily occupied with the exploitation of the crown resources in their own interests. The process of centralizing the administration which had gone on for so long was now reversed; local treasuries, local systems of taxation, local courts of justice increasingly replaced those of the Crown. When one reads of the increase of the revenue of the House of Burgundy from 100,000 francs in 1375 to 500,000 francs in 1400, and reflects that a greater part of this increase was due to the misappropriation of the funds of the Crown, it is not surprising that the latter's plight became desperate. Forced loans, mortgages, debasement, no amount of fiscal devices could save it from bankruptcy.

This indeed is one explanation of the bitter civil war that was to follow. Once the Crown had been plundered, the plunderers were bound to fall out among themselves. Louis of Orleans and Philip of Burgundy became the chief opponents in a clash which extended over the whole range of policy. If Louis supported the Avignon popes, Philip must withdraw his allegiance; if Louis wanted war with England, Philip must stand for peace.

The quarrel moved through murder to civil war. After John the Fearless (1404-1419) had succeeded his father as Duke of Burgundy, he hired assassins to cut down his chief rival (1407); a few days later he fled from Paris to Lille. France was divided between those who supported Burgundy and those who held to the house of Orleans, henceforth known as the Armagnacs, from Bernard of Armagnac, the new leader of the faction. None could support the mad king, and the Dauphin, the future Charles VII, had none of the qualities to heal so vicious a quarrel. Fluctuating warfare between Burgundians and Armagnacs continued for six years (1407-1413). At first a Burgundian victory seemed likely, but, as in 1358, violence over-reached itself; the fierce rising in Paris, led by the butcher Simon Caboche and supported by John the Fearless, frightened noble opinion enough to produce a reaction. The Dauphin and the Armagnacs, newly united by the Peace of Pontoise (1413), came once more to control the capital at just the moment when Henry V mounted the English throne bent on war.

A France so divided stood little chance in face of a determined attack. The Armagnac leaders tried desperately to avoid war, but Henry was insisting on terms which in name or in fact would make him the sole ruler of France. There is no doubt that he wanted war; even before the negotiations had broken down in 1415 English attacks from Guienne had begun. Later in the same year Henry crossed to Normandy to capture Harfleur as a base for future operations. The battle of Agincourt, the last and strategically the least important of the great English victories, arose from the interception of his army on its march back to the north. Agincourt only proved how little the Armagnac leaders had learnt of the military lessons of the war; a more significant but less lauded achievement was Henry's systematic reduction of lower Normandy two years later.

Between John the Fearless on one hand and Henry V on the other, the Dauphin was now practically without hope. His plight was not improved by the conduct of his mother Isabella, who now took it

upon herself to broadcast the opinion that the Dauphin was not
Charles VI's son. Since her own sex life had long been notorious,
there was nothing improbable in a story on a subject on which

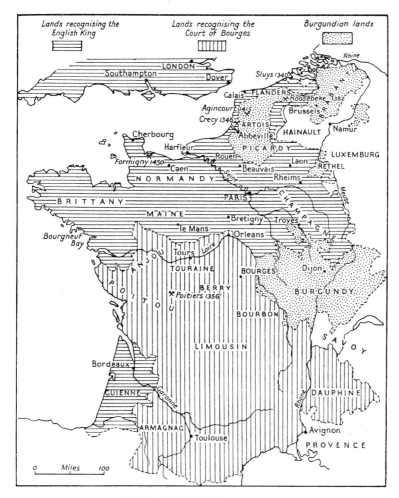

FRANCE AT THE TREATY OF TROYES

inevitably she was better informed than her son; there reason is to
believe that the Dauphin himself came to believe it. At any rate
the belief hastened the reconciliation between the English and the
Burgundian causes. John the Fearless was murdered in 1419, and the

new Duke of Burgundy, Philip the Good (1419–1467), at once entered on the negotiations which were to result in 1420 in the Treaty of Troyes between England and Burgundy.

Accepted everywhere north of the Loire, the Treaty of Troyes dismissed the claims of the 'bastard' Dauphin, whose alleged powers were declared to be vested in Henry V. For the moment France would be divided into that part which would come under direct English rule, Aquitaine and a Normandy enlarged to include the Vexin and the northern half of Maine, and that part which would be administered as a joint Anglo–Burgundian condominium. Henry himself would marry Charles VI's only daughter, Catherine of France; when his father-in-law eventually died, Henry's rights to the French throne would be unquestionable. The rights of Philip to his own lands were of course unaffected.

South of the Loire the future Charles VII, surrounded by the survivors of the Armagnac faction, did his best to maintain his cause at Bourges. He had no hope of regaining Paris by force of arms, and indeed he had little confidence in his ability to lead an army. Only the prospect that his victors might fall out among themselves gave him any hope.

Yet this hope was not remote. Normandy remained an occupied province. For all the attempts to make English rule popular there, it could only be held down by garrisons of English knights, an arrangement which fed the growing national feeling which was to destroy the English cause. In the Condominium an unwieldy council, on which only a few Englishmen sat, tried to administer an area which was never fully reconciled to Burgundian rule. Joint rule is always hard to apply, and quarrels between the English and the Burgundians were frequent. It was a situation which called above all for unity in the English camp; the death of Henry V (1422) when his son was an infant of eight months destroyed that unity.

John, Duke of Bedford, who was acting as regent in Normandy, did his best to preserve the English position in France, but the weakness of his home government, hopelessly split between the Beauforts on the one hand and the faction of Humphrey of Gloucester on the other, much weakened his position. Gloucester's ridiculous marriage (1432) to Jacqueline of Holland, the legality of which was more than questionable, was a serious blow to Anglo-Burgundian relations, since it bore the appearance of a deliberate English attempt to split the Burgundian lands. By 1423 secret negotiations had already started between Philip and the Court of Bourges, where the Dauphin could now style himself Charles VII; the old mad king had died in the winter of 1422. But Philip was understandably reluctant to switch alliances until Charles VII had shown in action that he had cast off the spirit of defeatism which had so long infected the court at Bourges.

This was the cue for the appearance of Joan of Arc. Her personal share in the liberation of Orleans from the English siege in 1429 may have been exaggerated, for the besiegers were already in difficulties and contemporary sources remain curiously silent of one who was to become the figure of French nationalism. But the instinct which has identified the raising of the siege of Orleans as the final turning point of the war is sound. At Orleans Charles took the Maid's advice to move on Rheims rather than Paris. Fortified by coronation and the anointing with holy oil at Rheims, Charles seemed to gain a new confidence that he really was King of France. That Joan's subsequent military ventures were less fortunate, that in 1430 she fell into Burgundian hands and was handed over by them to the English for trial and execution, were of little significance. Indeed, Joan's final service of martyrdom was the best she could have rendered to the House of Valois. Alive she would have been an embarrassment; as a martyr she formed a telling witness to the brutality of the English. The rival coronation of Henry VI in Paris in 1431 seemed what it was, a belated expedient to try to check a tide which was bearing Charles to the capital.

The reconciliation of Charles with Burgundy came out of the discussions opened at Arras in 1435. The English regent, Bedford, was himself a dying man, and his representatives were not prepared for the very substantial concessions by which alone English power in France might have been saved. After the English delegation had withdrawn, the chancellor of Burgundy, Nicholas Rolin, arranged the details by which Philip and Charles were reconciled. Burgundy was to lose nothing; all the lands by which England had purchased her support were to remain in her keeping, and Philip was even exempt from the obligation of homage to his new king. It mattered little; the new alignments had put the English forces at a hopeless disadvantage, and the tense struggle for power that was going on round the ineffective person of young King Henry VI precluded the prospect of an English revival. In the next year Paris fell, and a determined effort might well have cleared the English from Normandy as well as from the Condominium. Charles rather cravenly failed to exploit his advantage, being fearful of the loyalty of his own son, the Dauphin Louis. Instead, he preferred to try and come to terms with England; in 1444 the Truce of Tours was signed by which a six years cessation of fighting was guaranteed by a marriage between Henry VI and Margaret of Anjou.

In 1449 he felt strong enough to resume fighting, and the English regent Edmund Beaufort was rash enough to give him a good pretext. Dunois, the victor at Orleans twenty years before, advanced into Normandy in the autumn. Rouen and Harfleur were both captured, and a campaign of great brilliance was crowned by the defeat of the reinforcements landed at Cherbourg under Sir Thomas Kyriel at the battle of Formigny in April 1450. This was the major French victory in battle during the war, but, unlike Crécy or Agincourt, it was decisive. By the end of the summer the entire English civil and military administration had been withdrawn from Normandy. Guienne followed fast on Normandy. The English monarchy was quickly sinking into the turmoil of the Wars of the Roses and could make no effort to save even its oldest possessions in France. The defeat of the Earl of Shrewsbury at Castillon in 1453 was followed by the evacuation of the remaining English garrisons from Bordeaux.

And there, surprisingly, ended the Hundred Years War, not with a bang but a wimper. There was no peace treaty, Calais remained in English hands for more than a century, and for centuries after that the kings of England would continue to style themselves kings of France. Yet there was no doubt who had won. In the closing phases of the war the institutions of monarchy once more grouped themselves round the king in Paris as they had not done since the days of Philip the Fair. The *Parlement* of Paris and the royal *Chambre des Comptes* acquired once more the status of national institutions, while their local equivalents either perished or survived with much diminished importance. Taxation raised to win the war was retained once the fighting had finished, as a royal prerogative in no way dependent on local estates. Even the army, for most of the war a blend of feudal host with mercenary companies, shared the same process. The cavalry was divided into twenty Companies of the King's Ordinance, each of a nominal one hundred lances with their attendant men-at-arms, and a beginning was made through the Companies of Free Archers in the task of organizing the infantry along similar lines. A national army, paid by the Crown and dependent in the last resort on royal orders, was growing from the ruins of the old feudal host.

The Hundred Years War in its origin and for most of its course was no national conflict. Yet paradoxically the very humiliations it brought to France hastened the growth of a genuine French nationalism; the England whose armies had so proudly dominated most of the fighting gained from the war only a generation of sterile baronial conflict.

17

The Later Medieval Church

When Clement V had refused to restore the papal court to Rome after his coronation at Lyons in 1305, nobody can have expected that this was more than a brief French interlude in the history of the Papacy, the reaction of one pusillanimous pope to an unusually disturbed condition in Italian politics. Yet the self-imposed exile of the bishop of Rome from his see was to last for seventy-three years; only for one short interval (1368–1370) was the attempt made by Urban V to reside again in Rome. From 1309 onwards the papal administration was firmly centred on Avignon, and it is from that city that the period has taken its name.

The Avignon Papacy has sometimes been known by less complimentary names. To Dante, who saw only its first stages, it was clear that residence at Avignon was merely a matter of 'covetous Gascons, striving to rob the Romans of their renown',[1] while later Petrarch (1374), who lived for much of his youth in papal Avignon, saw it simply as a 'hell on earth' and the exile of the Church on the banks of the Rhône as a 'Babylonish Captivity'. It is easy to read too much into such contemporary criticisms of the Avignon Papacy, particularly when they come from Italian sources. Italians naturally enough saw in the absence of the popes from Rome and from Italy a blow at once to their material well-being and to their pride, but an examination of the careers of the popes of the previous one hundred and fifty years shows that there was nothing novel about the absence of the pope from Rome; several had never visited the Holy City. Absence from Italy was rarer, but the exiles of Alexander III and Innocent IV in France provided precedents. Moreover, while these earlier exiles had been in the territory of the French Crown, the popes of Avignon lived in a city which was held in name by the Angevin kings of Naples, themselves vassals of the Holy See, and a city surrounded by a papal county. Clement V apart, none of the Avignon popes could be regarded as the puppets of the French monarchy, nor would it be

---

[1] Dante's letter to the cardinals of the Church after the death of Clement V, 1314, quoted A. C. Flick, *The Decline of the Medieval Church*. Kegan Paul, 1930. Vol. i, p. 211.

easy to see in the unfortunate Valois kings who ruled France during the Hundred Years War a power capable of controlling the Church; they had more urgent political and military concerns.

Nor is it fair to bring accusations of exceptional moral depravity against the Avignon court. Petrarch might call it 'the sewer of the world' and S. Birgitta of Sweden accuse it of 'the foulest pride, insatiable avarice, execrable wantonness, and all-devouring simony',[1] but the one was an Italian and the other a saint speaking with the voice of prophetic righteousness. The truth is not that Avignon was without faults, but that those faults it showed in good measure had already become characteristic of the Papacy long before it left Italy. An excessive concern with financial matters, an organization so large that it gave every opportunity for corruption to remain undiscovered, the extensive practice of nepotism by which great churchmen and sometimes the popes themselves aided their own kin at the expense of the good government of the Church, these were faults as characteristic of the court of Innocent IV as of that of Innocent VI. The Avignon popes in their worst moments were never to approach the unbounded licence and cynical depravity of the later popes who had the full benefits of the occupation of Renaissance Rome.

But generalization about the Avignon period is unwise; seven popes ruled there, and no one of them was like his predecessor. The outstanding defect of Clement V had been a lack of firmness of purpose; no such accusation can be brought against his successor John XXII (1316–1334). John was a small man whose lack of stature was compensated for by a remarkably intransigent character. At times he was prepared even to resist the wishes of the still powerful French monarchy, and to other European rulers he spoke with all the old assumption of superiority over all secular powers which Boniface VIII had attempted so unsuccessfully to implement. The Emperor Lewis of Bavaria was excommunicated and declared deposed (1324), an action which had the predictable result of producing an anti-pope and a renewal of schism within the Church, and John did not hesitate to intervene in the affairs of other European kingdoms, such as England. In Avignon itself he was notable above all for the scale of his nepotism; offices in the papal entourage from the cardinals down to the humblest clerks tended to be filled by the pope's relations or fellow-countrymen.

John's self-confidence led him into the most notorious of his conflicts, that with the Spiritual Franciscans. The 'Spirituals' believed

[1] *Revelations of S. Birgitta*, as quoted in Flick, *op. cit.*, p. 183.

themselves to be the proper custodians of the genuine spirit of S. Francis, in that they taught the necessity of absolute poverty by those who would be his brethren, as against the more numerous 'Conventuals', who held that practical considerations made it expedient that the Order at least should hold property. The quarrel was already of long standing, and both sides had already committed themselves to extreme viewpoints. The Spirituals had come to hold that complete poverty had been the characteristic, not only of their founder, but of his master Christ. From here it was only a short step to the view that the whole Church should share this belief; such a belief could not but involve them in criticism of the papal court and the luxuries commonly associated with it. Yet a more tactful pope might well have avoided the extremities to which John hastened. The flat condemnation of the doctrine of the absolute poverty of Christ contained in the bull *Cum inter nonnullos* (1323) unloosed a fierce persecution against men who were at worst misguided, and drove many of the Spirituals, whose right to exist had now been removed, into fierce opposition to the Papacy.

John's successor, Benedict XII (1334–1341), presents another contrast; where John had been too worldly Benedict was perhaps not worldly enough. A sincere Cistercian of simple origins, he turned his main attention to the reform of the many internal abuses which marked the Church of his day. The monastic orders were to be reformed, a task now overdue, and abuses like non-residence, pluralism and the system of expectancies, by which the right to occupy a living in the future was often sold two or three times over in the lifetime of its present occupant, were to be swept away. Unfortunately Benedict could back these excellent intentions with none of the administrative skill which might have suggested alternative measures by which the Church could be financed. Simply to abolish its existing machinery would have produced not reform but chaos, and in consequence his reforms remained only hopeful dreams. In the same way he seems to have been sincere in the protestations he made of his intention to restore the Papacy to Rome, but the practical difficulties or the nearly unanimous voice of the French cardinals caused him to abandon the attempt, and he ended by starting work on the *Palais des Papes* at Avignon. This when it was completed was to prove a massive obstacle to the return of the Papacy to Rome; nothing could more clearly suggest that the Avignon Papacy was intended to be permanent.

The later popes of the Avignon period show a similar variety.

Clement VI (1342–1352) was far from the humble origins of his predecessor. A French nobleman by birth, he had become archbishop of Rouen; to the papal office he brought a taste alike for high diplomacy and for luxurious living and extravagant building—whatever the state of the papal exchequer. Clement did not lack the virtues of such a nature; his personal courage and good sense when Avignon suffered a severe attack of the Black Death were most praiseworthy, but his pontificate saw no progress either towards a reform of the Church or towards a return to Rome. But it was perhaps unfortunate that he died when he did. His successor Innocent VI (1352–1362) was an elderly canon lawyer of poor health and somewhat timid disposition; his election is said to have been the result of the cardinals' desire to have a pope whom they might run without difficulty. If Innocent proved not so much of a cypher as they had hoped, he was still not the man to deal effectively with the vast problems of a Church financially ruined by the drastic fall in income caused by the Black Death, or of Avignon itself, a city threatened with physical destruction by the mercenary bands which, thrown out of employment by the collapse of French resistance after Poitiers, now roamed the country. Residence in Avignon thus rivalled even the perils of Rome itself.

To Innocent's successor Urban V (1362–70), the abbot of S. Victor, belongs the distinction of making the first serious attempt to bring the Papacy back to Rome. Disregarding the wishes of the French king and the loud complaints of his French cardinals he left Avignon for Rome in the spring of 1367. But he was to regret this intrepid act. The Romans received him warmly and put themselves to great expense in repairing the papal apartments to receive again their pope, but it required more than the presence of Urban to quiet the turbulence of the city. Within a few months the pope was finding himself endangered by the chronic Roman factions, while the members of the Curia made no secret of their preference for the Rhône as against the Tiber. Ignoring the warnings of S. Birgitta, he re-embarked for Avignon in the summer of 1370; his death before the end of the year seemed a confirmation of her prophecies.

The honour of bringing the 'Captivity' to an end thus rests with Gregory XI (1370–1378), the last of the Avignon popes. Gregory's career demonstrated some of the abuses of the Church. By the age of eleven he was already a canon of two French cathedrals. But personally he was a devout man of good intelligence, who understood the overwhelming need for the Church Universal to restore its traditional capital at Rome. The difficulties of such a move remained considerable; they had not been lessened by his predecessor's failure. But at last in October 1376 the convoy which was to convey the papal court to Rome was ready to sail. As a favourable wind filled the sails Gregory is said to have burst into tears; there must have been many in his party who hoped that his grief was premature and that within a few months they would be comfortably settled once more at Avignon. Possibly Gregory himself might have come to be of their number, but he did not live long enough to show Urban's indecision. Within eighteen months he had died—in Rome.

This brief summary has suggested that it would be wrong to take too low a view of the characters and capabilities of the Avignon popes. Some of them were men of real ability; most tried according to their lights to do their best by the Church over which they ruled; none can be written off simply as a thoroughly evil and selfish man. Moreover, on the administrative side the Avignon papacy saw considerable improvements. The Curia took on a highly efficient form. It was sub-divided into four separate bodies, each with its own clearly defined functions. To the *Camera Apostolica* fell the supervision of the whole complicated financial machinery of the Church. Under two permanent officials appointed by the pope, the 'camerarius' and the 'thesaurarius', a permanent check could be kept on all the dues owed to Rome. The financial difficulties of the Church were not caused by any weakness in the central machinery. Next there came the papal Chancery, which was charged with the handling of the vast bulk of correspondence with which the centralization of the Church had burdened the Curia. An efficient registry was kept in which copies of all letters received and issued were filed, so that the Chancellor was in a position to see that his servants did not omit to issue any necessary document.

The supreme judicial function in the Church was exercised by the Pope himself, but the great multiplication of judicial business which came to the Curia through the constant extension of the canon law had led to the creation of a whole structure of courts, of which the most important was the Consistory. Finally there was the Penitentiary, the department concerned with exercising the papal prerogative of granting dispensations, absolutions in cases reserved to the Holy See, and similar functions, now greatly increased in number. Each of these administrative departments had a staff of civil servants, trained and experienced in the type of work peculiar to itself. Of course it is arguable that the Papacy would have been better off without so much organization and with an altogether simpler and more spiritual view of its functions. But granted that the papal system was to be one of centralized autocracy, and the decision to make it so had not been taken at Avignon, it was well that the bureaucracy which served it should be efficient; it was during the exile that the administration of the Church reached its most developed form.

Yet there is little doubt that the Church *was* weakened during the papal residence at Avignon, and that the institution which Gregory XI restored to Rome had less prestige and less real power than that which Clement V had established at Avignon. There are three main causes for this decline. The residence at Avignon coincided with, if it did not produce, a financial crisis in the affairs of the Church which forced the Papacy to measures which made it seem in many parts of Europe little more than a glorified machine for the extraction of money. Secondly, at Avignon, if the Papacy did not in fact become a French institution, it appeared in the eyes of many in other nations to be one; for its reputation this was as bad as the reality. Thirdly, it was at Avignon that a large part of the conditions which could later produce the Schism, a far more damaging and direct blow to medieval papalism, were formed. Together they form a formidable indictment against the Avignon Papacy.

The financial crisis was not the direct result of the move to Avignon. In one sense the whole development of the Papacy since the twelfth century had produced it, by steadily increasing the papal need for revenue. The combined need to staff a civil service and to indulge ever more deeply in the expensive occupations of war and politics had caused difficulties enough in the days of Gregory IX and Innocent IV, and the vulnerability of Boniface VIII to financial pressure has already been seen.[1] The move to Avignon seriously worsened the problem of revenue. Extravagance among some of the popes and many of the cardinals certainly played its part. The building programme at Avignon was unnecessarily lavish if the popes were in earnest about their intention to return eventually to Rome, and there was even less to be said for the elaborate palaces constructed by some of the cardinals in the surrounding countryside from money which can only have been diverted from other more fitting purposes. They served only to strengthen the vested interest against a return. Serious dishonesty certainly existed, though the most flagrant example of it, Clement V's impudent attempt to treat the fortune he had saved out of the exercises of his office as his personal estate, and to leave it to his relatives, was promptly annulled by his no less

[1] See Chapter 14.

financially-minded successor. John XXII indeed possessed great skill as a money maker, and he too was widely believed to have amassed a large personal fortune. But personal dishonesty and extravagance were only a part of the story. The collection of revenue from the papal estates in Italy had long played an important role in filling the coffers of the Papacy. Now that the pope was no longer in Italy this task became much more difficult. The Avignon popes did not altogether lose control over their Italian property, but the revenue from this source dwindled to a small fragment of what it had been, and it was balanced by no corresponding increase elsewhere. Certainly it did not suffice to pay for the increasing expense of the wars necessary to retain any control in Italy. A much more serious problem was presented to the Papacy, along with the national monarchies, by the Black Death. A very much reduced population could not be expected to pay as much in taxes and dues as before the pestilence, but the administrative machinery to be financed remained much the same. Reductions had to be made in the case of dioceses, such as Tours, which had suffered particularly severely from the plague, and the balance could only be made up by an even more strenuous attempt to extract the last penny of revenue from the other sources. Proceedings which two hundred years before would have seemed the grossest simony were by now coming to be the standard practice. The higher clergy, for instance, were subject to the *servitium commune*, a species of severe tax payable on entering on a new appointment; objectionable in that it bore a close resemblance to the purchase of spiritual office, the tax became even more so through the curiously uncertain means by which it was assessed. Prominent churchmen were expected to engage in a prolonged process of haggling, in which they tried to beat the authorities down to what seemed a reasonable sum. Annates, a similar system applying to the less exalted clergy, were similarly abused. Other devices, such as provisions and reservations, which had originally been designed for other purposes, were now increasingly used with purely financial aims in mind. Avignon did not create new abuses, but it saw the worsening of many existing ones. There is no doubt of the extent of feeling aroused throughout a Europe where national feelings could now exacerbate the natural resentment to paying money. Papal tax collectors were lynched in Germany; in England the statutes of *Provisors* (1351) and *Praemunire* (1353) bore witness to a rooted objection to interference from Avignon. The Hundred Years War indeed was scarcely likely to make the English

Crown or its subjects look with favour on government by a French pope.

The national element about Avignon, indeed, was one of its most damaging features. The whole theory of papalism depended on the catholicity of the Church and of its pontiff. Only a pope genuinely raised above the nations could claim to control the universal church. Broadly speaking it had been true of earlier popes that they had not been unduly influenced by national considerations, even if the clash between 'French' and 'Italian' popes in the later thirteenth century did give an ominous hint of the dangers to come. The popes of Avignon certainly did not consciously abandon the idea of catholicity, nor were their policies, with the possible exception of Clement V, dictated to them from Paris; if this had been the case the Papacy would never have left Avignon. But the fact remains that they were all French, and that out of a hundred and thirty-four cardinals created by the seven popes of the exile no less than a hundred and thirteen were Frenchmen. By contrast two Englishmen received the purple and not a single German. If this is not evidence of an attempt to make of the Holy See a national institution, it is at least eloquent testimony to the belief of the popes in the superior merits of their own countrymen, and a sufficient explanation of the view increasingly held outside France that the Papacy was a French institution whose powers it behoved other nations to curtail. The abuses of the court at Avignon were very widely condemned indeed by many of whose general orthodoxy there could be no doubt. S. Catherine of Siena (†1380), for instance, besought Gregory XI to drive from his sheepfold the wolves, 'those demons incarnate, who think only of good cheer, splendid feasts and superb liveries', while S. Birgitta (†1373) referred to another pope as 'worse than Lucifer, more unjust than Pilate, more cruel than Judas'.[1]

Most of these critics were devout Catholics aiming their shafts at the abuses of the Avignon Papacy, and hoping to see the day when, restored to Rome and with a court purged of its offences, the Pope would take the lead in a general reformation of the Church over which he ruled. But there were not lacking more sinister undertones, voices questioning not merely the present abuses but the whole system of papal authority which had allowed those offences to take root. Michael of Cesena (†1342), who as vicar general of the Franciscans championed the cause of the Spirituals against both John XXII and their own brethren, had every reason to oppose John;

[1] Quoted in Flick, *op. cit.*, p. 182.

the latter had imprisoned him in Avignon. But after his escape from prison and flight to Germany Michael became a radical critic of the whole papal position, suggesting that ultimate authority in the Church should rest with a council on the lines of the great councils of the early Church, and not with the pope. He suggested also that his present protector, the German emperor, should take over the leadership of a Church so shamefully misled by its present pastors.

This last suggestion revived old unhappy memories of the struggles of the eleventh and twelfth centuries. William of Ockham (†1349), also a Franciscan and a friend of Michael, made his own contribution with an idea which as clearly reaches forward to the post-Reformation period. In what seems to have been his last work,[1] the last great scholastic philosopher suggested that the ultimate authority in the Church could be neither pope nor council nor any other work of man, but the gospel of Christ Himself; the biblical Protestants of the seventeenth century would have approved most heartily.

Michael's work was most clearly the product of his own immediate situation, while Ockham considered the situation of the Church only in one minor work, his deeper interests lying on a more philosophical plane. The fullest destructive criticism of the medieval papacy for which Avignon can be regarded as indirectly responsible was contained in the *Defensor Pacis* by Marsiglio of Padua (†1343). Like Michael and William of Ockham, Marsiglio became an adherent of the Emperor Lewis, and the opposition to the Avignon popes in which this involved him no doubt coloured his work as it did theirs. But the *Defensor Pacis* is a very full consideration of the origins of power in both Church and State. Finding Petrine authority a fabrication, Marsiglio was prepared to envisage a condition in which papal authority was found to be not even a convenience. The ultimate authority in the Church came from the believers who made it up and not from the shepherd to whom it was entrusted, just as the ultimate authority in the State came from those who were ruled. In the last resort the temporal ruler (and Marsiglio had the Emperor in mind), whose concern is with the whole welfare of his subjects, must be above a spiritual ruler whose attention is, or should be, confined only to their religious activities. That Marsiglio found it possible to combine a strong belief in the rights of the people as a whole with a claim to almost unlimited sovereignty on behalf of the ruler who 'represents' them will surprise no one who knows of the actions of his most distinguished disciple, Henry VIII of England.

[1] *De imperatorum et pontificum potestate.*

In his own age he pointed the way to a day in which the Church universal might be replaced by a number of national Churches and the office of pope necessarily lapse. At Avignon indeed the popes had already gone some way towards establishing a national church.

In their own day these were but radical voices crying in the wilderness; widespread as was the discontent against the Church, few were as yet ready to envisage the possibility of a revolutionary answer. But their words would be remembered in the following generations, when the Great Schism had further undermined men's faith in the traditional Church.

The death of Gregory XI so soon after the return to Rome created unusual difficulties for the papal election which followed. Eleven of the sixteen cardinals who assembled to elect his successor were French, and among them the dominant feeling seems to have been that the sooner the Papacy was removed from the discomforts and alarms of Rome to the security of Avignon the better they would be pleased. On the other hand an immediate announcement of another withdrawal to Avignon would be sure to scandalize European opinion and cast the most unfortunate reflections on their own motives. Moreover, it would not be unattended with risk; Roman sentiment, inflamed by well-founded rumours that another flight was meditated, was demonstratively in favour of a Roman pope who would keep the papacy where it belonged, and the cardinals in conclave could hear noisy shouting from the city outside in favour of a Roman. The election of another Frenchmen would certainly lead to some violent demonstration of anger. Their eventual choice of the Archbishop of Bari as Urban VI (1378–1389) can be seen as an attempt at compromise. The new pope was Italian and not French; on the other hand he was not a Roman, but came from the south with all its traditional Angevin connections with France, and there was nothing in his past career to suggest any hostility to French influence in the Church. The peculiar difficulty about the schism that was to follow is that the claims of the rival popes hinged on the motives in the minds of the cardinals when they elected Urban; since these were probably not at all clear in their minds even at the moment when they cast their votes, it is not surprising that men who were not there could have no certainty as to whose was the better claim. If the cardinals were right in their subsequent claim that the election was made in fear of immediate violence at the hands of a mob whose prejudices had been inflamed by the contents of the papal wine cellars into which they had broken, it was invalid; no promise extracted by threats can be considered binding.

The danger of violence certainly existed, but the later behaviour of the cardinals cast doubt on the belief that it was the major factor in their decision. Instead of immediately withdrawing themselves from Rome and denouncing the election they had been forced to make, they proceeded to do homage to their new pope. They informed of the result those cardinals still in Avignon who had not come to Rome for the election, and they in their turn expressed obedience. Urban received the recognition of the whole Church, and three months passed before his election was questioned. This suggests that what caused the cardinals to change their minds was not the circumstances in which Urban had been elected, but his conduct once in office. It is difficult to forecast the effect of office on a man, and in Urban the Sacred College had made a serious error. He showed himself a holy terror, and the cardinals who had so recently been working with him in the Curia now found themselves treated like a bunch of disobedient schoolboys. Ignoring the wise advice of S. Catherine of Siena to 'mitigate a little, for the love of Christ, these sudden impulses', Urban proceeded to order the cardinals to surrender at once all the perquisites of their offices; if they refused he threatened to extinguish the French influence in the Curia by swamping the college with new Italian creations of his own. Criticism was met with sharp rebukes, and the resentment of the cardinals grew. The cardinal of S. Marcello is said to have answered an accusation of bribery with the words 'Since you are Pope, I cannot answer you, but if you were still the little Archbishop of Bari, I would tell you that you lied.'[1]

Reform was certainly needed, but such tactless measures merely produced revolt. It was not long in coming. The cardinals withdrew themselves from Rome to Neapolitan territory, and at Fondi in September 1378 they proceeded formally to depose Urban and to elect one of their own number, Cardinal Robert of Geneva, in his place as Pope Clement VII (1378-1394). Three Italian cardinals abstained from voting in this second election, but except for them all the cardinals who had voted for Urban now proceeded to vote for his rival. There had been schisms enough before this in the history of the Western Church, but always it had been reasonably clear to an impartial observer which was the pope and which was the

---

[1] Quoted from A. C. Flick, *The Decline of the Medieval Church*, London, Kegan Paul, 1930, vol. I, p. 258.

anti-pope. The present situation, in which both candidates had been elected almost unanimously by one and the same body of cardinals, was without precedent. While both 'popes' solemnly excommunicated each other, and Urban furnished himself with a new set of cardinals, European opinion was understandably perplexed. Both parties could claim the support of good theologians and even of saints; ordinary laymen could have no certain guide as to whether they were supporting the true Church or a diabolical schism. Clement's attempt to secure a rapid victory over his rival in Rome failed (1379), and he withdrew to Avignon; the Schism was established.

It split Europe into two camps. The very ambiguity of the ecclesiastical issue enabled national and dynastic rivalries to have full scope in determining allegiance. That Charles V of France decided naturally enough to give his support to Avignon meant that England supported the Roman cause; this in its turn secured Scottish recognition of Avignon. The Emperor Charles IV gave his backing to Urban, but Francophile German princes who opposed imperial authority were drawn to Clement. Castile and Aragon were in the same camp as their northern neighbour, but this was enough to make Castile's old rival Portugal Roman in her sympathies. All Europe was ranged in one camp or the other, for neutrality was an impossible attitude; there could be but one pope, and hence it followed that the other must be an imposter.

The results for the Church throughout Europe were disastrous. In purely practical terms the Schism meant that the already overstrained financial resources of the Church had to be stretched to cover two different papal courts, each supported by only half Europe. Moreover each pope was necessarily involved in a struggle to try to overthrow his rival, and for this weapons other than his own possibly illusory powers of excommunication were needed. Both sides employed mercenaries, who found in the battlefields of Italy a rival source of employment to those of the Hundred Years War. The process of secularization, already far advanced by the time of the captivity, was carried to shameful lengths by popes who had few other aims than the destruction of the rivals.

If the practical results of the Schism were bad, the less tangible effects were even worse. For over three hundred years unity had been the proud boast of the Western Church, the mark by which the true Church might be distinguished from the multiform heresies of the East; it had been no new teaching of Boniface that 'this one and only

Church' has 'one body and one head—not two heads, like a monster'.[1] Now it had become a monster, a reproach to the faithful and the laughing stock of the heretics.

It was easier to bemoan the plight of the Church than to see what could be done about it. The most obvious remedy, that both claimants should abdicate leaving the way clear for a new election which could be recognized by both sides, was blocked by the unwillingness of either pope to take the first move, and their deep suspicion of any form of co-operation with their rivals. Nor did the mortality of the popes offer a way of escape. The death of Urban in 1389 merely caused the election of Boniface IX (1389–1404) and that of Clement in 1394 the election of Benedict XIII (1394–1423). The cardinals of both sides seemed to have no alternative to perpetuating the schism short of the tacit admission that their opponents were in the right. Both Benedict XIII at Avignon and Gregory XII, the Roman pope from 1406 to 1415, solemnly promised both before and after their elections that they were willing to abdicate to further the cause of unity, and there is no reason to doubt their sincerity, but when it came to the point neither was prepared to fulfil his promise.

Failing abdication, the best hope seemed to lie in the appointment of some impartial commission of theologians to examine the respective claims. The doctors of the University of Paris, generally recognized as the leading theological school of the West, were prominent in supporting this proposal, and indeed generally took the lead in all attempts to restore unity. But the difficulties in the way of securing unity by arbitration were very great. Successful arbitration depends on the existence of genuine neutrals, and just as in the contemporary world arbitration on issues between East and West is rendered nearly impossible by the lack of nations regarded by both sides as genuinely neutral, so in the conciliar period there were very few individuals who were unbiassed and, which was more difficult, seen to be unbiassed. Nor was it at all clear that the findings of any such commission could be put into effect. When in 1398 a synod was called in Paris by the French king and attended by many of the doctors of the university, its findings were against Benedict XIII and the Avignon line; robbed of his strongest secular support there seemed every hope that Benedict would be forced into capitulation. The hope proved vain. Benedict made good his escape from the French troops moving on Avignon, and continued to maintain his

[1] See Chapter 14.

claims in Provence. The very fact that the theologians of Paris seemed to oppose his claim served to win him sympathy from those of Toulouse, Montpellier and the other universities of the south, while many even of the Parisian doctors came to regret a move which seemed to have increased the control of the French crown over them; as the monk of S. Denis, a witness at close quarters of royal methods of collecting revenue from the Church, has it: 'the first fruit of the withdrawal of obedience was to expose the Church to the persecution of the secular arm'.[1] Nor could Charles VI feel satisfied with a measure which, failing in its purpose of stripping Benedict of his European supporters, had only succeeded in further dividing his own kingdom. In 1403 French recognition was restored to Benedict.

The failure of both simultaneous surrender and arbitration as techniques for solving the schism caused men's minds to move reluctantly towards more revolutionary solutions. The idea that the claims of both papacies might be submitted to a general council of the whole Church could find little support in the history of the medieval Church. The Lateran Councils which had met at intervals since 1123 had been composed of those who came to Rome by papal invitation; they provided no useful precedent when the occupancy of the papal office itself was in question. But very much earlier precedents could be found in the great oecumenical councils of the Early Church. Here, before the Papacy had evolved to fulfil any of its more modern functions, questions of doctrine and practice had apparently been submitted to the collective wisdom of the assembled Church. Such an idea ran completely contrary to the general movement towards papal autocracy which had marked the development of the Church in the West; without the stimulus of this particular crisis it would certainly not have found acceptance. But anything was better than the apparently endless schism, and a new interest came to be shown in writers of earlier generations, such as Marsiglio, who had seen in councils a vital form of Church government. As early as 1379 Conrad of Gelnhausen, a canonist of the University of Paris, was suggesting that necessity justified the extraordinary measures of a general council to deal with the extraordinary crisis.[2] The same theme was taken up in 1381 by another German doctor at Paris, Henry of Langenstein. In his more full *Epistola Concilii Pacis* Henry argued that both the spiritual and the temporal leaders of the Church should combine in summoning a general council as the only way to

---

[1] Quoted from *Cambridge Medieval History*, Vol. VII, p. 297.
[2] Conrad of Gelnhausen, *Epistola Brevis*.

restore unity. As the schism dragged on this idea gradually gained wider acceptance. But it was easier to approve in abstract the idea of a general council than to suggest a practical means whereby such a council could come into being. Churchmen themselves were already committed to one or other faction, and there was no secular ruler who had the prestige necessary to take the initiative, until 1410 the German Empire itself was in dispute between Wenzel of Bohemia and Rupert the Elector Palatine, both of whom claimed to be King of the Romans.

The first attempt at a conciliar solution came in 1409 from churchmen, and was entirely unsuccessful. In that year thirteen cardinals, nine of whom had defected from the 'Roman' camp and four from Avignon, summoned a general council of the Church to meet at Pisa. Their suggestion had been treated with scorn by both popes, but it received powerful support from the Chancellor of Paris, the most distinguished theologian of the day, Jean Gerson. More than five hundred delegates assembled at Pisa; they represented most areas of the Church, and most of the great powers were also represented, along with thirteen European universities. Much time was spent in rehearsing the misdeeds of the existing popes, a process which culminated in their deposition on the grounds of schism, heresy and perjury. Having done this the Council was free to replace them by a new pope; the cardinals present, who now numbered twenty-four, went into conclave, and elected the Cardinal Archbishop of Milan. He took the title of Alexander V (1409–1410).

The new pope received nothing like the universal support which would be necessary if he were to gain a swift triumph over both his adversaries. The only immediate result of Pisa was that the two-headed monster had sprouted yet another head. Nor in office did Alexander satisfy those who had hoped optimistically that the new pope would verify his own credentials by showing a concern for true religion in contrast to the secular ambitions of his two opponents. Instead he concentrated on attempting to regain control of Rome from the forces of Ladislas of Naples, a supporter of the Roman line. In this he came to rely increasingly on the services of that ordained condottiere Cardinal Baldassare Cossa, a master of diplomatic intrigue with an unequalled knowledge of the muddy waters of Italian politics. When Alexander died suddenly at Bologna in the next year many suspected poison; the suspicious speed with which Cardinal Cossa got the cardinals into a conclave, which proceeded to elect him pope as John XXIII (1410–1415), did nothing to allay their doubts. The Pisan line could certainly now claim no moral superiority over either of the other two.

The crucial event in bringing the Schism to an end was the election in 1411 of the Emperor Sigismund. At last the Empire seemed to have emerged from the anarchy in which it had been submerged since the death of Charles IV. In appearance and ability the new emperor seemed to measure up to the responsibilities of his office. He was, indeed, by nature a man who thought in grandiloquent terms, and the reunification of the Church was certainly a project large enough to satisfy such a taste. Practically, too, he could hope that the prestige he would gain from accomplishing a task which for so long had defeated Christendom would be of the greatest value to him. Despite the fiasco at Pisa, educated opinion in Europe still held that a council offered the only hope of escape from the Schism. His position as emperor gave him an unique claim to be heard should he summon such a council; all that was needed was some encouragement from the side of the Church, so that he should not fear the risk of another Pisa.

The most recent of the popes provided him with it. John XXIII had not found his task as Vicar of Christ an easy one. He had begun well by regaining control of Rome in winning the support of Ladislas from Gregory XII, but the alliance proved short-lived. In the summer of 1413 John found himself suddenly expelled from Rome by the treachery of Ladislas. To regain it he would need powerful temporal support; rashly he approached Sigismund for aid. The emperor was willing to provide it, having no great desire to see Ladislas control the whole Italian peninsula, but only on condition that John consented to summon a general council. Reluctantly the latter agreed, evidently hoping that a council summoned in his name would prove to be malleable to his own interests. His ambassadors had expected that an Italian meeting place would be chosen for the council; there it might well be that the council could be packed with his own supporters. But Sigismund insisted that Constance should be named as the location of the council, and in December 1413 John issued a bull summoning the council to meet there on November 1st, 1414. That Ladislas should die earlier in 1414, thus from the viewpoint of John removing the main purpose of the assembly, only ensured that the pope who had summoned the council would attend it with no very good grace.

During the summer of 1414 the little city of Constance gradually filled with delegates to the conference. Three patriarchs and twenty-nine cardinals, nearly two hundred archbishops and bishops, a massive representation from the universities—the Catholic world had seen nothing like it before. With their attendant retinues the delegates must have outnumbered many times the six thousand inhabitants of Constance, many of whom deserted the city, like citizens of Edinburgh on the eve of the Festival. Besides the manifold problems of accommodating so large an host, the problem of procedure had to be settled before effective work could commence. Nor were these mere matters of detail; as in the United Nations Assembly, the procedure would largely determine where power rested. In particular there was the question of voting. John had hoped that even in Constance it might be possible to pack the assembly with his own supporters. But the size of the assembly turned out to be much greater than he had expected, it being decided for instance that all graduates in theology might attend as full members, a decision which opened the door to large numbers of delegates from· the North over whom he had no influence. Moreover, the adoption of a suggestion made by an English representative, Robert Hallam, that the members of the Council should not vote as individuals but should follow the precedent of university organization in voting as 'nations', virtually excluded his hopes of extracting a vote of confidence, since he could not hope to control more than one of the four nations.

At the start the Council was set a threefold target of Unitas, Fides, and Reformatio. Briefly it can be held to have succeeded triumphantly in the first, to have secured a temporary and partial success in the second, and to have failed in the third. As with many experiments which start with high and almost Utopian hopes, its failure to achieve all it set out to do should not be allowed to obscure the reality of its achievements.

To take the three aims separately, Unitas at least presents no problem of definition. It meant the restoration of a unified papacy. John XXIII proceeded to play into the Council's hands. Foiled in his attempt to control the assembly he proceeded to declare the Council dissolved, and then fled to take refuge with Frederick of Habsburg in the Tyrol. His action merely rid the Council at Constance of an embarrassing encumbrance and allowed it to put forward a more exalted view of its own nature than would otherwise have been possible. In the decree *Sacrosancta* (1415) the Council laid it down that 'This holy Council of Constance . . . has its authority immediately from Christ; and that all men, of every rank and condition, including the Pope himself, are bound to obey it in matters concerning the Faith, the abolition of the Schism, and the reformation of the Church of God'. However revolutionary the implications of such a decree, no substantial body of European opinion was prepared to rally behind John XXIII in opposing it. Hunted down to Freiburg he was captured there, and accused of so formidable a list of crimes that he was glad to ratify his own deposition lest a worse fate should befall him.[1] As it was he was permitted to finish his days under the protection of the Medicis in Florence.

The fall of John put an end to the Pisan line; the 'Roman' succession was more easily wound up. Deserted by his chief secular ally, Carlo Malatesta of Rimini, Gregory XII had the sense to read the writing on the wall. In 1415, in return for a promise that the cardinals he had created should retain their rank, Gregory abdicated; he himself was permitted to remain a cardinal until his death two years later. The 'Avignon' popes proved more intractable. Benedict XIII refused to come to terms with the Council, and indeed on his death in 1423 his cardinals elected a successor, Clement VIII (1423–1429). But the Avignon Papacy had become a poor shadow of its former self. Driven out of France it was forced to take refuge in Aragon. Here more and more it took on the nature of a purely local deviation; as such it could be ignored. The way was open for the election of a new pope to rule over the united Church, although national jealousies made it very difficult for any candidate to secure the required majority. At length in 1417 Cardinal Odonne Colonna was elected as Martin V (1417–1431), tactfully taking a title not associated with any of the popes in the period of dispute. Unitas had been achieved.

Fides in 1414 meant first and foremost the protection of the Church from the Hussite and Wycliffite heresies. Both were satisfactorily extinguished,[2] but little was done to touch the roots from which those heresies had sprung. In particular nothing was done at Constance —perhaps nothing could have been done—to reconcile the conflicting claims of nationalist sentiment and catholic religion. Nor did the clerical assembly pay any attention to the needs of those devout and educated laymen who were becoming ever more conscious of the contrast between scriptural Christianity and the ecclesiastical realities of their day.

[1] The incident gave Gibbon an opportunity he did not miss. 'Of the three popes, John the Twenty-third was the first victim; he fled, and was brought back a prisoner; the most scandalous charges were suppressed; the vicar of Christ was only accused of piracy, murder, rape, sodomy and incest.' The Decline and Fall of the Roman Empire, ed. Bury, vol. VII, p. 288.
[2] See Chapter 18.

But it was Reformation which provided the chief failure of the Council. Here there was a real difficulty of definition. Reformation might mean a reform of the constitutional mechanism of the Church, designed to turn it from an autocracy into something analogous to a limited monarchy. Equally it might mean what reform had meant in the past, the abolition of pluralism, simony, and clerical marriage, the reform of the monastic orders, and the correction of the multitude of day to day abuses. Whereas there had been complete agreement as to the desirability of Unitas and Fides, there was not such agreement about constitutional reform. Moreover, many of the delegates to the council themselves benefited from the abuses, and it was impossible to get unanimity as to where such reform should start.

In practice constitutional reform received the greater attention. Before proceeding to the election of Martin the Council had issued the decree *Frequens* (1417). This was an attempt to make the conciliar system of government perpetual; the next General Council was to meet five years after the dissolution of the Council of Constance, the next seven years after that, and thereafter councils were to meet at intervals of ten years. Combined with *Sacrosancta*, *Frequens* would have turned the Church into an oligarchy in which ultimate control rested with those who attended the councils; the pope would have become the head of an administration charged with carrying out the decisions formed by the councils. Such suggestions had appeared highly revolutionary when they had been made in the previous generation. Even now they were probably more extreme than most churchmen really intended. To agree to a General Council as an extraordinary measure to restore the Papacy to sanity was one thing; to uproot the whole traditional order of things, and incidentally to cast doubt upon all the decisions taken since the oecumenical councils of the Early Church, was another. In any case it must be doubted whether a regular conciliar organization could have worked in the conditions of the fifteenth century. It presupposed an ability to think in universal rather than national terms which was becoming increasingly unlikely. In the event the members of the councils tended to break up into mutually antagonistic groups divided largely on national lines. There is no lack of depressing modern parallels in the world of politics.

The popes of the period, heirs to a whole tradition of autocracy, were understandably hostile to the institution to which they owed their origin. Martin V watched with approval the sterile proceedings of the Council of Pavia in 1423; his successor Eugenius IV (1431–1447) was to find himself in open conflict with the Council of Basle (1431), the second and last of the councils summoned under the terms of Constance. At Basle the Council resisted an attempt made by Eugenius to dissolve it, and showed itself ready to conduct its own policies. It was, for instance, ready to ignore papal policy and negotiate on its own account with the Hussites. Along with this independence of action, the members of the Council of Basle showed a marked independence of thought. In its proceedings are to be found the expression of a number of highly radical views, as for instance that the Council only held its authority by virtue of the acceptance of its rulings by the whole body of the Church, clerical and lay alike. Such dangerously democratic ideas could not but arouse suspicion in conservative breasts. Nevertheless, at first it seemed that the Council might triumph in its struggle with Eugenius. Ignoring a flurry of bulls directed against it, the Council seemed in no hurry to dissolve itself. In 1433 Eugenius's bull *Dudum Sacrum* admitted a conciliar victory; revoking his earlier bulls it promised full papal co-operation with the council for the future.

The conciliar victory was short-lived. Although there is no reason to think that *Dudum Sacrum* marked any change of heart on the part of Eugenius, the Council must carry the blame for its own destruction. For many years the West had turned a deaf ear to even more urgently worded appeals for help from Byzantium; now the remnant of the Eastern Empire was in such straits that the embassy which arrived in the West was prepared to offer even ecclesiastical submission as the price of aid. The question was really a theoretical one; nothing which the West was likely to do now could save Byzantium, nor, events were to show, would eastern opinion be prepared to ratify the surrender made by its representatives. But in its effect on the conciliar movement the eastern move was decisive. The delegation was confronted by conflicting demands as to where and with whom it should negotiate. The majority party at the Council of Basle, headed by the Cardinal of Arles, insisted that the negotiations should take place at Avignon, geographically an unsuitable place for the Greeks, but a substantial minority under Cardinal Cesarini supported the papal view that the negotiations should take place at Ferrara. The eastern delegates were well aware of the Papacy: the papal supremacy was indeed one of the issues on which they had come to negotiate. But they did not know what to make of this novel and divided body. Not unnaturally they chose to make their approaches to the papal party. The discussions, which were carried on at Ferrara and Florence

(1438–1439), were crowned with apparent success. The Greeks were willing to accept papal terms, pledging their Church to an acceptance of the supremacy of Peter and of the western form of the Nicene creed. All the credit of healing this ancient wound in the Body of Christ went to the papacy; the Council at Basle was futilely engaged in denouncing this step towards the unity it had been created to serve.

In the summer of 1439 the Council of Basle took the step which sealed its ruin. By electing Amadeus Duke of Savoy as pope Felix V (1439–1449) it removed all justification for its own continued existence. Felix would have been a curious choice in any age; it was necessary for him to take priest's orders after his election. But that the Councils, formed to end the scandal of anti-popes, should themselves turn to the manufacture of superfluous popes was a clear indication that their utility had vanished. That what was now clearly the Conciliar Schism lingered on for another ten years was not the result of any widespread belief in Felix, but of the determination of various secular rulers to drive as hard a bargain as possible before switching their support to Rome. When Nicholas V (1447–1455) purchased the allegiance of the Emperor and most of the German princes by promising them a goodly share of clerical pickings in the Concordat of Vienna (1448), the Council was left without secular support. It came to an ignominious end by dissolving itself at Lausanne in the next year. It only remained for a later pope, Pius II (1458–1464) to declare the conciliar doctrine itself a 'pestilent poison' in the bull *Execrabilis* (1460). The attempt at constitutional reform had failed.

Probably it could never have succeeded. The worst result of the conflict over conciliar principles was undoubtedly that it led to a complete neglect of reform in the other less spectacular but more necessary sense. A Church preoccupied by the intense struggle over its own leadership had had no time to spare for the problems of simony and pluralism, of secularization and immorality. Indeed the struggle in many ways itself worsened those evils. The Concordat of Vienna saw a grave extension of the evil by which the high offices of the Church became merely pawns in the game of international politics. The moral authority of the Papacy, by which alone in the last resort it could justify itself, had been already badly dented by 1378; by 1449 it had been so long and so deeply involved in the filth of Italian politics that it seemed that the papal hands could never again be clean. The way was open for the more spectacular excesses of the popes of the later fifteenth century. Piety was not dead; the Council of Constance had coincided with the publication of Thomas à Kempis's *De Imitatione Christi*, the greatest devotional work of the later Middle Ages, and in northern Europe at least through such bodies as the Brethren of the Common Life the religious life continued to flourish. But there was an intense and understandable pessimism about the Church as an institution which led men increasingly to cultivate more personal forms of devotion. The Council of Constance was perhaps the last moment when, for all its difficulties, a widespread reform of the Western Church was still possible. The loss of this opportunity ensured that when reform did come it would take the form of revolution.

18

The Diminishing Empire

After the collapse of the Hohenstaufens the German Empire did not again form the main focus of power in central and eastern Europe until 1871. The Crown indeed was still coveted by many rulers for the traditional prestige and opportunities of enrichment which it might yet bring to those who held it, but it could fill no longer its role as the dominant force in the eastern half of the Catholic world. Nor could the Empire play any larger part; with another five hundred years of history before it the Holy Roman Empire was already an antique. Within Germany itself interest shifts to the lands of the various princes, independent in all but name, who filled the gap left by the royal decline. Outside the traditional borders of Germany attention is fixed on those areas of mixed Slav and German population, such as Bohemia, which were attempting on the fringes of the Empire the difficult passage into statehood, or, further to the east again, on Poland and Lithuania, now staking their claim to recognition in the European community.

Lacking the central imperial theme the history of the fourteenth and fifteenth centuries does not easily lend itself to brief description. The death of Conrad IV in 1254 had ushered in a period of exactly twenty years which is commonly known as the Interregnum. During all that period there was no ruler in Germany who received any significant recognition, let alone support, from the German nation. The two claimants to the throne after the death in 1256 of William of Holland, the papalist opponent of the Hohenstaufens, were Richard of Cornwall, the brother of Henry III of England, and Alfonso of Castile. That both candidates should be foreigners is a fitting commentary on the level to which the prestige of the monarchy had sunk in the eyes of the German nobility, and on the scope which Germany now gave to interference from outside. The principal beneficiaries of this weakness over the next hundred years were to be the kings of France. In 1257 both candidates could claim to have been elected by German diets which included some of those normally accustomed to elect German kings; neither had any of the realities of power. The only difference between them was that Alfonso of Castile acquiesced in that situation; he had only wanted the title as a means to Mediterranean power. Richard, on the other hand, sought German power, and was lavish in his grants of lands and privileges designed to win him support. But the recipients were not impressed by gifts which they knew the donor had not the power to retain, and Richard's efforts were unavailing.

These two decades were a black period in the history of the German monarchy; it does not follow that they were therefore a period of growth in princely power. As in the twelfth century under Lothar and Conrad III, the princes found that the absence of any effective imperial power had to be paid for by the absence of any effective arbiter in their disputes. The period was one of incessant warfare, not only between the principalities themselves, but between individual princes and their own overmighty subjects, against whom they could no longer summon the aid of an overlord. When Richard died in 1272 and Alfonso at last withdrew his claim, the electors ignored the claims of two foreign candidates, Ottokar II of Bohemia and Philip III of France, in favour of a German candidate, Rudolf of Habsburg (1273–1291). Fortified by unanimous election, by a coronation in time-honoured style at Aachen, and by papal approval of his elevation, the Emperor Rudolf I began his reign.

It is tempting to read too much into this first appearance on the scene of the most illustrious and long-lived of all the ruling families of Europe. The election of Rudolf points to a realization by the princely families that something more than a vacuum was necessary in the place of royal power, but it does not indicate any desire for a centralized monarchy, which by now was in any case probably an impossibility. At this period of their history the Habsburgs were a family of considerable local importance in south-western Germany, with lands extending from Alsace in the north to Switzerland in the south. But Rudolf had none of the scattered possessions elsewhere in Germany by which alone a real revival of the monarchy might have come. In practice he was to prove a shrewd and effective statesman, but the cause he served was that of his own family interests rather than that of Germany. He had immediately to face the challenge of the defeated candidate, Ottokar of Bohemia; in conquering it he was able to lay the foundations of that power in the south-east of the German speaking lands where the future greatness of his house was to lie. By his two victories over Ottokar in 1276 and 1278, the second of which resulted in the death of the Bohemian king, he was able to remove the anomaly of a Slavonic ruler over German peoples; Ottakar's successor Wenzel II was to turn Bohemian ambitions to the east. More important, he was thereby enabled to distribute the duchies of Austria and Styria to his own sons, thus raising his family for the first time to a situation of importance in its own right in German affairs. Rudolf was prepared to adjudicate between his vassals, but he made little attempt to assert his will in central or northern Germany.

Rudolf's very success in the limited aims he set himself probably explains the refusal of the electors, among whom his family was not represented, to consider the claims of his son on his death in 1291. Instead, by choosing an obscure Rhineland prince, Adolf of Nassau (1291–1298), they condemned the throne to another period of insignificance as well as impotence. Adolf counted for little in German affairs, and his efforts to remedy this defect by opposing French intervention from the west, and by intervening himself in the affairs of central Germany, led to his destruction by Albert of Habsburg at the battle of Gollheim (1298).

Even before the death of Adolf the electors had met to depose him and had replaced him by Albert, who as the Emperor Albert I was to rule for ten years (1298–1308). His reign stands in logical succession to that of his father Rudolf. He too was far more interested in the prospect of extending Habsburg power in the unstable, and therefore promising, lands of the south-east, than in defending the Empire as a whole; indeed, at his meeting with Philip IV of France at Quatrevaux in 1299 he seems to have given the French king a guarantee that he would not hinder the gradual French advance in the west if the French would support his own plans in the east. Treachery from an imperial standpoint, this was a realistic arrangement from a Habsburg point of view. Nor did Albert's sacrifice of the Empire go unrewarded. Although assassination brought his reign to a premature end in 1308, he had succeeded in securing the election of his eldest son Rudolf as king of Bohemia and in installing his second son, Frederick the Handsome, in neighbouring Moravia. The first gain was only transitory, Rudolf dying in 1307 before his father, but Habsburg control over Moravia remained.

On Albert's death the electors once more refused to continue with the same dynasty. Their choice of Henry of Luxembourg as Henry VII (1308–1313) gave the empire a ruler who not only lacked the family lands which might have made him formidable, but had the added disadvantage of being as much a Frenchman as a German.

In addition Henry had the misfortune to be the possessor of a fertile imagination. Together these two factors led him to suppose that he could desert Germany altogether for the old romantic quest of an empire which should in fact as well as name be Roman. The scheme was, of course, hopelessly impractical. Although many Italians, now deprived of their papacy, might genuinely desire a restoration of their empire, Henry had none of the practical resources which might have made his scheme of an Italy united under the Empire successful. The Papacy was prepared to support him at first, in the hope that he would prove useful as a regainer of papal lands, but any prospect that Henry might succeed would alarm Clement V as much as any Italian ruler. All the old Welf opposition to imperial intervention was resurrected, and the emperor was confronted by a powerful league headed by Florence and backed by Robert, the Angevin king of Naples. Against such opposition Henry could only muster a few hundred German supporters (and he had little enough hope of paying them) and the doubtful support of some of the Lombard cities. Curiously, this ill-fated venture stimulated Dante to write perhaps the most cogent of all the multitude of literary defences of imperialism, the *De Monarchia*. But the gap between the theory and the reality must have been difficult to stomach even for this age, accustomed as it was to such discrepancies.

Once Henry had crossed the Alps only defeat could await him. Yet he was not without ability as a ruler, and earlier in his reign he had secured a considerable triumph by gaining for his son John the throne of Bohemia, through marriage to the surviving daughter of the popular king Wenzel II (1310). It can at least be said that the house of Luxembourg was to figure more prominently in history as a result of his reign.

After Henry's death at Siena in 1313 there followed another prolonged period (1313-1346) of doubt and confusion in the affairs of the Empire. The heads of two of the leading German houses, the Wittelsbachs and the Habsburgs, were both elected as emperor by separate diets in somewhat dubious circumstances. Lewis IV (1313-1347), Duke of Bavaria, himself controlled two electoral votes; Frederick III (1313-1330), the surviving son of the emperor Albert, could call on the resources of the Habsburg family as well as those of his own duchy of Austria; neither could claim any widespread support outside the areas they directly dominated. For this reason the struggle between them for some years resembled shadow boxing; each 'emperor' found it easier to discharge high-sounding manifestoes at his adversary than to mobilize the forces to dethrone him. But eventually the issue was tested at the battle of Mühldorf (1322), and Lewis emerged victorious with Frederick as his prisoner. But Mühldorf was far from settling the question of who was to rule Germany; it continued to plague the country even after Lewis's tactful gesture three years later in associating his one-time prisoner with him in the government of the Empire. This might satisfy Frederick until his death in 1330, but Lewis had to face the continued suspicion and intermittent hostility of both the house of Luxembourg and the Habsburgs for the rest of his reign. Neither wished to see Germany dominated by the Wittelsbachs, and the very fact that Lewis was using his office to help him in the game of dynastic aggrandizement, at which they themselves were old hands, served to increase their resentment. The attempt made by Lewis in 1342 to attach the Tyrol and Carinthia to the Wittelsbach lands by means of a peculiarly brazen manipulation of the marriage law was just such a device as the Habsburgs themselves were accustomed to use; it was correspondingly unpopular with them.

Nor was this all. The disputed succession to the Empire had enabled John XXII at Avignon to revive the old papal claims to overlordship of the Empire. Certainly this claim was not likely to find much support inside Germany, but there was always the danger that behind John might be ranged the forces of the French Crown. An imperial collapse would serve French interests well, and it had already been suggested in the reign of Philip the Fair that the ultimate solution might be to join the imperial title to the French monarchy. John proceeded to excommunicate Lewis and to declare him deposed (1324), and Lewis retaliated by declaring John heretical; it was against this background that Lewis's support of Michael of Cesena and the Spiritual Franciscans developed.[1] The dispute between Lewis IV and the Avignon popes, the last in a great series of conflicts between Empire and Papacy, only serves to illustrate how far both had fallen. Papal bulls had little effect in Germany. In 1338 the German electors, the Luxembourg John of Bohemia alone excepted, met to issue the Declaration of Rense, indignantly repudiating the suggestion that the pope had any say in the question of who was to be emperor. The extent of their differences on all other questions of policy only strengthens their testimony that papal policy was hopelessly outdated. Similarly, when Lewis IV had carried out the traditional invasion of Italy with an anti-pope in his train in 1327. he had succeeded only in

[1] See Chapter 17.

demonstrating at once the tenuous nature of imperial resources and the lack of European prestige now commanded by the imperial title.

The fall of Lewis of Bavaria when it came, although it was applauded by Clement VI at Avignon, sprang from entirely secular causes. In attempting to secure for his own family the succession to Holland and Hainault with their attached territories by an exercise of his imperial rights, he deeply alarmed the house of Luxembourg, itself possessed of extensive lands in the Netherlands. The five electors who were not Wittelsbachs met, again at Rense, and declared Lewis deposed (1346). In his place they elected the emperor Charles IV (1346–1378), the effective head of the house of Luxembourg who had already succeeded his blind and exiled father John as king of Bohemia. The danger that this might lead only to another prolonged period of civil war was averted by the death of Lewis himself in the next year (1347).

Charles IV must be reckoned the most effective German emperor of the later Middle Ages, but paradoxically his claim to be considered as such rests on his realization that his imperial title was not the first claim in his attention. In an often-quoted remark a later emperor, Maximilian, described him as 'the father of Bohemia and the step-father of the Empire'; the phrase neatly sums up the ideas of a ruler whose actions were characterized by a realistic sense of his own limitations. Certainly Charles had no time for an empire which was in any sense Roman. Lewis IV had shown how little was to be gained by expeditions to Italy in pursuit of this impossible ideal. Instead his only expedition to Italy, in 1355, was made without an army for the sole purpose of receiving coronation from papal representatives, and he was happy to withdraw as soon as the ceremony was completed.

He was even prepared to accept in theory what he must have known in practice to be a myth, that his office was dependent on papal confirmation; in return he received the considerable benefit of papal support. This acceptance of a real, if limited, advantage in return for a large but meaningless concession is very typical of his practical approach to all his problems.

In Germany he is known above all as the author of the 'Golden Bull' of 1356. An imperial diet summoned to Nuremberg in 1355 laid down the main lines of the document the emperor was to issue in the next year. Again it is possible to criticize a settlement by which the Empire was condemned to remain perpetually elective, and

Charles has been said merely to have legalized chaos. Undoubtedly it is true that the elective system put Germany at a great disadvantage in her dealings with other states, in which the hereditary system had for centuries been generally accepted. But the issue was not one of the theoretical advantages of the hereditary principle. The German monarchy *was* elective. The whole history of Germany since the collapse of the Hohenstaufen dynasty had demonstrated that no attempt to change that system was likely to succeed. Certainly Charles himself did not possess the strength to make him succeed where so many had failed. But, accepting that this was so, there was everything to be said for so organizing the elective procedure that every election did not bring with it the very real threat of civil war. The two main defects in the existing electoral machinery were the doubt surrounding the question as to who the electors were, and the failure to recognize clearly any majority rule. In early times the German emperors had been elected by very varying assemblies, in theory consisting of the tenants-in-chief of the Crown, but differing widely in composition from occasion to occasion. Somewhat mysteriously, from the mid-thirteenth century onwards the electors seemed to have become settled at the number of seven, but the precise composition of the seven continued to vary. For instance Bavaria and the Palatinate alternated in their control of a vote, but sometimes, as in 1273 at the election of Rudolf, both would vote at the same election. The electoral college was now stabilized at seven members, three of whom, the archbishops of Cologne, Mainz, and Trier, were ecclesiastics, and four, the King of Bohemia, the Elector Palatine, the Duke of Saxe-Wittenberg, and the Margrave of Brandenburg, were lay. To avoid future confusion by the sub-divisions through inheritance of the lands attached to a particular electorate, the vote was now conferred not on the persons of the electors, but on the lands they controlled, and these lands were declared indivisible. This belated adoption of primogeniture came too late to save the power of the Empire itself, but once adopted by the electors it had a tendency to spread to the other German powers. In this way it did something to check that excessive fragmentation of Germany into ever-smaller units which was the chief threat to the power of the princes themselves. The distribution of votes in the Golden Bull was not faultless. In particular, the ecclesiastical representation was greater than the actual size of the ecclesiastical lands in Germany would justify, while both Bavaria and the Habsburg lands might be considered unfortunate not to be awarded votes. Nevertheless the electoral system did not succeed in giving some representation to all four of the geographical quarters of the country.

The other frequent cause of electoral disputes in the past had been the lack of any clear majority rule. Imperial elections were in theory unanimous, and in consequence, when the electors failed to achieve unanimity, both factions could feel that, whatever the division of votes, their candidate had as much right to be considered emperor as the other. Now a bare majority rule was laid down; the electors were all expected to vote, and, their number being odd, there should no longer be any ground for dispute.

The supreme justification of the Golden Bull is that it worked; it could not restore power to the Empire, but it did free Germany from the recurrent menace of disputed imperial elections. This alone is ample justification. The rest of his policy in his imperial lands carried the same stamp of realistic appreciation of his own limitations. He made no attempt to check French penetration into the western lands of the Empire, for the good reason that he would have had no hope of success. Instead, he concentrated on trying to retain at least the form of legal sovereignty, for instance by receiving the homage of the king of France for the Dauphiné and of the duke of Burgundy for Franche Comté. A more fortunately placed successor might be able to make something of these claims. In the same way he recognized that he could not control the various leagues of German towns, but by granting them charters he might turn the situation to his financial profit and hope to retain their support.

Meanwhile it was in Bohemia that Charles found the greatest scope for his talents; a parallel might be found in Frederick II's regard for Sicily as the real heart of his domains. Like Sicily, Bohemia had presented a chaotic picture when Charles had succeeded to its throne, before ever the imperial dignity had come to him. Just as Frederick had restored order and good government to Sicily, so Charles succeeded in turning Bohemia into an efficient kingdom in a remarkably short time, and even in installing some degree of national pride into its diverse elements; in both cases the achievement, though real, proved to be short-lived. At first Bohemia must have seemed an unpromising field in which to sow the seeds of national monarchy. Its population was a mixture of Germans and Czechs, each speaking their own language. Nor was the division between the two peoples at all clear-cut; while the Germans were predominant in the north and west near the German frontier, pockets of them were to be found distributed throughout the country. Religious unity was no more

375

noticeable. Originally converted to Christianity by missionaries of the Orthodox faith, Bohemia had long been a somewhat unruly member of the Western Church. The reforming decrees of Rome had been resisted in many instances. For instance, nowhere in Europe was the clerical concubine a more accepted part of the social scene. Nor had the Bohemian Church showed itself either enthusiastic or successful in the persecution of heresy. Nearly obliterated elsewhere in Europe, in Bohemia heresies of both Albigensian and Waldensian extraction continued to flourish. The social scene revealed similar tensions between urban populations living by trade or mining and a baronage which had proved largely unable to support itself as country landlords, and instead had made use of the weakness of the Crown to indulge in predatory attacks on the towns.

Charles's solution to these problems was to attempt the creation of a Czech state. The outlying provinces of Moravia and Silesia, the latter rich in mineral wealth, had by no means always been attached to Bohemia; now they were declared permanently incorporated into the Bohemian kingdom. Royal diets were held at intervals to try and instil in the nobility a loyalty to their king. Ecclesiastical unity was sought by persuading the pope to make of the whole country a new province of the Church under the archbishop of Prague. Prague itself was largely rebuilt and greatly enlarged to serve as a capital for the whole country. Its law courts were encouraged to act as a final court of appeal from the feudal courts in the rest of the country. The creation of the new university of Prague in 1348 was another sign of the deliberate cultivation of prestige around the new national capital. Every encouragement was given to the industries and agriculture of the country, which in its turn began to reward the Crown with greater revenue. By 1378 Bohemia was not yet a national monarchy; there were still tensions between Germans and Slavs, and the heretical tendencies within the Church had certainly not been checked by its new degree of autonomy. But the progress made in one reign had been remarkable.

Despite Charles IV's constitutional reform of the Empire, the general picture of the German scene at the time of his death is a gloomy one. Politically the problem created by the disappearance of imperial power, a problem acknowledged rather than solved by the Golden Bull, had not been met by any corresponding increase in the power of the princes. Rather the tendency was for large areas of the country to become detached altogether from Germany. Where a powerful neighbour existed, as in the case of Franche Comté, this simply meant that they passed under the control of some non-German power. Where there was no such powerful neighbour they might achieve partial or complete independence. The Hanseatic League is one example of this process,[1] and the various leagues of towns in various parts of Germany (*Landfrieden*) can furnish others. Their large degree of independence from outside control was not the result of any statesmanlike appreciation of the value of towns to the community as a whole, but simply of the inability of the princes to control them. But the most striking example of this process of erosion from Germany was to be found in the Swiss cantons, for here, eventually, a new sovereign state was to be born.

There was no natural unity about the Swiss cantons. Some spoke French dialects, others German. Some, such as Zürich or Bern, had considerable interests in manufacture or trade; others, such as the so-called Forest Cantons of Uri, Schwyz and Unterwalden, were almost wholly rural. High ranges of mountains separated their narrow valleys from each other, so that no more than a mile or two on the map might see a totally different world of customs. Most of the German speaking territory in the future Switzerland had come under the control of the Habsburgs in the days when that family was still a power in Suabia, rather than an aspirant for imperial honours or for lands in the east; some of the towns, such as Bern, had become free cities, possessed of charters which guaranteed them independence of all but the emperor. As early as 1291 the three Forest Cantons had begun a struggle for independence against the Habsburgs, now increasingly seen as alien rulers from the east. In 1315 the citizens of these cantons, even more formidable on their own terrain than they were later to become on the battlefields of Europe, won the battle of Morgarten against Habsburg troops. This was the beginning of a struggle which was to continue intermittently until the final recognition of the whole Swiss Confederation as a power independent alike of the German Empire and the French Crown in 1648. By their military prowess and by cleverly exploiting the differences between their Habsburg overlords and non-Habsburg emperors the cantons continued to resist successfully. By 1378 the original three cantons had grown to eight. The double defeats of Sempach (1386) and Näfels (1388) finally discouraged the Habsburg dukes from the expense and danger of attacking such difficult country; at Zürich in 1394 they recognized the independence of the eight cantons. In the meantime the cantons, too small for independent existence, had

[1] See Chapter 15.

begun to forge for themselves the instruments by which they could become something more than a defensive alliance. The idea of independence from the Empire was always secondary for the Swiss to that of freedom from the Habsburgs, but in effect they were already far along both roads before the fourteenth century was over.

Socially, too, Germany in the later fourteenth century was fraught with difficulties. The Black Death had not passed her by, and the same troubles that had afflicted England and France in the decades after 1350 were to be found here. The blow was felt with particular strength in the east. Areas of subsistence agriculture often found that the effects of the Black Death more or less cancelled each other out; fewer hands were now producing for fewer mouths. But eastern Germany had never been an area of subsistence agriculture; very many of its farms were organized for the production of one crop for the export market. The sudden contraction of that market could not but spell acute economic distress, for the complete reorganization of the agricultural methods of a region is inevitably a slow and painful process. This is the background against which many of the activities of the 'robber barons' of the later Middle Ages are to be seen. It is true that the decadence of the Empire removed from many of the lesser nobility of Germany such administrative functions as they had possessed; the so-called 'Knights of the Empire' are a case in point. But sheer economic necessity was the most potent of all forces in driving small landholders to a life of disorder.

These very conditions of disorder acted as a further stimulus to the formation of ever larger *Landfrieden*. The town itself was, partly at least, in origin a defensive association against the disorders of the countryside; by the same token the association of towns might guarantee a much larger area of peace even in generally disturbed conditions. In 1376, for instance, fourteen cities in Suabia responded to the call of Ulm to form a Suabian League for the protection of them all; at about the same time a similar league was being formed in the Rhineland. There were several other such associations in other parts of Germany, and if the Hanseatic League, the greatest of them all, owed its origin to more purely commercial causes, it certainly also performed this function of protection for its members. Certainly it is in the cities that the most vital forces in German life in the fourteenth and fifteenth centuries are to be found; many of them handled a considerable bulk of trade and were rich enough to indulge in lavish public expenditure. Yet even here all was not well. The very desire to form into ever more extensive associations is evidence of a fear in each city that it might not continue to get its share of what was a much diminished cake.[1]

There were those who profited by German decline. In particular it brought very welcome relief to those Slavonic peoples to the east of Germany who for centuries had been accustomed to act as the recipients of German expansion and western over-population. The

THE HANSEATIC LEAGUE AND THE BALTIC LANDS

outstanding political facts of the fourteenth and fifteenth centuries in eastern Europe were the revival in the fortunes of the kingdom of Poland, and the sudden appearance of Lithuania, hitherto outside the community of European nations, as a power of the first magnitude.

For much of the fourteenth century expansion towards the east from northern Germany continued as before. The chief agents of this expansion remained the Order of Teutonic Knights. The religious motives of this organization had become more and more questionable; its military effectiveness remained undimmed. By 1350 the

[1] See Chapter 15.

379

Order had already conquered most of the southern coast of the Baltic from Danzig as far east as Reval in Esthonia. In so doing it had cut off the kingdom of Poland and the duchy of Lithuania from any access to the sea. The Poles at any rate had learnt much from the example of their new German neighbours, in particular the use of the heavy plough with which they could cultivate their own waste lands. But they were now prohibited from reaching western markets with what they produced. Nor were the Slavs to be left long in the enjoyment of their lands. Wisely shrinking from the prospect of a direct invasion of continental Russia to the east, the strategists of the Order now decided that the attack should be directed to the south against Poland and Lithuania. To accomplish this they sought to make use of the rivers Vistula, Niemen, and Dvina, all of which led south-east from the territory of the Knights into the Slavonic lands.

Of the two, the Lithuanians formed the more tempting target, if only because as they were still pagan their destruction could be made to square with the original purpose of the Order. Moreover, Lithuania itself was a most tempting prize. The Mongol conquests of the thirteenth century had passed to the south of the central Lithuanian lands, leaving them untouched. But the forces of the Khan had smashed the ancient principality of Russia. Its traditional capital at Kiev had been captured, and its rulers were either destroyed or made tributaries of the Great Khan. Only Novgorod in the north had retained virtual independence of the Tartars. When the Mongol pressure eased towards the end of the thirteenth century, the Lithuanians were in a position to profit from the resulting political vacuum. Expanding rapidly to the south they had come to control first Galicia and Podolia, and then the Ukraine itself. Kiev became a Lithuanian city, and the Lithuanians gained access to the Black Sea.

It was thus no trivial adversary that the Knights now encountered. Nevertheless for thirty years, under their Grand Master Winrich von Kniprode (1351–1382), they pressed home an attack on the northern Lithuanian province of Samogitia. It was a war of peculiar ferocity. The chronicler of the Order records without surprise that in 1378 the Livonian Master 'for nine days and nights killed, burnt, laid waste, and destroyed everything',[1] and the Lithuanians for their part made a habit of roasting captured knights alive in their armour. But the Knights made no significant progress against the Lithuanian prince Keystut, and the difficulties of gaining new recruits from the West was steadily growing. In 1386 occurred an event which was finally

[1] See *Cambridge Medieval History*, Vol. VII, p. 259.

fatal to the Order's hopes of further expansion to the south. By the treaty of Volkovysk the Lithuanians agreed to accept Christianity, and Jagiello, the heir to the Lithuanian Grand Duchy, was married to Jadwiga, queen of Poland. Jagiello took the title of Vladyslav II (1386-1434) on his accession to the Polish throne, and his joint dominions now represented an insuperable barrier to further German expansion. When war was resumed again in 1391 the question was no longer whether the Knights would make further conquests, but whether they could hold on to what they already had. For nearly twenty years the Knights held on successfully, busily stirring up the latent hostility between Lithuanians and Poles to supplement the efforts of their armies in the field, but in 1410 they suffered the crushing disaster of Tannenberg. Not for the last time in their history the desolate marshes to the east of the Vistula became the scene of a great battle between Germans and Slavs. There was something symbolic about the varied contingents which went to make up the army, vast by medieval standards,[1] which defeated the Knights at Tannenberg. With Poles from Cracow and Lithuanians from Vilna rode Russians from Smolensk, Ukrainians from Kiev, even Tartars from Asia. It was the final assertion that one era of European expansion was over. Within fifty years Byzantium would have fallen, and armies from the East would again be threatening central Europe. When next the West sought to expand, overseas empire would be her chosen method.

After Tannenberg the war dragged on through a series of truces until the final Peace of Thorn in 1466. The Teutonic Knights, even in decline, had shown much skill and ferocity in the defensive campaigns they had been forced to wage. Now the Poles remained content with West Prussia, including the great castle at Marienburg which had been the headquarters of the Grand Master of the Order. The Knights were allowed to retain East Prussia, although even for this they had to do homage to the Polish Crown. By this curious arrangement, in effect detaching a German speaking and controlled area from the rest of Germany, the difficulties caused by the irregular nature of the German advance were legalized into permanence and left to plague future generations. But the age of the Knights was over. Poland and Lithuania never really succeeded in fusing their crowns into a single monarchy, let alone fusing their peoples into one nation; the joint monarchy was only to last until 1492. But each was now strong enough to resist any attack likely to come from Germany.

[1] It seems to have numbered about 100,000.

Charles IV had succeeded in securing the election and coronation of his son Wenzel II (1378–1410) as King of the Romans during his own lifetime. His hope that this might lead to a Luxembourg dynasty was frustrated, and Wenzel's own character is largely to blame for this. A constitutional indolence gradually worsened as he gently subsided into chronic alcoholism. That he neglected the mirage of imperial power in favour of Bohemia cannot be held against him; Charles IV after all is praised for just this. His real failing was that his 'favouring' of Bohemia amounted to little more than a preference for living there rather than elsewhere in his lands. No more in Bohemia than in any other portion of the empire did he show any talent for leadership. Now that the German monarchy had been stripped of most of its effective permanent powers it was more than ever necessary for its continued survival that it should not only justify itself, but be seen to justify itself, in terms of its services to the rest of the country. Above all this meant that it must be prepared to offer effective mediation in internal German disputes.

This Wenzel most blatantly failed to do. His reign was marked by a series of civil wars, of the Suabian league of cities against the discontented knights of south Germany, of the Wittelsbachs against the Archbishop of Salzburg and the Suabian towns, of Saxony against the surviving Welf faction. All these were issues in which royal mediation was necessary; indeed, that they had broken out at all was to some extent evidence of lack of royal leadership. Wenzel's conduct was an unconvincing blend of impotence and inertia. He made no attempt to call the various parties together to settle their disputes; when he committed himself to one side or the other he took no effective steps to see that his support was of any military value, nor was he in the least averse to switching his loyalty to the other side if it seemed that his original choice was mistaken. To most German rulers he must have seemed a useless and not particularly dignified figurehead, whose sole practical activity consisted in the support of the quest for the crown of Hungary by his apparently more able brother Sigismund. Their loyalty soon evaporated, and the electors came to regret the choice into which Charles IV had rushed them. Within the first ten years of his rule suggestions of a regency were being made, and in 1396 Wenzel gave heed to them by suggesting that his brother should be recognized as his successor to the throne and should act as his regent in Germany. This proposal, humiliating enough in itself, did not placate the electors, some of whom were disturbed by the growing power of the Luxembourg family. Wenzel was unable to take any decisive action to end the papal schism or to resist the encroachments of the French monarchy, the two big public issues by which he might have regained his lost prestige. Now he was faced with open civil war in Bohemia which fully engrossed his limited energies.

In the summer of 1400, after many premonitory rumblings, the deposition issue at last exploded. Instigated by the Archbishop of Mainz, the three ecclesiastical electors, the Elector Palatine, and the Margrave of Brandenburg summoned Wenzel before them to answer for his misdeeds. On his failure to appear he was declared deposed. The next day the three archbishops announced that they had elected Rupert III, the Elector Palatine, to fill the vacancy as king.

The Golden Bull gave no justification for such an action, but if they had settled the issue by giving Germany an effective king this would have been overlooked. But in practice all that had been achieved was a guarantee of civil war. For Rupert proved no more fitted for his responsibilities than Wenzel. A fatuous expedition to Italy in search of an entirely useless coronation from the Roman pope, which incidentally he failed to obtain, showed how small was his grasp of political realities. Both men were totally unfitted for the Crown, and neither commanded respect from the German princes, who had learnt that there was nothing to fear or to hope from the Crown. The death of Rupert in 1410 put an end to the dispute by removing one of the contestants, but the futility of them both is shown by the fact that it did not lead to the triumph of the other, and that there were few who thought that it should.

It is refreshing to turn from the sterile and meaningless history of Wenzel's reign in Germany to the equally turbulent but far more significant record of Bohemian affairs. The development of what was later to become the Hussite movement owed everything to Charles IV's decision to encourage the development of Bohemian nationalism. In this he had succeeded perhaps too well. The exaltation of Prague as a Czech capital with its new university and its new archbishopric, the encouragement given to the Czech language, the frequent recourse had by Charles to both local and national Estates, the extensive new building carried out under royal aegis both in the capital and elsewhere, all had contributed to an entirely new national self-confidence. In so far as this strengthened the position of the Crown this was the result which Charles had planned, but there were other and less wholly favourable results. Bohemia was a country of mixed

German and Czech population, and the new policy was bound to increase the racial antagonism; every exaltation of Czech was necessarily also a degradation of German. Also, the deliberate stimulation of nationalism in a country which already had something of a tradition of religious non-conformity was very liable to breed a national religious discontent. It is this which was the really new element in the Hussite heresy. The Bohemian Church was full of abuses, but all medieval heresies had fed on the abuses of the Church. Bohemia contained many pockets of heresy fed from many strangely heterodox theological sources, but all earlier heresies had contained this element of genuine theological protest. Wycliff was certainly not as unorthodox as the Cathars of twelfth-century Languedoc. The really new thing about Huss, and what made him far more dangerous to the Catholic Church than any of his predecessors, is the ability he showed with his followers to blend national and religious protest into one movement. It is genuinely difficult to say of Huss, as it is genuinely difficult to say of Luther, whether he is a national leader masquerading as a religious reformer or a religious reformer skilfully making use of national sentiment. That neither man probably recognized any difference between the two roles only made them both the more dangerous to the Catholic Church.

Before Huss appeared on the scene there had already been a number of voices raised in criticism of the condition of the Church in Bohemia. Some of these, like Conrad of Waldhauser and Milič, were themselves churchmen speaking largely to their own kind, but there were also laymen who indulged in criticism of the Church. Thomas of Stitny (†1401) was a country landowner speaking and writing in Czech, and thus possessed of a larger hearing among his own countrymen than those who used Latin. Among these early critics there is no sign of any desire to raise a standard of rebellion. Their theme is the necessity of moral reform by the whole Bohemian people, and in particular by their clergy. There are other characteristics of a Puritan kind in their writings. Great stress was laid on the value of the Bible as a guide to Christian conduct and belief, and one reformer, Matthias of Janow, lays particular stress on the spiritual danger involved in the use of pictures and statues as an aid to worship. Several of the reformers made considerable use of the pulpit as a means of getting their views across to the laity. None of this was in itself heretical; the Catholic Church was accustomed to accommodate some puritans in her fold. Nor was there anything heretical in the view often expressed that frequent reception of the Communion by the laity was much to be commended, eccentric as this was by the standard of normal practice elsewhere.

John Huss was born in 1369 of Czech peasant parents. His early career took him by the normal route which could lead men of low birth to high office in Church and State. He went to the new Prague University, distinguished himself there, and in 1402 became its rector. He had taken orders, and was appointed to the charge of the Bethlehem Chapel in the capital. This brought him into the public eye, for the chapel was a fashionable centre of worship, often attended by members of the court. His sermons there did not differ markedly in content from many which had already been preached from Czech pulpits, but they reached a wider public. His reputation as a forceful and critical preacher was soon established.

A political event was the ultimate cause of Huss crossing the borderline into heresy. In 1382 Anne, sister of the Bohemian king, had married the English king Richard II. One by-product of the increased cultural contact between the two countries had been that Wycliffite teachings current at Oxford had appeared also in the University of Prague. Intellectually and temperamentally Wycliff and Huss were poles apart. The Englishman was a genuinely original thinker, but he was possessed of the scholar's distaste for any but academic conflict; this valuable gift enabled him to die in his bed. Huss was a much less original and radical thinker; much of his theological writing was in fact a mere transcription of Wycliff's own work. But he had what Wycliff lacked, a desire to apply his views beyond the academic sphere, and to make out of them a popular movement. Again the parallel with Luther suggests itself. The issue of Wycliffite teaching came before the university of Prague in 1403; the resolution was then taken, against the wishes of Huss, that the new doctrines should not be taught. The voting on the issue revealed a dangerous split on national lines between Germans, who were insistent on outright condemnation, and Czechs. Huss himself was discontented with the decision, and his preaching and writing continued to reflect Wycliffite views.

At this stage of the conflict Huss appeared to have the confidence of the court and of Archbishop Zbynek of Prague, and no doubt gained additional morale from his appointment as court chaplain. But neither Zbynek nor Wenzel himself were anxious to create doubts about their own orthodoxy or to encourage a dangerous religious disunity in the country. An appeal from the clergy of Prague, many of them Czechs themselves, to the archbishop in 1408 that he should restrain Huss from his incessant attacks on them, though it led to no action, no doubt served to sap the archbishop's confidence in him, and the king cannot have appreciated the migration of all the Germans from Prague University to found a new university outside Bohemia at Leipzig. The step was a direct consequence of the dispute over Wycliffite doctrine, and was a most damaging blow to the prestige of his new institution. A dispute between the archbishop and the king in 1410 further complicated the issue, and when Zbynek transferred the allegiance of the Bohemian Church to the Pisan pope Alexander V in that year, the suppression of Wycliffite teaching was one of the conditions of the union. Heretical books were to be destroyed and all preaching was temporarily to be suppressed. Refusing to obey this ruling, Huss continued to preach and was duly excommunicated for the first time (1410).

Violent anger greeted the announcement in Prague, and street fighting broke out. Wenzel was not anxious to alienate the Bohemian national feeling he had so sedulously cultivated, while the new pope, John XXIII, would have stomached a great deal of heresy rather than run the risk of losing a secular ally. Wenzel played the part of mediator between Zbynek and Huss, and a compromise was patched up, saving the archbishop's face but allowing Huss to continue preaching.

It was not to last. If John XXIII was careless of doctrinal issues, any question of finance touched him most acutely. In the very next year there appeared in Prague papal representatives to preach the virtues of the papal plenary indulgence. The purpose for which the money was required, a 'crusade' against Ladislas of Naples, was even less sanctified than was to be the case at Wittenberg just over a hundred years later. Huss reacted with the same hostility that Luther was to show. Here was a squalid clerical abuse practised, not by the clerics of Prague, but by the alleged Vicar of Christ himself. He preached violently against the indulgences, and the streets of the capital were once more filled with demonstrators. John XXIII reacted sharply. The money was essential to him, and he conjectured rightly that Wenzel would not wish to add the Church to his already not inconsiderable circle of enemies. Huss was again excommunicated, and the city of Prague was placed under an interdict until it should hand him over for punishment. Wenzel, in an agony of indecision (a condition more or less normal in his life), was more than relieved when Huss left the capital, and took refuge with the Bohemian nobility who shared his views and with whom he would be safe.

Luther, in hiding among 'the Christian nobility of the German nation', must have pondered on the parallel. But Bohemia itself remained simmering at the point of revolt.

When the Council of Constance met in 1414 the Bohemian question naturally figured on their agenda. They were the more ready to tackle it since it was an issue on which the delegates were united. Whoever might be pope, there was no question, except among Czechs, that this Bohemian heretic should be suppressed. Huss, for his part, was anxious to put his case to the assembled Council of Christendom. The Emperor Sigismund gave him a safe-conduct, and in the autumn of 1414 Huss arrived at Constance. On his arrival he was at once arrested and kept in close custody for examination. Sigismund arrived at Christmas, and expressed surprise that one to whom he had given the imperial safe conduct should be chained to a post in the sewer dungeon of the Dominican Friary. But it was represented to him that heresy was a purely ecclesiastical matter, in which he, as a layman, had no standing. To have let the whole council founder over the case of one individual heretic would have seemed a scandal. In any case it was a truism that no faith was owed to heretics, men who by their very nature did not know the meaning of faith; Ferdinand of Aragon wrote to Sigismund in shocked surprise that there could be any question of his promise being fulfilled. So Huss was not released, and in the next year his public examination and trial before the Council took place. The accused refused to abjure any of the heresies of which he was accused, on the ground that to do so would be tantamount to admitting that he had held heresies. In point of fact he was certainly guiltless of some of the charges the enthusiasm of his accusers brought against him. It scarcely mattered. The real issue at the trial of Huss, as at the trial of Joan of Arc, was the refusal of the accused to submit his personal judgment to the correction of the Church, and by this test Huss was clearly guilty. Immediately after sentence he was handed over to the secular arm in the person of the emperor and duly burnt. His ashes were tipped into the Rhine; his chief disciple, Jerome of Prague, suffered a like fate in the next year, and the whole incident seemed satisfactorily closed.

Yet the death of Huss was the beginning rather than the end of the Hussite problem. Bohemia flared into revolt when it heard of the fate of one who had only needed martyrdom to become a national hero. For twenty-one years this small country maintained a successful resistance to the Catholic and German world around it. Moreover, it did this even though ranks of its armies were greatly divided. Once Huss was dead it became increasingly difficult to tell what it was that he had championed. Those who now called themselves Hussites were of many different beliefs. Some, the so-called Utraquists, were really but reforming Catholics with a nationalist bias. They took as their war aim that the laity at the Communion should be allowed to partake of the chalice as well as of the Host. Since at one stage of its history the Catholic Church itself had decreed this, there was nothing impossibly revolutionary about such an aim, and for the rest they stood merely for the elimination of what they believed to be foreign abuses in the Bohemian Church. Others, the Taborites, advocated a strictly puritan morality, and, like the Calvinists of the next century, called for the severe and public punishment of all sinners. Along with these two main groups went many other fragments, each holding its own exotic beliefs culled from that depository of strange faiths, the Bible. The Adamites, for instance, with their insistence that their new-found innocence necessitated that they too should go as naked as Adam before the Fall, would have been embarrassing allies for most causes.

How then did the Hussites resist for so long? The answer is to be found partly in the difficulty of finding any secular ruler to carry out their destruction, partly in their own enthusiasm and in their discovery of two generals who would have led most armies to victory. For four years after the death of Huss Wenzel refused to take sides, and strove incompetently to reconcile his Bohemian rebels with the Church. When he at length decided to support Catholicism and to attempt their reduction he died almost immediately (1419), a clear sign of divine support for the Hussites. His successor as king of Bohemia was the Emperor Sigismund, who had many other worries beside the Hussites. His invasion of Bohemia with notably unenthusiastic German troops was confronted by the Hussite general Zizka (†1424). By a skilful use of the wagons in which his army moved as fortifications in battle and by a realization of the use of firepower in the field, Zizka achieved both mobility and strength. Throwing the Germans back at the battle of Vyšehrad (1420), Zizka succeeded in gaining such a moral superiority over his enemies that he was able not only to win such defensive victories as Saaz (1421) and Deutchsbrod (1422), but even (1423) to take the offensive by invading Hungary. That Zizka had lost the sight of his one remaining eye in 1420 only added to the mystique which surrounded his name. After his death the Hussites found in Procop the Great another excellent general to maintain his tradition. But Utraquist opinion had been slowly alienated by the excesses of the more extreme factions in the Hussite ranks, and fighting between Hussite and Hussite became increasingly common. After Procop's death in 1434 Sigismund was at last able to capture Prague, and the Utraquists were then ready to negotiate a peace. By the Compacts of Prague (1436) they made peace at once with their king and with the Church. In return for Sigismund's promise to keep the government of the country in the hands of Czechs and to support them in keeping the high posts of the Church in Bohemian hands, their leaders did homage to the emperor. By a similar compromise the Church permitted the Utraquist demand for the chalice; in Bohemia alone this was to be permitted to the laity. Now Utraquists, reunited with Catholics, would join with them in stamping out the embers of the more radical heresies. The Hussite wars were over, but the hope of a prosperous and united Bohemian kingdom had long been dead.

It is right that any description of the reign of the emperor Sigismund (1410–1437) should concentrate on Bohemian affairs and on his dealings with the Council of Constance.[1] Sigismund had the personal qualities which might in happier times have made him a notable emperor. But the days when the power either of the Empire or of the German monarchy might have been restored were past. His mind was full of grandiose schemes for the conclusion of treaties with the other great powers and for their union under him in a great crusade against the Turks. In one sense he was right; the Turks were soon to be again the supreme European problem. But his complete inability to meet even the expenses of his own court, a standing jest among contemporaries, was sufficient comment on the likelihood of these plans seeing fulfilment. The problems of his two kingdoms of Bohemia and Hungary were more than enough to engross all his time and more than all his money. In the politics of Germany itself he was an insignificant figure. To the west of his empire lay the Duchy of Burgundy, that composite body of territories, many of them traditionally part of the German Empire. Their rapid rise to, and equally rapid fall from, statehood forms a central theme of the history of the fifteenth century, but one which falls outside the scope of the present book. Sigismund was powerless to hinder or to advance this development.

It is fitting to leave the history of the medieval empire with Sigismund. The Carolingian ideal of universal dominion in the West,

[1] See Chapter 17.

the Ottonian achievement of strong monarchy in Germany, both alike in him display their final bankruptcy. His successors, Albert II (1438–1439) and Frederick III (1440–1492), were to be as powerless as Sigismund, but they at least bore the Habsburg name. In that name lay the promise of a new Empire, Austrian and dynastic, to rise from the ashes of the old Holy Roman Empire.

19

The Spanish Peninsula

In planning a history of medieval Europe the temptation to omit all mention of the lands of the Iberian peninsula is strong. Even today the Pyrenees seem to form a frontier so well-designed that Spain and Portugal are cut off from the rest of the European community, not in their political systems alone but in their whole way of life. Like Britain itself they are in, but only partially of, Europe. In the Middle Ages the Pyrenees were among the very few frontiers which marked a clear division. Again, for the greater part of the period covered by this book more than half the peninsula belonged, not to Christian Europe, but to that rival world order whose centre, unacknowledged though it might be, lay in Baghdad; as such it seems to be the proper preserve of historians of the Muslim world. Medieval Spanish history, too, seems to be of less immediate relevance to an understanding of what comes after it. In England or France the development of the medieval monarchies can be seen as a necessary part of the whole process which produced their modern history. Even in Germany the story of the medieval Empire, doomed though it was to destruction, is yet an indispensable factor in the making of modern Germany. The history of the various and changing kingdoms of medieval Spain has no such apparent relevance; a knowledge of the turbulent narrative of the kingdom of Leon will cast no great light on the history of modern Spain.

Yet medieval Spain cannot be dismissed as an irrelevance. The very existence of the Moorish occupation gave it a deep significance for the whole European culture. For by this means Spain became one of the very few points of contact between the two rival world orders, a point through which the medieval world could constantly refresh itself with the accumulated treasures of classical Greece, so miraculously preserved by Islam. Nor can the future of Spain be left out of account. With the marriage of Ferdinand of Aragon with Isabella of Castile in 1469, and the resulting union of their kingdoms ten years later, Spain at once assumed a leading role among European powers; within fifty years as a part of the Habsburg empire she had become the leading European power, and for another hundred years after

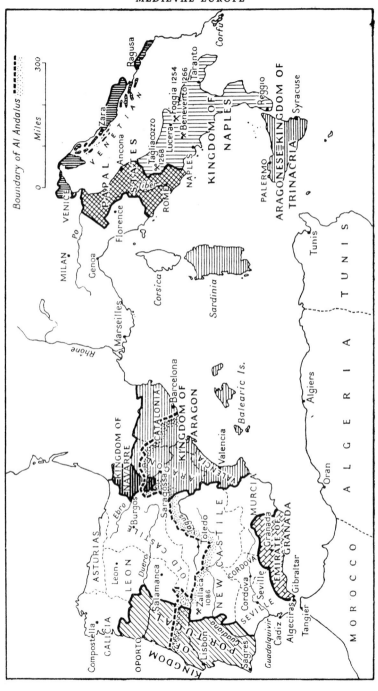

THE WESTERN MEDITERRANEAN IN THE LATER MIDDLE AGES

that there is little doubt of her primacy. No European nation of the Renaissance period so successfully combined political strength with cultural achievement. In all of this chance had its usual historical importance, and the successful exploitation of the newly discovered areas of the world played a most important part in the exaltation of both Spain and Portugal. But the nature and form taken by the Iberian states in the sixteenth century can only be explained in the light of their medieval experience; nations like men are subject to heredity as well as environment.

Geography is the vital clue to much Spanish history. The Iberian peninsula is large: well over five hundred miles separate Gibraltar from the north coast, and, unlike France, at its widest point in the north Spain is considerably broader from east to west than it is long from north to south. But it is a comparatively infertile country. Much of its area consists of arid plateau intersected by ranges of barren mountains. Apart from the fertile land in the extreme south, only the river valleys are capable of maintaining anything but a sparse population. This ensured that it would be a country which long resisted the demands of political centralization, for each area of relatively high population was separated from neighbouring areas by wide expanses of near-desert. Even today the persistence of four different languages in the peninsula, Portuguese, Basque, Spanish, and Catalan, reveals the strength of regional divisions. The map shows another point of importance. The highest points in the central Iberian plateau lie well to the east. Four out of the five great Spanish rivers empty into the Atlantic rather than the Mediterranean. This, allied with the natural strength of the Pyrenees, helped to turn the Spanish kingdom away from European affairs and to give medieval Spanish history its introverted character. Later, in the fifteenth and sixteenth centuries, both Portugal and Spain were to profit from this westward inclination, for by then the Atlantic was no longer merely the inevitable edge of Europe; it had become the path to worldwide dominion.

Spain shared the common fate of the Roman world by falling victim in the fifth century to barbarian invasion. The particular German tribesmen who chose the peninsula as their dwelling place, the Visigoths, cannot have been numerous, but they seem to have encountered little difficulty in taking over as much as they wanted of the land. Centuries later Spanish writers, enthused by the picture of united Spain painted by S. Isidore of Seville (†636), would look back to the Visigothic period as a golden age of Spanish unity. But

Isidore's was the voice of exhortation rather than description, and the truth was far different. Visigothic Spain resembled Merovingian Gaul in the weakness inherent in the control of a large, partially Romanized population by a numerically much smaller Germanic caste; it too was subject to a paralysing series of quarrels over the succession. In one important way the Visigoths were less fortunate than the Merovingians. Clovis and his successors had been able to use the Catholic faith as a bond of unity in their divided lands. But the Visigoths had originally been converted to Christianity of the Arian persuasion; thus for them, until King Reccared's conversion to Catholicism in 589, religion was yet another cause of division.

The weakness of Visigothic Spain was shown conclusively enough by the speed with which it capitulated to its first serious foreign invasion. The Muslim force which crossed the straits of Gibralter to land near Algeciras in 711 was not large; its leader, Tariq the Ziyad, was himself only the lieutenant of the Muslim ruler of Tunis, and the expedition had not been countenanced by Damascus, which still retained some measure of control as capital of the Muslim world. But, insignificant though he might be, Tariq was yet strong enough to defeat the main forces of the Visigoth king Roderic at the battle of Arcos de la Frontera (711). Tariq had revealed an obvious point of military weakness in the Christian world, and his coreligionists were not slow to exploit it. Under pressure the Visigothic kingdom disintegrated. Using the excellent Roman roads which still remained the Muslim armies, largely composed of north African tribesmen who were themselves recent converts to Islam, spread rapidly north. Within two years the Visigothic kingdom was no more; its place had been taken by the Muslim state of Al-Andalus.

To say that the Muslims occupied Spain is only a partial truth. Organized resistance to their armies ceased for the time, but the numbers of the invaders were very small, perhaps not more than one hundred thousand in the first wave of conquest. Systematic settlement of the whole peninsula was clearly impossible, and even the military reduction of the more remote and mountainous regions was not undertaken. The real aim of the Muslim armies soon became the more fertile lands beyond the Pyrenees, and the route to them by the eastern coastal plain, along with the fertile regions of the south, was thoroughly subjugated. But the Christian victory at Poitiers in 732 put an end to the Muslim penetration of the north. The central plateau was much more sparsely held than the coastal plain, and no serious attempt was made to reduce the barren Asturian mountains in the north-west. Nor did occupation by any means spell the end of the Christian population of Al-Andalus. Many of the Christian princes had collaborated with the invaders, and subsequent conversions to Islam were not uncommon. But they were unnecessary. Both Christian and Jews received tolerant treatment from the conqueror, the latter indeed profiting greatly from this temporary cessation of Christian persecution. The Catholics were allowed to retain their identity, not only as individuals but in the form of Christian communities; the occupying power preferred to deal in such matters as taxation with the counts who were the recognized leaders of their fellow Christians. Slavery indeed assumed considerable proportions, but the slaves for the most part were not Catholic Spaniards, but captive Slavs from the eastern frontiers of Europe imported into Spain. By neither exterminating nor converting the major part of the people they had conquered, it can be said that the Moors of Spain were endangering the stability of their state. They were never numerous enough to resist a determined Christian counter-attack, particularly if Al-Andalus was to lose its own somewhat precarious unity.

Spain gained much from the Moorish occupation. In particular, in a country in which the poverty of much of the soil makes destitution always the major social problem, the Spanish economy benefited greatly. For the followers of a religion which had started in the desert the Moors accustomed themselves to the possibilities of industry and trade with surprising rapidity. Settling largely in towns, the Moorish population brought into Spanish life qualities of industry and technical ingenuity which could not fail to benefit the whole of Spanish life. Moreover, the Moors were part of a highly developed civilization of their own, and through their links with it were able to introduce new industries and new crops which by their scarcity could command a profitable market in the West. The oranges of Seville and the Mediterranean coast, the cotton and silk of the south, the dried fruits of Malaga, the leather work of Cordova, the iron work of Toledo, all these were assets which no Christian kingdom could equal. In architecture too Moorish influence was strong and beneficial. The Romans in Spain had accomplished some of their most remarkable building, particularly in the field of public works: the Roman aqueducts at Segovia and Tortosa are among the finest survivals of that materialist civilization. But, as elsewhere in Europe, the Roman architectural tradition was by now moribund, and no Gothic tradition had as yet arisen to take its place. With the

Moors came a new architectural style, with its roots in the Near East; in Spain this developed into a national style practised by Christians as well as Moors, and leaving a permanent impression on the architecture of much of Spain. The Great Mosque at Cordova and the minarets of Toledo have more in common with the buildings of Cairo and Baghdad than with the Gothic cathedrals of France, but there is no denying the architectural quality of much Moorish work in Spain. In being thus able to draw alike on the Gothic and Christian tradition of the North and the Muslim styles of the South Spanish culture became doubly rich.[1]

The same characteristics can be seen in the intellectual field. The comparative tolerance of Islam allowed the Moors to make use of the inheritances of both Christian and Jewish civilization in a way alien to the more rigid beliefs of the Christian world. But this was not all. The chance of history had made the Arab world itself custodian of much of the Greek learning. Several of the works of Aristotle, for instance, were unknown to the West but known to the Arabs, who had gathered them from translations extant in the world of Syrian Christianity which they had overrun. Their new custodians had developed to the full the scientific and philosophical interests of the Greeks. In the eleventh century they produced in Avicenna (†1036) a philosopher of the first rank, at a time when the West was still taking its first faltering steps towards abstract thought. The Moors of Spain shared in this development. Averroes (†1198), an Arab who passed much of his life in Al-Andalus, was perhaps the most original thinker produced anywhere in the Islamic world. He was to have followers in the western world in his attempt to separate entirely the teachings of religion and philosophy, and the challenge of his teaching was largely responsible for the Christian affirmation of the unity of all knowledge by the Parisian masters of the thirteenth century. For good measure, twelfth century Spain also produced in Moses ben Maimon, known as Maimonides, one of the greatest of all Jewish thinkers. All this is evidence of a society of vigorous intellectual interests fertilizing not only itself but its northern neighbours as well.

Politically the Muslim world was no more successful than Christianity in preserving its unity. At first the Moors of Spain, in name at least, were subject to Damascus, but that link did not last long.

---

[1] The ribbed vaulting, so characteristic of 'Gothic' architecture in the north, is believed to have entered the Christian world through the example of the Moors in Spain.

The reigning dynasty in Syria, the Umayyads, were overthrown and massacred. Only one of the family, 'Abd ar-Rahmān, survived, and he at length made his way to Spain. At Cordova in 756 he was proclaimed Emir of Al-Andalus. The dynasty he set up was to last through many vicissitudes of fortune till 1031, and its rulers were to repudiate all connection with the East by establishing their own Caliphate of Cordova in 922. After it had disintegrated, Al-Andalus was twice revivified by new strength from Africa. In the eleventh century the Almoravids, who drew their strength from the recent converts to Islam from as far afield as Nigeria, flooded into Spain and threw the Christian kingdoms once more upon the defensive. At the battle of Zallaca in 1086 the forces of Alfonso VI of Leon, who was them claiming with some justice to be Emperor of all Christian Spain, were routed, and for fifty years the Almoravids controlled Al-Andalus with a firm military hand, making a number of conquests from the Christians.

The Almoravids were little but efficient military conquerors from Africa, and their power could not survive the appearance of weak rulers at the top. But no sooner had Almoravid power gone into decline than it was replaced by that of the Almohads. In origin these were the followers of a rigidly puritanical Islamic sect in the Atlas mountains. Their leader, making the traditional claim to be the promised Mahdi, put great stress on the obligation on the faithful to wage holy war. By the middle of the twelfth century they had broken Almoravid power in north Africa, and from there they proceeded to invade Spain. They too won quick successes alike against Christians and against their fellow Muslims, for Muslims in Spain, like crusaders in Outremer, often pursued the course of co-existence with the Infidel. Politically the Almohads were less successful than the Almoravids in establishing Muslim unity in Al-Andalus, and their rule was to prove no more permanent. But, particularly during the reign of Abu Ya'gub (1163–1184), the second Almohad caliph, they showed to a greater degree than their predecessors the ability to fuse the Arabic and the Greek elements in their cultural heritage. Abu's court was intellectually alive to the same philosophical problems that were currently exercising men's minds at Paris, and the unity of the Godhead was as likely to be discussed in terms of Plato as in those of the Koran. Moreover the Muslims had the advantage over the Christians of a more complete, if no more accurate, knowledge of the writings of the Hellenic past. Military and religious hostility could not altogether obstruct this community of interest, and the Spain of the Almohads played its part in feeding the cultural renaissance of western Europe.

The final decline of Al-Andalus began with the defeat of the main Almohad army at the battle of Las Navas de Tolosa in 1212. For another two hundred and eighty years, until the final conquest of Granada in 1492, some of the peninsula was to remain under Muslim administration, but there was no real revival in Muslim fortunes at any stage. Such unity as Al-Andalus had possessed was lost as the rulers of different cities each sought their own salvation, some by resistance and some by negotiation. Of those who chose the latter method some indeed were successful in purchasing their independence for long periods of time. The so-called Nasrid kings of Granada, for instance, secured nearly one hundred and fifty years of immunity by their agreement with Ferdinand III of Castile (1217–1254) in 1246, but the price of their safety was not only the tribute they now paid regularly to Castile, but the use of their own forces against their fellow believers in Seville. By the thirteenth century political and economic rivalries in the world of Muslim Spain had become more important than religious unity, and in such circumstances what had always been a minority religion could not be expected to survive.

That the Moors remained an important element in Spanish political life for so long was the result of the quarrels of the various Christian kingdoms far more than of their own strength, and it is now time to look at Christian Spain. It has been seen that the conquest of the whole peninsula was neither wholly achieved by the invaders, nor in the remote areas at any time seriously attempted. But the surviving Christian territories, only very loosely knit together in Visigothic times, were now often divided from each other by Moslem forces as well as geographical obstacles. They thus developed into the separate kingdoms which gave to medieval Spanish history its complexity, and to modern Spain its strongly regional character. To trace the very intricate story of the changing relationships between the different kingdoms is not for the purpose of this book necessary, but some account must be given of how each came into being.

The five kingdoms around which medieval Spanish and Portuguese history was constructed sprang from three main areas. In the north-west the mountainous and unprofitable country of Galicia and the Asturias had deterred the original invaders from attempting conquest. This was the area of the kingdom of Leon, a kingdom which could reasonably claim to be the only true descendant of the Visigothic monarchy. But it Leon could claim to be ancient, it had inherited also the Visigothic tradition of political ineptitude. As soon as the reconquest began to increase the lands owing allegiance to the crown of Leon, the monarchical institutions showed themselves incapable of holding that allegiance. Both Castile, with its first capital at Burgos, and Portugal, which found its earliest capital in Oporto rather than Lisbon, were in origin dependents of Leon, ruled by counts responsible to its king. First Castile, while Sancho the Fat (957–966) reigned in Leon, and then much later Portugal, severed all connection with Leon, and grew into separate kingdoms. Indeed military incompetence against the Moors and a series of disputes over the succession made the history of Leon a sad story of decline, and it ended by losing its identity to the Castilian kingdom. It was to be Castile that took the lead in the long crusade against the Moors. Castilian troops had the main part in the recapture in 1086 of Toledo, the first great Muslim city to be liberated; it now became the capital of New Castile. It was a Castilian king, Alfonso VIII (1158–1214) who commanded the Christian forces at Las Navas de Tolosa, and to Castile fell the major share of the broken state of Al-Andalus.

To the east of Castile lay the little mountain kingdom of Navarre. It owed its survival to the rugged nature of the western Pyrenees and to the equally rugged independence of the Basque people who inhabited it. Perhaps the same qualities go to explain why the kings of Navarre showed much more reluctance than the other Spanish kings to lead their country along the path of expansion to the south. They did not altogether stand aside; a king of Navarre for instance took his share at Las Navas de Tolosa. But they were markedly less active than either the kings of Castile to the west or those of Aragon to the east. But, refusing to play for high stakes, the kings of Navarre found themselves excluded from the rich prizes which the peninsula offered. Navarre remained a small mountain kingdom, and its ruling house eventually involved it more in the affairs of France to the north of the Pyrenees than of Spain to the south.

The third area, that of the eastern Pyrenees, was not dissimilar geographically from Navarre, except in so far as it contained the Mediterranean coastal plain. By this the Muslims had launched their main attack on the Franks in the eighth century; it was not surprising that it should become a springboard for an important part of the Christian counter-attack. The kingdom of Aragon, the last of the five kingdoms, had a different historical origin from the rest of them. In Carolingian times the Franks had occupied a Spanish March, extending as far south as Barcelona, with the idea of keeping a secure hold on the main line of the Pyrenees. As might be expected the zone was the scene of much fighting, and its defence was entrusted to a number of counts, of whom Aureolus of Jaca, the founder of the future Aragonese kingdom, seems to have been one. Aragon was thus early in its existence linked to the rest of Europe in a way which was not true of any of the other kingdoms. This difference was to persist. As the process of reconquest proceeded Aragon, even more than Castile, came to be a kingdom composed of very varied peoples. The original counts of Aragon in the central Pyrenees must have had local and circumscribed interests, and indeed Aragon did not become a kingdom until 1035, when it was conferred upon a bastard son of the Navarrese line. But a century later Aragon became united with the County of Barcelona. The joint monarchy which was thus established linked two peoples with very little in common. Not only did they speak different languages, but the Catalan population of the county of Barcelona had strong links with the outside world. Through their territory ran the main link between the peninsula and France, and a considerable confusion of allegiance existed, with Catalan nobles claiming lands north of the Pyrenees and French nobles with claims in Catalonia. Moreover, Barcelona was fast developing as a Mediterranean trading port. As such it was much more akin to Italian ports such as Genoa than to any Spanish town, and, like them, it became committed to a career of colonial and mercantile expansion overseas. The conquest of Majorca from the Moors (1228–1231) was only the earliest of a series of adventures in which Catalonia was to involve the Aragonese kingdom. The addition of yet a third element to the association, when James I of Aragon (1213–1276) finally reconquered Valencia, added another discordant element, for Valencia had a large Moorish population and a variety of industries unknown in the north. The Aragonese kingdom had become quite unlike its fellows; its highly diversified population and occupations made it at once stronger and more vulnerable than them. Its kings, who had taken Saragossa as their central capital, could command the possibility of far more revenue than their rivals, but the danger that the three sections of their kingdom would simply fall apart was very real.

Until the completion of the greater part of the reconquest with the capitulation of Seville to a Christian army in 1248, the constant struggle against the Moors is the central theme of the history of all the kingdoms. This is the heroic period of Spanish history, a period in which legend and history get mixed in the stories of such legendary but historical heroes as El Cid. The religious conflict gave to the struggle all the glamour of a crusade, and it was not unknown for crusaders from other lands to engage in the Holy War in Spain rather than in the East. If the reality was a less romantic story than the legend, so that, instead of the simple story of the soldiers of the Cross in arms against its enemies, the truth often showed Muslim allies of the Christian kingdoms and even Christian supporters of Al-Andalus, the same can be said of the story of the eastern crusades. During this period of Spanish history the affairs of the peninsula are very much detached from those of the rest of Europe. Even the Christianity which was being defended was for long significantly different from the Catholicism of the West as a whole. In early times the Visigoths had embraced Arianism, and although Catholicism, particularly in the person of S. Isidore of Seville, had proved largely triumphant in the seventh century, the Church in Spain had retained a flavour of its own. For nearly four hundred years it had very little contact with Rome; its liturgy, the rite of Toledo, differed widely from that of the Roman Church, and its bishops depended neither for election nor in office on Rome. In the ninth century the alleged discovery of the tomb of S. James the Greater at Compostela in Galicia seemed to place the Spanish Church in the direct tradition of the apostles, and to justify its independence. The reforms of the tenth and eleventh centuries had spread only slowly to Spain, where the Church had for long been run on lines which to an Hildebrandine could only be simoniacal. For a time there was a serious danger of a Spanish schism under the leadership of the bishop of Compostela, whose shrine was fast becoming a place of pilgrimage rivalling for the western world Rome itself. It was only averted by a settlement which included the exaltation of Compostela to an archbishopric and the conferment on it of a number of unusual privileges. Elsewhere in Europe independence of the secular powers was the aim most sought by the Church, and, in the thirteenth century at least, it came near to being achieved. In Spain independence never seemed to be of the same importance, and it is not difficult to see why. The main object of the Spanish kings was the expansion of their kingdoms at the expense of Al-Andalus; the main purpose of the Church was the christianization of the Moors. These two aims were very largely the same.

A new age in Spanish history opened in 1248. Apart from the relatively small state of Granada, which the kings of Castile decided to tolerate for the present, the reconquest was complete. The common purpose was gone, and every kingdom was now faced with the problem of finding itself a new destiny. In so doing their paths diverged, so that Spanish unity came to look less rather than more probable; at the same time they lost their parochial nature and came to be involved in the affairs of the rest of Europe.

Portugal, Castile, and Aragon were now the three surviving kingdoms of importance in Iberian affairs. Of the three, Portugal had fared least well in the era of reconquest. The Castilian expansion to the west of Gibraltar, which had been marked by the capture of Seville and Cadiz, had effectively blocked Portuguese hopes in this area, and south of Cape S. Vincent there was for the present nothing to conquer. The kingdom was thus fated to be much the smallest of the three. The history of Portugal from the middle of the thirteenth to the beginning of the fifteenth century is not particularly striking. During the reign of Afonso III (1248–1279) an interminable dispute with the Church sprang from the king's decision to subject the Military Orders to taxation. Since there was now no very real need for their presence in Portugal the decision is understandable, but neither Church nor monarchy profited from the argument. The real lines along which Portugal might gain prosperity were shown by his successor Dinis (1279–1325). He was thoroughly to earn the title of 'the Cultivator'. Eschewing thoughts of increasing the size of his small kingdom by attacks on its neighbour, he concentrated instead on increasing the fertility of what he already had. By royal command swamps were drained, forests planted, merchants given every encouragement. In a country noted neither for good government nor for prosperity the reigns of King Dinis and of his grandson Peter I (1357–1367) form happy exceptions. The other Portuguese kings of the fourteenth century concerned themselves mainly with sterile attempts to annex Castilian territory. Sometimes they claimed the Castilian throne for themselves, sometimes they supported the claim advanced by John of Gaunt on the strength of his Castilian wife Constance, thus bringing into existence the ancient and often-criticized Anglo–Portuguese alliance. In neither case were their efforts in the least likely to be successful against their much more powerful neighbour. All they achieved was the exhaustion of a Crown which had never been particularly well endowed, and a growing discontent among the nobility, manifesting itself at successive meetings of the Cortes. This discontent culminated in 1385 when a meeting of the Cortes declared the dynasty overthrown and the Crown to be elective. They then conferred it on John the Bastard, who acceded as John I (1385–1433).

With the reign of King John, Portugal entered upon new policies which were to succeed within a hundred years in turning her from an insignificant Iberian kingdom into one of the most powerful and feared of all European powers. John had the sense to see that no profit was to be found from constant warfare with Castile. Instead he turned to overseas expansion. At first the north African coast formed the field for the Portuguese attempts, and the capture in 1415 of the port of Ceuta on the south side of the straits of Gibraltar seemed to give Portugal the chance of becoming a Mediterranean power. But it was not there that her future lay. Mediterrranean trade was already declining, but the same forces which were threatening Venice and Genoa with decline spelt opportunity for those nations which possessed what until then had been the disadvantage of an Atlantic seaboard. John's third son, Prince Henry the Navigator (†1480), gave the movement to explore the possibilities of ocean travel the patronage and encouragement it needed from his palace at Sagres. By the middle of the century Portugal was already beginning to reap the fruits of this entirely new policy. Madeira and the Azores had been colonized, and Portuguese seamen had rounded Cape Verde and made landfall on the coast of what was to be Portuguese Guinea. There they had found negroes and gold, the raw materials for two profitable trades of the future. The greater prize, the discovery of a route to India which should be free from all Ottoman interference, still lay in the future, but by 1450 this had become the foreseeable future. Portugal was establishing her right to be the first European colonial power, and in so doing serving notice on the historian that the Middle Ages, in one of their manifold aspects, are at an end.

If the kings of Portugal had regretted the smallness of their portion from the spoils of Al-Andalus, those of Castile by contrast suffered from surfeit. So much had come to Castile in so short a time that the process of digesting what had been won was to occupy its rulers for the rest of the thirteenth and fourteenth centuries. The population was very mixed. Not only were there large numbers of Muslims and Jews, some of them alleging conversion to Christianity, but the Christian population itself was deeply divided, there being no tradition of, or indeed good cause for, unity among the very varied lands which now went to make up the kingdom. The prolonged war against the Muslims had served to produce a military society in which the nobleman with his own armed men in his company was the most valuable of beings. Now that peace had come that same nobleman had become a grave menace. The history of Castile after the reconquest is full of turbulent baronial wars. Nor was the overmighty lay subject the only danger to royal power. The Church, particularly, as in Portugal, through the military orders, had enriched itself greatly through the reconquest. All its old subservience to the Crown was gone, and its present power was a political danger as well as something of a special problem. Nor could the kings of Castile look for aid to those champions of monarchical power in other countries, the smaller country gentry and the bourgeoisie of the towns. In Castile the hidalgo class attached itself firmly to the more powerful of the nobility; in the Cortes, for example, there was no hint of that alliance between squire and bourgeois which could make the House of Commons formidable. The towns, though of some value in supporting the monarchy, often gave their first loyalty to the local landowner, who was so much more real to them than a distant king.

The kings of Castile, therefore, ought to have concentrated on establishing the Crown in a dominant position. Alfonso X (the Wise, 1252–1282) rightly identified the great variety of local laws and customs in his kingdom as one factor which was hindering the work of unification; his attempt in 1254 to produce a single code for the whole country in *Las Siete Partidas* was an attempt to remedy the situation. But this was a diagnosis rather than a cure, and it was to be many centuries before a Spanish law which was effectively enforceable throughout the country came into existence. Moreover, Alfonso's long and inevitably unsuccessful attempts to become Holy Roman Emperor did not assist him to retain Castilian loyalty. By the end of his reign Alfonso was facing not only a dangerous Muslim revolt, but widespread opposition from his own nobility, who formally deposed him in favour of his younger son Sancho IV (1282–1295). The reigns of Sancho and his successor Ferdinand IV (1295–1312) were an unhappy period of internal and external strife; a regency for Ferdinand, who succeeded at the age of nine, did nothing to improve the prospects of the monarchy, which had its own disputed succession problem to add to external pressure from the Moors, Aragon, and France. Not until the reign of Alfonso XI (1312–1349) did Castile again have a king who commanded any general respect, and his reign too opened with a long regency. Alfonso did his best to improve the Crown's control over the towns, sending royal officials known as 'corregidores' to supervise their governments. By the institution of a purchase tax, known as the *alcabala*, he sought to give the Crown that financial strength which

alone might give it supremacy over the nobility, and, like his name-
sake Alfonso X, he did what he could to aid the cause of legal
uniformity.

But these intervals of good government did little to improve the
long-term prospects of the Castilian monarchy. The resources of the
Crown were so small in relation to the problem which confronted
it that what was needed was not an occasional able ruler, but a
constant succession of kings of exceptional ability. This it is not in the
nature of an hereditary system to produce. When the throne was
occupied by rulers of mediocre talents, as happened after the death
of Alfonso XI, the country simply relapsed into faction. The worst
feature of these struggles, which make up the bulk of Castilian history
from the reign of Peter the Cruel (1349–1369) to that of Henry the
Impotent (1454–1474), was the regularity with which Castilian
territory was subject to foreign invasion. For instance Henry of
Trastamara, half-brother to Peter the Cruel and eventually both his
murderer and, as Henry II (1369–1379), his successor, brought the
forces of Aragon and the free companies of Duguesclin to his aid.
Peter for his part retaliated with an English army under the Black
Prince, so that for a time Castile became the main scene of the
Hundred Years War. The arrangement gave needed relief to the
long-suffering populace of France, but for Castile it meant that the
destruction involved in this fraternal struggle came to be out of all
proportion to its real importance.

This indeed is the pattern of Castilian history for the rest of our
period. Under a succession of incompetent kings whose names,
'Ailing', 'Impotent', and the like, fitly reveal their governmental as
well as physical failings, the prestige and power of the monarchy
dwindled. The kings themselves were driven to all the devices of
debasement and other financial chicanery with which impoverished
monarchies were accustomed to attempt solvency, and the prestige
of the Crown inevitably ebbed. The claim put forward by repeated
sessions of the Cortes to exercise the royal prerogative through a
small royal council nominated by themselves is one indication of the
extent to which the power of the Crown was disappearing. When
Isabella of Castile brought her kingdom with her to her marriage
with Ferdinand of Aragon in 1469, it must have seemed a damaged
offering. Yet, as is often the case, political incompetence had not
destroyed the potentiality of the kingdom. Not only had Castile been
preserved intact, but the raw material of future growth was there. The
wool trade, by which wool esteemed of finer quality than any in

Europe was widely exported, had flourished, and throughout the southern half of the kingdom the large element of Jews and Moors brought valuable skills to the economic life of the country. For two hundred years Castile had played a passive part in European affairs, a country suffering from the policies of others rather than herself making history; nothing dictated that so it must always be.

The third Spanish kingdom played by far the most active role of the three. Certainly Aragon's position and the extent to which in the past she had had contacts with other European kingdoms made this intrinsically likely, but early in the thirteenth century there seemed no likelihood that she would come to be the pivot of Mediterranean history in the later Middle Ages. The history of Italy, disunited and stateless as she was in medieval times, always suggests treatment in terms of some external power. Earlier this is without question the Holy Roman Empire, but in the fourteenth and fifteenth centuries there is good cause for taking Aragon as the central theme. Nor is this all. Citizens of the eastern Spanish kingdom were to play a significant part in such distant communities as Constantinople and Athens. For a small country this was a great—perhaps too great—achievement. If the story of Castile is one of passivity, that of Aragon suggests an intense and febrile activity.

As has been seen Aragon was really not one kingdom, but a loose federation of three. The traditions of Catalonia and the recently conquered Valencia were very different from those of Aragon proper. Nor did the separate kingdoms move closer to each other. This can be seen in the history of the Cortes. All the Spanish kingdoms had these assemblies, which appear somewhat earlier in Spanish history than the parliaments and estates with which they suggest comparison elsewhere. As early as the second half of the twelfth century the kings of Castile can be found summoning to their presence representatives of the three main estates of their kingdom. The Spanish Cortes never obtained the positive role of the English Parliament. Except in a constitutional crisis, such as a disputed succession, they never achieved legislative power; the most they could do was to make suggestions which might subsequently be turned into law by the king and his council. Nor did they gain recognition as the supreme court of their respective countries. Their inability to get united action from their three estates except on the rarest of occasions was another check on their utility. But they could have a considerable negative importance through restraining royal actions by withholding extraordinary supply, and they could act as national institutions which by their very existence could counteract the excessive localism which was the bane of all the Spanish kings. In Portugal and Castile they performed this latter role; no more, for instance, is heard of a separate Cortes for Leon after 1300. But in Aragon all three Cortes retained their separate identities, and, partly for this reason, disintegration of the whole state remained a very real possibility.

The end of the main period of reconquest from the Moors coincided for Aragon with the final liquidation of her hopes of an expansion in Languedoc by the Treaty of Corbeil.[1] James I of Aragon (1213–1276), who signed the treaty and had taken the major share in the recapture of Valencia, was also responsible for the new direction of Aragonese policy. He had already pointed the way to a Mediterranean empire by his annexation of the Balearic islands; by marrying his heir to the daughter of King Manfred of Sicily he set in train the chain of events which was to end in the recognition at the treaty of Caltabellotta in 1302 of an independent Sicily under an Aragonese monarch.[2] The successful defiance of the Papacy and of the Angevins was a remarkable tribute to the military skill of Aragonese and Sicilians alike. But if the extent of Aragonese acquisitions in the Mediterranean was coming to be considerable, the empire was no more united than the homeland itself. Sicily was independent, and on his death in 1285 James I had split off Majorca with certain mainland territories to form a separate kingdom for his younger son James II (1311), an act of folly since it made certain disputed successions in future years. After peace had come to Sicily, a large number of Aragonese troops who had been fighting there took service under the Byzantine emperor, who was seeking in the fashion of his predecessors to find western troops to combat the Turks. The Aragonese contingent proved a bad investment. Soon falling out with their new master, most of them escaped an attempt by the Byzantine authorities to bring a final solution to the problem by massacring them in 1305. Four years later they transferred themselves to a new master in the person of the Duke of Athens. There they soon succeeded in taking over the duchy, and maintained themselves with help from Sicily for many years as a curious western outpost in eastern Europe.

So vigorous a policy of Mediterranean expansion inevitably brought Aragon into conflict with the Italian trading cities, and hence into the whole orbit of Italian politics. In 1322 James II (1291–1327) proceeded to annex Sardinia. His action aroused the greatest hostility in Genoa, which had many colonists in the island, but in securing Genoese opposition the Aragonese had almost automatically secured also the support of Genoa's oldest enemy, Venice. In the reign of Peter IV (1336–1387) the joint fleet of Venice and Aragon carried on a war against the Genoese throughout the whole length of the Mediterranean. Aragon had become deeply involved in the affairs of both northern and southern Italy, and in 1377 Peter was able to unite Sicily once more with the mainland of Catalonia by installing his younger son Martin as king. The process of building up Aragonese power in the Mediterranean was complete.

The success of this whole remarkable operation is obvious; its principal defect is equally clear. The exploits of the Grand Catalan Company in obscure parts of the Balkans might enthuse Barcelona, but they were totally foreign to the wishes and traditions of Aragon and Valencia. Their nobility only saw what seemed to be the dissipation of the meagre resources of their kingdoms on remote adventures. Peter IV had to face dangerous rebellions in the other two kingdoms. At Epila in 1348 he had been able to lead a Catalan army to victory over the rebels of the other two kingdoms. But victory in the field had done nothing to increase the popularity of his house outside Catalonia or to commend Catalonian policies in Valencia or Saragossa.

In 1410 the other two kingdoms got their opportunity. King Martin of Aragon and Sicily died only a few months after the death of his heir, and all his thrones became vacant. Several candidates appeared, and their rival claims were discussed, not by full meetings of the Cortes, but by a special commission of theologians and lawyers from the three mainland kingdoms. Finally they decided on the election of Ferdinand, a member of the Castilian house of Trastamara and younger brother of the reigning king of Castile. Their choice was full of significance for the future, since it prefigured the eventual alignment of Aragon with Castile. Until this time a union between Castile and Portugal had seemed both more probable and more logical. The choice also reflected a reaction against Catalonian policies. Ferdinand was accepted by all the lands which had acknowledged Martin, but his Castilian past must have suggested that he was likely to pursue a more Spanish and less expansionist policy.

If this was indeed their motive, then those who elected Ferdinand were disappointed in their intention. Ferdinand only ruled from 1412 to 1416, during which time his main energies were devoted to coaxing Aragon away from its allegiance to Benedict XIII and back to the united church.[1] During his short reign he also gave signs of wishing to turn Aragon from the course she had been following; certainly the introduction of numbers of Castilian advisers into Catalonia aroused much resentment. But after his death Ferdinand was succeeded by his two sons, Alfonso V (1416–1458) and John II (1458–1479). With them the Mediterranean policies of the earlier dynasty were taken up again with redoubled energy. During the closing years of the independent Aragonese monarchy it would be fair to describe it as more Italian than Spanish. From 1420 onwards Alfonso flung himself into a career of Mediterranean conquest which was in the best traditions of Catalonia. Corsica was captured from the Genoese, and after many vicissitudes the kingdom of Naples was eventually captured in 1442. Ignoring the protests which reached him through the mouth of the *Justicia* of Aragon, the supreme legal authority of his Spanish possessions, Alfonso proceeded to move the seat of his government to Naples. While he ruled in great state there, the charge of Aragon was left to his brother, an arrangement which not unnaturally provoked resentment in Spain. Nor did the character of John as regent, and the violent quarrels within his own family in which he indulged, do anything to allay their fears. The Aragonese state was in great danger of dissolution under a king with little interest in its affairs, and with discontent at home threatening to reduce it to its component parts. Nor would it be long before an even greater threat to its security appeared. The France of the Hundred Years War had lacked the strength to make any serious attempt at conquest in the peninsula. But that war was now drawing to a close, and a revived French monarchy, soon to be occupied by one of the most ruthless and efficient of all French kings (Louis XI, 1461–1483), would be able to challenge the interests of Aragon in both Spain and Italy. The marriage of Ferdinand of Aragon and Isabella of Castile was to be the means by which the united state of modern Spain came into being, but the separate medieval kingdoms it replaced were already doomed. In a real sense that marriage was one of necessity rather than of convenience or of love.

It is time now to look at the Italy into which Aragon made such deep penetration in the fifteenth century. Its most striking characteristic was the absence of any development in the direction of statehood. To some degree this was the result of geography; the Apennines sliced the country in half. But even Spain, with much greater geo-

[1] See Chapter 17.

graphical obstacles, eventually overcame them. The past history of the country is a more relevant consideration. For centuries Italy had known two different authorities in the Empire and the Church, both claiming the allegiance of its citizens and both inhibiting the growth of any national monarchy. The Italian cities had sided, though often in the most bewilderingly fluctuating manner, with one or other of these supra-national organizations. During the fourteenth century both had become obsolete. Emperors who were little more than ineffective German princelings, popes who were constrained to hide themselves in Avignon, these were not figures to lead the Italian people. The terms Welf and Ghibelline continued to be used, but they had lost all their original meaning. With the practical disappearance of the two powers which had at different times claimed to exercise sovereignty over Italy, there had disappeared also what had been the main stimulus to association among the cities; there was no longer the need to organize leagues to resist emperor or pope. In consequence the Italian political scene reached a level of political anarchy among the differing hostile cities approached nowhere else in Europe; reflective minds such as Dante, Petrarch, and Marsiglio all deplored this, but they were powerless to prevent it. Elsewhere in Europe the merchant class was still encountering sufficient opposition from the non-capitalist forces in society to retain a certain unity. In Italy the very extent of its domination ensured that the latent hostilities which existed between trade rivals could find full expression.

To trace the story of the innumerable wars between the Italian cities in the fourteenth and early fifteenth centuries would be a tedious task. But two important consequences followed from them. Firstly, even more than in earlier centuries, Italy became a field that invited foreign intervention. Secondly, the chaotic political conditions favoured the production almost everywhere of that type of despotism which forms the characteristic political background of the Italian Renaissance.

Although the Italian scene showed a picture of innumerable communes, all jealously guarding their independence behind their walls, it was not to be expected that they would all come to exercise an equal influence in Italian affairs. A good deal of cannibalism took place, and by the early fifteenth century Italy consisted of five predominant states, with most of the other cities, while retaining almost complete internal self-government, associated more or less closely with one of the big five in external matters. Milan, Venice,

Florence, the Papacy, and Naples between them provided most of the political initiative in the peninsula. The relative decline of some of the great trading cities of the past, such as Genoa and Pisa, is an indication of the increasing difficulties besetting the trade with the East. But the big five were unable and unwilling to take the further step of associating with each other. Apart from economic rivalries they were completely different in their past histories and traditions. The Papacy, for obvious reasons, was set apart from the rest in its aims if not in its methods. Venice, secure on her Adriatic lagoon, had always been in Italy, yet in a sense not of it; with her curious constitution and her extensive preoccupation with the East she belonged as much to the world of Byzantium as to the West. Naples, again, with a tradition of non-Italian rule, Byzantine, Norman, Angevin or Aragonese as the case might be, was very different from the normal Italian pattern. Milan and Florence, the chief cities of Lombardy and Tuscany respectively, had inherited the hostility which had long existed between the two areas. No one of them was regarded with anything but hostility by the other four, and none of them seemed in any way marked out to give leadership to the whole country.

The disunity inevitably invited foreign interference. The very fact that it existed against the background of what was still considerable economic well-being only increased the temptation for countries which had been more successful in solving their own internal problems to intervene. In one sense it is surprising that it was not until 1492 that Italy finally became the prey of continuous foreign invasion and the battlefield where the dynastic quarrels of the sixteenth century were to be fought out. Only the preoccupations of the neighbouring great powers saved her independence for so long. The Aragonese capture of Naples was indeed foreign intervention, but in an area where this was no novelty, and by a kingdom which had already stretched its resources nearly to the limit. When in the next century the Aragonese line there came to be supported by the whole might of Spain it would prove a real danger to the entire country.

The development of tyrannies in most of the Italian cities has attracted much attention from historians. Only Venice, where the power of the doges never became despotic and was checked by the Grand Council, remained oligarchical; elsewhere, though at different speeds and in different ways, almost every city produced rulers with no hereditary claim to their offices and with almost unchecked powers. The tyrant most frequently appeared as the answer to a general desire for order to replace constant internal strife; as the statutes of the city of Cremona had it 'To be without a prince is impossible; cities and all else without a prince are in confusion'.[1] In the eleventh and twelfth centuries the struggles within Italian cities had generally taken the form of conflict between the *Grandi*, the feudal nobility on whose lands the towns had grown up, and the *Popolo Grasso*, the merchants and employers whose wealth was assisting their growth. But this phase passed fairly early; by the thirteenth century control in most of the city states rested firmly with the more wealthy of their inhabitants. The earlier conflict was replaced by one in which the power of the urban oligarchs was challenged by a substantial section of those whose labour they at once employed and exploited. The successful tyrant was the man who had successfully mobilized this popular discontent behind himself.

Thus, like most effective dictators, the tyrants were also demagogues. Sometimes they sprang from the ranks of the proletariat itself. More often, like the Visconti in Milan, the new leaders were drawn from the ranks of the old aristocracy, or, like the Medici in Florence, from some particular merchant or banking family which had mastered the technique of controlling the state to its own advantage. The nominal offices held by the tyrants varied greatly, and mattered little. Some were titled *Podesta*, an office of chief magistrate which they had succeeded in making permanent, others had vested themselves with the title of Captain of the Commune. The Medici, perhaps the most effective of them all, held no formal office, preferring, as do bankers in all ages, to work in the shadows. Despotic power was perfectly compatible with frequent apparent recourse to elections and other means of securing expressions of popular assent. In the twentieth century there should be no difficulty in understanding this.

One important factor in establishing, and still more in maintaining, a tyrant was the increasing use of professional *condottieri* in Italian warfare. In earlier times war between the cities had normally been carried on by citizen armies; it had been in just such a war that S. Francis had been taken prisoner in his youth. But the citizen army had now become obsolete, and war had become a matter settled by the professionals in accordance with a well-established code, in which manoeuvres were everything and bloodshed cut to a minimum. The capacity of some of the *condottieri* generals to fight 'battles' which lasted for days with scarcely any loss of life was remarkable. At the end of the century Machiavelli was to see it as intolerably spiritless

[1] Quoted from M. V. Clarke, *The Medieval City State*, Methuen, 1926, p. 126.

and unpatriotic; alternatively it can be viewed as a relatively civilized machinery for the settlement of disputes. But two things are certain. The system made the maintenance of the power of a tyrant within the Italian political system very much easier. At the same time it made the whole system very much more vulnerable to external attack. With a citizenry which had lost all knowledge of and inclination to arms, military power rested with the man who was able to hire the army. Once a tyrant had secured financial power, there was no very good reason why he should lose military control, unless indeed the *condottieri* general himself developed political ambitions. Such cases were not unknown. The most celebrated example came in Milan in 1450 when, the direct male succession of the Visconti having died out, Francesco Sforza was able himself to succeed as duke by dint of his control of the army.

Equally it was true that the Italian professionals, engrossed in their code of warfare, had had no need to keep up with military developments elsewhere. The lessons of the Hundred Years War had passed them by; and disciplined masses of infantry and the destructive force of gunpowder had no place in Italian warfare. Thus in a sense the whole system of Italian statecraft rested on a system of mutual confidence among the generals. If it were challenged from outside by national armies who were prepared to violate that confidence, it would collapse.

Politically there is little to be said for the Italy of the later Middle Ages. The exceptionally complicated system of states succeeded in giving the country neither external security nor internal peace. But that is not the whole story. The same criticism could very reasonably be brought against the Greek city states of the fifth and fourth centuries B.C. But their practical, as opposed to theoretical, incompetence in politics was the least important thing about them. The very defects of the Italian political system helped to achieve the glories of Renaissance Italy. To seek to explain the Renaissance entirely in terms of patronage would be foolish, and a fuller explanation lies outside the scope of the present book. But there is little doubt that a world of many rival communities, each seeking to outdo its rivals in the splendour and taste of its public buildings and in the excellence of its music and art, provides an environment peculiarly suitable for the artist. The music of eighteenth-century Germany, the artistic achievements of fifth-century Greece and Renaissance Italy, were all paid for by political ineptitude. Perhaps here is to be found the reason why the creative ages in man's history are so short.

20

The End of the Story

The problem of when medieval history ended and modern history began is a riddle without an answer. Convenience demands that some line must be drawn between the two, even if any suggested date can easily be shown to be absurd. For many years 1492 has continued to cast its spell, if not over English historians, at least over those who determine the content of historical examination papers. The prime responsibility rests with Lord Acton. By starting his lectures on European History at the end of the fifteenth century and by planning the original *Cambridge Modern History* to start from the same point, this founding father of Cambridge historical scholarship determined the limits of modern history with no less authority than some years earlier Bishop Stubbs at Oxford had determined the content of English medieval history. In his inaugural lecture, delivered at Cambridge in 1895, Acton described as 'Modern History that which begins four hundred years ago, which is marked off by an evident and intelligible line from the time immediately preceding, and displays in its course specific and distinctive characteristics of its own'. This Great Divide between medieval and modern history has proved durable.

Stubbs and Acton were both great men. Their solutions were not absurd; their very longevity demonstrates this. Stubbs's *Charters* do contain the real skeleton of English constitutional history, in itself a subject which, if not a part of the divine revelation, is at least worthy of serious study in any age; in the same way Acton's choice can be seriously defended.

The year 1492 saw the discovery of America, and with it the first possibility of a new Europe beyond the Atlantic. In 1492 too, began that long period of Italian wars between France and Spain which was to form the main content of western diplomatic history for the next fifty years. It can be said that one of these events was so long term in its consequences as to be almost useless as a guide, while the other was merely a recurrence of something which had long been a part of European history. For the discovery of America had little immediate significance for most of Europe, and even its psychological effect can be overestimated; Portuguese sailors had already demonstrated the vastness of the world and destroyed for ever the old medieval *Mappa Mundi*. As for the Italian wars, little knowledge of medieval history is needed to know that foreign invasions of Italy had nothing new about them. But Acton had more in mind than the events immediately connected with the year he had chosen. For him 1492 could be seen as a central date for that Renaissance which was transferring men's minds into modern ways of thought. By 1492 the use of the new discovery of printing was already beginning to assume the proportions which would guarantee that in future even the most heterodox of opinions might win the immortality of an edition. Moreover 1492 formed a convenient point from which to watch the growth of the two great processes which were to shape the Europe he knew. The first of the Tudors was already reigning in England, and, in Saxony, Martin Luther was growing up. Protestantism, with all the undertones of religious liberty and toleration which it carried even for the Roman Catholic Acton, and Nationalism, with its promise of new and powerful political organizations to replace the wreckage of the medieval Empire, these were the forces of the future, and it was from the end of the fifteenth century that their rise could best be observed.

Today the picture can no longer be seen in Acton's terms. The difficulty is in part that we can no longer accept the valuation or the descriptions of growth assumed by him for protestantism and nationalism, in part the appearance on the historical scene of other factors no less potent than they.

Protestantism no longer can be seen as an expression of a desire for liberty in religion, and Luther and Calvin appear in the modern world of wholly secular states as anomalies. Not only did they not desire to create anything of the kind but, more important, it is difficult now to see them as anything but very indirect causes of its being. The Protestant leaders of the sixteenth century seem now not so much to be the new figures of a new age as the legitimate heirs of the Waldensians, Wycliff, and Huss.

Much the same can be said of nationalism, a subject which after two world wars based on it has lost some of the glamour it possessed in the days of Victorian security and British hegemony. The nation state no longer appears as the unique creation of the sixteenth century. Certainly in Spain the latter part of the fifteenth century and that which followed it saw the creation of a fierce nationalism, the very ardour of which betokened its novelty. In England too a rediscovered political unity made of the sixteenth century a nationalistic age, and in both countries the potential divisive effects of the religious conflict of the period were skilfully turned to the service of states they might well have destroyed. But in France and Germany the story was to be very different. A history of French nationalism might well start with Philip Augustus and S. Louis, who with medieval tools made something nearly approaching a nation state out of France; it would extol Philip the Fair, and, after the destructive interlude of the Hundred Years War, it would hail Louis XI as the restorer of the French nation. In contrast the latter half of the sixteenth century, with the country torn by religious dissensions and incompetently governed by a foreign regent, would seem anything but an age of nationalism. Medieval Germany had been far from a nation, but, until the fall of the Hohenstaufens in the thirteenth century, the Empire had given it some of the characteristics of statehood. The sixteenth century was to see only the increasing tensions of religious and political disunity which were to culminate in the Thirty Years War. Not until 1871 was Germany to become 'modern'. In Italy indeed nationhood had been far distant in 1300, but it was no nearer in 1600. Judged by the test of nationalism there is no supreme significance in the closing years of the fifteenth century.

If nationalism is left aside, what of the other supposedly modern characteristics of the later fifteenth century? It would be foolish to belittle the Renaissance either in terms of artistic achievement or as a movement in the minds of men. But in as far as it is possible to date anything as fluid as a cultural movement it can be said with confidence that 1492 is too late a date. Renaissance Man, if he existed, had certainly come into existence well before then. If the term is looked on in its narrowest sense as applying only to pictorial art, the change to a three-dimensional and naturalistic technique in painting can certainly be seen at work in Giotto (1337), and the mosaics of the former church of San Salvator-in-Choro in Constantinople, most of which belong to the period immediately following the restoration of the Byzantine Empire in 1261, show that in the East the change had been coming at an even earlier date. If, by contrast, the term is interpreted more widely to cover a whole attitude to life, an attitude of unrestrained curiosity about the possibilities of both mind and body, derived from the classical Greek ideal, the date of 1492 still seems far too late. The revolutionary speculations of Marsiglio of Padua in the fourteenth century and of the writers of the conciliar period somewhat later are testimony to this curiosity in one field, and the intellectual freedom and moral anarchy of the Italian city states in the fifteenth century show that on this definition the Renaissance was a medieval movement. Indeed an intense interest and desire to emulate the great figures of the classical past was a lasting facet of the minds of medieval men from the first primitive strivings at the court of Charlemagne down to the full glories of the Italy of the fifteenth century; only in degree did 'the Renaissance' differ from what had gone before. Here, as elsewhere, there is no chasm to separate 'modern' from 'medieval' times.

It can be argued that the real gulf between the two ages should be sought in the field of science. The modern world is as it is because of the profound capacity man has gained to alter the environment and physical conditions in which he lives, while scientific curiosity, if rarely the most esteemed, has yet been always the most vital part of modern culture. It is certainly true that of experimental science, as opposed to deductive reasoning about the universe, the Middle Ages knew very little. For the most part men were prepared to accept their scientific knowledge from the accepted authorities of other times and places, from the Arabs, from the Bible, and above all from Aristotle, so that scientific advance came to be equated with the rediscovery of ancient lore. The awkward thing about taking this scientific interest and ability as the mark of modern European man is that to do so means extending the Middle Ages far beyond the normally accepted limits. If artistic change is taken as the touchstone they did not survive the age of Dante, but by the scientific test they must be prolonged to that of Newton, for the scientific ideas of Shakespeare and Milton belong to the world of the schoolmen rather than that of the laboratory. The Aristotelian thought barrier was not broken down until the seventeenth century, and even then it was to be another hundred years before the new ideas came to be at all widely reproduced in the form of technological change.

Another line of division between modern and medieval times can be found in the contrast between what can be called, in the most general sense, a secular and a religious culture. The light of medieval learning, whether blazing out in the strong confidence of the thirteenth-century universities or guttering obscurely in the remote monasteries of the Dark Ages, was always an ecclesiastical light. The great majority of those who tended it were churchmen, and even those who were not in orders could not escape from the fact that they lived in a world in which questions about the nature of God were as important as questions about the nature of Man. To many, indeed, they were the only questions of ultimate value. By contrast the last five centuries have seen a steady movement towards the dethronement of Theology from her place as queen of the sciences to that of the tenant of a distant and peripheral holding coveted by few. On the one hand stand the Venerable Bede and Gratian, Alcuin and Aquinas, on the other Machiavelli and Marx, Voltaire and Darwin. Here surely there is a classification to divide the two worlds from each other?

Moreover, at first it looks a simple matter to date the first appearance of this rift. The first successful exploitation of the art of printing by Gutenberg of Mainz in the middle of the fifteenth century would seem to mark the division. By creating the possibility of cheap books Gutenberg both made possible, indeed certain, an eventual increase in literacy to a level far beyond anything that the Middle Ages could have achieved, and conferred upon all heterodox beliefs, and eventually upon unbelief itself, the gift of immortality. There was no shortage of heterodoxy in the later Middle Ages, but the beliefs in the last resort could rarely survive the believers. But it is far easier to burn a manuscript or to silence a teacher than it is to destroy an edition. In this perhaps is to be found the explanation of the failure of the Hussites in the fifteenth century and the success of the Protestants in the sixteenth.

The defect of this dividing line is its imprecision. Dante, layman though he was, described an universe constructed round the Christian faith, yet it can be questioned whether Christianity was any more central to him than it was to Milton writing more than three hundred years later. Few if any of the apologists of the secular societies of the sixteenth and seventeenth centuries argued more cogently for their rights than Marsiglio of Padua, a contemporary of Dante in the early fourteenth century. Isaac Newton was not to die until the eighteenth century, yet it may well be that he would have preferred to be remembered for his commentary on the Book of Daniel rather than for the *Principia Mathematica*. Such contrasts as these show that the discovery of printing marked no sudden transformation in the very gradual process by which a religious was changed into a secular society.

The attempt to define the limits of the Middle Ages by reference to the appearance of specifically modern characteristics in society is a hazardous business, for some 'modern' roots go deeply down into the remote past while others are of very recent growth. Moreover, the variations from area to area as well as from subject to subject are very great. A man standing his trial before one of Frederick II's courts in Palermo in the thirteenth century was assured of a trial more free from medieval trappings than an Englishman at a twentieth-century assize confronted by a sworn jury of his peers. Does it then follow that twentieth-century England is 'medieval' and that thirteenth-century Sicily was 'modern'?

A more profitable line of investigation might be to concentrate, not on the emergence of 'modern' characteristics, but on the decay of specifically medieval ones. This method has the advantage of being less subjective. As between the relative importance of Renaissance art and modern science there can be no impartial test, but there is no gainsaying the importance of the Roman Church or of the manorial economy, to take two obvious examples, within the framework of medieval society; value judgments on them both are not called into question. Now it is clear that both these two vital institutions were in a state of grave decay by the time of the Black Death. No historian could question that the Papacy at Avignon, with its commands disregarded by half Europe and its operations hamstrung by a shortage alike of manpower, money and reputation, was but a poor shadow of the institution which Innocent III had made feared and respected throughout the Western world. In the same way the operation of agriculture throughout much of western Europe was clearly changing fast even before the Black Death came everywhere to accelerate the process. Large estates of the old type were breaking up, and traditional patterns of labour service were being replaced by a relationship based on money rents. It might be said that this makes a clear case for considering that the Middle Ages were ending, and indeed there would be much to be said for ending such a book as this with the Black Death. Yet even here there is need for caution. What was decaying in the fourteenth century was not so much the Church as that particular organization of the Church which had been inspired by Cluny and Gorze, fashioned by Hildebrand, and perfected by Innocent III. To identify the Middle Ages with that development in the Church which began only in the tenth century and had already achieved its consummation by the early years of the thirteenth would be to take altogether too limited a view.

In the same way, manorial economy, although undoubtedly a central feature of the economy of the high Middle Ages throughout much of Europe, was never the unique or sole expression of their economic life. In large areas, such as England, it only made its appearance in any complete form comparatively late, in others, such as Italy or the colonial lands in the East, it never took root. Moreover, even in those regions where it took a firm hold it was rarely if ever the sole form of economic life; the existence of some money rents even in such areas as central France is the proof of that. From the year 1000 the steady growth of urban life throughout Europe is clearly recognizable; later centuries, in so far as they saw a growth of the practice of commutation and the gradual erosion of the manorial system, were not witnessing any new cataclysm but merely the steady growth of one feature which had long been present in European life at the expense of another. In any case the change was a very gradual one. While it is now common form to regard the Black Death as merely the sensational interment of the corpse of a feudalism which had already died, it is worth remembering that the destruction of feudalism was still a cause of interest to the English House of Commons in the seventeenth century, that the destruction of 'feudal privileges' was a feature if not a cause of the French Revolution, and that elsewhere in Europe the issue remained alive until well into the nineteenth century. If feudalism was buried by the Black Death its spirit certainly did not rest in peace.

The same objections will be found to any attempt to establish the limits of the Middle Ages by reference to any particular institution or event. Watersheds in history dividing one period sharply from another are rare and certainly none exists in the history of western Europe separating medieval from modern times. Indeed it is well that it is not otherwise, for a large part of the justification for the study of medieval history lies in its relationship to our own age. The Middle Ages are the upper reaches of the stream of contemporary western civilization.

But when all is said, books, if not history, must have an end. The selection of the middle of the fifteenth century as the date at which this book should end was not wholly a fortuitous matter of convenience. For the middle of the fifteenth century is perhaps a better point than its end from which to look backwards and forwards.

The fall of Byzantium in 1453 is the outstanding public event of the period. It was not in the least unexpected, except in so far as men will cease to expect an event which in all logic should have happened many years ago. That Byzantium had held out for so many centuries was one of the wonders of the world, and her final collapse must be laid to the charge, not of the infidels from beyond Europe, but to that of her fellow-Christians from the west. The wounds inflicted by the soldiers of the Fourth Crusade never healed. True, the outward show of an eastern empire had been restored in 1261, but its real strength had never returned. When a new tribe, the Ottoman Turks, entered the empire of the Seljuks, and, having taken to Islam, brought a new vigour to the Muslim opponents of Byzantium, her tired body lacked the strength to repel yet another attack. Her death agonies were slow indeed; as early as 1357 the Ottoman forces crossed into Europe by the Dardanelles, thus severing the main line of communication between Byzantium and the West and putting the city into a condition of blockade. Sultan Murad I (1358-1389) established his capital at Adrianople, in what is today European Turkey to the west of Istanbul, and under his successors the conquest of the Balkans was carried through systemtatically.

Still Byzantium held out, saved partly by her own military and diplomatic efforts, partly by a series of fortunate distractions, such as the intervention of Tamerlane against the eastern provinces of the Ottoman Empire. But appeals to the West brought no sufficient help, and in 1451 the accession of Sultan Mehmet II (the Conqueror) brought to the Ottoman throne a ruler determined that his people should no longer be baulked of their legitimate prey. During the next year his construction of a great castle at Rumeli Hisar on the north shore of the Bosphorus, only some four or five miles to the east of Byzantium, completed her isolation; now a miracle greater even than those customary in Byzantine history would be needed to save the city. It was not forthcoming. On the night of 28 May 1453 the janissaries succeeded in breaching the massive walls on the west side of the town, and within a few hours all was over. The last eastern emperor had perished and the new Rome had at length gone the way of the old.

It must be said that although S. Sophia and most of the other great churches of Byzantium were now fated to become mosques, the city as a whole suffered far less in 1453 than it had from Christian hands in 1204. The new rulers of the city were eager to preserve as many as possible of the Christian inhabitants as their subjects, and a whole quarter of the town was set aside for their use. Indeed, as capital of the new and expanding Ottoman Empire the prospects of what had once been Byzantium were brighter than they had been for many centuries.

But the practical advantages which many even of her Christian population were to reap from the new regime does not rob the event of its real and symbolic importance. The concern of this book has been to tell the story of the medieval West, but at every stage the East has been shown to play a vital role. From the East came the original tribes which were to destroy the classical Empire, but in that very act to fertilize the seeds of Western culture; from the East again came the Muslim invaders of the seventh and eighth centuries who, by their act of surgery in severing the Mediterranean, compelled the formation of a specifically western Christendom. At a later stage, when that society was growing to maturity, it was the East which acted as a magnet to attract most of the surplus vigour of an expanding society. The whole crusading movement, drawn alike by the fabulous stories of the riches of the Orient and by the real wealth of Byzantium, was an elaboration on this theme. In the East too the German colonizers built out their new extension of western Europe. From the riches of the East Venice and Genoa and Pisa themselves grew rich, and through them came much of the wealth of medieval Italy. In the East Angevins and Aragonese alike sought to build up their imperial dreams into reality. The Genoese quarter of Istanbul, the Catalan castles of the Aegean islands, the Venetian settlements on the Peloponnese, the Templars' castles on Rhodes, the whole eastern Mediterranean bears witness to the power of the East to excite the acquisitive instincts of western Europe.

From the East the scholars and universities of the twelfth and thirteenth centuries drew the greater part of the material they were to weave into the fabric of western Christian civilization. Finally, it was from the East that much of the inspiration and the written sources which were to stimulate the scholars and the artists of the Italian Renaissance were derived.

In all this there is no cause for surprise. Both Eastern and Western Europe, and indeed the lands of north Africa and the Near East, had a common root in the Roman Empire, that empire which had united all the lands which surround the Mediterranean. The constant urge in the Medieval West to seek out towards the East can be seen as a largely unconscious urge to restore this lost unity.

The rise of the Ottoman Empire and the consequent destruction of Byzantium can be taken as the signs that this dream is now over. Not only is there now no longer any independent eastern Christianity left with which to unite, or over which to dominate, but in future the lands of the Near East, and the very Balkans themselves, will be under the sway of a strong and aggressive government aiming at control of Europe.

In some ways this situation was the same as that which Charles

Martel and Charlemagne had confronted in the first Muslim attacks on the West, but there was an important difference. No Charlemagne now appeared to lead a united West, and, for all the talk of concerted Christian action and of a new crusade against the infidel, there was never any real possibility that such would materialize. Instead the new Ottoman invasion was regarded as being the concern only of those rulers whose lands were directly threatened. Those whose lands lay further to the west and who stood in no immediate danger were not slow to recognize that Muslim victories might be to their advantage. The stage was being set for what was to be a long-lasting tradition of modern diplomacy, by which the rulers of France and other states which had no reason to love the Habsburgs did not scruple to make all use of Ottoman assistance to embarrass their Catholic rivals. This can be regarded either as sad proof that the idea of Christendom is at last dead or as a bracing demonstration of the real self-confidence of the nation states which had taken its place. Both attitudes have some justification, but it should be said that the reality of combined western action, as opposed to the idea of it, had long ceased to be practical politics. Even in the thirteenth century the only expedition to have a genuinely international flavour had been the Fourth Crusade, and it could scarcely be counted as a recommendation for united Catholic action. By contrast it is certainly true that by the sixteenth century at least the western nations were strong enough to contemplate Turkish invasions with equanimity. Even when the Turks were at the gates of Vienna in 1526 the danger of the whole of Europe being overrun was more apparent than real. In the eighth century Christendom had really been in dire peril.

But of course one consequence of the new distribution of power in the eastern Mediterranean was that proximity to the East, the advantage on which Venice had grown fat and on which Sicily had once flourished, had now become a liability. The trade routes were almost completely stopped, and all that was gained by being close to these traditional arteries of western commerce was the danger of Turkish attack. It is this which explains the sudden rise of the Spanish kingdoms discussed in Chapter XIX. Nothing in the next century speaks more eloquently of this new distribution of power than the gradual decision of the conservative Charles V, at once Holy Roman Emperor and Spanish king, to treat his Spanish lands and his Spanish crown as his first responsibility. In the circumstances of the sixteenth century there is no doubt that he was right, but it is impossible to imagine that any medieval ruler who had chanced to find himself in a similar position would have preferred the affairs of the remote peninsula to the imperial crown of Germany, for all its difficulties a country at the heart of European affairs.

The new political situation had created opportunities for the states of the Atlantic seaboard. To take advantage of them would require more statecraft and a higher degree of internal organization than any of them displayed in the middle of the fifteenth century. They were to respond to the challenge by producing rulers of exceptional ability in the second half of the fifteenth century. Ferdinand and Isabella in Spain, first Edward IV and then Henry VIII in England, Louis XI in France, to discuss whether these rulers were modern or medieval is a somewhat sterile occupation. The aims of strong government are much the same at all times, and even its methods are curiously repetitive. What must be noted is the contrast between western Europe, with its new and reviving states unconsciously preparing to reap the full benefits of a New World in the next century, and their neighbours to the east. There is no sign of a revival in the fortunes of the Empire, and Italy remains a constant example of the dangers of political disunity and foreign intervention. Even the Duchy of Burgundy, that fortuitous collection of territories around the basin of the lower Rhine whose sudden rise and equally sudden fall have been omitted from this book, never really looked likely to solve the problems its unexpected existence had created. All the political initiative of Europe, along with most of its economic hopes, have passed to the western seaboard. Even culturally, though nothing breaks the attractive power of Italy over the European mind, the century of Cellini and Leonardo, of Valla and Botticelli, is succeeded by that of Rabelais and Cervantes, Montaigne and Shakespeare. These men made full use of what Italy had to offer, but they made of it something which was not itself Italian.

Throughout the centuries which separated the fall of the classical empire from the fifteenth century the minds of men in western Europe, and the political policies they followed, were subject always to the tug of the memory of that great empire which had passed. Sometimes this would be a crude and unsophisticated emotion, a simple feeling that the golden age of prosperity had passed and the hope that perhaps one day it might return. So, for instance, the romanized Franks of Merovingian Gaul must have felt about the past. At other times it assumed more sophisticated forms, and led rulers to deny the fact, and proclaim that the Empire had not been dead but merely slept awhile, and that now it was high time that it was roused from its sleep. In this spirit Charlemagne assumed the imperial crown, and Otto III fashioned his imperial dreams on the Aventine; thus too the popes of the thirteenth century saw in themselves the inheritors of imperial as well as of apostolic power. But as men had grown to know more, so inevitably they had come to realize that the Empire they sought to revive had been an empire of the East as well as of the West; so too they had become more conscious of another Empire and another Christendom to the East. With this recognition came the desire to end this awkward duality. Whether by negotiation or by force, unity must be restored and a really Roman Empire at last established; with it of course would go a restoration of the unity of the Church. In this dream such very different men as Urban II, Henry VI, and Frederick II had all formed their schemes.

With the decline of both Empire and Papacy any hope that this might even be achieved dwindled, but nevertheless the new aspirants after European power used the same ideas and still looked to the East. Only with the fall of Byzantium to the Turks was it made clear that the quest after yet another new Rome was vain. With this recognition the way was clear for the powers of the West, never well placed in the imperial chase, to assert their claims to sovereignty in word and deed. 'Our realm of England is an Empire.' The proud assertion of Henry VIII's 'Act in Restraint of Appeals' could be taken as the text of all the new rulers of the West, whose actions were to form the stuff of politics in the first modern age. In this sense at least the rise of the Ottoman Empire, symbolically manifested in the capture of Byzantium in 1453, can be seen as the decisive factor separating modern from medieval Europe. Greece might still dominate men's intellects, but in politics the ghost of Rome had been laid at last.

Further Reading

The following list is in no sense a bibliography of the Middle Ages. Those who wish a select bibliography of medieval history will find one in a pamphlet published for the Historical Association in 1955. The aim here has been to provide a short list of some eighty books, all of them readily available in English. Some, such as Professor Southern's *The Making of the Middle Ages*, are rewarding for any student of the period; others, for instance Dean Rashdall's monumental study of the medieval university, are by their nature specialist works dealing with particular aspects of medieval life. No work has been listed which is not of real merit.

The limitation of the list to works in English is not meant to suggest that the period can be studied at any depth by those whose knowledge of languages is confined to that tongue. Recent years, happily, have seen a marked increase in the number of English translations available, but it will always remain true that the student of medieval Europe who completely lacks the gift of tongues is at a serious disadvantage.

Translations of medieval works have been entered under the name of their translator, those of modern works under the names of their original authors.

GENERAL WORKS
The Cambridge Medieval History. Cambridge U.P., 1911–36. 8 vols. The only large-scale history of the whole Middle Ages in English. This is a work of composite authorship which was initiated in 1911. Parts of it are badly dated and parts well-nigh unreadable but it remains an indispensable source of information on many topics on which other sources in English are very scanty.
The Shorter Cambridge Medieval History. Cambridge U.P., 1952. 2 vols. This is in part an abridgement of the larger work.

Much has been lost in the process, but it is considerably more readable, and its later date of publication has enabled more recent views to be included.

C. W. Previté-Orton. *Outlines of Medieval History*, 2nd edn. Cambridge U.P., 1930. This is still a useful summary of the whole period.

R. H. C. Davis. *A History of Medieval Europe from Constantine to Saint Louis.* Longmans, 1957. A survey of nine hundred years of European history in a short compass, this makes no attempt to be comprehensive, but it is refreshingly written, makes admirable use of source material, and is an excellent introduction to the period it covers.

H. Pirenne. *A History of Europe from the Invasions to the Sixteenth Century.* Allen and Unwin, 1939. An English translation of a work by a great Belgian medievalist written during its author's internment during the First World War. The circumstances of its production made this book remarkably free of factual overloading; it is a work of ideas and 'views' rather than of narrative. Many of its conclusions are now widely challenged, and it is noticeably better on the earlier period than on the later centuries, but it remains easy and useful reading.

The Methuen History of Medieval and Modern Europe.
I. 476–911. M. Deanesly. 2nd edn. 1960.
II. 911–1198. Z. N. Brooke. 3rd edn. 1951.
III. 1198–1378. C. W. Previté-Orton. 3rd edn. 1951.
IV. 1378–1494. W. T. Waugh. 3rd edn. 1949.
This series is the only attempt at covering the whole period in reasonable detail at moderate length.

C. BROOKE. *Europe in the Central Middle Ages: 962–1154.* Longmans, 1964.

J. HALE and R. HIGHFIELD. *Europe in the Later Middle Ages*, ed. B. Smalley. Faber, 1965.

D. HAY. *Europe in the Fourteenth and Fifteenth Centuries.* Longmans, 1956.

CHURCH HISTORY

G. BARRACLOUGH. *The Medieval Papacy.* Thames & Hudson, 1968.

R. F. BENNETT. *The Early Dominicans.* Cambridge U.P., 1937.

P. SABATIER. *Life of St Francis of Assisi* (trans. L. S. Houghton). Hodder & Stoughton, 1920.

W. ULLMANN. *The Growth of the Papal Government in the Middle Ages.* Methuen, 1955.

J. R. WHITNEY. *Hildebrandine Essays.* Cambridge U.P., 1932.

THE CAROLINGIAN PERIOD

H. W. C. DAVIS. *Charlemagne.* Putnam, 1900.

C. DAWSON. *The Making of Europe.* Sheed and Ward, 1948.

A. J. GRANT, trans. *Early Lives of Charlemagne by Eginhard and the Monk of St Gall.* Chatto & Windus, 1922.

H. PIRENNE. *Mahomet and Charlemagne* trans. B. Miall. Allen & Unwin, 1939.

J. M. WALLACE-HADRILL. *The Barbarian West, 400–1000.* Hutchinson, 1957.

THE EMPIRE

G. BARRACLOUGH. *The Origins of Modern Germany.* Blackwell, 1947.

J. BRYCE. *The Holy Roman Empire.* Macmillan, 1864.

J. HALLER. *The Epochs of German History*, Eng. trans. Routledge, 1930.

B. JARRETT. *The Emperor Charles IV.* Eyre & Spottiswoode, 1935.

E. KANTOROWICZ. *Frederick the Second, 1194–1250.* Constable, 1958.

FRANCE

J. EVANS. *Life in Medieval France. 1925* Phaidon, 1957.

J. EVANS, trans. *De Joinville's History of St Louis.* Oxford U.P., 1938.

R. FAWTIER. *The Capetian Kings of France*, trans. L. Butler and R. J. Adam. Macmillan, 1960.

C. H. HASKINS. *The Normans in European History.* Constable, 1959.

E. PERROY. *The Hundred Years War.* Eyre & Spottiswoode, 1951.

H. WAQUET, trans. *Suger's Life of Louis VI.*

J. BRYCE. *The Holy Roman Empire.* Macmillan, 1864.

J. HALLER. *The Epochs of German History,* Eng. trans. Routledge, 1930.

B. JARRETT. *The Emperor Charles IV.* Eyre & Spottiswoode, 1935.

E. KANTOROWICZ. *Frederick the Second, 1194–1250.* Constable, 1958.

G. MASSON. *Frederick II of Hohenstaufen.* Secker and Warburg, 1957.

FRANCE

D. C. DOUGLAS. *The Norman Achievement.* Eyre & Spottiswoode, 1969.

J. EVANS. *Life in Medieval France.* 1925. Phaidon, 1957.

M. R. B, SHAW, trans. *Chronicles of Joinville and Villehardouin.* Penguin, 1967.

R. FAWTIER. *The Capetian Kings of France,* trans. L. Butler and R. J. Adam. Macmillan, 1960.

C. H. HASKINS. *The Normans in European History.* Constable, 1959.

E. PERROY. *The Hundred Years War.* Eyre & Spottiswoode, 1951.

R. VAUGHAN. *Philip the Bold.* Longmans, 1962.

R. VAUGHAN. *John the Fearless.* Longmans, 1965.

H. WAQUET, trans. *Suger's Life of Louis VI.*

THE MEDITERRANEAN WORLD

N. H. BAYNES. *The Byzantine Empire.* Thornton Butterworth, 1925.

M. V. CLARKE. *The Medieval City State.* Methuen, 1926.

B. LEWIS. *The Arabs in History.* Hutchinson, 1950.

D. MACK-SMITH. *Medieval Sicily: 800–1713.* Chatto & Windus, 1968.

G. OSTROGORSKY. History of the Byzantine State, trans. J. M. Hussey. Blackwell, 1968.

S. RUNCIMAN. *Byzantine Civilisation.* E. Arnold, 1933.

S. RUNCIMAN. *History of the Crusades.* Cambridge U.P.: Vol. I, 1951; Vol. II, 1952; Vol. III, 1954.

S. RUNCIMAN. *The Sicilian Vespers.* Cambridge U.P., 1958.

J. B. TREND. *The Civilisation of Spain.* Oxford U.P., 1944,

Home University Library.

ECONOMIC AND SOCIAL HISTORY

The Cambridge Economic History of Europe.
Vol. 1. *The Agrarian Life of the Middle Ages,* ed. J. H. Clapham and E. Power, 1941.
Vol. 2. *Trade and Industry in the Middle Ages,* ed. M. M. Postan and H. J. Habbakuk, 1952.

M. BLOCH. *Feudal Society,* trans. L. A. Manyon. Routledge, 1961.

M. BLOCH. *French Rural History,* trans. Sondheimer. Routledge & Kegan Paul, 1966.

M. BLOCH. *Land and Work in Medieval Europe,* trans. J. E. Anderson. Routledge & Kegan Paul, 1967.

G. DUBY. *Rural Economy and Country Life in the Medieval West,* trans. Postan. Arnold, 1968.

F. GANSHOF. *Feudalism,* trans. P. Grierson. Longmans, 1952.

G. LUZZATO. *Economic History of Italy from the Fall of the Roman Empire to the Beginning of the Sixteenth Century.* Routledge & Kegan Paul, 1961.

H. PIRENNE. *Economic and Social History of Medieval Europe,* Eng. trans. Kegan Paul, 1936.

H. PIRENNE. *Medieval Cities,* Eng. trans. Doubleday, 1925.

E. POWER. *Medieval People.* Methuen, 1924.

C. STEPHENSON. *Medieval Feudalism.* Cornell U.P., 1942.

INTELLECTUAL AND CULTURAL HISTORY

C. BROOKE. *The Twelfth-Century Renaissance.* Longman, 1969.

J. EVANS. *Art in Medieval France, 978–1498.* Oxford U.P., 1948.

C. H. HASKINS. *The Renaissance of the Twelfth Century.* Harvard U.P., 1927.

J. HUIZINGA. *The Waning of the Middle Ages,* trans. E. Arnold, 1924.

D. KNOWLES. *The Evolution of Medieval Thought.* Longmans, 1962.

M. L. W. LAISTNER. *Thought and Letters in Western Europe, 500–900.* Methuen, 1957.

G. LEFF. *Medieval Thought.* Penguin, 1958.

C. H. MCILWAIN. *The Growth of Political Thought in the West.* Macmillan, New York, 1932.

D. OATES, ed. *The Dark Ages.* Thames & Hudson, 1965.

N. PEVSNER. *An Outline of European Architecture*. Murray, 1947.

R. L. POOLE. *Illustrations of the History of Medieval Thought and Learning*. 1884. 2nd edn. S.P.C.K. 1921.

H. RASHDALL. *The Universities of Europe in the Middle Ages*, ed. Sir M. Powicke and A. B. Emden. 3 vols. Oxford U.P., 1936.

R. W. SOUTHERN. *The Making of the Middle Ages*. Hutchinson, 1953.

R. W. SOUTHERN. *Medieval Humanism and Other Essays*. Blackwell, 1970.

W. ULLMANN. *History of Political Thought: The Middle Ages*. Penguin, 1965.

W. ULLMANN. *The Principles of Government and Politics in the Middle Ages*. Methuen, 1966.

P. VINOGRADOFF. *Roman Law in Medieval Europe*. Oxford U.P., 1929.

H. WADDELL. *Peter Abelard*. Constable, 1933 (Novel).

H. WADDELL. *The Wandering Scholars*. Constable, 1927.

Two convenient sources of translations of some of the more important documents of the Middle Ages are:

Select Historical Documents of the Middle Ages, ed. and trans. E. F. Henderson. Bohn's Antiquarian Library, 1847.

Documents of the Christian Church, ed. and trans. H. Bettenson. Oxford U.P., 1943, World's Classics.

GENEALOGICAL TABLES

I. THE CAROLINGIANS

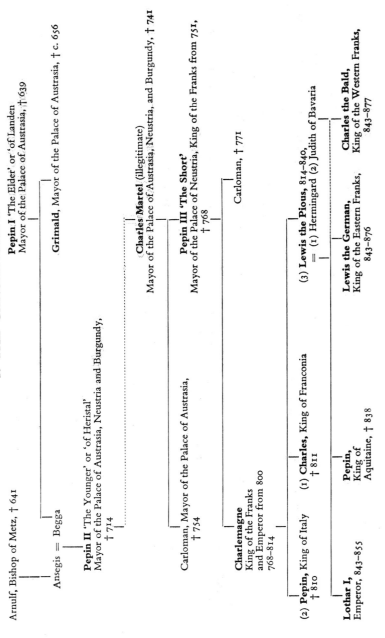

Arnulf, Bishop of Metz, † 641

Pepin I 'The Elder' or 'of Landen'
Mayor of the Palace of Austrasia, † 639

Ansegis = Begga

Grimald, Mayor of the Palace of Austrasia, † c. 656

Pepin II 'The Younger' or 'of Heristal'
Mayor of the Palace of Austrasia, Neustria and Burgundy, † 714

Charles Martel (illegitimate)
Mayor of the Palace of Austrasia, Neustria, and Burgundy, † 741

Carloman, Mayor of the Palace of Austrasia, † 754

Pepin III 'The Short'
Mayor of the Palace of Neustria, King of the Franks from 751, † 768

Carloman, † 771

Charlemagne
King of the Franks
and Emperor from 800
768–814

(1) Charles, King of Franconia
† 811

(3) Lewis the Pious, 814–840,
= (1) Hermingard (2) Judith of Bavaria

(2) Pepin, King of Italy
† 810

Pepin,
King of
Aquitaine, † 838

Lewis the German,
King of the Eastern Franks,
843–876

Charles the Bald,
King of the Western Franks,
843–877

Lothar I,
Emperor, 843–855

2. THE SAXONS AND SALIANS

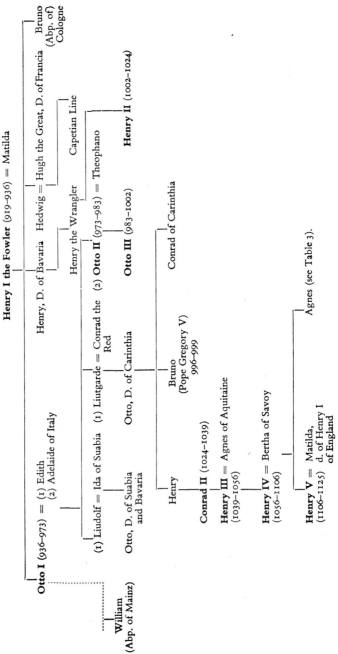

3. THE WELFS AND HOHENSTAUFENS

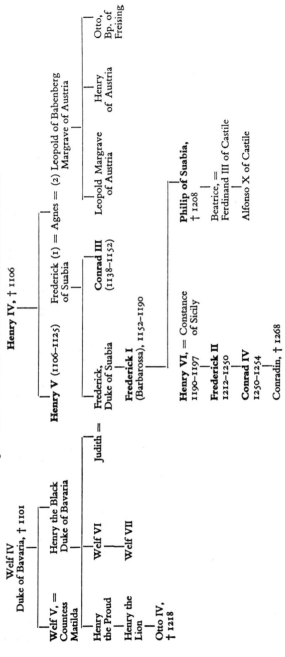

Henry IV, † 1106

Welf IV, Duke of Bavaria, † 1101

Henry V (1106–1125)

Frederick (1) = Agnes = (2) Leopold of Babenberg of Suabia, Margrave of Austria

Henry the Black, Duke of Bavaria

Welf V, = Countess Matilda

Welf VI

Judith =

Frederick, Duke of Suabia

Conrad III (1138–1152)

Leopold Margrave of Austria

Henry of Austria

Otto, Bp. of Freising

Henry the Proud

Welf VII

Frederick I (Barbarossa), 1152–1190

Henry the Lion

Otto IV, † 1218

Henry VI, 1190–1197 = Constance of Sicily

Philip of Suabia, † 1208

Frederick II 1212–1250

Beatrice, = Ferdinand III of Castile

Conrad IV 1250–1254

Alfonso X of Castile

Conradin, † 1268

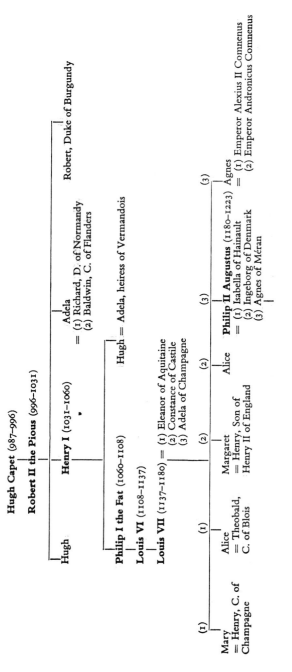

Hugh Capet (987–996)

Robert II the Pious (996–1031)

Henry I (1031–1060)

Adela = (1) Richard, D. of Normandy (2) Baldwin, C. of Flanders

Robert, Duke of Burgundy

Hugh = Adela, heiress of Vermandois

Philip I the Fat (1060–1108)

Louis VI (1108–1137)

Louis VII (1137–1180) = (1) Eleanor of Aquitaine (2) Constance of Castile (3) Adela of Champagne

Hugh

(1) Alice = Theobald, C. of Blois

(2) Margaret = Henry, Son of Henry II of England

(2) Alice

(3) Philip II Augustus (1180–1223) = (1) Isabella of Hainault (2) Ingeborg of Denmark (3) Agnes of Méran

(3) Agnes = (1) Emperor Alexius II Comnenus (2) Emperor Andronicus Comnenus

(1) Mary = Henry, C. of Champagne

5. SUCCESSION TO FRENCH THRONE IN 1328

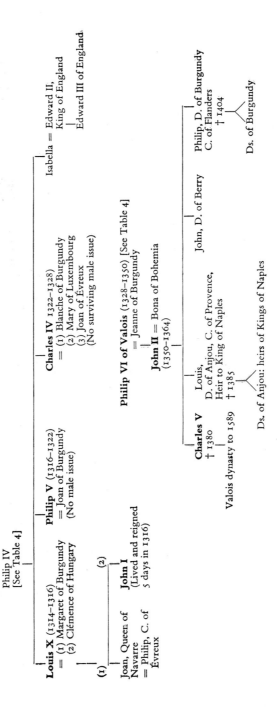

Philip IV
[See Table 4]

Louis X (1314–1316)
= (1) Margaret of Burgundy
  (2) Clémence of Hungary

(1)

Joan, Queen of Navarre
= Philip, C. of Évreux

(2)

John I
(Lived and reigned 5 days in 1316)

Philip V (1316–1322)
= Joan of Burgundy
(No male issue)

Charles IV 1322–1328
= (1) Blanche of Burgundy
  (2) Mary of Luxembourg
  (3) Joan of Évreux
  (No surviving male issue)

Philip VI of Valois (1328–1350) [See Table 4]
= Jeanne of Burgundy

John II = Bona of Bohemia
(1350–1364)

Charles V
† 1380

Valois dynasty to 1589

Louis,
D. of Anjou, C. of Provence,
Heir to King of Naples
† 1385

Ds. of Anjou: heirs of Kings of Naples

John, D. of Berry

Philip, D. of Burgundy
C. of Flanders
† 1404

Ds. of Burgundy

Isabella = Edward II,
        King of England

Edward III of England

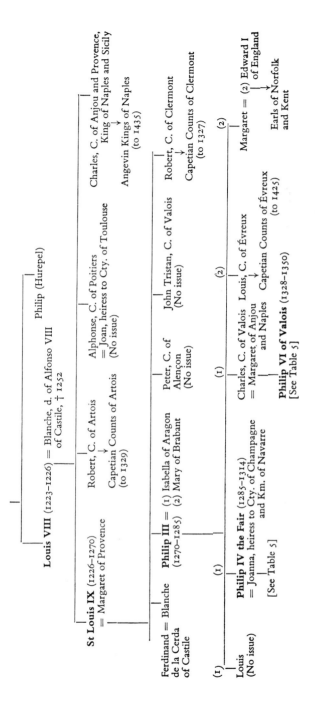

INDEX OF NAMES

Where given the dates are those of birth and death, except in the case of the popes where they are those of their pontificate.

36; his marriages, 34–5, 42; and the Lombards, 34–5; protects the Papacy, 35–8, 82; nature of his Empire, 38–41, 60; crowns his successor, 42–3; death, 43

Charles II, the Bald, Emperor (823–77), 48–9, 51; his inheritance, 49–50; and Viking invasions, 57–8

Charles III, the Fat, Emperor (839–88), 58

Charles IV, Emperor (1316–78), 357; his policy, 373, 375; and Germany's elective system, 373–5; and Bohemia, 375–6; attempts to create a Czech state, 376

Charles III, the Simple, King of the Franks (879–929), 61, 157; and the Vikings, 58–9

Charles IV, King of France (1294–1328), 292, 322

Charles V, King of France (1337–80), as Dauphin, 333, 334–6; leads partial recovery, 336, 338; character, 337; death, 338; supports Avignon, 357

Charles VI, King of France (1368–1422), France at her lowest ebb, 338–9; effect of his madness, 339–40; governs through Marmosets, 339; death, 343; and Great Schism, 359

Charles VII, King of France (1403–61), as Dauphin, 340; proclaimed a bastard, 340–2; and Hundred Years War, 342, 343; at Bourges, 343; and Joan of Arc, 343; crowned at Rheims, 343; reconciled with Burgundy, 343

Charles, King of Navarre (d. 1387), 332–3, 334–5, 337; and the Jacquerie, 336

Charles Martel (c. 688–741), 23–4

Charles of Anjou (1225–85), 187, 190, 194; his Angevin Crusade, 278–9; defeats Conradin, 279–80; expedition against Byzantium, 280–1; provokes Sicilian Vespers, 281; and Philip II, 284

Charles of Castile, 333

Childeric III, King (d. c. 751), 23, 24

Clement II, Pope (d. 1047), 95

Clement III, Pope (1080–1100), 106, 107, 112

Clement IV, Pope (1265–8), 278, 279–80

Clement V, Pope (1305–14), 301–2, 371; and the Templars, 303; and the Avignon Papacy, 346, 347; personal dishonesty, 351–2

Clement VI, Pope (1342–52), 349, 373

Clement VII, Pope (1378–94), his election, 356

Clement VIII, Pope (1423–9), 363

Clement of Alexandria (c. 150–c. 215), 8

Clovis, King (465–506), 155; his conversion, 19, 20, 394

Coeur, Jacques (d. 1456), 313–14

College of Cardinals, and papal election, 99, 100, 117, 202; Alexander IV and, 277; the move to Avignon and, 302; and the election of Urban VI, 355–6; depose Urban and elect Clement VII, 356; and Great Schism, 360

Conrad I, King of Germany (d. 918), elected King, 61; his policy, 61–3

Conrad II, King of Germany (c. 990–1039), 116; his Italian policy, 91–2; and the Church, 92, 94; German policy, 92; his administration, 92–3; succeeded by Henry III, 93

Conrad III, King of Germany (1093–1152), 117; elected King, 119; his reign, 119–20; death, 121; and Second Crusade, 143, 144, 149; the Empire at his death, 242; his successor, 243

Conrad IV, King of Germany (1228–54), 268, 368; struggle with Innocent IV, 276; and Henry of Hohenstaufen, 276

Conrad of Gelnhausen (c. 1320–90), 359

Conrad of Montferrat (fl. 1192), 148

Conrad of Waldhauser, 384

Conradin, King of Jerusalem and Sicily (1252–68), nominated King of Regno, 277; comes to Italy, 279

Constance of Sicily, 251, 255, 256, 258

Constantine I, Emperor (*c.* 274–337), 1, 3, 8; and Constantinople, 4; his conversion, 9, 35

Constantine V, Emperor (741–75), and the Papacy, 27

Constantine VI, Emperor (d. 797), 36

Cossa, Cardinal Baldassare, *see* John XXIII

Damian, Peter, S. (*c.* 1007–72), 84, 99–100, 101, 295

Dandolo, Enrico (*c.* 1120–1205), and Fourth Crusade, 206–7, 208

Dante Alighieri (1265-1321), 5, 88, 306, 346 and n., 371, 410, 417, 418

de Garlandes family, 163

Desiderius, King, 35

Dinis, King of Portugal (1261–1325), 402

Dominic, S. (1170–1221), 215, 216

Duguesclin, Bertrand (*c.* 1320–80), 337, 405

Dunois, Jean (1402–68), 334

Duns Scotus, Johannes (*c.* 1265–1308), 218, 317

Edward I of England (1239–1307), dispute with France over Guienne, 289; and *Clericis Laicos*, 297–8

Edward II of England (1284–1327), 321

Edward III of England (1312–77), claim to French Crown, 322–3, 325; supported by Gascons, 323; use of economic means to provoke war, 324–5; renounces homage to Philip VI, 325; and Flanders, 325–7; his leadership, 327; intervenes in Brittany, 330; and Crécy campaign, 330–1; besieges Calais, 331; death, 338

Edward, the Black Prince (1330–76), 327, 405; his leadership, 327; at Poitiers, 333; and Aquitaine, 338; death, 338

Einhard (*c.* 770-840), 28, 31, 33, 37

Eleanor of Aquitaine, Queen (1122?-1204), 144, 165; relations with Louis, 166–7

Eugenius III, Pope (1145–53), 120, 121, 123, 244; and Second Crusade, 143, 212; Frederick I and, 246

Eugenius IV, Pope (1431–47), and Council of Basle, 364–5

Euric, King (d. 485), 10

Felix V, Pope (1439–49), 366

Ferdinand of Aragon (1373–1416), 408–9

Ferdinand II of Aragon (1452-1516), 391, 405

Ferdinand III, King of Castile (d. 1254), 398

Ferdinand IV, King of Castile (d. 1312), 404

Ferrand, Count of Flanders, 181

Flôte, Pierre, 286, 287, 292, 298, 300

Francis, S. (1181/2-1226), 86, 200, 215, 216–18

Frederick I (Barbarossa), Emperor, (*c.* 1123–90), 121, 126, 156; and the Crusades, 148, 149, 177, 251, 255; death, 149, 255; situation at his accession, 242 ff.; his character, 244; his imperial policy, 244; and Germany, 244–5, 248–9, 251; and Hadrian IV, 246, 248; Italian expeditions, 246, 247, 248, 249; and Diet of Roncaglia, 247–8; and papal schism, 248; and Peace of Constance, 250–1; relationship with German Church, 252; and Henry the Lion, 252–4; breaks the power of the Welfs, 254

Frederick II, Emperor (1194-1250), 45, 255; opposed by Otto IV, 181, 259; and Louis IX, 190; Innocent III and, 201, 258–61; birth, 256; crowned emperor, 261; grants Golden Bull of Eger, 261, 266; character, 261–3; organization of Sicily under, 263–5; German policy, 265–9; policy towards German Church, 266–7, 268; revolt of Prince Henry against, 267–8; struggle with Papacy, 268, 269 ff.; and the Fifth Crusade, 270–1; and Lombard League, 272; and Innocent IV, 273–4; defeat and death, 274

Frederick III, Emperor (1415–93), 390

Widukind, *Res gestae Saxonicae*, 65 and n.

William I of England (1027–87), and France, 155; Henry I and, 159–60

William I, the Bad, King of Sicily (d. 1166), 246

William II, King of Sicily (d. 1189), 148

William V of Aquitaine, Count, founds Cluny, 82–3, 94

William X, Duke of Aquitaine (d. 1137), 165

William of Ockham (d. 1349?), 218, 317, 354

Winrich von Kniprode (d. 1382), 380

Wycliff, John (*c.* 1320-84), 317, 363, 384; compared with Huss, 385; dispute over his teaching, 385–6

Yolande de Brienne, Empress, 270

Zacharias, Pope (d. 752), 24, 103

Zangi, Emir of Mosul, 142

Zbynek, Archbishop of Prague, and Huss, 385–6

Zizka, General John (*c.* 1376–1424), Hussite leader, 388–9

SUBJECT INDEX

rediscovery of Aristotle and, 196, 197; and dualism, 211–12; the Friars and, 217; Frederick II and, 261–2; its expansion in Europe, 304; effect of the Black Death on, 315–16; its development in Spain, 401; debt to the East, 422

Church, the, monopolizes education, 7; relations with the Empire, 9, 80 ff.; assumes political power, 9–10, 20; her early bishoprics, 10–11; doctrinal differences between East and West, 11, 97, 134; Roman influence in, 11–12; and Arianism, 19; relations with the Franks, 20, 22, 23–5; and Kingship, 25; the Carolingian Renaissance and, 30, 32–3; and the crowning of Charlemagne, 37–8; Lewis the Pious and, 44, 46; relationship with the Crown, 44–5, 295; reforms of S. Benedict, 45–6; Conrad I and, 62; Otto the Great and, 68–70, 82; election of bishops, 68–9, 115–16; subject to invasions, 80–1; her feudal nature, 81–2; corruption in the tenth century, 82; influence of Cluny on her history, 84–7, 93; the Lorraine movement and, 87, 89; and simony, 88–9; and concubinage, 89; her reform in Germany, 94, 99; Gregory VII and, 96–7, 103; reconciled with the Empire, 115–16; opposition to her wealth, 120; supports the colonial movement East, 126; attitude to war, 129–30; and the German monarchy, 152; and the French monarchy, 152, 156, 162, 166, 185–6, 190–1, 294–5; development of the Inquisition, 192; and education, 195; growth in her moral authority, 199; tendency to centralization, 200, 219; attitude to heresy, 209–14; and S. Francis, 216–17; and the Friars, 219; imposes fealty ceremony, 221; and urban communities, 239; her need of administrators, 295; Benedict VIII asserts her unity, 300; unity under Innocent III, 304; effect of

Black Death on her doctrine, 315–16; and the Avignon Papacy, 346, 351; schism of 1324, 347; Benedict XII's reforms, 348; critics of her ultimate authority, 353–5; effect of Great Schism on, 357–9, 366; her oecumenical councils, 359; Concordat of Vienna and, 366–7; her character in Spain, 401, 404. See also Papacy

Church, Eastern, monasticism and, 14; doctrinal differences with West, 97, 134; attempts to unite the two Churches, 97, 130, 208; worsening relations with the West, 121, 134; the Crusaders and, 207; nominal unity restored by Gregory X, 280

Churches, founded by feudalism, 81, 94; Black Death and, 315–16

Cistercians, 85, 86, 126, 168–72, 297, 348; their constitution, 170–2; growth of lay brethren, 172; rapid growth, 172

Cîteaux Abbey, 168–72

Cîvetot, Battle of, 136

Clerical concubinage, 88, 89, 94, 99, 102, 376

Cluny, its foundation, 82–3; early abbots, 83, 108; its influence on monasticism, 83–4, 93, 168–9, 419; influence on western Europe, 84–5; first monastic order, 85–6; becomes a landowning corporation, 86, 168–9, 170; churches of the order, 87; and the Crusades, 127; its liturgy, 170–1; Cistercians and, 172

Cologne, 115, 123, 312

Colonial movement in East, to the Slavonic East, 122, 123–4; methods of achieving, 124–5; importance of, 125–6, 226; the Crusades and, 131; growth of Flemish trade and, 229; its decline, 307, 379; Black Death and, 310

Commissions of Array, 328

Communications, in the Roman Empire, 3, 5; effect of barbarian invasions on, 6; decline in, 225; between northern and southern Europe, 233

first settlements, 56, 57; and Charles the Bald, 57–8; do homage to Charles the Simple, 58–9; converted to Christianity, 59; as traders, 225
Visigoths and Spain, 393, 401. *See also* Goths
Vitry-sur-Marne, 143, 166
Vivarium, monastery of, 7, 15

Welfs, the, 92, 108, 117, 119, 245, 252–4, 382
Wittelsbachs, the, 371–2, 373, 382

Ypres, 228, 325

Zallaca, Battle of, 397
Zoroastrianism, 211